THE *LONDON JOURNAL*, 1845-83

To LJH

The *London Journal*, 1845-83

Periodicals, Production and Gender

ANDREW KING

Canterbury Christ Church University College, UK

ASHGATE

Published by
Ashgate Publishing Limited
Gower House
Croft Road
Aldershot
Hampshire GU11 3HR
England

Ashgate Publishing Company
Suite 420
101 Cherry Street
Burlington, VT 05401-4405
USA

Ashgate website: http://www.ashgate.com

British Library Cataloguing in Publication Data
King, Andrew
    The London Journal 1845-1883 : periodicals, production and gender. – (The nineteenth century series)
    1. London Journal – History 2. Periodicals – Publishing –
    Great Britain – History – 19th century 3. English literature
    – Periodicals – History – 19th century 4. Books and reading
    – Great Britain – History – 19th century 5. Books and
    reading – Great Britain – Sex differences
    I. Title
    052'.09034

Library of Congress Cataloging-in-Publication Data
King, Andrew, 1957 –
    The London journal 1845-1883 : periodicals, production, and gender / Andrew King.
        p. cm – (The nineteenth century series)
    Includes bibliographical references and index.
    ISBN 0-7546-3343-8 (alk. paper)
    1. London journal. I. Title. II. Nineteenth century (Aldershot, England)

PN5130. L6K56 2004
052'.09421'09034–dc22

2003065069

ISBN 0 7546 3343 8

Printed and bound in Great Britain by MPG Books Ltd, Bodmin, Cornwall

Contents

List of Figures

List of Tables

The Nineteenth Century Series
General Editors' Preface

The aim of the series is to reflect, develop and extend the great burgeoning of interest in the nineteenth century that has been an inevitable feature of recent years, as that former epoch has come more sharply into focus as a locus for our understanding not only of the past but of the contours of our modernity. It centres primarily upon major authors and subjects within Romantic and Victorian literature. It also includes studies of other British writers and issues, where these are matters of current debate: for example, biography and autobiography, journalism, periodical literature, travel writing, book production, gender and non-canonical writing. We are dedicated principally to publishing original monographs and symposia; our policy is to embrace a broad scope in chronology, approach and range of concern, and both to recognize and cut innovatively across such parameters as those suggested by the designations 'Romantic' and 'Victorian'. We welcome new ideas and theories, while valuing traditional scholarship. It is hoped that the world which predates yet so forcibly predicts and engages our own will emerge in parts, in the wider sweep, and in the lively streams of disputation and change that are so manifest an aspect of its intellectual, artistic and social landscape.

Vincent Newey
Joanne Shattock
University of Leicester

Preface

> It starts when the child is as young as five or six, when he arrives at school. It starts with marks, rewards, 'places', 'streams', stars – and still in many places, stripes. This horserace mentality, the victor and the loser way of thinking, leads to 'Writer X is, is not, a few paces ahead of Writer Y. Writer Y has fallen behind. In his last book Writer Z has shown himself to be better than Writer A.' From the very beginning the child is trained to think in this way: always in terms of comparison, of success, and of failure. It is a weeding-out system: the weaker get discouraged and fall out; a system designed to produce a few winners who are always in competition with each other.
>
> (Lessing, 1962: 15)

One of the major themes of the 'Preface' to Doris Lessing's *Golden Notebook* concerns the reception of her work by critics, academics and students. It criticises us, accusing us of a 'horserace mentality', and asks readers instead to envisage a flat, autodidact culture independent of institutions. Even if I no longer accept the possibility of realizing such a utopian space, I still consciously refuse to image writers as competitors in a horserace. This refusal constitutes my intervention here.

I came to Lessing late, first reading *The Golden Notebook* while I was teaching in Sicily in the mid 1980s. I read it in a cool blue-grey flat, in a baronial palace in which a baron still lived. It looked out onto a flight of dark steps that climbed sedately up to two churches, one flamboyantly baroque and the other a classical reprimand. At the base of the steps was a communist nightclub, and on hot summer nights beer-drinkers would spill out onto the steps and talk and shout. Opposite my flat there was a lava-block convent with a thick grating over each opaque and dirty window. The nuns would come out once a year, to sing in the Easter Sunday night, candles making a festival of their faces. Beneath my balcony there was an excavation of black-and-white geometry, a Roman mosaic. An Apollo and a Venus had been dug up so I was told, neither of great value. I never saw them. The archaeologists kept them locked up.

I had left Britain believing – no, hoping – that there must be something else, another way of thinking the world, but I was not even sure what I disliked about the twenty-year attempt to route my thought. Lessing's novel put my vague unease into language. It focussed my discontent and moved it from the personal into the social. It gave my dissatisfaction the more concrete form of a question mark which opened a space for words gradually to form before it: affect emerged into cognition.

Why did I so intensely want to know yet feel alienated by Books of Knowledge? How and why did what I was supposed to hear not speak to me? Why did I feel left out of this vast chatter of Learned Books, so vast as to make me feel there was nothing else? Why did these Books of Knowledge not love me, while my love for them remained?

Sicily, an edge of Europe like my native Wales, helped me form the questions that offered a respite from unrequited love. It was in Sicily, far from Wales, that I had time to reflect on how cultural hierarchies had shaped the Books and my reactions to them, and on how specifying these hierarchies might help me to move on. Distance provided a satirical mirror in which to see my British experiences and then also to scrutinize the nature of such reflection itself. For Sicily was hardly a narcissistic mirror comfortably offering self-satisfaction. There was an anxious irony in questioning consecrated culture in a baronial palace so close to churches and nuns. And the archaeologists had snuck away the gods, the beer-drinkers kept me awake, the convent was ugly, the steps mostly in shadow.

In place of a sweepstakes in which the competitors are our Great and Famous literary forebears (respectable ancestors for those of us who have no portraits on our walls), it would be possible, I imagine, to propose a rival horserace, using a different course and different fences. Studies of class, gender and 'race' have been key in mapping alternative routes which have allowed us to hear the marginalized and silenced. But what of that great mass that is both central and silenced, the occluded norm beyond the Books of Knowledge – *Readers Digest* and its ancestors?

The novels of, say, Henry James command a few thousand readers. The even smaller number of readers with high status have produced letters and books and periodicals that let us know how these novels were and are read, and create that vast chatter that still largely sets the parameters of knowledge. Such thoroughbreds are not my forebears. Although I love many, I will not hang their portraits on my walls. The *London Journal* was bought by 500,000 people a week for over twenty years between the 1850s and the 1870s. If alternative horserace we want to set up, then sales figures offer a criterion for determining the winner. The *London Journal*, as perhaps the best-selling publication of mid-nineteenth-century Europe, offers the temptation of a massive reality, vaster, at least in echo, than the voluminous chatter of up-market in-groups legitimating their own lineage.

Yet the metaphor of an alternative race still offends me. Must I enact the violence of a snobbery – structural, even if disavowed – that is merely inverted? Is there no other reason to study the mass market? If there were not, I could not have written this book. While inversion of the terms in a violent hierarchy is necessary, there is also a beyond, a deconstruction of the violence that shuts up and out.

This book treats a nineteenth-century periodical as a case study to explore various methods of writing about mass-market media in general. My fundamental thesis, however, concerns the necessity for an interdisciplinary vision that recognizes that periodicals are commodities that occupy shifting but specific places in a constantly mobile market. They are not only produced and distributed commodities though, but consumed as magical, fantasmatic *commodity fetishes*, aesthetic objects that give imaginative pleasure. Hence the need for a constant oscillation between the 'hard' facts of production and hypothesized gratification.

Part 1 begins to form the questions in the blank spaces of the books, and the first chapter offers an initial theoretical engine with which to move through the terrain. Chapter 2 discusses nineteenth-century accounts of the *London Journal*, treating it not as a material body but as a discursive entity that participates in battles over the definition of the cultural field. In Part 2 I map the magazine through production – circulation figures, labour costs, and profits. I visit its offices, editors, proprietors and authors. I navigate the effects of rivalry with competitors in the same cultural zone and of relations with other now more canonical literary areas, connecting them to changes in the magazine's contents. Just as important are the changing pleasures the magazine offers in its bid to be loved and exchanged for a penny. In other words, I analyse the magic tricks of the fetish, proposing an aesthetic of the nineteenth-century mass-market text (there is no escape from the fetishizing aesthetic: I lived in a cool blue-grey flat after all, not a pure machine for living in). Part 3 traces the *London Journal*'s transitive and tangled relation to gender, weaving it into politics, consumerism and interpretation itself. This part includes chapters on two narratives sold and read today as discrete volumes, Braddon's *Lady Audley's Secret* (1863) and Zola's *The Ladies' Paradise* (1883). I explore these novels as embedded in local periodical landscapes, taking the first to query the glamorous notion of the inherent 'subversiveness' of a text and the second to tease out issues of control over the meaning of a commodity.

Despite its metropolitan title, the *London Journal* was read all over Britain, the British empire, and Europe. Maybe even in Sicily too, where in the nineteenth century there were notable British commercial ventures. Marsala was first shipped to England by John Woodhouse in 1773; a hundred years later the Avelines of Bath set up sulphur mines around Etna. There are certainly records of the *London Journal* being bought in the Welsh mining valleys. Since it folded as late as 1928, when it was still recycling stories from the 1850s and 60s, my grandparents and even my parents might have read it. Margery Allingham, the 'Golden Age' detective novelist, certainly did: her father edited the *London Journal* for almost two decades and around 1911, when she was seven, she put together a magazine modelled on it (Thorogood, 1991: 36-7). On the whole though, readers of texts such as the *London Journal* were of little status and their writings, if any, are hardly accessible to us. People without the charisma of learning or radicalism, these are my ancestors. Besides an alternative horserace (for I do not believe in complete escape from the *déjà connu*), this book is then also a family album, a compilation of crazed and faded *cartes de visite*, fragments of calotype stuck together with modern theory and recent technologies, a collage of people and events and above all stories that contributed to forming the imaginary I inherited. Like Richard Hoggart's, mine is an address to the dead, an *ave* and a valediction to a past that I left physically long ago. As a farewell, it is also a move into the future, and into yet another unknown country.

Such a path is not trod alone: neither my questions nor my motive force could exist without other people and the kindness of many. First of all, I want to acknowledge my debt to accounts by previous cartographers of the nineteenth-century mass-market in general and of the *London Journal* in particular – Altick (1998), Dalziel (1957), James (1963), Mitchell (1989), and Anderson (1994). Their explorations have provided me with valuable leads and background knowledge; my specific obligations to them will be acknowledged as appropriate in succeeding pages.

List of Abbreviations

BL	The British Library
Boase	Boase, Frederic, *Modern English Biography,* London: Frank Cass & Co, 6 vols., 1965 (1892-1921)
BUCOP	*British Union Catalogue of Periodicals.* ed. James D. Stewart et al., London: Butterworth Scientific Publications, 4 vols with supplements, 1955-
DLB	*Dictionary of Literary Biography*, ed. Joel Meyerson et al., Detroit: Bruccoli Clark/ Gale Research Co., 1978-
DNB	*Dictionary of National Biography*, ed. Leslie Stephen, Sidney Lee et al., Oxford: Oxford University Press, 1917-
ILN	*Illustrated London News*
LJ	*London Journal*
LSJ	*London Saturday Journal*
MLAA	Modern Languages Association of America
N&Q	*Notes and Queries*
n.d.	undated publication
n.s.	new series
NYPL	New York Public Library
OED	*Oxford English Dictionary*, 2nd edition, 1989
PMLA	*Proceedings of the Modern Language Association*
SDUK	Society for the Diffusion of Useful Knowledge
Sullivan	Alvin Sullivan, ed., *British Literary Magazines*, 4 vols, London: Greenwood Press, 1984
TLS	*Times Literary Supplement*
VPN	*Victorian Periodicals Newsletter*
VPR	*Victorian Periodicals Review*

Where only volume and page number are given, the reference is to the relevant part of the *London Journal*.

Errata

The following page should be inserted as page xiv

I want to recognize publicly how much I owe to Laurel Brake for her lessons in map reading and her sage warnings about pits in the road. She it was who brought me to realize that a periodical is a medium that constitutes its messages in very particular ways.

Birkbeck College of the University of London provided a liberating and challenging environment for my intellectual passage. Ana Parejo-Vadillo, John Plunkett, Joanne Woodman and Andrew Wyllie read drafts of this manuscript in various forms: especial thanks for their guidance and friendship.

Two on-line discussion lists have provided invaluable leads and models of hard work and intellectual generosity: Bloods And Dimes and VICTORIA.

Louis James supplied me with some photocopies of *Spare Moments* and a transcription of a letter in his possession from G.W.M. Reynolds. Brian Maidment sent me a copy of *Into the 1830s* and gave helpful advice on an earlier form of this book. In response to my homepage, John Phillips emailed me private information about his relation, Israel Watts Phillips, a *London Journal* novelist.

Toni Johnson-Woods, with her characteristic open-handedness, early on in my research spotted connections between stories in the *London Journal* and the *New York Ledger* and supplied me with early versions of her indexes: without many conversations with her, both bodily and virtual, I might otherwise never have escaped the confines of Europe.

A version of Chapter 9 has appeared in the *Journal of Victorian Culture*, 7:1 (2002), to the editors of which go my thanks for permission to use the material.

And to Lesley Hayman, with whom I have travelled much – literally and metaphorically – far, far beyond the perils of the Sicilian straits, and even the Hesperides, the word is not enough: nonetheless, *mulţumesc*.

Throughout the index there are title entries which should have been italicized, for which the publisher apologises.

Part 1

Periodical Discourse

Chapter One

Periodical Questions

Questions of Enquiry

The London Journal. The Encyclopedia Britannica puts the circulation at 170,000 in 1850 (11 ed., [sic] s.v. »Periodicals«); Fox Bourne (2, 228) gives the figure in 1855 as 510,000, which agrees with the Leeds sample and with the estimate of a writer in Household Words (1858, Aug. 21, 218). In 1869, a writer in the St. James' Magazine (Vol. 3, p.4) put it at 120,000. At first a journal of the Family Herald type, though even more trashy in its contents, it eventually (after 1865) gave more and more prominence to women's fashions. Readers lower to middle class women, educational standard low.   (Ellegård, 1957: 37)

At a time when many previously unexplored areas of print culture are being charted – the American dime novel, the 'Other Tradition' of mass-market American woman writers, the globally-circulating newspaper novel – there is no full-length account of one of the most pervasive print media, the nineteenth-century British penny fiction weekly. This study is concerned to fill this gap by focussing on the first series of the most popular illustrated example, *The London Journal and Weekly Record of Literature, Science and Art* between 1845 and 1883. I shall treat this magazine not as an isolated entity but as a case study and vantage point from which to explore both the wider field of Victorian periodicals and issues concerning mass-market culture in general.

In recent years, a discipline whose primary educational aim is literacy in present-day media has appeared in the academic firmament with all the apparent suddenness and glamour of a super nova: media studies. Taking literacy to mean ability to use various hermeneutic techniques, it has tended to prioritize theoretical speculation and textual analysis over history, paying the merest lip-service to long-term transformations in its object of study – when they are mentioned at all. On the other hand, and all too often ignoring the theoretical insights of media studies altogether, positivistic histories of print and reading are also burgeoning under the general category of 'History of the Book'. The present study aims to address both hermeneuts and historians. Those in search of biblio- or biographical descriptions of products and producers will certainly find them here, but those interested in theorization of mass-market media consumption will find that too.

I do not seek an easy synthesis of these different and, to many, antithetical approaches. Rather I use each methodology, the 'media studies' and the 'historical', to activate and critique the other. As I suggested in the 'Preface', it is oscillation between the two that I value, not one side isolated from or prioritized above the other in what is by now a conventional but still emotionally fraught debate. For it is oscillation that enables analysis of how a periodical might operate as a particularly luminous example of what is itself multiple and mobile, the *commodity fetish*.

Towards the beginning of *Capital*, Marx commented on how complex and indeed 'metaphysical' a commodity is, suggesting that the material alone is inadequate to describe its operation:

> A commodity appears, at first sight, a very trivial thing, and easily understood. Its analysis shows that it is, in reality, a very queer thing, abounding in metaphysical subtleties and theological niceties ... [in the marketplace] it is a definite social relation between men, that assumes, in their eyes, the fantastic form of a relation between things. In order, therefore, to find an analogy, we must have recourse to the mist-enveloped regions of the religious world. In that world the productions of the human brain appear as independent beings endowed with life, and entering into relation both with one another and the human race. So it is in the world of commodities with the products of men's hands. This I call the Fetishism which attaches itself to the products of labour so soon as they are produced as commodities, and which is therefore inseparable from the production of commodities.
>
> (Marx, 1887: 76-7)

The commodity fetish has then a double nature, as physical 'product of men's hands' and the metaphysical magic we attribute to the product. Even though this orthodox Marxist notion underlies the whole of the present book, I have not found it necessary to take on board Marx's thought *in toto*. Indeed, as will become clear, I do not accept the utopian Hegelian division of society into two opposing classes whose conflict will eventually bring about a revolutionary *Aufhebung*. It seems to me, however, that employing the commodity fetish as a governing concept allows alternation between 'soft' media studies and 'hard' historical data. While I consider it vital to uncover who produced, sold and bought what, when, where and for how much, this nonetheless does not entirely explain the 'social relation' between producer and consumer, or indeed between that pair and the social totality. A fiction periodical such as the *London Journal* has less obvious use value than the table Marx talks of elsewhere in his chapter. Its use value comprises in fact its stimulation and permission of fantasy of various kinds – 'the mist-enveloped regions of the religious world' – even when, as I shall show in Part 3, it is communicating what seem the facts of 'news'. Its identity as a medium is then precisely equivalent to its status as a commodity fetish indicative of a 'definite social relation' between people. It is this varying and complex relation, apparently with a will of its own, independent of the producer but which the producer is constantly trying to control, that I shall explore in my speculations concerning the pleasures of the text, all the while bearing in mind the material conditions of textual production.

As a medium, a periodical is most obviously concerned with communication between writers and readers. But these are not the only elements involved in the periodical as social relation. As Robert Darnton (1990: 111-13) has pointed out, the communication circuit also involves publishers, printers, paper suppliers, shippers, booksellers, binders, and all their workers and variants, not to mention the complexities of legal, cultural and political sanctions and encouragements, and the various intellectual histories, aspirations and competencies of all involved.

In the Preface, I acknowledged my debt to accounts by previous writers of the nineteenth-century mass market. I feel it now necessary to suggest that the reader turn to them for a panoptical historical overview of mass-market reading, for although such a general history is conventional as an introduction in a book of this genre, I shall not offer one here. I am instead more concerned to formulate the questions such studies have provoked. For through their gaps, ironies, refusals and silent assumptions, they have helped me frame the theoretical questions I shall address and which my historical research will seek to answer. Besides the overarching enquiry into the implications of the periodical as commodity fetish, these questions fall under three main heads: the usefulness, nature and role of class, gender and geography as descriptive categories for a study in this area; the nature of reading; and the operation of the cultural status and location of texts.

The necessity of asking these questions is evident in especially concentrated form in the few lines of the epigraph to this chapter. Ellegård's magisterial description of the *London Journal* in his much-cited monograph, *The Readership of the Victorian Periodical Press*, starts with a bare recital of a few circulation figures that indicate the periodical's mass-market status. He implies through bare juxtaposition that the periodical must perforce be 'trashy', the figures acting as 'proof' of his value judgement. His high-culture attitude towards the text is unabashed; his juxtaposition of literary worthlessness with the 'lower to middle class' and with femininity is unproblematized and unconcealed. But were the *Journal*'s readers simply 'lower to middle class', female and uneducated? And even if they were, what do these terms mean? Is the 'lower to middle class' a unified social grouping? And if so, unified by what? Does it employ the same decoding practices in Leeds as in London? Are all women in that social group alike? Does uneducated inevitably mean stupid and easily led? The remainder of this chapter seeks to refine these lines of enquiry and to sketch out how I shall pursue them in the rest of the book.

Questions of Class, Gender and Geography

Although it is still a commonplace to use the terms working, middle and upper class in work on nineteenth-century media, I regard this terminology as inadequate to describe cultural consumption. Consumers of mass-market products should not be defined by 'class' in the strict sense of head-of-household income or place within the means of production, but should be classified mainly by their places within the means of cultural consumption. Louis James realized this in the early 1960s. Discussing readers of mass-market publications in the 1830s and 40s, he queried the idea that they were necessarily 'working class'.

But what were 'the working classes'? The factory hand and the miner certainly, but where should one place the small tradesman, or educated and generally respected lower-class men like William Lovett and S.T. Hall? There was a large and growing intermediary class. What was 'the reading of the lower classes'? Starting with the *Poor Man's Guardian* and *Cleave's Penny Gazette* we move up the range until with *Chambers's*

Edinburgh Journal and the *Family Herald* one realizes that some periodicals span two fields. Then, the young Rossetti read [the penny serial] *Ada the Betrayed*, while workmen in coffee houses read *Blackwood's*. There is no neat definition. Fortunately, the problem is less acute here than it would be even ten years later, for the working classes were closely unified by political and class feeling, and poverty meant that the price of literature largely determined the class of the reader, the poor buying the penny part, the middle classes feeling cheap literature had a social stigma. We are therefore reasonably safe to take as 'lower class', literature published at a penny, and some at three half-pence, largely omitting *Chambers's Journal* after 1840, and the *Family Herald...*   (James, 1963: xii)

Clearly of the same thinking as E.P. Thompson (1963) in this passage, James did not want to jettison the political implications of 'class' terminology, even while his evidence contests it. Almost three decades later, Sally Mitchell also found a class-based social organization highly problematic when explaining what group magazines such as the *London Journal* appealed to. '[P]eople between the two nations', 'the petty bourgeoisie and the labor aristocracy' characterized by 'aspiration for respectability' (Mitchell, 1989: 29, 33, 34) – these are descriptors that fit uneasily a vision of society organized in terms of place in the cycle of production. Later again, Patricia Anderson (1994: 156) wrote that the consumers of penny fiction magazines were 'a socially diverse cultural formation of women and men, the youthful and the mature, the middle and the working classes. It was in this sense that the mass made itself. Working people had played a large part in this process ...'. Like Mitchell and James, then, Anderson continues using the terminology of class even though for her it has become vague and almost detached from a politicized analytic framework.

As Patrick Joyce (1994, 1995) amongst many others has observed, 'class' has become increasingly problematic as an explanatory category, even when describing place in production, let alone consumption. This has been brought about in the late twentieth century both by huge shifts from production to consumption in employment and investment patterns in wealthy regions of the world, and, more recently again, by changes in the nature of communications technology. Realization that a much more complex social organization and hierarchy exists in the present than the old tripartite or even binary structure has also enabled us to see the multifariousness and hybridity of nineteenth-century society. Not only income levels and how these were generated, but also gender, geography, ethnicity, religion and attitudes to specific cultural formations were key determinants in their constitution. If we are to concern ourselves with the historical study of the markets of cultural consumption – in other words media history from the point of view of the consumer, reader or audience – then we need to heed the lessons of business studies and social anthropology on the social as comprising mobile overlapping structures. One has only to consider the 54 categories of ACORN neighbourhood segmentation, a sociological mapping much in use for product placement in 2004 and easily available on the Internet. While I am not at all suggesting a simple retrospective application of these 54 or any other categories to the nineteenth century, I do think that either a more precise sociology of consumption is necessary, or, as I do here, at least an attempt to identify the imaginary relations that the product as commodity encourages. Jonathan Rose's magisterial *Intellectual*

Life of the British Working Classes (2001) actually concentrates on the reading habits of a very specific social group, the poor male industrial autodidact, who was much more likely to try to legitimate himself by consuming what he thought high-status texts. Although Teresa Gerrard (1998) and Patricia Anderson (1994) have combed correspondence columns of nineteenth-century penny fiction magazines, material on mass-market textual consumption remains very scarce and unreliable. While I have made use of what there is, I have mainly concentrated on the imaginary, fetishistic, relations that the commodity text encourages.

The *London Journal*, when it was successful as a mass-market magazine, refused to ally itself with any income group and reached out beyond specific geographical areas. Its complex relation to gender changed as perceived demography and the political landscape mutated. Its readers can instead be characterized in terms both negative – by their non-consumption of the exclusive culture of the quarterlies and other representatives of 'difficult' culture – and positive – by their desire for a literary culture that welcomes them. The common term in this opposition is the ambiguous and contested one of 'culture', key both for the many nineteenth-century groups who assigned themselves the attributes of either present or desired power, and in the repeated insistence in the late twentieth century on the *Journal*'s unstable, ambiguous but always median cultural position. 'Salisbury Square Fiction' and its non-respectable ilk took on board the techniques of material production from respectable producers of culture, but then used them to broadcast images and narratives that resisted the cultural codes issuing from their respectable ancestors. This resistance, rather than any notion of 'incompetence', is what is indicated by the extremely non-naturalistic prints and stylized narratives that James (1963, 1976) and Anderson (1994) reprint and comment on. Consumption of such culture meant rebellion, at least for the duration of the consumption. The *Journal*, on the other hand, discovered a reader that wanted the exclusivities of neither the resisting nor sanctioned cultures. Obvious as that may be as a general conclusion, its specificities are complex and unexpected, and my analysis has created the necessity for a new terminology that will be introduced and defined in due course. As befits the mobility of the market, this terminology is only local in its explanatory effects and requires constant redefinition if it is to be applied to different areas of the field and to different time periods.

Now in arguing that we move on from the language of class when analysing cultural consumption, I am not suggesting we abandon politics as a social engagement that seeks more equitable distribution of power and resources. On the contrary, my concerns about the many books today that continue to use terms such as 'middle-class periodicals' or 'working-class serials' lie precisely in the contradiction between the attenuation of such engagement while still clinging on to its language. Employment of the language of class seems an archaism, a residuum of a previous age whose politics have become tame, dutiful, a badge of belonging to specific academic sectors of the arts (cf. Bourdieu, 1988: 66-9). My rejection of the language of class is based not only on its descriptive inadequacy for my purposes, but also on my belief in the urgent necessity for the revival of political intervention in specific and focussed areas.

Just as class has proved inadequate as a descriptive category for the reader of the mass-market text, so the category of gender also needs refinement away from a simple binarism of products labelled as either 'men's' or 'women's'. As exemplified by the epigraph from Ellegård, the London Journal has usually been described in the twentieth century as 'feminine' in some way. But just because the *Journal* published a coloured fashion plate as an optional supplement from 1868 (not 1865, *pace* Ellegård), this does not mean that it was in any easy sense a 'woman's magazine' by then – which is what Mitchell (1989) later claims. Patricia Anderson (1994) is less direct in her gendering of the *Journal*. Although she maintains that mass culture is not class- or gender-specific, she feminizes its reader in a way suggestive of the melodramatic seduction of an ambiguously willing or stupid heroine by a villain skilled in the arts of pleasure. In the overall narrative that Anderson tells, the *Journal* jointly plays the role of villain with *Reynolds's Miscellany* and *Cassell's Illustrated Family Paper* in perverting the artistic taste of the masses that the virtuous *Penny Magazine* had started to educate and raise. But are the illustrations of these later publications as 'low' as Anderson claims? Elsewhere I have shown the *Journal*'s indebtedness to gallery art (King, 1999 and 2000). In the same way that Mitchell repeatedly describes the *Journal*'s fictional women, Anderson concludes that the illustrations in penny fiction magazines present an unambiguous vision of women as helpless and pneumatic sex objects (Anderson, 1994: 124-9). Even if this is true, is the reader necessarily a virtuous victim who reads as she – or he – ought to? Can a reader not gain pleasure by resisting, twisting or ignoring an overt message, as Menocchio did in Carlo Ginsberg's *The Cheese and the Worms* (1980)? One is tempted to see in this feminization the subtle influence of the twentieth century's pervasive and implicit gendering of the mass market as documented by Andreas Huyssen (1988).

At this point I need to clarify what I intend by gender. As I use the term in this book, it comprises three interrelated components: the gendering of the implied reader (and thereby of the periodical itself); the gender dynamic between producers and the implied reader; the discursive construction of gender ('Man' and 'Woman'). To these I append a fourth, closely related to gender even if, strictly speaking, not subsumed into it, the textual construction of sexual desire.

What I mean by these components can most easily be explained by referring to how they will be used. In the last four chapters of the book, where I concentrate most on gender and sexual desire, I shall show how the *Journal* was initially a magazine implying predominantly masculine readers and writers who colluded to control a gender-ambiguous domestic space and language. As a gendered discursive object, 'Woman' fulfilled two main functions at this time, as an image that was passed between men to create homosocial solidarity and as an allegory for the condition of the unenfranchised male. I shall argue that state regulation of the periodical field was a major determinant in these gender relations between readers and producers, with the market as another. As long as profits resulted, gender blurring could quite easily be accommodated, together with what may seem to us as constructions of sexual desire at variance with common images of Victorian morality (King, 1999). In Chapter 9, *Lady Audley's Secret* (serialized in the *Journal* in 1863) will be considered in this light, with attention to how homosocial elements common in fiction a decade previously were revisited, as well as to how the figure of the supposedly 'subversive woman' was actually a well established part of the mass market. In Chapter 10 I shall suggest that the debates around the time of the 1867 extension of the male franchise, along with demographic changes and the commercial success of new rivals aimed specifically at women consumers, caused the demise of vestigial appropriations of 'Woman' as allegories of unenfranchised men. The *London Journal* now locked the signifier 'Woman' more firmly onto the female (as opposed to the earlier feminine), offering women consumerism in place of enfranchisement. In the last chapter, I shall look at Zola's *The Ladies' Paradise* (serialized in the *Journal* in 1883) as an exploration of sales strategies that the *Journal* itself employed. By examining the original French version I show how masquerade and narcissism were as key to the *magasin* as to the magazine. I shall end by comparing Zola's original with the *Journal*'s considerably rewritten version. This enables me to reconsider the struggle between the consumer and the producer over knowledge, and to show how, by the 1880s, gendered producer-consumer relations had metamorphosed from an uneasy homosocial expulsion of 'Woman' as third-person Other to a troubled second-person address to women.

There remains the question of the gendering of the literary field in terms of production, a sub-set of the second component of gender. What proportion of *London Journal* novels was written by women and by men in which periods? Tuchman (1989) suggested that the novel was increasingly colonized by male writers who raised its status, while the devalued mass market was left to women – a material investigation by sociologists that supports Huyssen's more literary approach. While my bibliographical research on penny fiction weeklies has confirmed this, related biographical work has enabled me to determine how much men and women authors were paid, clearly a key aspect of gender differentials. This I explore in Part 2 where I concentrate on the *Journal*'s production history. Furthermore, bibliographical techniques I outline there help to determine the status of each novel and novelist within the periodical. What has emerged is the huge importance of American women authors in the British mass market more or less continuously from 1855. This is the year that 'Fanny Fern' started to receive $100 per column in a New York fiction weekly modelled in many ways on the *London Journal*, the *New York Ledger*. Prefigured by the extraordinary sales of *Uncle Tom's Cabin*, this turn to America was caused not least by changes in the 1852 copyright agreement with France, the country that had previously been the principal source for (pirated) cheap fiction.

Fifty years ago, in a neglected but exceptionally well-informed book, Mary Noel pointed out the close connection of British and American literary markets, and Louis James soon after remarked the popularity of American literature in Britain in the 1830s and early 1840s. There has been in fact a two-way traffic in mass-market fiction between London and New York in continuous operation since the 1830s, intensifying from 1855. In the second half of the nineteenth century, not only was work by American women imported in large numbers into Britain, but British writing was as much, if not more, imported into America (Johanningsmeier, 1997; Law, 2000a). Recent work on the Australian mass market has confirmed a globalization of mass-market fiction from the 1860s, with the massive import of American and British fiction into Australian periodicals, (Morrison, 1995; Johnson-Woods, 2001). The ongoing work of Law and Morita (2000) on the global syndication of serial novels in newspapers is revealing the importance of translations of western mass-market fiction, including Braddon, Dumas and Hugo, as far afield as Japan from the 1880s. By the early 1870s, the *London Journal*, like other major British penny weeklies, was on sale all over the British Empire and North America. Advertisements on its monthly covers from 1870 (volume LI) list the 'Colonial Agents':

Australia – Castlemain, Mrs E. Vale, Mostyn St
Victoria, Mr W.M.K. Vale, Jas. T. Hall, Sandhurst
Melbourne, Geo. Robertson, Robert Mackay
Sydney, Gordon and Gotch, F. Kirby, G. T. Sandon, Reading & Co.
Cape of Good Hope – J.C. Juta, Cape Town
Canada – A.S. Irving, Toronto
Jamaica – Geo. Henderson, Kingston
New Zealand – Mr Jesse Hounsell, Trafalgar Street, Nelson
New York – Willmer & Rogers, Nassau Street
Tasmania – J. Walch & Sons Hobart Town, Walch Bros & Birchall, Launceton
Nova Scotia – G.E. Morton & Co.

I do not wish to suggest that similar gender or other dynamics of social hierarchy operated the same throughout the world. Though many of the same serials were circulated in different magazines, they were inserted into different contexts, surrounded by different advertisements and miscellaneous matter, juxtaposed with other stories and news items, placed in relation to various narrative traditions. Often the names of characters and the setting of the plot were changed when a serial migrated from one publication to another: the Adirondacks in the American versions of Southworth novels usually became Wales in the British (see Figure 6.5 for a striking visual example); New York was renamed London, and so on. More disturbingly, slaves became servants even while their original and characteristic patois was retained. Then again, while the *London Journal*, like other similar British periodicals, tended to import woman-centred romances by American female writers, the *Australian Journal* preferred adventure narratives with male heroes, written by authors with masculine signatures (Johnson-Woods, 2000). The same broad set of authors and stories may have been read around the globe, but in different proportions, with different emphases, different connotations and contexts.

Even when we are talking of the same periodical or novel, I cannot think that their depictions of social relations, in all their complexity, operated in the same way in Castlemain as in New York, Nova Scotia, or London. What of issues of 'race', that third element in the hellish trinity of inequality? That would certainly have had widely different political resonances in the Cape and Jamaica, Toronto and Manchester. While 'race' is discussed to some extent in Part 3 (and nationality figures in Part 2), I have chosen not to concentrate upon it in this work, as it is a much less frequent issue than gender during the time-frame I cover. This is most assuredly not the case in the last two decades of the nineteenth century in the related cultural zone of the syndicated newspaper novel, as Law (2000) and numerous studies of the fin-de-siècle adventure romance remind us. Even though the *London Journal* survived until 1928, it still continued the kind of fiction – and indeed often repeated the very same novels – that had been new in the 1850s, 60s and 70s. In that sense it never moved on from the third quarter of the nineteenth century. Furthermore, most of the material about reading I have uncovered was written by and about white British city-dwellers, for whom 'race' probably operated as little more than an allegory of social oppression in general. As a result, I have read mainly as a literate white British urbanite since, while the *Journal* and its fellow fiction magazines were certainly consumed in the country as well as abroad by a wide variety of social groups, it is such a reader with a corresponding imaginary that the magazine invokes and through which it defines and sells itself.

Questions of Interpretation

One of my *a priori* assumptions is that meaning lies not in a text but is an effect in readers created through their interactions with texts. Even if meanings vary from place to place, and from person to person, this does not imply that they are entirely arbitrary or irrecoverable. Modern-day empirical studies, in which readers and audiences are interviewed, find general tendencies in meanings generated from a text according to a variety of factors: age, gender, socio-economic group, education, geographical location, and so on (see, for example, Radway, 1984; Taylor, 1989; McCracken, 1993; Hermes, 1995). I do not intend to engage here in depth with arguments about the validity of the various ways audiences can be conceptualized and studied (see Ang, 1991, 1995, 1996; Abercrombie, 1998) except to say that I agree in my own way with Ang that the context of media consumption is vital (cf. King, 2000) and that I disagree with the Althusserian leanings of Feltes (1986), for I do not believe meaning to be entirely coextensive with the magic of the fetish although it is certainly closely related to and overlaps with it.

A major problem for the cartographer of the nineteenth-century mass market lies in the dearth of sources for direct qualitative research of readers which might reveal context and decoding strategies. *What* was read is guessable, for circulation figures provide quantitative data (of varying reliability); *how* readers read or what else they did with the texts they bought is much less certain. We know that illustrations were cut out and pasted on the walls of a cottage, a trapper's shanty, and a county asylum (Mountjoy, 1985: 51-2), but what precise meanings were adduced from them remain hypothetical. Kate Flint (1993) has comprehensively discussed 'The Woman Reader' in the nineteenth century, but her sources for 'real readers' are almost exclusively taken from those with sufficient cultural confidence and education to write down their reading. Such people were unlikely to admit to enjoying mass-market periodicals. 'Slumming', whereby a culturally respectable reader takes pleasure in mass-market reading, was in the nineteenth-century a love that dare not speak its name. When the great psychiatrist Sir Shadwell Rock in

Sarah Grand's *The Heavenly Twins* (1892) derives pleasure from detective novelettes with female criminals, this marks him out as both exceptional and of dubious credibility when he is supposed to advise on curing the hysteria of a woman who as a girl had read the classics and John Stuart Mill. More typical is the silence of E.S. Dallas, the otherwise notable theorist of pleasure, who, when writing about 'Popular Literature' in *Blackwood's*, omits the mass market altogether to concentrate on works just below his own cultural preferences. This is not to suggest that Dallas was a closet consumer of penny fiction, but to mark that silence was the norm. Rose's (2001) study has one incidental reference to a penny fiction weekly in 534 pages. Similarly, if Flint's section on the reading of the 'working class' is only four pages long (and there is no mention of the mass-market periodical), this need by no means indicate an indifference to this area of the market; there is simply little material that reveals how 'real readers' read such publications. While there has been an attempt to use correspondence columns in mass-market magazines to determine reading strategies (Gerrard, 1998), there are actually very rarely any comments on reading that reveal information that is not already well known: most published comments comprise queries about when a particular serial started. As with circulation figures, the columns can be used as a gauge of what was read, then, not as a window on readers' decoding strategies.

In any case, studies of recent media suggest extreme caution here. For instance, despite a plethora of correspondence with readers published in today's women's magazines, it is impossible to tell from that alone that substantial numbers of men read them (Ballaster et al., 1991: 45, 113). While I discuss the little I have glimpsed of the decoding strategies of 'real readers' at various points in Parts 2 and 3, most of my comments regarding reading and readers must perforce operate in the subjunctive mood, hypothesizing the complex, often contradictory and vaguely structured roles of a modified version of Wolfgang Iser's 'implied reader'.

Iser (1978: 36) proposed a 'conditioning force' that the text sets up, a transcendental, ideationally structured field within which a real reader is offered a choice of roles and positions. Iser's implied reader is a transhistorical concept that seeks to answer the question of what enables us today to read and enjoy texts written in the past. Under the influence of later reader response criticism I have tended to localize my version of the implied reader to one situated in a particular cultural field at a particular moment. Thus I read *Lady Audley's Secret* as a serial read after others in the *London Journal*. In this sense my model of signification has elements of linguistic pragmatics, influenced in general terms by the criticisms and modifications made by Fish (1980), Said (1991) and Eagleton (1983). Such a model seeks negotiation between the real and the abstract, historical empiricism and media studies theory, and, following the *Journal's* similar median cultural location, recognizes its instability and its need for constant refinement.

The periodical I describe throughout Part 2 is an artefact located through an investigation of its production: origins, costs, market conditions, networks of writers, determination of authorship, and so on. I wish this materialist approach not only to contrast with the discursive orientation of Chapter 2 but also to resonate over those sections of Parts 2 and 3 that deal at length with the metaphysics of reader-text relations that the implied reader depends on. Although reading and consuming, I do not wish to fetishize the fetish and forget the commodity. A good deal of Part 2, then, and especially Chapter 4, is intended to stick in the throat, a burr preventing the easy consumption and assimilation of yet more textual interpretation.

Further expanding my point concerning the necessary interrelatedness between the commodity and the fetish, I feel it incumbent upon me to add that the claim that a production history should offer an exclusively producerly and positive perspective, somehow more 'real' than the hermeneutic, forgets that producers of a successful commodity must constantly shift their viewpoints to those of consumers and to speculation. To be successful, producers must have bifocal vision shared between production costs and possibilities on the one hand, and actual or potential consumer desires, fantasies and interpretations on the other. An interesting example of the interplay between the two is available in Chapter 8, where legal constraints and the consumerly aspects of 'news' are put into play against and with each other in an edgy, seductive tension.

Of course one can object that the hypothetical pleasures of the implied reader that I propose below are grounded ultimately in a personal – my – subjectivity. I would argue that it is necessary to reflect upon the subjective experience of reading these texts and to try to abstract general principles from it. In order to do that I engage directly in interpretation, for all the risks it runs of further fetishing the text (Feltes, 1986), for it is only thus that the magic seductions of the fetish can be understood. In other words, what I am aiming to do is offer a phenomenology of the nineteenth-century mass-media fetish, as exemplified by the *London Journal* and its fellow magazines.

Questions of Culture

In order to explain the specific cultural status of the mass market in general and of the *London Journal* in particular, I have found Pierre Bourdieu's example of mapping cultural consumption in France the most illuminating model. According to Bourdieu, every society is organized according to sets of 'fields', economic, cultural, political, geographical, and so on. Each field has its own laws that determine the position of its participants in a hierarchy. It is firmly situated in time and space and is not necessarily applicable anywhere else. Each field is relatively autonomous, but exists in dialogue with others. For example, the analysis of Flaubert's *L'Éducation sentimentale* (Bourdieu, 1996) locates various kinds of cultural production in different parts of Paris, overlaying the cultural field with the geographical – a procedure I adopt most intensively in the last part of Chapter 3. In theory, it might also be possible to extend such work to mapping decoding practices, not just production, onto a global geography, but so far there is insufficient evidence to permit this.

As Bourdieu portrays it, the literary and artistic field is a sub-set of the 'field of power', which is itself a sub-set of the 'field of class relations'. The literary field is governed by two principles. The first is concerned with the hierarchization caused by market forces. This Bourdieu calls 'the heteronomous principle' which rules the mass market: here economic capital – money – rules. The second principle he terms 'autonomous'. This creates a hierarchization based on prestige, which Bourdieu also calls 'symbolic capital' or 'consecration'. Symbolic capital is granted by limited groups who, to use Bourdieu's deliberate solipsism, 'recognize no other criterion of legitimacy than recognition by those whom they recognize' (Bourdieu, 1996: 38). In its ideal form this kind of hierarchization is autonomous and independent of normal market forces, being a market for objects created by producers of culture for their fellow producers. Nineteenth-century France came to produce a field determined largely by a logic of 'loser wins'. Poetry, from which there was usually little financial gain to be made, was granted the most symbolic capital (one thinks of Mallarmé's wonderfully impenetrable experiments), whereas the theatre, which was economically profitable, had the least prestige (a Feydeau farce). The novel hovered over a wide area in between these two extremes. Although rather too simple a mapping – there was, for example, commercial poetry in France (as described by Kavanagh, 1847) – the general principle remains helpful in understanding how certain texts are granted status and others not.

Beside economic and symbolic capitals, there are two other forms of capital that Bourdieu describes: social and cultural. Social capital comprises that power conferred through belonging to certain families or other social networks that lend support of various kinds. As repeatedly emerges in Bourdieu's work, France is still governed by quite a small set of 'great families', but there are many less powerful social networks that also struggle to maintain or advance their positions. Cultural capital consists in educational or intellectual qualifications, experience or knowledge that can be deployed and converted to other forms of capital. It should not be confused with symbolic capital, although the two are intimately related, for cultural capital comprises a set of skills that a person might 'own' and exploit, while symbolic capital is the status that is granted by others to those skills and their products. A form of capital that Bourdieu tends to play down but which has been commented on in recent years is 'gender capital' (Fowler, 1997, esp. ch. 6; Armstrong, 2000: 156). Obviously, I think this so important that I have already devoted a separate section to it, although I do not tend to use the language of capital when referring to it. It work in ways that analogy to finance does not always illuminate.

Each sub-field (which I prefer to call a 'zone') is related to what Bourdieu calls a 'habitus'. A habitus is a system of 'principles which generate and organize practices and representations that can be objectively adapted to their outcomes without presupposing a conscious aiming at ends or an express mastery of the operations necessary to attain them' (Bourdieu, 1990: 52). The habitus is learnt unconsciously from early childhood from a variety of sources, from institutions such as schools, but also from the family and from all kinds of social and cultural contact. It determines a person's rhetoric concerning and attitudes towards objects, and indeed, to a large extent their perception and actions in relation to them. A recent book (Hillier and Rooksby, 2002: 5) has summed up the habitus as 'a sense of one's (and others') place and role in the world of one's lived environment ... an embodied as well as a cognitive sense of space'. Thus people whose habitus supplies them with criteria which predispose them towards the restricted market of learned (consecrated) periodicals, will probably dismiss as invalid the heteronomous periodicals of the mass market, which operate according to different criteria. They will regard them as a foreign country perhaps. They will also have a defined range of positions to adopt in relation to political and economic power. Lest it be thought that Bourdieu be setting up a *ballet méchanique* of social automata whirring through pre-set programmes – and implicitly claiming godlike status for himself outside this ballet – it is important to stress that he only talks of the habitus as creating *dispositions*. There is always the possibility of alternative action and thought, including those based on reason which, writes Bourdieu, escape the routes laid down by habitus.

An issue that is less explicit in Bourdieu is how people can inhabit, and be constituted by, several different zones simultaneously. Postmodern notions of hybridity would have it that identity is never perfectly self-consistent and monolithic, but comprises an enormous number of contradictory historical lines always in process, proliferation, degradation and tension with each other. Such a notion is clearly appropriate for times and places where technology enables the rapid diffusion of habitus outside their originary geographical and cultural zones – such as occurred in urban Britain of the 1840s when the railways and print media profoundly altered migration and communications practices. Bourdieu (1993: 262) does point out, however, that people who are 'richest in economic capital, cultural capital and social capital' tend to be those who most readily move to new positions vis-à-vis consecration. A powerful economic, cultural and social position enables the adoption of radical or avant-garde ideas and life-styles, for these can be invested with the prestige the producer already feels s/he carries. G.W.M. Reynolds is a good example. From an impeccably upper-middle-class background, in his youth he travelled to France, appropriated notions of French romanticism, wrote *soi-disant* radical fiction and became prominent in Chartism. On the other hand, the 'badly placed' – for example, economically poor, provincial cultural producers – tend to stick to the already consecrated. This is very visibly the case with the majority of *London Journal* poetry written by correspondents, which is almost without exception what Brian Maidment (1987) has called 'Parnassian'. In fact, one of Maidment's examples of a Parnassian, Charles Swain, was the *Journal*'s favourite paid poet in the early 1850s. As I shall show, most *London Journal* serial writers had even more ambiguous social backgrounds than either Reynolds or reader-contributors. Comparatively rich in cultural capital from their education, association with journalism or the book trade, they yet require financial and social capital.

The 'literary field' I chart may be modelled on Bourdieu's, but, specifically concerned with periodicals, it departs from it in many ways. For instance, I refer to the 'habitus' of a zone in which a periodical is located, referring not just to sociological location but the cultural practices of a text and its consumers. If, as Margaret Beetham (1990: 21) has remarked, periodicals are always commodities, then, according to Bourdieu's macro-analysis, the periodical field should be entirely on the side of the heteronomous, aiming for as high a circulation as possible. Yet, unlike the *London Journal*, most nineteenth-century periodicals that are commonly quoted and studied today – those in the Wellesley index to Victorian periodicals – had remarkably small circulations and did not wish to move into the mass market. They glitter with high and intimidating cultural capital, echoed in their high prices. The very fact that they are still regularly quoted suggests their ability to survive through their consecration: they are not disposable reading, but bound in covers as sacred reliques in our library pyxes, preserved for repeated consultation. Conversely, periodicals with truly large circulations are not quoted or studied nearly so much, largely because they survive in very low numbers. Unlike the unique auratic artwork that Walter Benjamin (1968) famously described, their very scarcity today confirms their low prestige.

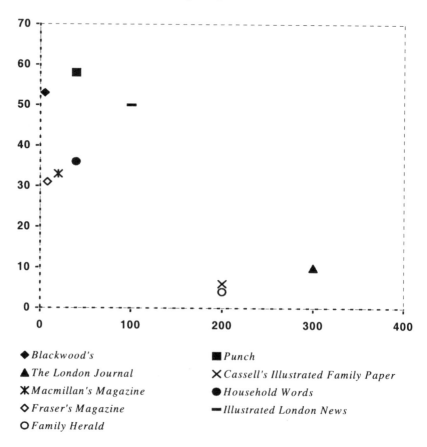

Figure 1.1 The Periodical Field in 1860: a Selective Ideograph.
Vertical axis: the number of runs (even incomplete) available in British libraries; *Horizontal axis*: circulation in thousands in 1860. *Sources*: BUCOP, 1986; Ellegård, 1957: 32-3, 35; Lohrli, 1973: 23

Figure 1.1 shows the relationship between survival and circulation very clearly. To plot it I deliberately used data concerning survival rates and circulation that has been readily available for over thirty years. It by no means represents an iconic scale topography of literary-periodical space in 1860, and, to mark that, I do not give precise figures for any publication. At best, both circulation and number of copies that survive are estimates rather than reliable statistical data. While the descending line of survival plotted against circulation confirms the logic of 'loser wins', I strongly suspect that the line should extend further. To my knowledge only one run of the *London Journal* survives (more or less) complete, that in the British Library. The other runs mentioned in *BUCOP*, when checked against library catalogues and in libraries themselves, are even less complete than *BUCOP* suggests. Furthermore, some contemporary sources indicate a circulation of at least 100,000 larger than that suggested by Ellegård.[1] The *Journal* should be placed even further from, say, *Blackwood's*, than Figure 1.1 draws. Finally, it needs to be said that a graph like this is only an out-of-focus snapshot that does not take into account changes in the composition and configuration of the field, which can be very rapid. The chart has value, therefore, only as a polemical ideograph that illustrates the huge gulf between the *London Journal* and the periodicals in which most descriptions of it have come down to us. Offering a *gestalt* of the fundamental epistemological problem this book is concerned with, the graph is a peculiarly appropriate opening in another way too, in that it imitates the advertorial practice of separating image and commentary that was standard in the *Journal*– you could only properly decode the image on the magazine's front page by reading several pages into it: the opening image sets up a mystery that in theory encourages you to read on.

If the distance between described and describer that Figure 1.1 so forcefully shows raises problems for the academic cartographer of the mass market who is dependent upon consecrated sources, it also created difficulties for nineteenth-century travellers over the field. While the availability of the mass-market periodical would not have been an issue, a more insidious problem was endemic. High-prestige zones risk seeing everything as a reflection of themselves and describing the entirety of the literary field in their own image. This is perceptible in the rhetoric of the article that Ellegård referred to in the epigraph above, a piece often cited as authoritative in discussions of 'Victorian popular reading', Wilkie Collins's 'The Unknown Public' in *Household Words* of 1858. Collins described mass-market serials as all of an 'extraordinary sameness', written by people who did not have any idea of how to write:

> Each portion purported to be written (and no doubt was written) by a different author, and yet all five might have been produced by the same man. Each part of each successive story, settled down in turn, as I read it, to the same dead level of the smoothest and flattest conventionality. A combination of fierce melodrama and meek domestic sentiment; short dialogues and paragraphs on the French pattern, with moral English reflections of the sort that occur on the top lines of children's copy-books; incidents and characters taken from

---

[1] For details of *London Journal* circulation figures, see the Appendix and Chapter 4 below.

the old exhausted mines of the circulating library, and presented as complacently and confidently as if they were original ideas; descriptions and reflections for the beginning of the number, and a 'strong situation', dragged in by the neck and shoulders, for the end – formed the common literary source from which the five authors drew their weekly supply; all collecting it by the same means; all carrying it in the same quantities; all pouring it out before the attentive public in the same way. After reading my samples of these stories, I understood why it was that the fictions of the regularly established writers for the penny journals are never republished ...   ([Collins], 1858: 443)

Such flattening rhetoric is a constant temptation for those of us disciplined to derive greater and more refined pleasures from the culturally exclusive. We are either unable to see complexity in what is different and/or we judge the other by our own criteria of value. Adorno and his followers have certainly been accused of this failure so many times it has become a commonplace that often overwhelms the many valuable insights they had. I have no intention of setting up straw men to burn. Rather I want to interpolate a brief consideration of the implications of such narcissism in terms of a related but different politics.

In an important justification for the study of history, Gillian Beer linked it to the project of feminism. Starting from how men have tended to regard women as failed copies of themselves, denying that women are radically Other, her conclusion took the form of an ethical imperative: historical contextualization is necessary if we are to escape the destructive and oppressive possibilities of such narcissism.

We shall read as readers in 1987 or 1988, or, with luck, in 1998, but we need not do so helplessly, merely hauling without noticing, our own cultural baggage ... the study of past writing within the conditions of its production disturbs the autocratic emphasis on the self and the present, as if they were stable entities ...   (Beer, 1989: 80)

What 'the study of past writing within the conditions of its production' means in practical terms is highly variable and always fraught. I propose and enact several different methods below. I have called this book a family album, and while never claiming to be able to represent the Other as fully as she deserves, nonetheless, it is possible to see even family members as different from oneself, even while acknowledging one's similarity and indebtedness to them. Engaged difference is what I am attempting here.

The Wilkie Collins article was not alone in the nineteenth century. The title 'The London Journal' was often used as a collocation voided of reference to the actual artefact, instead metonymically standing for the penny fiction weekly in general. Chapter 2 starts to engage directly with the otherness of the nineteenth-century mass-market by considering the nature of the sources upon which twentieth-century writers have based their accounts. In other words, I shall consider the periodical not as a material body – as the *London Journal* – but as a discursive construct – 'The London Journal' – employed in local attempts to formulate and control the cultural field. The tactical nature of these descriptions of mass-market periodicals is precisely what has not hitherto been considered.

Lest I seem to be suggesting that the narcissism I decry above be due to some notion of personal failure of vision or psychology, I want to stress how the refusal of otherness can be an effect of structural constraints of various local and general kinds. What I mean can be explained by reference again to Collins's 'Unknown Public' article. Now Bourdieu (1993: 47) attributes 'special lucidity' to bohemians (meaning that they are able to give more accurate descriptions of society). Yet even though his decidedly bohemian status should allow Collins to travel more easily over the social field and observe it more accurately, his article remains constrained by the space it appears in. For all their ideological differences, the proto-feminist Langham Place periodicals, which claimed to be advanced, and the quarterlies that had so much prestige that they could afford sometimes to look *de haut en bas*, all operated on the supposition that sales were less important than the 'quality' or ideological value of what they contained (characteristics of 'autonomy'). *Household Words*, however, where 'The Unknown Public' appeared, had to balance 'quality' with sales much more carefully. In such an uncertain space, Collins chose to operate within a distancing frame narrative when dealing with material that was all too obviously heteronomous. He employed the familiar topos of the anthropological or travel writer exploring unknown zones of the metropolis and country, 'discovering' by chance a strange, incomprehensible artefact from an unknown people. This is exactly consonant with the habitus of the periodical.

> Do the subscribers to this journal, the customers at the eminent publishing-houses, the members of the book-clubs and circulating libraries, the purchasers and borrowers of newspapers and reviews, compose altogether the great bulk of the reading public of England? There was a time when, if anybody had put this question to me, I, for one, should certainly have answered, Yes.
>
> I know better now. I know that the public just now mentioned, viewed as an audience for literature, is nothing more than a minority.
>
> The discovery (which I venture to consider equally new and surprising) dawned on me gradually. I made my first approaches towards it, in walking about London, more especially in the second and third rate neighbourhoods. At such times, whenever I passed a small stationer's or small tobacconist's-shop, I became conscious, mechanically as it were, of certain publications which invariably occupied the windows ...
>
> ([Collins], 1858: 439)

Collins moves from the comfort of the familiar household ('readers of this journal') into 'second and third rate neighbourhoods', overlaying the literary field onto the geographical. But he will never meet a single reader of the artefacts he describes. They remain elusive despite his supposed searches for them. Unlike Mayhew, he does not even pretend to allow them to speak, marking a net separation between observing subject and observed object. He remains within the zone that *Household Words* has created and is maintaining for itself by applying the same criteria for the zone he writes for to the zone he writes about. This is especially the case in the marked emphasis he places on 'Answers to Correspondents', with an amused horror that several twentieth- as well as nineteenth-century commentators echo. Public interaction with the consumer was not a feature found in periodicals of higher symbolic capital at this time, and it is portrayed as so bizarre that Collins has to insert several declarations concerning his veracity:

> At the risk of being wearisome, I must once more repeat that these selections from the Answers to Correspondents, incredibly absurd as they appear, are presented exactly as I find them. Nothing is exaggerated for the sake of a joke; nothing is invented or misquoted to serve the purpose of any pet theory of my own ...   ([Collins] 1858: 442)

Collins's article is characteristic of a position in the field that fetishizes the art object as unique, uniquely sourced, new and exclusive. This is a technique deriving from what Bourdieu calls 'distinction' whereby what is available to most people is dismissed as without value by those with more capital, be it social, cultural, financial, or symbolic. Indeed, such dismissal is a key component of cultural capital, and one which infects and inflects almost all descriptions of the nineteenth-century mass market and indeed, as I shall show, the mass-market text itself.

Commitment to oscillation and refusal of discrete boundaries are characteristic of the present study, as summed up in the term commodity fetish. Hardly a treatment of the 'mass market' as an undifferentiated 'mass', this book stresses the extremely local conditions under which meanings are made and transformed, and how each utterance, interpretation and, indeed, silence is necessarily an intervention in a field of power.

Chapter Two

Periodical Titles; or,
'The London Journal' as a Signifier

Querying the Major Source

The nineteenth-century description of the *London Journal* that has undoubtedly been the most influential on twentieth-century accounts occurs in the autobiographical reminiscences of Henry Vizetelly, the colourful writer, publisher and *bon viveur*. To appreciate how profoundly his remarks have influenced the received vision of the periodical (cf. Dalziel, 1957; James, 1963; Anderson, 1994), it is worth quoting the relevant passage at length. The magazine was set up in 1845, wrote Vizetelly, by an unsavoury 'lank, cadaverous-looking' character called George Stiff:

> Originally a very bad wood engraver earning little more than a pound a week, [Stiff] added a trifle to his income by starting a portrait club at some 'public' which he frequented. Subsequently, by dint of putting a high estimate on himself, he managed to secure the direction of the 'Illustrated London News' engraving establishment in its early days, but his incompetency soon manifesting itself, he was sent to the right about. He took his revenge by talking some ambitious printer into starting an opposition paper, and persuaded a few draughtsmen and engravers to assist in the enterprise; but the affair proving a miserable failure in the course of a few weeks he was again adrift. The 'Family Herald' had at this time secured a very large circulation and Stiff puzzled his brains how he could best cut into this. Finally, he determined upon bringing out a somewhat similar sheet with illustrations, and thereupon planned the subsequently well-known 'London Journal'. (Vizetelly, 1893, II: 10)

Stiff had no capital so he talked a printer into lending him money and a wholesale stationers into opening an account with him.

> I remember being told by one of the firm who supplied Stiff with paper, that they first began to press their customer for thirty odd pounds, but that his account with them gradually increased, until it amounted to £13,000 odd before any attempt was made to reduce it. It was part of a regular system in those days for impecunious publishers and proprietors of struggling periodicals to get sufficiently deep into a wealthy stationer's debt as compelled him to find them both cash and paper, in the hope of saving the amount they already owed him from being irrecoverably lost. When by pleading and cajolery Stiff had succeeded in getting a few hundred pounds into his stationers' debt, he knew that the game was in his own hands, and before long, on the score of effecting certain necessary

economies, he prevailed on them to advance him large sums, first for the purchase of printing machinery, and next to enable him to build a printing office of his own.

Eventually Stiff worked up the weekly circulation of the 'London Journal' to several hundred thousand copies, for he allowed nothing to turn him aside from his one set purpose – the increasing sale of this publication; not, however, by means of bogus prizes and illusory insurance tickets after the favorite practice of the present day, but by providing his factory and servant girl readers with lengthy and exciting stories, telling how rich and poor babies were wickedly changed in their perambulators by conniving nursemaids, how long-lost wills miraculously turned up in the nick of time, and penniless beauty and virtue were 'led to the hymeneal altar by the wealthy scion of a noble house,' after he had gained the fair one's affections under some humble disguise.

In the early days of the 'London Journal' the radical G.W.M. Reynolds furnished Stiff with his fiction, but he subsequently resigned the task, and started a miscellany of his own, when Stiff luckily came across J.F. Smith, who, although he had failed as a three volume novelist, succeeded with his well-known novel of Richardsonian proportions, called 'Minnegrey' [*sic*], in raising the circulation of Stiff's journal to half a million copies – an unheard of number in the days when cheap publications were heavily handicapped with a paper duty which positively doubled the price of the material they were printed on.

So cleverly did J.F. Smith pile up the excitement towards the end of the stories which he wrote for Stiff, that the latter told me his weekly circulation used to rise by as many as 50,000 when the *dénouement* approached. He surmized [*sic*] that the factory girls in the north, the great patrons of the journal, were in the habit of lending it to one another, and that when their curiosity as to how the story would end was at its greatest tension, the borrowers being unable to wait for the journal to be lent to them, expended their pennies in buying it outright.

Eventually John Cassell enticed J.F. Smith away from the 'London Journal' on to some publication of his own, and the pair kept the affair a profound secret. Smith, who always wrote his weekly instalment of 'copy' at the 'London Journal' office, chanced to be in the middle of a story for Stiff at the moment he had chosen for abandoning him. In this dilemma he decided upon bringing the tale to a sudden close, and to accomplish this artistically he blew up all the principal characters on board a Mississippi steamboat, and handed the 'copy' to the boy in waiting. Then, proud at having solved a troublesome difficulty, he descended the office stairs, and directed his steps to La Belle Sauvage yard to take service under his new employer. When Stiff saw the number after it had been printed off, and recognized how completely he had been tricked, he was thunderstruck, but he speedily secured a new novelist – Pierce Egan, the younger, I believe – who ingeniously brought about the resurrection of such of the characters as it was desirable to resuscitate, and continued the marvellous story in the 'London Journal' for several months longer.   (Vizetelly, 1893, II: 11-13)

Vizetelly's entertaining narrative suggests a vision of a repetitive fiction weekly for gullible, young, working-class women, produced by ingenious though rather seedy crooks who had failed in the more respectable publishing world of the triple-decker and the *ILN*. While any recall of events that took place fifty years earlier is liable to distortion, envy seems to colour this particular story, for it follows on from, and seems suggested by, a memory concerning the failure of Vizetelly's own attempt at a mass-market publication, the *Welcome Guest* (1858-64). This had been a 'kind of cross between the "London Journal" and Dickens's "All the Year Round"', was brought out by the *Journal*'s own publisher, George Vickers – and

Vizetelly had lost 'between two and three thousand pounds' on it (Vizetelly, 1893, II: 9-10). Then again, Vizetelly's version of the *Journal*'s sale to Ingram and of J.F. Smith's departure from Stiff's magazine are not confirmed by other sources. Perhaps even Stiff's own name led to Vizetelly's description of him as 'cadaverous-looking'. The *OED* records that a 'stiff' was slang for 'corpse' from the mid-nineteenth century and that 'a stiff 'un' meant the same at least twenty years earlier than that. Distorting influences are clearly at work.

When considering any description there are multiple factors that need to be taken into account, not least historical precedent, established generic codes, and the complex of elements that make up the describer's political and cultural alliances and his or her relations to the object described. To understand the Vizetelly account therefore it is necessary to trace the ways in which the mass-market periodical, of which 'The London Journal' is a prime example, was described.[1] This task is less daunting than it sounds. There is no great amount of material to cover since mass-market publications were on the edge of the threshold of description. Secondly, maps of the periodical field have been sketched by several scholars.

Most of the surviving nineteenth-century descriptions of 'The London Journal' and its analogues come from comparatively high-status journalistic sources, from a limited range of periodicals and books with small circulations. They thus come mainly from outside the cultural zone of the mass market, yet still within the field of literary production. This distance-in-proximity has its own variable effects, mainly, but not exclusively, of a competitive and anxious nature. A previously unexploited site of descriptions I shall excavate lies in fiction of the 1860s that appeared in volumes. Some of this was written by authors who were associated with the *London Journal* (Mary Braddon, George Augustus Sala and Emma Robinson), yet nonetheless, like the non-fiction accounts, this also tries to distance itself from penny weekly.

To 1852. 'The London Journal' Enters the Literary Field: From Revolution to Crime

While I have found no trace of 'The London Journal' in literary sources before 1847, I begin my narrative a generation before the *London Journal* actually appeared, for it was then that the options for describing magazines crystallized out (cf. Parker, 2000). As is well known, in the 1820s and 1830s the impact of radical politics and of the French revolution and its aftermath led both to denunciations of mass-market reading as socially inflammatory (mainly a Tory discourse), and to

---

[1] Since this chapter is concerned with the deployment of a periodical title as a sign in discourse, I have elected to highlight this by writing of 'The London Journal'. When I use the *London Journal* (or *Journal*) in italics, I refer to the material reality of the magazine. Of course the two fade into each other and there will be instances where the reader will disagree with my usage, thinking I should use one where I have used the other. But I maintain the value of this distinction as a polemical reminder of the difference between the two.

support for it as raising the mental level of the nation as a whole (mainly Radical and Whig). The first tended to emphasize the need for a supply-led version of the literary field in which the market was centrally controlled and restricted, and the second to a demand-led version in which the market was free. In general terms, this can be related to attitudes concerning the regulation of other commodities: activists against the stamp duty moved easily into the Anti-Corn-Law League (Jones, 1996: 21) and the process extends even to temperance. As Brian Harrison (1994) has explained, many activists thought that removal of taxes on beer and the abolition of the licensing system on the sale of alcohol would encourage temperance by denying them the glamour of the regulated and forbidden. In terms that are applicable as much to the periodical press as to temperance and the Corn Law reform, Whigs, many Radicals and Temperance activists thought that 'free trade extended choice, cheapness and purity of government, and thereby promoted national prosperity' (Harrison, 1994: 63). Free trade would result in a form of social improvement. This, in turn, meant reliance on a strategy of incorporation into an increasingly dominant power structure. In other words, rather than violently setting oneself against a threat in quasi-military fashion by erecting exclusionary walls and doing battle (as promoted on the whole by the Tories), charming rationality and negotiation, not to mention charity, might well disarm opponents and encourage them to accept your point of view (cf. Curran, 1978 and Curran and Seaton, 1991: 5-48). Mutant forms of these differing economic visions, which initially followed party-political lines, continued throughout the century and beyond.

A combination of factors caused developments in discourses about popular reading in the 1830s. Fears of revolution dissipated: the stamp duty on newspapers was reduced, and prosecutions of those papers that appeared without paying it became rarer. The *Penny* and *Saturday Magazines*, both sponsored by ruling élites, were claimed by them as marvellous successes and proof of the 'elevated nature' of the reading public. Then, although by no means new in form, Dickens's *Pickwick Papers* and its successors showed how the part-issue novel could yield high profits. Penny part-issue novels continued this work, gradually replacing and surpassing sales of the older forms of popular printed matter such as chapbooks. The high sales of such fiction 'in pieces' were confirmed by the serialization of novels in French and, later, in British newspapers. New cheap weekly miscellanies that were not sponsored by the élite reached and sustained high circulations. Finally, new technologies of print and distribution, having by now proved their worth, became much more widespread. In effect, the Whig method of social control through incorporation proved more effective than Tory attack: as a French historian of the British and American press realized in 1857, the British press in the nineteenth century owed its form to the *besoins nouveaux qu'épreuvent les grands interêts mercantiles ou industriels* (Clarigny, 1857: 66).

While the literary field had been divided for hundreds of years into interest and price groups, it was not yet so complexly divided into separate zones as would occur later in the century. Nor had the rules of distribution within the field yet been fully established. Those with high cultural capital still preferred to imagine that the whole field was unified. Thackeray noted in 1838 how the circles he moved in had no idea of what the majority of people were reading, a state of affairs which allowed them an illusion of a greater cultural unity than actually existed. While he was willing to explore and expose regions that no respectable person might have cared to be associated with, an anonymous article in the *North British Review* (1847a) was more typical in the way it corralled under 'Popular Serial Literature' a diverse collection: *Punch, Dombey and Son, Vanity Fair, Chambers's Miscellany of Entertaining Tracts*, the *Christian's Penny Magazine* and the *Churchman's Monthly Penny Magazine*. The omission of the *London Journal*, the *Family Herald* and *Reynolds's Miscellany*, at a time when they are individually already far outselling Dickens, is indicative of a blind spot towards the actual division of the market. The collocation, in other words, suggests the continued fantasy of a panoptical vision over a unified field.

The 1848 revolution in France was perceived as largely caused by the *roman feuilleton*, and the resultant backlash by the French administration killed off the genre (Bory, 1962: 320, 350-51). While panic in Britain never reached this level, concern over the mass-market press nonetheless resurfaced at the demands of the Chartists in the 1840s. This stimulated anxiety about the safety of the state and drew attention to what the majority of people were actually reading, as it might prove socially inflammatory.

This is the situation in which the first account of 'The London Journal' of any length appeared. It formed the last of a series of jeremiads against popular reading by J. Hepworth Dixon in the up-market *Daily News* of November 1847. After fervidly condemning Lloyd's publications and the works of Eugène Sue, Dixon cited 'The London Journal', together with 'The Family Herald' and 'The London Pioneer', as examples of the 'perceptible improvement' in popular reading. While he claimed 'The London Journal' belonged ultimately to Lloyd's wicked 'Salisbury Square type' of publication, it was nonetheless a cut above them.

> It is also illustrated with wood-cuts, some of which are not without a rough, striking merit of their kind. The mass of contents is translated from the French – a source which will not of itself offer any guarantee of its purity. 'Monte Christo' by Alexandre Dumas forms a prominent feature in the work; and a still more useful translation of 'Thiers's History of the Consulate and Empire of France under Napoleon' appears in its columns. Amongst the more reprehensible matter is a series of 'Love Letters of Remarkable Persons' – in which are printed several disgusting epistles attributed to Lord Byron, but which were never written by him, and his mistress C— L—. Others of Pope and Swift are also given, which modesty might well have spared. But a dash of the sensual is considered by the editors or proprietors of all these low works as essential to their success. They call it the seasoning of their made dishes ...   (Dixon, 1847: 2-3)

There are several things to consider here. The first point is particularly interesting for the genealogy of both nineteenth- and twentieth-century descriptions of the penny fiction weekly: in a continuation of the passage quoted above, Dixon goes on to explore and ridicule the 'Notices to Correspondents', and in so doing initiates a fascination with this department that mixes the delight and horror of encountering other epistemologies, aesthetics, knowledges and manners (see, for example, [Oliphant], 1858: 210; [Collins], 1858: 439; Strahan, 1870: 445-46; Hitchman, 1881: 392-95; [Johns], 1887: 54; Altick, 1998: 360-61).

Second, the reference to the 'sensual' is a reflex of an older trope, more visible elsewhere in these articles, which equates mass-market reading with the pornographic. Since sex was considered an 'appetite', a link was easily made to that other appetite, hunger, and thence to food and other substances taken into the body. This is the discourse that links the 'sensual' to 'the seasoning of their made dishes' and the very many references to such phrases as the 'moral poison' of popular reading that date mainly from the first half of the century (see Mays, 1995). By the end of the 1840s, however, such elision of the pornographic and mass-market literature was becoming less common. 'The London Journal' and its fellows mark a fault-line between the two that will gape wider with the eventual passing of the Obscene Publications Act in 1857 and, in 1868, the notorious Regina v. Hinklin case in 1868 when the 'pornographic' was more specifically defined. Throughout Dixon's description of the mass-market, this fault-line is manifest in a tension between Tory-style condemnation and Whig narratives of progress, a double vision that fits the politically ambiguous readership of the *Daily News*: wealthy Whig that utters conservative views.[2]

Thirdly, the references to the specific letters from 'Love Letters of Remarkable Persons' permit the dating of the issues Dixon must have read to early October 1847: what he read by chance had a significant impact on his description of the magazine. For instance, he thinks the *Journal*'s selection of Dumas acceptable, while Sue's *Martin the Foundling* in the *Family Herald* a 'disgusting tale'. He was unaware that *Martin* had already been serialized in the *London Journal* and that Sue's *Seven Cardinal Sins* would begin there on 27 November. Neither did he come across the potentially seditious *Memoir of the Life and Times of Daniel O'Connell* (19 June – 18 Sept 1847). More surprising is Dixon's description of the *History* by Thiers as 'useful', when British comments in the high-status reviews on the French original roundly condemn it for its bias and its extreme inaccuracy ([Croker], 1845; Kirwan, 1845; cf. [McNeill], 1841). Dixon's positive response may have been caused by the fact that the *Journal* version had been considerably rewritten to make it more agreeable to an English audience: certainly what the *Journal* printed in October 1847 would have been unlikely to cause him offence. The comment on the immorality of French literature in general on the other hand is much more usual: I read this and the many similar remarks over the century as a kind of literary Corn Law, an attempt to erect barriers against foreign imports which might lower the price of home-grown products, and which might be infected or infectious.

G.W.M. Reynolds's reply to Dixon's series bears out the commercial basis of the descriptions, brilliantly exemplifying several of my main points in this chapter.

> [W]e will explain the reason wherefore Messrs. Bradbury and Evans, the proprietors of the *Daily News*, have directed their literary scrub to pen the articles entitled "The

---

[2] On the readership of the *Daily News*, see Ellegård (1957: 16-17), who gives a circulation of 5,000. Koss (1973: 34) gives a circulation of 53,000 in 1853 and a much more sanguine view of the 'advanced liberalism' of the paper. My reading of the paper agrees more with Ellegård in this case.

Literature of the Lower Orders." The motive was purely a *trade* one. Bradbury and Evans are the proprietors of numerous works, which, being very dear, do not sell; and they therefore vent their spite on the cheap and successful rivals... in denominating cheap works "The Literature of the Lower Orders," Bradbury and Evans put a gross, vile, and base insult upon the Industrious Classes of these realms. They wantonly throw dirt in the face of the honest artizan, and working man of every class and description. They moreover propagate an infamous falsehood when they represent such periodicals as THE MISCELLANY, the LONDON JOURNAL, and the FAMILY HERALD to be read only by the *lower orders*; for they circulate widely amongst the middle class, and the Volumes obtain a sale in the richer sphere.

(G.W.M. Reynolds, 'The 'Daily News'', *Reynolds's Miscelleny*, III: 63-4)

If, in parts of this piece not quoted, Reynolds directly insults Bradbury and Evans publications with aspersions not altogether true (*Punch* was not 'going down as rapidly as possible' at this time), his comments on the low sales of *Vanity Fair* ('of extraordinary talent and great originality') and *Dombey* are spot on, at least compared to the sales of truly mass-market penny publications. Later in the same article he goes on to show how Gilbert à Beckett, who was now writing for Bradbury & Evans's *Punch*, had previously owned the *Evangelical Penny Magazine* and the *Gallery of Terrors*: 'Religion for the Millions on one hand – and Murder for the Millions on the other!' His point is that Bradbury and Evans are by no means uncontaminated by what they affect to despise. A second article on the Dixon series is equally fascinating (*Reynolds's*, III: 95). After furiously defending his wife from attacks on her serial *Gretna Green*, Reynolds dissects the economics of 3d newspapers such as the *Daily News*, finding them lacking in the ability to sustain genuine 'news'. He should know. In the next two chapters I shall comment on the effects of economic management on the contents of a penny paper he edited.

Other accounts of the mass-market periodical press around this time generally avoid the economic, however, preferring to use colourful tropes derived from 1820s Tories, with politics replaced by morality (see, for example, Anon, 1845c: esp. p. 81; Green, [1850]: 123-24; [Mayne], 1850; [Mayne, n.d., 1851?]; [Burn], 1855: 210-11). Sometimes, though, this can mask an animosity occasioned by failure in the market analogous to Vizetelly's and what Reynolds claims about Bradbury and Evans. In the last issue of his continuation of the *Penny Magazine* in 1846, Knight inveighs against the 'moral miasma' spread by 'the most vulgar and brutal fiction'. Circulation of his magazine had dropped because of the newer fiction weeklies such as the *Family Herald* and the *London Journal*, and Knight could no longer keep his magazine afloat (Knight, 1863-55, II: 328-29). Even though the *Penny Magazine* was written from within the earnest improving traditions of the 1830s and constituted a material enactment of the Whig hope of incorporation, this did not prevent Knight's appropriation of once Tory language for use against a more successful rival. A less well-known case occurred in the *Family Journal*, a sixteen-page penny weekly that lasted for only two months over 1846 and 1847. The magazine opened by proclaiming Whig progressivist tropes and ended by denouncing, Tory-style, the 'deluge of cut-throat literature which has emanated from Salisbury Square, Seven Dials and the vicinity of Smithfield' ("To the Readers of the Family Journal", *Family Journal*, p. 120). Clearly, a magazine's stage in its life-cycle has an effect on how it describes the system it is part of. Sometimes, of course, there is no time to change: issue 1 of the *Bee*, a 2d miscellany which existed for just two issues in 1833 only had time to celebrate the 'Present Taste for Cheap Literature'.

Cassell's *Working Man's Friend and Family Instructor*, a pioneering temperance venture that in 1850 had yet to make its name, offered a variant of the Tory topos in order to do so, by linking 'The London Journal' (and 'Reynolds's Miscellany') to Newgate penny serials such as *Jack Sheppard*, *Paul Clifford* and *Claude Duval* as causes of crime.[3] After the fiascos of the 1848 Chartist agitation had proved themselves very unlike their continental counterparts, the British cultural élites and those that aspired to join them no longer felt the association of collective social action with the printed word to be quite so threatening. Instead, an allied topos comes to the fore wherein popular reading was linked more to individual social disruption, to crime and to religious 'infidelity' than to collective revolution.

Man, by nature, is a being of imitative sympathy ... Tales of imagination ... that deal in murders, and in other species of iniquity, lead to the actual commission of similar sins. The history of a sceptic will lead others into scepticism. We cannot help being drawn, as it were, into the mind of the narrator, whither he narrate actions or feelings. Are the million to be fed with the moral poison of tales of crime, and of open or insinuated infidelity?

([F. Mayne], 1852: 266)[4]

Bussey (1906: 74-5) relates the story, unfortunately undated, of how a double murder was supposedly caused by a rival to the *London Journal*. An old couple who regularly took the *Family Herald* were murdered by their grandson and a page of the magazine was used for wadding in the gun with which he shot them. Such was the belief in the criminal influence of the mass-market press that this was taken as evidence of a link between the paper and the motivation for the murder. It is the same connection between literature and crime that caused Dickens to write 'The Author's Introduction to the Third Edition' to *Oliver Twist* in 1841. He of course denied such a relation through claims he was only writing the 'TRUE' (see Bowen, 2000, ch. 3). A decade later, it was again to sever the connection between crime and mass-market entertainment that Dickens's famous series 'Amusements of the People' was to appear in *Household Words* in Spring 1850.

The connection remained, however, as evidenced by how other 'experts' similarly kept questioning the link. When, Cassell and the Manchester bookseller Abel Heywood mentioned the *London Journal* in their evidence for the *Report from the Select Committee on Newspaper Stamps* of 1851, they had to define it (and its fellow penny weeklies) for the benefit of the Committee, who seem to have had almost no direct knowledge of the world of cheap publications – exactly the situation that Thackeray had described in 1838. Cassell and Heywood both took

---

[3] Cassell's should not be confused with the more famous radical *Workingman's Friend* (22 December 1832 to 3 August 1833). Rather it is an appropriation of the title which ran 5 January 1850 to 26 March 1853.

[4] Cf. [Mayne], 1850: 620-21; Talbot, 1853: 102; [Burn] 1855: 210-21.

advantage of their inquisitors' ignorance and drew on Whig tropes to further their own economic interests in the field. 'The London Journal' was an example of the improved morals of the penny press, claimed Cassell, in stark contrast with the indignation vocalized in his *Working Man's Friend*. And he would soon found a direct rival to Stiff's magazine, *Cassell's Illustrated Family Paper*. Heywood drew a more elaborate picture of this supposed improving publication, claiming that 'The London Journal' was historical in nature rather than just light reading, and that the quality of the writing was very good (*Report*, 1851: 216, 377). He did not tell the Committee he was then making a profit of about £10 a week from the *Journal* alone, selling over 9,000 a week. A respectable penny press strengthened the case for a free literary market, and profits for those who dealt in it.

From 1852. 'The Literature of the Kitchen': 'The London Journal' Established in the Field

By the mid-1850s, the *London Journal* had come to be perceived mainly as a member of what Dalziel (1957) called the 'purified penny press': even rivals did not now use the language of moral poison in any unequivocal way. While never mentioning the *Journal* or its fellows by name, the penny weekly *Family Friend* is nonetheless clearly referring to them.

> [They are] made up of love and mystery, and matters of idle and silly gossip, by which servant maids, footmen and cabmen, are held in continual excitement. The question is sometimes discussed whether these works exercise a demoralising tendency; or whether by creating an appetite for reading they develop faculties which gradually aspire to higher tastes. We will dismiss the question here, and content ourselves with this assumption, that if six hundred thousand sheets of the character described can be disposed of weekly, it is a national disgrace if such a work as the FAMILY FRIEND cannot find a large weekly sale.
>
> ('Preface', *Family Friend*, 11 June 1852, IV: iii).

However, even if it had exchanged its discursive location from 'evil Salisbury Square' to 'silly' – an adjective that George Eliot famously was to make the mark of a cultural Cain in her self-promotion – 'The London Journal' had still not made a proper appearance in 'society'. Mentioned in accounts of a few trials in *The Times* only as a chattel, it is not described. But in 1855 it visited Parliament as part of the drive to eradicate the Stamp Tax. The Chancellor of the Exchequer, Cornewall Lewis, cited it in a speech as an example of the newly moral press that needed no fiscal regulation. Yet again an audience's ignorance of zones of the market other than its own proved handy, for it enabled Lewis to adduce apparently novel evidence for his case. He claimed that he had never heard of the magazine before and that he supposed many other MPs would be in the same position. It was rather like the *Penny Magazine*, he said, though with a far higher circulation – 510,000 weekly, equivalent to 26,520,000 a year, some 10 million more than the annual circulation of *The Times*. It was 'perfectly unexceptionable in point of morality' and, together with the *Family Herald*, altogether disproved the notion of the wickedness of the popular press (Hansard (1855), col. 783).

A few months later, the Stamp Tax was made optional, and the following year 'The London Journal', now eleven years old, made its first full entrance into the world of more consecrated magazines. The *Saturday Review*, despite its reputation as the 'Saturday Reviler', placed it in a constellation of penny weeklies that were treated moderately, if patronisingly.

> The Family Herald, the London Journal, Reynolds's Miscellany, Cassell's Illustrated Paper [*sic*] and a great many others, give every week, at the small cost of a penny, column on column of stirring and spirited romance. The stories are not indeed specimens of very high art, and it is difficult to mistake the class for whom they are especially written. They are obviously meant to find their way into the kitchen: and if mistresses want to know what are the evening studies of their cooks and housemaids, they have only to devote a few minutes to turning over the fascinating pages in question.
>
> They may do so in perfect safety; for, if these romances have one characteristic more striking than another, it is that of an exuberant propriety. They overflow with virtue and are models of poetical justice. ... These stories are not very like real life, but they depart from it in a way that is not much to be regretted. Melodramas are not altogether unwholesome food for the half-educated mind. Hard and mechanical labour is an antidote strong enough to carry off most of the pernicious effects of fanciful exaggeration; and the worst fruit of reading these romances is probably a transient fit of unreal excitement and overwrought sympathy. It is evident that the stories are not written for a bad set of people; for they do not appeal to bad passions or pique morbid curiosity. And in this sphere of literature, it is the readers who determine the spirit of the publication, and not the publication which creates the taste of the readers.
>
> ('Weekly Romance', *Saturday Review*, I, 8 March 1856: 364-65: 365)

There follow outlines of tales from the *Family Herald* and the *London Journal* proving the points made in the quotation. Mayne's previous assertion of the potential dangers of 'imitative sympathy' is here neutralized by reference to the effects of labour, and, indeed, the influence of the mass market is reduced to zero. This is the first high-status article to cement the penny fiction periodical into the cultural zone of the 'respectable but *boring*', a development in the history of descriptive tropes of penny weeklies and their perceived location in the literary market whose effects are perceptible today. Ultimately a celebration of the Whig market-led conception of the press, the *Saturday Review*'s is also a description whose effect relies on its attribution of explicit class and gender markers to the penny market. When the *Family Friend* had used the idea of servant literature to dismiss penny publications, class, not gender, had been the distinguishing factor: 'servant maids, footmen and cabmen' had been lumped together as its consumers. It was the *Saturday Review* article that marked the penny weekly fiction magazine as reading for *servant girls* for the first time. This is the point at which 'The London Journal' and its fellows became the 'literature of the kitchen'.

Comments on servant-girl reading were not of course new, but what servant girls were supposed to read varied over time. In 1847 the Mayhew brothers had described Betsy, addicted to the *Penny Sunday Times* and part-issue sentimental and 'romantic' novels published by Edward Lloyd. She is the worst of all servants who causes her mistress to leave home in despair (see Figure 2.1). Yet from 1856, until it is redefined again in the 1880s, it is 'The London Journal' that will principally exemplify the category 'kitchen literature'. Over these decades it appears in both fiction and non-fiction as a conventional accessory that defines the servant girl as much as the servant girl defines it.

Figure 2.1 'The Sentimental Novel Reader', drawn by George Cruikshank
Source: Mayhew, 1847, plate opposite p. 214.

Betsy Jane, the scullery maid in *Lady Lisle*, a Braddon novel of 1862, 'leaned her head against the brass rim of the high fender [of the fireplace], and composed herself to the perusal of an interesting fiction in penny numbers, entitled 'Rodolph with the Red Hand'' (p. 273). This not only recalls the Mayhews' Betsy, but also the title of a recent serial in the *Journal*, *Violet Davenant; Or, The Red Hand* (1859) by Bayle St. John. The same year as *Lady Lisle* was published, the *Bookseller* (3 May 1862, LIII: 321) classed the *Journal* with the *Family Herald* and

Reynolds's Miscellany as servant-girls' reading. In 1869 George Walter Thornbury's *The Vicar's Courtship* used 'The London Journal' in a low-comic parody of the famous Paolo and Francesca scene in Dante's *Inferno* where the lovers realize their feelings while perusing chivalric romances. Bob, a good-natured, 'shambling pawnbroker's assistant', has bought 'The London Journal' for Susan, a sharp but affectionately presented 'little maid of all work' (a descendant of Susan Nipper from *Dombey and Son*). She has just told him off for talking to another girl and spied something he was carrying:

> 'What's that 'London Journal' you've got there? I dare say it's for some minx or other!'...
>   [Bob] produced the latest number of the London Journal [*sic*], and glowingly eulogized the thrilling story of the 'Red Diamond, or the Skeleton in the Closet', especially where (as he eloquently pointed out) Sir Algernon Fitzherbert Goswald confronts the wicked Duke of Mountgarret Chesney, and accuses him before his proud minions and pampered menials of bigamy, arson, poisoning, felony, treason, bad language, and strong drinks.
> (Thornbury, 1869, I: 62-3)

While it is Bob who has bought the magazine, Susan archly assumes it is a present for a rival. It cannot be meant for his reading *alone*, for 'kitchen literature' is women's reading. The ridiculing lack of accuracy in the reference is itself a reflex of the disregard for realism which high-status sources viewed as the norm in 'London Journal' novels. As purely generic and with no reference to reality, kitchen literature demands only generic and fantastical reference to itself. At the same time, the adversion to 'The London Journal' also functions as an affectionately droll puff of a periodical owned by a friend of the novel's publisher, Tinsley, in that the reader may be encouraged by the reference to allow such risibly harmless matter into his or her house as appropriate matter for 'downstairs'.

Boundaries are always crossed, however, and the *Journal*'s location in the kitchen was problematized the moment it arrived there. In 1864 Charles Knight commented that 'the unnatural incidents and slip-shod writing' of 'the Half-Penny and Penny Weeklies which have acquired the name of Kitchen literature [*sic*]... may be traced to the literature of the parlour' (Knight, 1863-65, III: 179). This inversion of Rae's now famous denunciation of Braddon as being able to 'boast of having temporarily succeeded in making the literature of the Kitchen the favourite reading of the Drawing room' ([Rae], 1865: 204) suggests that the notion of crossovers between the two had already become a cliché. Similarly, a few years later, when Alfred Austin (1870: 421) described 'The Sensational School' of triple-deckers, his comments on its links with the *London Journal* and *Reynolds's Miscellany* suggest that this was common knowledge.

Margaret Beetham (1999) has pointed out that the trope of kitchen literature often indicates a recurrent fear, found in manuals on domestic management, about servant reading as a theft of the time that the employer has paid for. In the late 1860s, such anxiety is also found in attitudes by men to the reading of working-class wives: indeed, 'modern servantgalism', the 'tale-tainted wife' and the 'lazy, lackadaisical, *London Journal* reading ladies with whom working men are more and more curst' can easily slide into one another (see [Wright], 1867: 189-93). In Marcus Clarke's *Long Odds* of 1869, the *Journal* plays a role in precipitating the disasters of the novel in a way that is intimately related to anxieties surrounding female reading and domestic management. At the same time, it plays on a narrative that Mayhew had brought out in the fourth volume of *London Labour and London Poor*: 'The ruin of many girls is commenced by reading the low trashy wishy-washy cheap publications that the news-shops are now gorged with' (quoted in Dalziel, 1957: 51). In *Long Odds*, the heroine, Caroline Manton, is the spoilt daughter of a lodging-house keeper who intends better things for her. Instead of working and helping her mother, Caroline becomes

> not unread in the fascinating pages of the *London Journal*, and had heard how pretty girls of humble birth were constantly being selected by the aristocracy as wives. Did not Mildred Mainwaring marry a Duke? And was not poor Lucy the Lone One rewarded for her perils ... Now Caroline had compared faces with Mildred Mainwaring, and had come to the conclusion that her own looking-glass reflected the prettier woman of the two, and she was convinced that she only wanted the chance to marry a duke in twenty-four hours.
>
> (Clarke, 1869, I: 4)

Encouraged by both her mother and by her reading of the *Journal*, she fantasizes that one of the lodgers has more money than appears. She flirts with him, and they marry. He is not, of course, a duke in disguise but instead ends up a bigamist, murderer and murdered. As for Caroline, experience teaches her the priority of work over romance reading and transforms her into a hospital-visiting saint. While this is an echo of the fate of Braddon's heroine in *The Doctor's Wife* (1864), it can also be read as a sales strategy for home-grown Australian literary fare: *Long Odds* was originally published in the Australian *Colonial Monthly* in 1869 and the *London Journal* was widely read in Australia at this time (Johnson-Woods, 2000: esp. ch. 2). It may be a cautionary tale about too great a dependence on the mother country's culture, of which the *Journal* was an example all too desired.

When the servant-girl trope is used in discussion of the literary field, then, it assumes a variety of strategic possibilities different from the fears Beetham spoke of. Marcus Clarke apart, the main variant that I am talking of, 'respectably boring servant-girl literature', I interpret as a sign that it poses no threat to the cultural zone of the informant. 'Objective' rational description of penny weeklies as a tame servant-girl pastime makes sure that it never will pose a threat to sales by voiding it of the potential for attraction that descriptions of a 'profligate' press might hold. It allows such literature to come in at the back door like a sack of potatoes or coal – kept in appropriate places within the domestic cultural economy.

The *Saturday Review* seems to have introduced this idea in 1856 less to denigrate penny fiction *per se*, however, than to police the literary tastes of the *mistress*, rather than of the maid. The article in its entirety had worked towards a comparison of the taste of both, to the advantage, surprisingly, of the maid. And it is here that the tactical purpose of the *Saturday Review*'s assessment of 'Weekly Romance' becomes plain. The mistress is reading fiction by an *American woman*, Susan Warner's *Queechy* and *Wide, Wide World* which were currently enjoying enormous sales on both sides of the Atlantic. According to Bevington (1941: 266), the attitude of the *Saturday Review* towards American literature until about 1868 ranged between 'amused contempt' and 'a sense of outrage at ... vulgarity'. The article can thus be seen not only as a containment of mass-market magazines and concern about women's relation to domesticity, but, anticipating Clarke's usage of 'The London Journal' in the Australian market, as part of a strategy to close British borders against transatlantic cultural invaders — and especially women, whose success in the shape of Stowe's *Uncle Tom's Cabin* had already been extraordinary in 1851-52. American women had just started to assume importance in penny weekly fiction: E.D.E.N. Southworth had been serialized in the *London Journal* the previous year, and the *Family Herald* had just run Fanny Fern's *Ruth Hall* and *Rose Clark*. In reality both mistress and maid were reading American women novelists. If the *Saturday Review* was able convincingly to ignore this, it was only because in the penny periodical American stories were still being pirated and the novelists' names not yet loudly and continuously broadcast.

1858-59. 'The London Journal' under Scrutiny

If one set of tropes allowed 'The London Journal' in by the back door, writers with cultural capital also dissected and sought to understand its commercial success. In 1858-59 there appeared a trio of very different articles of exceptional interest, occasioned, I believe, by the unpublicized joint purchase of the *Journal* by those publicly closer to the consecrated magazine zones: Herbert Ingram, the proprietor of the *ILN*, and Reynolds's *bêtes noires*, Bradbury and Evans. I shall have more to say about this purchase in Chapter 6; suffice it to say here that Ingram placed Dickens's friend Mark Lemon in the editor's chair, which caused Dickens much amusement in his letters.[5] Lemon sought to educate his new readers by serialising Scott, and his failed attempt to do so and thereby reunify the literary field became key for a general reconceptualization of the literary field: after this there seems much wider acceptance that it was now irremediably zoned.

Margaret Oliphant wrote her *Blackwood's* account of penny weeklies in July 1858, a month before Dickens wrote his letters mentioning the *London Journal*. Crucially she is unaware of Lemon's impending failure, offering instead a distinctive take on the issue of 'literature for the million' and apparently a stimulus for at least the third of the articles I shall discuss here.

Oliphant begins by recounting how, in order to kill time, she bought sixpence-worth of penny weeklies for a bored little girl on a hot summer's day and took her to a cathedral close to read them. Playing on notions of moral poison that the conservative *Blackwood's* audience could be expected to anticipate, this frame narrative offers the pleasures of scandal, a tactic to attract and maintain attention: the narrator seems to be about to corrupt an innocent child in a sacred space. The scandal will be diffused when Oliphant sets up a new binarism of progressive

---

[5] See Dickens to Sir Joseph Paxton, 11 December 1857; to Wilkie Collins, 6 September 1858; to Albert Smith, 16 September 1858, (1965- , VIII: 491-2, 651-2, 661-2).

materialism versus unchanging, eternal spirit. This she deploys to explain the disparity between what she sees as the static, old-fashioned world of the penny journals with the modernity of the tiny world of 'anybody who is anybody' which defines what real 'literature' is. In a wonderful rhetorical move that appropriates Ruskinian views of the Gothic *in favour of* the mass-produced (an argument that would no doubt have upset Ruskin greatly), Oliphant argues that the penny weekly remains within the stereotypical and chivalrous imaginative world of the Middle Ages when the cathedral was built, and is therefore a manifestation of spirit. Mass-market literature thus paradoxically *belongs* in the cathedral space and must logically be regarded as perfectly appropriate for children. Visiting the romantic trope of the noble savage and civilized corrupter, she implies that modern up-market literature does not represent 'progress' so much as a 'fall'.

Such virtuoso reversal of expected norms is singular in my reading. But lest it be thought Oliphant is suggesting that the desire that drives the mass market is *intrinsically* static and closer to God, it is important to remark her explanation of the apparent simultaneous existence of two versions of time and two markets. It is devastatingly simple and again Ruskinian in logic: the consumer's relation to labour.

So it comes about that these labouring multitudes stand somewhat in the same position as, perhaps, the very knights of romance held four or five hundred years ago. It is not that they differ in intelligence from the classes above them; it is not that the delf [*sic*] is duller than the porcelain; it is only that we have got so many centuries ahead by dint of our exemption from manual labours and necessities. They are still among the dragons and giants, where hard hands and strength of arm are more in demand than thoughts and fancies. We have gained the thoughtful ways of civilization, when we smile at Archimage, and find St George's hideous adversary a fabulous creation. Our leisure accordingly plays with all fancies, all inventions – all matters of thought and reason; whereas their leisure, brief and rapid, and sharpened with the day's fatigue, loves, above all things, a story, and finds in that just the amount of mental excitation which makes it somehow a semi-intellectual pleasure.   ([Oliphant], 1858: 205)

For Oliphant, this means that the project of the SDUK was always bound to fail since it did not understand that it was the material condition of the labouring masses that prevented them from progressing culturally. The 'spirit' she writes about at the beginning of the article turns out to be little more than a deployment of an emotive term intended to appeal to her conservative and pious readers. In actual fact her analysis is profoundly material.

The workers' existence outside progress is the fundamental reason for Oliphant's other main point: why the masses prefer fabulous creatures of enormous wealth and aristocracy to the realist depictions of themselves in *Alton Locke* and *Mary Barton*. Oliphant does not draw any definite conclusions about what is to be done about this split in the market: rather an impasse is reached that seems to me to result from the tension a recent biography has noted between her Radical perspective and the well-known Toryism of the magazine she wrote for (see Jay, 1995: 250-51). It is this impasse that causes the fascinating ambiguity of much of this article.

Oliphant refers to 'The London Journal' only briefly as 'less edifying' than 'Cassell's Illustrated Family Paper', but she makes space to remark on its serialization of a novel by Scott, which she regards as

> not only a praiseworthy desire to introduce into these regions the best literature, but a wise discrimination in the choice of its first venture – for Sir Walter is rarely so 'thrilling' as in this beautiful romance [*Kenilworth*].   ([Oliphant], 1858: 209)

Since Scott is up-market, the *Journal*'s practice constitutes a crack in Oliphant's main point about the necessarily split market, a fissure she seeks to seal by only briefly mentioning Scott's sensationalist appeal. What she did not know was that Scott would fail dismally and the market remain split.

I discussed Wilkie Collins's 1858 encounter with unnamed penny periodicals in Chapter 1. Here I wish to take a different tack and locate it historically with even greater specificity. While his piece may well be a response to the Oliphant which had appeared earlier in the month, a more immediate aim was, I suspect, moral support for Collins's friend Mark Lemon, under whose editorship the circulation of the *Journal* was now known to be falling drastically.[6] As such, it is both a defence of Lemon against the *Journal*'s new proprietors, whose losses on the magazine were now enraging them, and also an enquiry into the nature of What the Public Really Wants. In trying to establish the latter, it is as though Collins were ventriloquizing the desperation Mark Lemon must have felt. As I have said, Collins fails, constrained both by where his piece was published and by his assumptions about the intrinsic value of art works. When in the article the narrator tries to gain information from a newsagent, his question about the worth of the stories reveals his conviction that some literature is better than others – a mode of thought characteristic of those who wish to validate codes that keep the unconsecrated out of high-status cultural zones. The narrator is, however, baffled by the newsagent's refusal to play this game, by his insistence on what different consumers want, and by his concern for value for money that openly regards literature as a commodity. Since the natives will not tell directly, Collins has to examine the artefacts themselves. They are duly presented in the 'respectable but boring' mode familiar from the *Saturday Review*, aided by the trope of the manufactory: everything is mass-produced and therefore all the same. 'The London Journal' is now attempting a solution to this problem, says Collins, by serializing Scott – and Charles Reade. The inclusion of Reade is particularly interesting as he was not serialized under Lemon but under Stiff, and was a flop: Collins is deliberately blurring boundaries to exculpate Lemon.

He concludes with a hope that the prestige market of the 'great writer' will expand to fill the entire available literary space:

---

[6] When Dickens wrote to Collins about this a couple of weeks later (6 September), the falling circulation already seems well known (Dickens, 1965-, VIII: 651-2).

> The Unknown Public is, in a literary sense, hardly beginning, as yet, to learn to read ...
> When that public shall discover its need of a great writer, the great writer will have such
> an audience as has never yet been known.   ([Collins], 1858: 444)

The article maintains an uneasy balance between supply- and demand-led versions of the market, and between low- and high-status cultural commodities. The resolution lies only in a fantasized utopian space that cancels out the difference between them. It is as if Collins himself (or Lemon whom he may be ventriloquizing) hopes to be able to unify the kitchen and drawing room in yet another manifestation of the endlessly repeated longing for a single market which will grant unheard-of profits for both writers and publishers.

Less than a year later, the serialization of Scott would be reduced to a 'mistake' that put 'The London Journal' 'at some disadvantage amongst its rivals'. As I shall show in the next chapter, by the time this comment appeared in the *British Quarterly Review* (Anon., 1859: 341), the *Journal* had just been involved in court cases reported in *The Times*, where its falling sales were plain for all to see. Ignoring the Wilkie Collins, the article picks up and redefines Oliphant's main points about cheap literature, modernity and labour. Indeed, the term 'Cheap Literature' itself undergoes a redefinition: while admitting that the term usually refers to the clutch of penny weeklies listed at the beginning of the article – the *Family Herald*, the *London Journal*, *Reynolds's Miscellany*, the *Leisure Hour*, the *Home Magazine*, *Cassell's Illustrated Family Paper*, the *Guide*, Vizetelly's *Welcome Guest* – the first twelve pages are devoted to other and newer forms, to newspapers of various sorts, railway literature and shilling novels. In order to prove the writer's Whiggish progressivist thesis, discussion of the penny weeklies revolves around a labour theory of value very different from Oliphant's: these periodicals are sloppily edited (which results in execrable English) and easy to put together. The extraction of great thoughts from great writers in the form of *sententiae* comes in for especial attention:

> [S]omething more ought to be done in this way with a firmer hand and a more direct
> purpose. The whole of this work which we have been describing may be executed by a
> pair of scissors, with an incredibly small amount of intelligence to guide them.
>   (Anon., 1859: 330-31)

These periodicals are of low value not because they do harm but because they are the result of little labour. This theory is then used to explain the failure of the Scott novels:

> The old matter occupies space which ought to be devoted to new, and substitutes a
> speculation, which properly belongs to the province of the bookseller, for the original
> work of a miscellany presumed to be dedicated to the onward progress of popular
> improvement.   (Anon., 1859: 341)

In a last-gasp vision of market unity, the piece ends with a recommendation that more effort should be made to raise the 'moral and intellectual character' of the popular press, a pathetic echo of the efforts of the SDUK.

The *British Quarterly Review* devotes very little space to 'The London Journal' (or to its major rivals). All that is said about it is that 40 tons of unsold copies have reportedly been sold for waste and that both it and 'The Guide' are more pretentious and ostentatious versions of 'The Family Herald'. The real energies of the article are directed against the *Welcome Guest*, and, above all, its main contributor, Augustus Sala, 'the head of a new school of writers, which may be called the Fast School', for whom 'violence, excess, outrageous word-painting, and unblushing effrontery are all in all' (p. 343). Thereafter follows a puff of the *Leisure Hour*, described as a secular version of the *Sunday at Home*, a religious publication 'which cannot be too heartily commended' (Anon., 1859: 344-5). While this article remains anonymous there is no possibility of inserting it with any certainty within a network that might reveal alliances and hostilities amongst social groups. All that can be said is that it seems to make tactical use of Whig tropes as well as to address issues from the Oliphant in order to fulfill its main purpose, which is to puff the *Leisure Hour* and attack the *Welcome Guest*. The *Journal* and its ilk are no more than effortlessly silly, a backdrop before which self-confident cultural capital enacts an assault on perceived invaders.

'The London Journal' in the 1860s: Receipts for Profit

As Chapter 4 will detail, the losses incurred by the *Journal*'s serialization of Scott did not last and in the 1860s there was an increased amount of material that discussed mass-market reading as a source of immense profit. The now intensified awareness of a split market created a fractured discourse indicative of both attraction and repulsion to the lower-status zone. In 1861 Lawrence Oliphant, one of the owners of the *London Review*,[7] was worried that sales of his magazine would drop after a reader's comment that Trollope belonged to the world of 'The London Journal', a magazine whose readers were 'persons of morbid imagination and low moral tone'. No more of Trollope's novels appear in the *London Review* after that (Trollope, 1983, I: 140-41). Effects theory was by now hardly dominant, no doubt caused by the fact that many describers of mass market literary field now also produced for it. Sala had written a couple of articles for Mark Lemon's *London Journal* in 1859 and later noted in his 1862 novel, *The Seven Sons of Mammon*, that one of his characters, the clerk Buff, read melodramas and romances, went four times a week to the upper gallery of the Victoria theatre and still remained honest ([Sala], 1862: I, 300-301). If this picture agrees with Dickens's 1850 (Joe Whelks also visits the Victoria with no harmful effects), it does so because of its position in the field, not simply because it is following a convention that floats free of social context.

The term 'receipt' is particularly appropriate to name the concerns of this section. In the nineteenth century the term meant both 'recipe' (as in instructions for cooking) and the amount of money received in a commercial transaction. An

---

[7] This Oliphant was only a distant relation of Margaret Oliphant: see Jay (1995: 142-45).

anonymous 1866 *Macmillan's* article was concerned with both senses and may stand as representative for several similar pieces.[8] It opened by echoing Collins's colonizing trope and continued by listing the ingredients in the mental pabulum of the people. It also described Pierce Egan, at this time both editor of and novelist for the *Journal*, in a way similar to how Oliphant had described J.F. Smith. The profit to be derived from the recipe for 'the multitude' was difficult to ignore:

> There is a mighty potentate in England, whose name is Mr Pierce Egan, and whose realm is nearly as unknown as a few years ago was the district of Victoria Nyanza. Many among us fancy that they have a good general idea of what is English literature. They think of Tennyson and Dickens as the most popular of our living authors. It is a fond delusion from which they should be aroused. The works of Pierce Egan are sold by the half million. What living author can compare with him? ... that vast unheeded multitude, with their unrecognized king, Pierce Egan, are worth looking after ... we may still inquire with profit into the ingredients of that literary provender which satisfies the lower classes of our countrymen...
>
> Give the poor man sensation; let him sup full of horrors; initiate him in all the mysteries of crime: but always be it remembered that one condition is essential to the success of the dreadful tale – that it shall somewhat ostentatiously ally itself to morality ... we believe that one of the secrets of [*Egan's*] influence with the lower classes is that he professes to depict for them what is called high life ... mainly he directs his attention to the working out of his plot, and the heaping together of incidents ... an infinity of strong passion ... [*and*] morality...   (compiled from Anon., 1866: 96, 101, 104, 105)

Such articles discussed penny fiction weeklies with the rational tone familiar from the *Saturday Review* piece and in so doing they distinguished and distanced their own merchandise from it. At the same time, their analyses, like Collins's in *Household Words*, ambiguously offered instruction in how to produce such immensely profitable commodities. Such an approach was heavily overdetermined, above all by continued anxieties over American cultural imports and the sensation novel. It was commonly said that the Civil War had been fanned by literary and homiletic means, including the 'sensation sermon', a genre particularly associated with America. There were fears that fiction imported from or influenced by America might cause the same kind of social disruption in Britain[9] and, as with French fiction in the 1840s, invasion by foreign cultural imports might also depress prices for home-grown products. Then again, the triple-decker sensation novel was regarded as a virus that had arisen in the kitchen and was infecting the drawing room – where men seemed in danger of losing control over their women's reading

---

[8] See, for example, 'Penny Novels', *Spectator*, XXXVI, 28 March 1863: 1806-8, which cites the *London Journal* as one of the principal money-makers; [Scott], 1863: 359-76; James Bolivar Manson, 'Men of Letters as Men of Business', *Daily Review*, November 1863, quoted in Bussey and Reid, 1879: 235-37. James Payn (the editor of *Chambers's Edinburgh Journal*) offers a late example in 1881.

[9] See 'American Literature and the Civil War', *Fraser's Magazine*, LXIII, April 1863: 517-27, esp. 522-23; [Scott], 1863: esp. 364-5. Cf. [Mansel], 1863: 482, 512. Balée (1997) has argued that the American Civil War was a major determinant of anxieties about the sensation novel, using different evidence from that cited here.

(Flint, 1993: 274-293; and, for example, [Rae], 1865: 204, [Lewes], 1863: esp. 133-34; [Wise], 1866). Finally, opposing this constellation of anxieties was another, very different, compulsion, driven by the market: the need to understand what consumers wanted in order to deliver it before rivals.

Besides the novels in which 'The London Journal' is a servant girl's must-have accessory, the 1860s also produced a pair of novels in which the periodical occurs, disguised, by authors who had written for it. Mary Braddon's portrait of a penny-issue novelist in her version of *Madame Bovary* is caught between the instructive and the distancing in the same way as the *Macmillan's* article. She wrote *The Doctor's Wife* in 1864 at the same time she was writing *The Outcasts* for the *Journal*, and the appellation of her fictional novelist, 'Sigismund Smith', recalls the name of J.F. Smith, who had been famous in the *Journal* in the early 1850s when *The Doctor's Wife* (like *The Outcasts*) is set. The techniques of writing for the mass market that she describes recall Smith's rather than the kind of fiction that the *Journal* was offering in the 1860s. This difference may be partially explained by Braddon's concern to differentiate her culturally ambitious work from that for the penny weekly. As Pykett points out, the complex figure of Sigismund Smith can be read as 'a device by means of which his creator simultaneously satirizes and celebrates the sensation genre, attacks its critics, and at the same time distances her own 'artistic' narrative from the low genre(s) with which she has hitherto been associated and some of whose machinery and effects she continues to employ' (Braddon, 1864: x). To translate what Pykett is suggesting here into my terminology, Braddon was suspicious that the zones were not after all separated in terms of literary techniques – which renders all the more urgent the discovery of a way to keep them apart so as to justify their differing cultural status.

Emma Robinson had worked as a *London Journal* novelist between 1855 and 1856 and, like Braddon, incorporated her experience of its world in a novel. The differences and similarities are telling. Both have an ironic attitude to the penny weekly audience, which implies unease at the idea of a demand-led market, but Robinson's account specifically foregrounds the opportunities this market offered to penniless educated women. *Mauleverer's Divorce* of 1858 is an explicitly topical 'protest' novel about the condition of women under British marriage laws (which had changed the previous year). One of the unhappily married women tries to support herself by writing after leaving her satyr of a husband who has infected her with a venereal disease – anticipating by 45 years the supposedly first appearance of this topic in Sarah Grand's *The Heavenly Twins* (1892). The woman starts her career by trying to publish a three-volume novel. Told she will have to pay the costs while the publisher takes the profits, she moves down the cultural scale to drama, where her play is praised but refused because the female lead is too prominent and the principal actor of the troupe doesn't like to be outshone. She hits rock bottom by working for a 'cheap periodical' '[a]t a very modest salary, and with an infinitude of drudgery annexed'. The novel shows the ambiguous net such writing provided for women: it both saved them from falling further down the social scale but also trapped them with its meagre rewards. Nonetheless, as the narrator reports:

nothing apparently could exceed Sophia's satisfaction and triumph in this first permanent employment, and the prospect of maintaining herself independently. And she often expressed herself to me delighted to write for 'the people', so frank, so credulous, so natural in all save that they required a 'little' exaggeration in everything, and liked the colours to be laid on 'perhaps a trifle glaringly', without any of the finer hues and gradation! But how honest, how kindly, how chivalrously noble and tender hearted this good, rough, popular public was! What a yearning it had for love, still love! And what infinite allowances it made! How fearlessly might you set before it the coarsest of scene-painting, the most wild, incongruous, and even impossible inventions in character and events, provided only that you took care to show the whole under rapidly changing and variable lights, and roared through the gigantic tubes with some semblance to the human voice – and always at the most vehement pitch of excitement, whether of the tender and loving, or bellicose and stormy passions!   (Robinson, 1863: 233)

If I referred in Chapter 1 to the silence of readers, the same applies to writers. Whatever the democratic and patronising pleasures of 'writ[ing] for 'the people'', Sophia refuses to name the periodical she writes for. While she triumphs in her earnings, she does not want to her work judged by the standards of the zone she feels she ought to inhabit — one of many examples of reticence that is a major obstacle to the study of the nineteenth-century mass market. Braddon likewise hid her work for cheap periodicals (see Wolff, 1974: 11). Emma Watts Phillips (1891: 67) mentions the *Journal* only once in the biography of her brother Israel who wrote five serials for it between 1862 and 1870. She even implies, when she does mention it, that Israel did not write his *LJ* stories himself, but rather employed an amanuensis to write all but the general plot outline. Israel also wrote a couple of serials for *Cassell's Family Magazine* in 1870 and 1874, but Emma will refer neither to those nor to her six own anonymous and pseudonymous *London Journal* serials in the early 1880s. Such (self-)cancelling from history is a powerful sign that the zone I am dealing with acknowledged its absolute distance from cultural capital. It is in a markedly different position from younger mass-market writers such as Marie Corelli or Rider Haggard: a sales rhetoric of high status is incorporated into the very fabric of Corelli's and Haggard's portentous and pretentious narratives as well as their advertising. In their different ways and to varying degrees these two believed in the cultural value of their works. *London Journal* writers, by contrast, seem more cynically to have believed only in the financial value of theirs.

'The London Journal' and the 1870 Education Act

Alexander Strahan's 'Our Very Cheap Literature' in his up-market *Contemporary Review* takes as its occasion both the final repeal of the Newspaper Stamp Act in 1870 and the more famous Education Act of the same year. The article harks back to the 1830s philippics against popular reading, filtered through tropes exemplified by Charles Knight's denunciation of the 'stream of sewer literature'. It continues with an analysis in 'rational' but always condemnatory mode, to end by criticizing publishers for not producing cheap editions of 'our best authors'. Following the practices of so many others, Strahan's article can be viewed as part of a 'positioning strategy', visible too in his other publications, that emphasizes the purity of his own productions – particularly his 6d monthly *Good Words* – and the immorality of rivals (see also, for example, Strahan, 1875; Alexander, 1876; [Wright], 1876). Strahan's analysis of individual issues of penny weeklies rather than of complete volumes (or even tales) allows him to demonstrate the wickedness of penny weeklies, for as the *Macmillan's* writer had pointed out, one of the pleasures they offer lies in how each serial temporarily disrupts moral norms only to restore them at the end of the story — but not at the end of the episode. Even if, as a decidedly religious publication, *Good Words* was in a different cultural category, it nonetheless competed against the monthly parts of the *Family Herald* and the *London Journal* (the examples of 'very cheap literature' Strahan reviews) in so far as they cost the same. But what is happening is not so much a purely commercial as a cultural competition. Although employing a mutated form of the violent rhetoric once deployed by Tories for political ends and later taken over by publishers, with Strahan, as with the piece from the 1859 *British Quarterly Review*, it is also the religious attacking the lay.[10]

No market is ever static. By the 1880s 'The London Journal' was less associated with the kitchen, and there was a renewed perception of the failure of cultural incorporation caused largely by the success of the 'New Journalism'. There were two general ways in which the zone of the *Journal* was now described, one related to the Arnoldian educational mode and the other related to journalism itself.

As with the Strahan, the effect of the 1870 Education Act provoked many articles to appear and anxieties about a connection of reading to crime resurface. Now, however, these were no longer connected to the *Journal* and its fellows but to children's – mainly boys' – reading: thus James Greenwood on 'Penny Awfuls' (1873), John Pownall Harrison on 'criminal literature' (1873: esp. 71-8) as well as both Strahan (1875) and Wright (1876: 319) again. Control over children's reading set up by the School Boards with their prescribed syllabuses ("Requisition Lists") had caused a new barrier to be set up between licit and illicit children's reading. Every barrier invites transgression: hence this particular worry over children who were reading beyond their syllabus.[11]

By the 1880s and 1890s pupils had passed through the restraints of the school syllabus and emerged into the adult literary world where they could more freely control their own budgets. Unsurprisingly therefore, the 1870 Act is the starting point for an efflorescence of material on popular reading: a series of seven prize essays in the *Paper and Printing Trades Journal* between September 1873 and June 1876, Francis Hitchman (1890), G.R. Humphery (1893), Joseph Ackland (1894), Hugh Chrisholm (1895) and many others (see McDonald, 1997, ch. 1). What is particularly interesting is their similarity of argument and rhetorical structure. Like Arnold's earlier jeremiads against philistines and barbarians, they

---

[10] On *Good Words* in general, see Srebrnik, 1986: esp. 37-47, 57-63. For a succinct overview of Strahan's intentions as a publisher, see Maidment, 1992: 44-9.

[11] This point differs from, but is consonant with, Springhall (1990 and 1994) who gives a careful account of 1860s and 1870s boys' reading.

differ from previous writing on mass-market reading in their manipulations of the concept of 'cultural crisis'. Like earlier denunciations, they all begin by remarking the existence of such a crisis manifested by the 'New Journalism', a term whose coinage by Arnold in defence of his own cultural legitimacy Laurel Brake has discussed (1994: 83-100). All the articles agree on the urgent necessity for resolving the crisis but none now put forward as social curatives literary productions either of their own or of their social group. Nor do they posit a utopian resolution in some indefinite future inexorably brought about by Progress. As in Arnold, but even more insistently, they suggest that cultural incorporation should be the work of schools: adults are a lost cause. In the sense that schools were now more closely policed and curricula (and hence educational publications) were controlled by School Boards and the state Education Department (Harrison, 1990: 202), we can see such arguments as supporting bids for cultural power through a return to the ideas of a supply-led cultural alteration of society the Tories had called for earlier in the century. Now, though, it is emptied of party-political affiliation. Rather these arguments have been taken over by that fraction of the respectable bourgeoisie who are not sufficiently confident of their cultural capital to experiment *à la bohémienne*. Fearful of their own position within the cultural and social hierarchy, they wish (as Marx said in *The Communist Manifesto* of the entire bourgeoisie) to create the world in their own image.

Israel Zangwill complicates this discursive strand in his novel *Children of the Ghetto* (1892). There 'The London Journal' appears as the ground upon and walls with which a grotesque-pathetic character builds her own personal ghetto to isolate herself from the pain of external life. 'Dutch Debby' is a 'tall, sallow ungainly girl, who lived in the wee back-room on the second floor ... and supported herself and her dog by needlework'. She has virtually no friends, for it is rumoured she had given birth to an illegitimate child and been cast out by her parents. However, the heroine of the novel, the clever child Esther, befriends her, and to her great delight, finds that Debby keeps a stock of 'London Journals' under her bed. As Debby says:

'You see I used to save up all the back numbers of the *London Journal*, because of the Answers to Correspondents, telling you how to do up your hair and trim your nails and give yourself a nice complexion. I used to bother my head about that sort of thing in those days, dear; and one day I happened to get reading a story in a back number, only about a year old, and I found I was just as interested as if I had never read it before, and I hadn't the slightest remembrance of it. After that I left off buying the *Journal*, and took to reading my big heap of back numbers. I get through them once every two years.' Debby interrupted herself with a fit of coughing, for lengthy monologue is inadvisable for persons who bend over needlework in dark back rooms. Recovering herself, she added, 'And then I start afresh. You couldn't do that, could you?'
   'No,' admitted Esther, with a painful feeling of inferiority, 'I remember all I've read.'
   'Ah, you will grow up a clever woman,' said Debby, patting her hair.

(Zangwill, 1892: 91)

Esther persuades Debby to come to the park one afternoon in late autumn, but when Debby sees a young man and a girl in a rowing boat she 'burst into tears and went home. After that she fell back entirely on Bobby [her dog] and Esther and the *London Journal* ...' (Zangwill, 1892: 96). Esther grows up and leaves the ghetto, but is eventually drawn back to it and to Debby. At their reunion, Debby asks her to 'read some of ['The London Journal'] aloud ... It'll be like old times' (Zangwill, 1892: 441).

As with previous novels discussed in this chapter, Zangwill's use of 'The London Journal' legitimates his own fictional strategies (in this case naturalistic) by remarking their difference from what he offers. But he does so in a much more subtle way. While he picks up the liberal variant of the trope of mass-market fiction as children's reading which we saw first in Oliphant – for it is through 'The London Journal' that Esther learns her passion for literature – it is also through mass-market fiction that Esther discovers a version of the world that she will enter in the second part of the novel. There she is adopted by philanthropic wealthy and assimilated West End Jews – a plot device in any number of real *London Journal* serials, as the novel itself points out. Zangwill's distinction from the 'London Journal' plot lies not in how Esther comes to feel unhappy in the luxurious and high-culture West End – that is also a common trope, a transformation into narrative form of the adage 'All that glisters ...'. Rather, Zangwill distances his novel from the mass market by showing how when Esther tries to return to the ghetto she is no longer at home there either. In the end, she leaves on a trip for America in her search for true Jewishness, promising to return. Enabled by a gentile mass-market text to progress beyond the ghetto, she discovers she is exiled from her roots for ever. For Debby, on the other hand, the same text constructs a cyclical treadmill of memory that traps her in the ghetto and in an Oliphantine mythological stasis, realizing the *pathetic* potential of the trope of mass-market culture as industrial production. The mass market comforts but also disables the poor worker from progressing, even while for the gifted, like Esther, it can lead to a painful and problematic progression beyond itself into alienation.

Zangwill was a journalist but, born in 1864, he was a generation younger than many of the writers about 'The London Journal' and its fellows at this time. This older generation, like the pro-educationalists, was horrified by the notoriously prurient and profit-oriented 'New Journalism' and its huge circulation brought about by, according to the Vizetelly passage at the beginning of this chapter, its 'bogus prizes and illusory insurance tickets'. An elegiac, nostalgic tone entered the picture of 1850s and 1860s mass-market fiction now drawn by the clubbable veterans of the 'Old Journalism' or by those who (however temporarily) were allying themselves to that group.[12] In his *Recollections* published in 1880, Thomas Frost, who had written for *Cassell's Illustrated Family Paper* in the 1850s, redefined an earlier term of abuse from his youth, the 'Salisbury Square school of fiction': it 'did a good work in its day'. Then he formulated an indigenous genealogy of popular literature (which includes the *London Journal*) that distinguished itself from 'the sensualism of Eugène Sue and the mawkish

---

[12] Noel, 1954: 304-5 notes a similar nostalgia in this period in America. The much younger Robert Louis Stevenson (1888: esp. 339-40) also wrote nostalgically of the reading of his youth, which included J.F. Smith.

sentimentality of the Minerva library', having its roots instead in Smollett, Ainsworth, Godwin and Radcliffe (clearly he preferred to forget that the *Journal* published several of Sue's most 'sensual' novels). Frost on two occasions went to some lengths to show the respectability of the older penny fiction, even arguing against the kitchen literature trope: 'young women in the higher grades of the middle class' read it, he claimed, and the same authors were as popular in penny form as in the triple-decker borrowed from Mudie's (Frost, 1880: 317-30; Frost, 1886: 177-9). In 1893, the journalist and bookseller James Bertram recalled his time as a bookseller in Edinburgh when, '[f]rom personal knowledge... several of the best men in Edinburgh took in for the perusal of their families both *The London Journal* and *The Family Herald*, as well as some other papers absurdly denounced as "immoral"' (Bertram, 1893: 142). In this nostalgic vision, mistress and maid both read 'The London Journal'. Thomas Wright, who had denounced the 'London-Journal'-reading wife as the curse of the working man, now argued that the 'lady' classes were the largest audience of penny weeklies:

> the young ladies of the counters, of the more genteel female handicrafts generally, and the dress making and millinery professions in particular ...young ladies whose parents consider them, or who consider themselves, too genteel to go out to work.
>
> ([Wright], 1883: 282)

Caroline Mantons read it now with no ill effects. Still viewed as respectable, dull and feminine, this zone is now haloed with an autumnal glow and fantastically unified with the rest of the field.

The 1880s introduced tropes that worked against outright condemnation of magazines of the *Journal*'s generation and it is partly through them that Vizetelly's vision of 'The London Journal' is refracted. Although in the failure of his rival enterprise he was in the same position as Knight in the 1840s, and his resentment shows up in his ridicule of Stiff, Vizetelly's condemnation of circulation boosters used by new periodicals such as *Tit-Bits* and *Answers to Correspondents* also reveals an admiration for the supposed methods 'The London Journal' had used to increase circulation. This is the discourse of the old speaking affectionately of their erstwhile rivals, now pushed out by the new: *où sont les journaux d'antan*? We can also see the persistent effects of mid-century discourses concerning the femininity of the reader. Besides a brief reference to the old trope of the servant girl, Vizetelly suggests a Munby-esque thrill in a male writer's capacity to excite 'the factory girls in the north'.

By no means a description that points directly towards a material reality, Vizetelly's influential account is inflected in specific ways by its position in culture and history. It is typical in its use of 'The London Journal' as only a vaguely known locale to which meanings are dispatched and deployed as a skirmish in a much wider cultural war. But that does not mean that we must resign ourselves to a history of discursive tactics and strategies. Part 2 offers a more material mapping of the *London Journal* in the nineteenth-century periodical field.

Part 2

Periodical Production

Chapter Three

1845-49. Theoretical Issues; or, Genre, Title, Network, Space

Genre, Title, Network, Space

In its very first issue, the *London Journal* defines itself as a business venture. Unlike the one-and-a-half-guinea triple-decker, the six-shilling quarterlies or the half-crown and one-and-six miscellanies, it is an example of 'cheap literature ... the difference between the *cheap* and the *dear* consisting merely in the alternative whether profit shall be sought in a very large or a very limited circulation ...' ('Address to Readers', I: 16, 1 March 1845). The *Journal* celebrates its commodity status, justifying its nature through a Whiggish trope of the benefits of market enterprise. As we know from Feltes (1986) and Macherey (1978), the notion of the 'commodity text' is not a simple concept. While acknowledging my debt to them, I wish to unpack the notion differently, into eight major aspects, of which I shall discuss four in this chapter and four more in the next.

The first of the four here is *generic*. By this I understand the set of practices determining what kinds of material can be published and sold that define the 'character' of a publication. 'Character' in turn implies both confirming and defeating the expectations of an audience or reader, offering the new within a much more slowly changing general framework. It is under the generic that I place the evocation of an implied reader, as such a reader is an effect of defined and repeated textual practices that encourage certain expectations. The *Journal* was inserted into the market as a 'cheap illustrated miscellany', and to understand the expectations this aroused in the implied reader, it is necessary to sketch a history of the genre. What I shall term the 'parergic' falls under the heading of generic practices, as does the use of the Star Name which will also be a recurrent object of scrutiny. In a later chapter I shall make use of a concept I call the 'performative' which similarly comes under the heading of generic practices by, amongst other things, ironically and seductively drawing attention to the skill with which a narrative is told.

Second, a periodical is a *title*. It is important to deal with how producers choose a name in order to imply to purchasers a genealogy. Just as significant, a periodical title also has legal identity and status, implying boundaries between what belongs inside it and what not. This is naturalized by the possessive ('Ainsworth's Magazine') or by the deictic 'the' that commonly precedes titles ('The London Journal', 'The Times'). But the boundary between 'inside' and 'out' is always contested. This is apparent both in the difficulty the 1851 Stamp Committee had in deciding what newspapers and periodicals actually were and in the plagiarizing of materials from one periodical by another.

Third, a periodical occupies *space* both metaphorically in terms of its position in the cultural field and, in the sense that it is produced and distributed from specific locations, physically or geographically. In this chapter I shall look both at some of the larger-scale geo-cultural implications in the *London Journal*'s title and how the periodical utilized specific areas of the metropolis, overlaying the geographical with the textual in what I shall call a 'politography' of the city.

The last of the aspects I consider in this chapter concerns how a periodical is both the product and consolidation of a *social network* of producers who attempt to translate their cultural capital into economic and symbolic forms. In the sociological sense, a network is a social configuration in which some but not all component units maintain relations with one another, in an organisation with a centre and periphery but without a clear-cut and common boundary. Its components may be technological as well as human (see Knoke and Kuklinski, 1991: 173-183). This fourth conception of what constitutes a periodical fits traditional methods of describing them: developments in railway technology, the postal system, and printing are all regularly drawn on in periodical histories, as well as the influence of friendship and kinship groups. I shall not refer much to the impact of technology on publishing here as it has been explored elsewhere (see, for example, Bennett, 1990; Johanningsmeier, 1997; Lee, 1976; Reed, 1997; Ward, 1989). Suffice it to say that the *London Journal* took advantage of the stereotype both to produce large numbers of itself and to juxtapose pictures and type on the same page.[1] It must have used the railways and shipping for distribution. Of more interest to me are, however, the human elements of the network. If in the previous chapter I mentioned that consumers of periodicals comprised a network, in this and later chapters I shall instead concentrate on the changing topologies of personnel networks on the production side.

Social network and space cannot easily be split off from genre and title, and their separation is to some extent arbitrary: the positions and movements of individuals within the cultural field tend to keep them within the same discursive geographical areas, and publishing genres. As a result, my actual treatment of each of the four elements necessarily interpenetrates the others.

The Parergic, Plagiarism and the Cheap Illustrated Miscellany

The history of the 'cheap illustrated miscellany' has yet to be written: there is so far not even an adequate bibliographical map. In looking at possible models for the *London Journal* in this area I can only hope to synthesize and very slightly extend the preparatory work of Louis James (1963: esp. 14-31) and of Brian Maidment (1992). Maidment shows how the genre is an 1820s derivative of much more expensive eighteenth-century forebears, such as the *Gentleman's Magazine* (1731-

---

[1] On the *Journal* as stereotyped, see several comments in Notices to Correspondents: for example, 'J.R.S.', IV: 240; 'F.T.G.', IV: 352.

1906). In so doing, he goes against versions of periodical history such as the influential accounts of Dalziel (1957) and Altick (1998) that see the mass-market weeklies of the 1840s as having their roots firstly in the sensationalist press, such as the *Terrific Register* (1825) or *Police Gazette* (1828-34), and, secondly and more importantly, in the weeklies of the years of reform, 1831-32, especially *Chambers's Edinburgh Journal*, the *Penny Magazine* and *Saturday Magazine*. Instead of using a model based on a newspaper history that tidily dovetails political and periodical innovation, Maidment directs attention to what was possibly the first of the 1820s illustrated periodicals, Limbird's *Mirror of Literature, Amusement and Instruction* (1820-45). It cost 2d and, like the *Journal,* was a sixteen-page weekly that carried a woodcut on its front page. The *Mirror* is a paradigmatic miscellany in that it is compilatory (comprising mainly extracts from other publications) and in that its criteria for selection are those of the eighteenth century, stressing the antiquarian, the picturesque-topographical and the literary. Maidment also points out what seems a new development, the *Mirror's* inclusion of a department headed 'Useful Domestic Hints'. This foreshadows the inclusion of similar departments in later 'Chartist and artisan magazines of the 1840s and 1850s' (Maidment, 1992: 9). Anderson (1994: 46) remarked that the magazine's audience of 80,000 was mainly upper- and middle-class, but the sheer size of its circulation suggests readers of wider income bands than those labels suggest. Importantly, the *Mirror* also formed part of the network from which the *Journal* would spring. Its editor for sixteen years, John Timbs, was later to edit the *ILN* through which Stiff, as director of engraving, might have met him.[2] Furthermore, a later editor of the *Mirror, Percy B. St. John* – under whom, in 1844, it would carry fiction for the first time – was also called on by Stiff to write for and (briefly) edit the *Journal.*

The *London Journal* immediately claimed an ancestry in the 1820s illustrated miscellany through the typography of its masthead and the wording of its sub-title. These echo not the *Mirror* but other periodicals of the same type such as the *Portfolio of Entertaining and Instructive Varieties in History, Science, Literature, the Fine Arts, &c.* (1823-30). In the 1830s such typography was very common for respectable miscellanies, as witness the *Penny Novelist, a Weekly Magazine of Tales, Fictions, Poetry and Romance* (1832-34). But if the *Journal's* masthead suggests the stability of the well-established, over its first year its front-page illustrations experimented with a variety of artistic styles and modes, including the romantic and picturesque, though with a tendency towards the sensational vignette (see Figures 3.1, 3.2, 3.3). They only settled down into a mode derived from the historical anecdote picture when John Gilbert became the regular illustrator in March 1846 (see Figure 3.4).[3] Internal illustrations covered an even wider spectrum, from the Lloyd-like refusal of respectable modes to the most genteel

---

[2] Timbs was editor of *ILN* during the *London Journal's* first years: see I: 328, a piece that remarks Timbs's editorship of the *Mirror* as well.

[3] See King, 2000. While several illustrations to Soulié's *It Was Time* are in his style (for example, II: 297, 313), Gilbert became a regular front-page illustrator only from 14 March 1846 (III: 17). He rarely signed his contributions to any publication, but a few examples of his signature can be found in the *Journal* (see II: 241, III: 113, 145; VI: 209).

picturesque. Verbal contents likewise ranged over a wide gamut, from indirect denunciations of government corruption to essays on the civilizing power of art. This constant shifting suggests that Reynolds and Stiff had not yet established a stable set of practices that would appeal consistently to its vague target audience of 'the people' and 'the industrious classes' (cf. James, 1972: 17). Uncertainty of reader profile, comprising but always threatening the limits of the miscellany genre, is here brought clearly to the surface.

Figure 3.1 'The Castle of Aspiroz; or, The Spectral Banquet'
Source: I: 1.

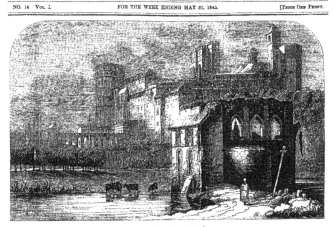

THE

LONDON JOURNAL;

And Weekly Record of Literature, Science, and Art.

NO. 14 VOL. I.   FOR THE WEEK ENDING MAY 31, 1845.   [PRICE ONE PENNY.

[THE PRISON OF THE INQUISITION.]

THE MYSTERIES OF THE INQUISITION.
CHAPTER XVI.
THE GRAND INQUISITOR'S LOVE.

Two months had passed away since the lovely Dolores, so miraculously delivered from the per- carnal enjoyments, nor satisfy those ardent and sensual desires, which the remembrance of the love-ly Andalusian created in the licentious breast of the Grand Inquisitor.

By overwhelming the late governor of Seville with his indignation and anger, the Grand Inqui- where was she? how had she contrived to elude his researches?

Vainly had the inquisitorial militia used all its exertions to discover the hiding-place of Dolores — vainly had the Order of Garduna received the most magnificent promises of money and pro-

Figure 3.2 'The Prison of the Inquisition', *The Mysteries of the Inquisition*
Source: I: 265.

THE

LONDON JOURNAL;

And Weekly Record of Literature Science, and Art.

NO. 15. VOL. I.   FOR THE WEEK ENDING JUNE 7, 1845.   [PRICE ONE PENNY.

NARRATIVE OF AN ARCTIC VOYAGE—A CREW OF ESQUIMAUX ATTACKED BY BEARS.

The good ship Van Tromp sailed from Flushing on the 29th of March, 1839, and, after encounter-ing various perils, entered the frigid confines of might be seen at one instant covered with foam, the next concealed from the sight by the waves, and instantly afterwards reared to a prodigious height above the surface of the sea. At 11 P.M. apparent damage to consist in the destruction of the most of the rudder works, a few slight bruises on the sides, and a cut on the lower part of the stern of the ship. These injuries being repaired, the

Figure 3.3 'Narrative of an Arctic Voyage – A crew of Esquimaux attacked by bears'
Source: I: 281

THE

LONDON JOURNAL;

And Weekly Record of Literature, Science, and Art.

No. 55. Vol. III.]   FOR THE WEEK ENDING MARCH 14, 1846.   [Price One Penny.

[THE CORPSE OF POPE ALEXANDER VI. THROWN FROM ITS COFFIN.]

FAUST.
By GEORGE W. M. REYNOLDS,
Author of " The Mysteries of London," &c.

principal houses were hung with black; the bells of the numerous towers of Rome tolled solemn knells; and all the shops were closed. The procession was opened by a number of the

The procession moved on : already had it left the Vatican a hundred yards behind, when suddenly the murky atmosphere was illumined with a flash o*

Figure 3.4 'The Corpse of Pope Alexander VI, Thrown from its Coffin', G.W.M. Reynolds, *Faust* Source: III: 17.

Besides its visual experimentation, the *Journal* departed from earlier miscellanies in several other ways. Firstly, it refused their octavo size and double-column layout. Thomas Frost suggested that one reason for the success of *Lloyd's Penny Weekly Miscellany* (1843-46) and the *Family Herald* (1843-1940) was their size: he claims they were easier to bind (Frost, 1880: 85). The *Journal*, like several other miscellanies of the late 1830s and 1840s, had virtually the same dimensions as these, suggesting at least the popularity of quarto for the miscellany in the mid-1840s, if not exactly confirming Frost's assertion. In adding an extra column to the two its most obvious rival, the *Family Herald*, employed, the *Journal* may well have been playing on the value-for-money trope that Wilkie Collins's informant insisted on. At any rate, in its wake, a triple-column layout afterwards increasingly became standard for entertainment periodicals.

Over the years, the *London Journal* copied other, basic, units of reading from the *Family Herald*, including the combination of serial novels and one-episode tales, poems, and departments headed 'Scientific and Useful' and 'Statistics'. 'Varieties', 'Random Readings' and 'The Riddler' in the *Herald* became in the *Journal* 'Miscellaneous' and the rather different 'Good Humour' (cuttings of jokes and humorous anecdotes). The *Herald*'s editorial was transformed into the weekly 'Essay' on general topics, redolent of an eighteenth-century magazine. At the same time the *Journal*'s early volumes compartmentalized reading far more than its model. In addition to its listing of serials, Volume I had no fewer than seventeen departments headed: 'The Arts', 'Biography', 'Diagrams' (distinguished from 'Illustrations' and 'Portraits'), 'Didactic', 'Essays', 'General', 'Good Humour', 'Historical', 'Miscellaneous', 'Poetry', 'Reviews', 'Tales', 'Useful Receipts', 'Voyages, Travels and Topographical Descriptions', 'Notices to Correspondents'. Later volumes added even more until volume XVII (1853), when departments became regularized. It is as if the *Journal* wanted to be seen to cover everything, haphazardly, it seems, prospecting over a wide range of the field to find the gold of 'a very large ... circulation'.

'Notices to Correspondents', renamed slightly from the *Herald*'s 'To Correspondents', is particularly interesting for the space it devotes to direct interaction between the periodical and its readers. Dating from the late seventeenth century and the rise of the periodical itself (Shevelow, 1989), by the 1840s such interaction had become a characteristic that defined newspapers and low-status periodicals – the quarterlies never deigned such open acknowledgement of the existence of consumer desire that producers might listen and respond to.

If the *Journal* exploited the notion of genre by aiming at established purchasers of cheap periodicals and trying to capture new ones with its innovations and its wide gamut of texts, its most important facet borrowed from earlier miscellanies was that it is meshed into contemporary and expensive literary zones. Its involvement with these zones took two forms, a sharing of personnel and a sharing of material.

In the previous chapter I referred to Emma Robinson's description in *Mauleverer's Divorce* (1863) of how authors tried their hand in the expensive zone and, when they failed to become established there, passed down the cultural hierarchy to end up in penny magazines. That this narrative of cultural descent existed in reality is evident from tracing relations of the *Journal* with *Bentley's Miscellany* (1837-68) and *Ainsworth's Magazine* (1842-54). At 1/6 and 2/6 respectively, they were well outside the market for the periodicals I have hitherto referred to. While plundered to provide material for the *Journal*'s early volumes,[4] they also fed personnel into them. Percy Bolingbroke St John is typical in this regard. Born in 1821, the eldest son of a family of journalists, he travelled extensively in America in his youth, contributed a few pieces to *Bentley's* and *Ainsworth's* in 1843-44 and 1844-45 respectively (together with one piece to the *Foreign and Quarterly Review* in January 1845), before editing the final years of the *Mirror* between 1846 and 1850. Meanwhile, he was writing a good deal for *Tait's Edinburgh Magazine*, and in 1847 published his first of four tales for the

---

[4] *Bentley's* was mined for three extracts in vol. I, only one of which is of any length; there are five in vol. II. *Ainsworth's* provided ten, most substantial.

Journal in this period. In 1853 he became the first front-page novelist for *Cassell's Illustrated Family Paper*, all the while contributing the odd tale to the *Journal*. He was persuaded to move, as front-page novelist, to the latter in early 1856. After reaching the zone of the penny fiction weekly, St John briefly attempted to run his own in 1861, the *London Herald* (*Bookseller*, 1861, XLIV: 522), before returning as contributor of serials and tales to the *Journal*. Simultaneously, he was employed to 'revise and edit' at least sixteen translations which appeared between 1858 and 1868 by the publisher of the *London Journal*, Vickers. He stayed with Vickers and the *Journal* until the end of the first series in 1883, pirated (as was quite usual) all the while in America.[5] St John died in apparently wretched circumstances in 1889.

The sociological narrative in which authors aim 'high', fail and end 'low', as exemplified by St John's biography, is not usually reversible. Having failed to maintain his position, St John did not return to higher-status periodicals or publishers. John Wilson Ross, the *Journal's* first named contributor and its second editor, is unusual in publishing a story in *Bentley's* in 1844, translating Paul Féval's *The Loves of Paris* for Vickers, and later managing to place one more story in *Bentley's* in 1851. Several years after leaving the *Journal*, he edited the second series of the *Universal Decorator* (1860). This was a ninepenny up-market magazine published initially by Vickers, intended to cultivate the senses and thereby improve 'moral action' ('Address', *Universal Decorator*, 1858, I), a common consumerist mutation of utilitarianism that the *ILN* also promulgated. When Ross took over, the publisher of the *Decorator* was in fact Houlston and Wright, but Vickers may have recommended him. He does not seem to have been successful, as the second series only lasted a few issues. Later, Ross published an anti-Darwinian pamphlet whose sensational title belies its dullness, *Biblical Prophecy of the Burning of the World: An Attempt to Fix the Day of the Coming Fire that is to Destroy Us All* (1869). There followed a curious historiographical tome, *Tacitus and Bracciolini. The Annals Forged in the XVth Century* (1878), which claimed that what we know as the Roman historian's work was invented in the Renaissance. While hardly placing Ross in the élite zone (the *DNB* dryly notes his erratic learning), this is still an unusual trajectory for a *London Journal* writer, and is due possibly to his colonial background and university education at the newly formed King's College, London. Given his interrupted publishing career, Ross may also have had another form of income.

A much more common pattern is perceptible in the career of John Parsons Hall, who, after one story in *Bentley's* in 1847, became a *London Journal* contributor for many years. Even G.W.M. Reynolds, the *Journal's* first editor, had placed one tale in *Bentley's* in 1837 (his biographical puff in the *Journal* refers to this in such a way as to suggest he was a regular contributor to *Bentley's*). Emma Robinson and Mrs Gordon Smythies, both significant novelists in the *Journal* in the mid-1850s and 1860s respectively, had previously managed to contribute a couple of works to *Ainsworth's* in 1844 and 1845. Ann Marie Maillard, who wrote many tales for the

---

[5] See St. John wrote a wry letter to *The Times* (9 November 1871: 8) in which he also complains about being called the author of *Lady Audley's Secret* in some American publications. St. John's biography appears in *DNB*, XVII: 647-8.

Journal from 1853 (most often as 'A.M.M.'), seems to have been trying to break into the more up-market zone with a story in *Ainsworth's* the previous year, but it remained an isolated success. Her novels in volume format from the early 1850s were published by Routledge, a firm specializing in cheap runs and one that authors were often wary of (Sutherland, 1976: 37).

The *London Journal* was thus a precipitate out of surplus labour which would prefer the greater symbolic (and at this stage usually economic) capitals of the up-market magazines. The desire for a unified cultural field that I discussed in Chapter 2 is visible here, supported sociologically by the very limited socio-cultural group that writers in general came from (Altick, 1989). In that sense, the impression gained from Vizetelly's description of the magazine as staffed by 'failures' is correct.

The longing for the high but exclusion from it that such career paths suggest results in what I term the *parergic*. This comprises a set of specific textual effects and practices, which, while underpinned by sociological narratives, does not inhere in specific bodies or corpora (a writer, artist, a periodical or even an article may display the parergic or not at various points). It is a system whereby texts are based on originals that are invested with greater symbolic capital and authority. Officially respectful and emulative, the parergic is tinged always with a resentment, caused by exclusion from desired cultural areas, that brings about mutation in what is supposedly emulated. The parergic sometimes raids authority aggressively and seems therefore to attack it, but nonetheless paradoxically buttresses cultural boundaries even in the act of transgressing them. Unlike parody, which always in some sense undermines the authority of its original even while being complicit with it, the parergic fully acknowledges and maintains this authority even when it effaces its model. Unlike straightforward imitation of the high, which depends on large cultural capital to judge its value, the parergic does not use the exclusive codes or high prices that cultural authority wraps itself in to keep out the uninitiated.[6]

---

[6] A 'parergon' according to the *OED* is a work 'secondary to or derivative of a larger or greater work, an opusculum', but the term is familiar in cultural studies today from Derrida (1987). Derrida discusses its use in Kant's *Critique of Aesthetic Judgement* as referring to those (sublunary) elements that are attached to a work of art or text but which are not, according to Kant, intrinsic to it. Examples include the frame of a picture, or clothing in a History Painting. Derrida then expands its meaning to include (foot)notes to a text, parentheses, or indeed the context of a work of art. Concerned to deconstruct the hierarchy of inside and out, essence and contingency, which defines the status differences between the work of art and its parergon, he argues that the parergon is essential to the work of art and defines it as such (in this sense it is a local manifestation of the well-known Derridean *supplement*). My usage is very different from Derrida's while yet related to it. Raiding philosophy in an attempt to make good a perceived lack of appropriate terminology to discuss the nineteenth-century mass market, I have reapplied the term to characterize the effects of status differentials amongst elements of cultural artefacts in print history at a specific moment. As will become clear, I am not suggesting a universal meaning for the parergic. Rather the parergic is itself contingent and sublunary, a local and always impure textual effect supported by modes of cultural production that eventually gives way to others.

The weekly 'Essays' furnish typical examples of the parergic in terms of that practice which is 'style'. Essay L on 'The English Language', signed by John Wilson Ross (III: 7-8), begins with the commonplace thesis that 'the progress of language marks the progress of the human mind', and swiftly interprets this in a nationalist sense. It continues by placing the 'rise' of the English language at the Reformation because then 'men began to argue' and to do so 'they [had to] express themselves with precision'. Thereafter,

> Addison was unquestionably the first of our writers who introduced elegance of expression into the composition of English prose. He found the writings of his predecessors disfigured by a loose, inaccurate, and clumsy style. He changed all this, and made himself a model for imitation. In his works we find no forced metaphor – no dragging clause – no harsh cadence, – no abrupt close. He is, also, a happy model for the use of figurative language. They seem to spring spontaneously from the subject: and are never detained till the spirit evaporates or the likeness vanishes. They are just like flashes of lightning in a summer's night – vivid, transient, lustrous, – unexpected but beautiful, – passing over the prospect with a pleasing brightness, and just vanishing before you catch a sight of all the beauties of the scene they gild. The copious and classic mind of that writer gave our language the greatest degree of elegance and accuracy of which it is susceptible. Since his time fine writing has not improved. Simply, because it cannot be. You cannot give the English language a nicer modification of form, or a greater beauty of feature than Addison gave it. But you can give it more nerve and muscle. And subsequent writers have done so.
>
> (III: 7)

It was Johnson, '[t]hat Colossus of English literature', who provided the muscle. Since his time 'there has occurred no variation in the style of English prose' except, possibly, by increased use of the 'Gothic, whence [English] sprung; and that is a feature in language which our readers will agree with us is more deserving of disgust than admiration, and a variation in style more worthy of punishment than praise' (III: 8).

The essay's claims to authority depend largely on the assumption of a common standard throughout the literary field: Addison and Johnson are set up as the authoritative models of excellence that *all* must imitate, including the essay itself. Its backward gaze towards a classical and smilingly rational eighteenth century is also bent towards an imagined lost unity of the literary market where economic, cultural, social and symbolic capitals coincide: that is, where you make money, become famous and sought after by producing a masterpiece. In seeking to imitate the model, however, even by its own standards of elegant and accurate writing, the

---

While in the body of this book I use 'parergon' and its derivatives 'parergic' and 'parergy' with particular reference to periodicals, I think the term is also useful to describe the works variously described as Dickens 'rip-offs', 'imitations' or 'parodies'– *Oliver Twiss, Pickwick Abroad*, and so on. The term is particularly appropriate to mark their relationship with their founding texts since the 'par' prefix of 'parergon' is sufficiently ambiguous to allow in 'parallel' (as in 'parallel universe', for example) as well as, where necessary, to mark status differences between the first and later works, however they may be conceived (παρά in Greek meant 'beside', 'running along with', 'towards', 'passing by', 'during', 'deriving from', and several other things, depending on what case it took and its context).

essay fails. Apart from its dubious historical thesis – questionable even in the 1840s, for Ross has had to omit Shakespeare – the style is 'loose, inaccurate, and clumsy', wordy even while sentences are brief to the point of abruptness. The comparison of figures of speech to lightning, no doubt meant to be both amusing and elegant in its self-reflexivity, is not only verbose but unclear. There is lack of agreement between grammatical subjects ('...figurative langauge. They...'). Even the typesetting indicates hasty and irregular punctuation.

This split between what is claimed and what is delivered, risible to those with more cultural capital, is exactly where the parergic resides. The style betrays symptoms of inability or *refusal* to 'write well'. Whether due to resistance, lack of time, money or education, what seems to me to underlie it is resentment at being caught up in and accepting structures of cultural authority while not being in a position to wield that authority. The 'economic literature' of which the *London Journal* is an increasingly successful example, does not have high cultural status, yet at the same time is struggling to validate through the terms of the high what it also and contradictorily imagines as a space for itself independent of the high. It is in such a fraught median space — that middle I described as so problematic in Chapter 1 — that parergy is found.

In the above example, the parergic operates on a micro-level, but there are more spectacular instances in which the *Journal* seeks to incorporate cultural and economic value, raiding it in a more aggressive manner. While I shall continue to explore the changing nature of parergy in later sections, I shall now discuss it under the rubric of plagiarism to reveal the ambiguity of its textual relations to authority. At the same time, I shall mix this theoretical discussion with the history of the *Journal's* first years to show the inextricable intertessellation of theory and history.

Now the legal definition of plagiarism in nineteenth-century England depended on the law of literary property (Saunders, 1992: 122-48). Copyright had begun in 1710 with the legal recognition of authorial property for a limited duration. The Copyright Act of 1814 designated the period as twenty-eight years or the life-span of the author, whichever was the greater. A further act of 1842 increased it to forty-two years or seven years after the death of the author. This later act also tightened contracts between authors and publishers (most of the twelve other copyright acts in the Victorian period were concerned with the international regulation of the book trade).

I define parergic plagiarism in slightly different terms. It takes three forms in the *Journal* (though all three are very common in publications near to it in the field). Two, covert and overt lifting of material, come under the laws of literary property clearly enough. But I want to start with another kind: faked personnel and the raiding of authors' names as if they were commodities in themselves. This kind has itself two forms. Firstly, the *Journal* may leave it unclear whether an author has written a piece specially for it, merely appending the author's name at the end. Sometimes it is obvious they did not – a prime example is Shakespeare, who anyway would not fall under the copyright laws – but often the practice leads to ambiguity. An instance is a two-part tale from February 1847 signed 'Camilla Toulmin', an author otherwise associated with magazines of higher cultural status, especially *Chambers's Edinburgh Journal.* The second form involves advertisements for the *London Journal* in the *Weekly Times*, another Stiff-Vickers publication. These suggest that certain authors have written pieces specially for the magazine, whereas inside the *Journal* it is acknowledged that the pieces are lifted from another publication. This is the case with James Whittle, whose tale 'Beatrice Cenci' is footnoted as originally in *Bentley's* inside the *Journal* (V: 394-6), whereas the *Weekly Times* (8 August 1847, I: 347) implies he is a *London Journal* author. In both types, what is important is that the 'name' is treated as a commodity: the zone operates according to a 'star system' in so far as it can, raiding constellations higher than itself.

Covert lifting is by its nature difficult to locate as its origins are deleted, but I have found an example in the series 'A Tour On The Rhine' in late 1845. This was a continuation of a previous series entitled 'Queen Victoria's Visit to Germany', the complexities of whose operation deserve initial comment to help understand how this plagiarism functioned. The earlier series, recalling the massive coverage of the tours in the *ILN* and elsewhere (see Plunkett, 2003: esp. ch.1), had not simply imitated its main model. In theory at least, as an unstamped publication the *Journal* was not allowed to carry news, and, instead of carrying details of what the Queen did, as in the newspaper, it had offered descriptions of the places she visited, in a topographical mode perfectly consonant with miscellany practice. The descriptions had, however, rapidly segued into romantic-gothic tales. Likewise, the series had been illustrated not with views of what the Queen was doing, but with picturesque scenes of what the Queen saw, again in the manner of a miscellany. Over August and September 1845 the *ILN* offered both pictures of the Queen performing her public offices and of what she saw, even reproducing picturesque art by Prince Albert. The *Journal* was therefore taking one side of *ILN* coverage and encouraging readers to displace an item in the authoritative news from the political to the literary, while at the same time offering the viewpoint not of a bystander to the spectacle of royal authority, but the vantage point of royalty itself. Such a practice both got around the authority of the Stamp Tax and incorporated the viewpoint of an even higher authority. The continuation of the first series, 'A Tour on the Rhine', developed this combination of topographical description, illustration and gothic tale, while appropriating yet another form of authority by lifting its descriptions silently from Murray's famous *Handbook for Travellers on the Continent.*[7] Murray's *Handbook* was *the* guidebook to use at the time, conceptually modern, replete with up-to-date information for the tourist with the money to travel (Buzard, 1993: 65-7). The *Journal's* plagiarism of it offered a cheap, virtual tour less into spaces that materially existed than into a realm of imaginative narrative, transforming its stolen descriptions of the real into atmospheric preludes to extended romantic legends. This was itself a mutant inflation of guidebook practice which provided appropriate quotations to read while viewing the scene. The *Journal*, therefore, through its mixture of plagiarism, topicality and recontextualization, was able to incorporate and reconfigure the

---

[7] Cf. II: 53, 73, 89, 185, 201, 217 with [Murray], 1836: 236, 235-36, 237, 229, 219-21, 213-16 respectively.

pleasures of several forms of authority in multiple ways. It is precisely in such complex combinations of aggressive raiding with simultaneous respectful acknowledgement of various authorities (either implicit or explicit) that characterizes parergy as textual practice and effect – a wonderful example of the prestidigitation of the commodity fetish.

Overt plagiarism is common from the beginning and is of course easy to locate. In the parergic version, its operation implies both aggression against the raided source and collusion with the reader over this. This is, I think, one of the particular pleasures that the *Journal* openly offered the reader, in contrast to less successful and less confident publications that also plagiarized the high. These (*New Parley's Library* – 9 March 1844 to 22 February 1845– is one) often reek of a tacit admission of cultural failure, as if the reader is offered such second-hand goods apologetically. Such embarrassed diffidence is certainly not resentful parergy, but rather a sign of a more thorough respect for and indeed awe of the consecrated.

It is abundantly clear that the recontextualization that plagiarism implies offers meanings that are different from those in the sources of the lifted texts. Recent critics have well explored the effects of recontextualization in periodicals (for example, Turner, 2000; Wynne, 2001) and I shall pursue this idea in Chapters 9 and 11. I shall not therefore enlarge on it here other than to say that overt plagiarism became ever more common from late 1846; extracts, and sometimes virtually complete works, were even serialized. This coincided with a noticeable redirection of the magazine. From the end of July 1846, Reynolds absented himself from his editorial duties, and by October John Wilson Ross was sitting in the editor's chair.[8] Although a contemporary described him as 'a really clever and extremely well-informed person... an acute thinker, a versatile writer, and a first rate scholar' (Dix, 1854: 287), Ross did not produce much original material apart from his regular weekly essay. Instead, he hugely intensified raids on French novels, and published a number of fine prints, including a set of penny supplementary engravings of famous English paintings available only to regular subscribers, called 'Cartoons for the People'. From Volume V (1847) he engaged the well-known engravers White and Bolton.

Under Reynolds, one of the most distinguished illustrators of the time had started to draw for the *Journal* on a regular basis: John Gilbert, most famous today as an *ILN* artist. His *London Journal* work comprised illustrations to novels, and maintained his internationalist hybrid style, which was perceived to combine Salvator Rosa, Rubens, Rembrandt, Velasquez, Pradilla, Poussin and a British watercolourist and illustrator favoured by Dickens, George Cattermole ([Spielmann], 1898: 53-64; Clayton, 1911). Gilbert's deliberate rejection of the low comedy of Cruikshank and the caricatures of Leech and others (a stance that caused Jerrold to eject Gilbert from *Punch*) was exactly right for a magazine which wanted to distance itself from the too overtly polemical. His generalized, *moralisé*, respectable yet non-exclusive style suited its parergy. Yet with rare exceptions,

---

[8] See Notices to Correspondents, III: 384; 'Address to Our Readers', IV: n.p.; advertisement for the *Journal* in the *Weekly Times*, 7 February 1847: 36 (also every week to 4 April 1847: 168).

such as the illustrations to Reynolds's *Faust*, Gilbert usually seems to have dashed off his contributions even more quickly than usual – and his execution was famously rapid – indicative perhaps of his low regard for the work. So different are they from his other work that Ralph Thomas (1913-14), an early twentieth-century expert on Gilbert, initially refused to believe that he had illustrated the Sue novels serialized in the *Journal* under Ross (despite the fact that some of these drawings are similar to Gilbert's work for the later volumes of *The Mysteries of London*). Even when the contributor has high status, then, the parergic means that there are marks of difference from the high – an important point that demonstrates how individual bodies cannot be too easily be associated with specific textual characteristics.

In addition to the French novels, Ross openly lifted massive amounts of material from London publications. This several times brought to court the magazine's publisher, Vickers. *The Times* (17 November 1847: 11) printed an account of a hearing whereby Richard Bentley, 'the well-known publisher', applied to restrain Vickers from reprinting in the *London Journal* 'several articles which had appeared in *Bentley's Miscellany* and which were the exclusive property of the plaintiff'.[9] The injunction was immediately granted. Less than a year later, Bentley again took Vickers to court for serializing excessively long extracts from Bulwer's *Harold, the Last of the Saxon Kings*. 'The Vice-Chancellor observed, that it was a matter of course to make the [restraining] order' (*Times*, 31 July 1848: 7), his attitude indicating both the low status of the *Journal* and *Bentley's* authority.

There are, however, other, less violent, ways to interpret such practices than raiding or theft: after all, the *Journal* never condemns anything it plagiarizes. Perhaps we might regard such lifting as publishers and authors puffing each other's work. A sociological approach might seek to establish the determinants behind the choices of works quoted – recurrence of publishers or authors might reveal a network. I have found little to support such a contention in the *Journal*. Amongst the authors, Bulwer Lytton and Disraeli rub shoulders with Archibald Alison and Frederick Douglass. Amongst the publishers, the disreputable Newby joins the rather more respectable Chapman and Hall, Saunders and Otley and the well established firms of Longman, Colburn and, of course, Bentley. There is no sense of a publicity campaign on behalf of anyone in particular. Curiously, under Ross even novels published by Vickers in other formats do not get puffed (though they are advertised), whereas Reynolds had decisively promoted them, including his own *Mysteries of London* and Dumas's *Three Musketeers*.

On the other hand, some departments, 'Good Humour' and 'Miscellaneous', which owe their whole existence to compilation, do repeatedly quote a limited number of periodicals. The most frequently cited include the *Clown* (38 short quotations in volume I; two only in II, as the magazine closed shortly after that volume had begun), *Great Gun* (54 short quotations in I), and *Joe Miller* (16 quotations in I and nine in II). All three magazines were competitors of *Punch*, and indeed products of related networks (Spielmann, 1895: 657). In fact, it is *Punch*

---

[9] Vickers is uniquely described here as the 'proprietor' of the *Journal*, but I have been unable to establish anything further about this possible ownership.

that is raided more than any other source: 64 times in volume I with 45 longer quotations in volume II. This intensely parasitic relationship indicates how the *Journal*, like the many publications that also raided *Punch*, still saw itself as part of the same field of entertainment. Altick (1997: 36) has claimed that readers of *Punch* were unlikely to read the *London Journal* or the *Family Herald*, but the *Journal*'s producers certainly assumed that its readers would delight in what was already the authoritative *speculum stultorum*, quoted in *The Times* and the House of Commons. The *London Journal* series 'The Newspaper Press of London' (the very conception of which indicates a belief that readers would be interested in the entire field) described *Punch* in exceptionally favourable terms (I: 407). Perhaps mindful of *Punch*'s prosecutions of plagiarists in 1843 and 1845, the *Journal* also turned to analogues to avoid lifting too much. If this is the case, then its quotations from the *Clown* and others can be regarded as raids *manqués* on authority.

Co-operation with others outside the network is not part of parergy. It was safe, culturally if not always legally, to praise and lift passages from three-volume novels by Bulwer or from expensive magazines, for the *Journal*'s readers were not expected to be able to buy these. Even *Punch* at 3d was too costly. It was safe, of course, to advertise Vickers's own publications, household products, reference works, music or 'class' periodicals like the *Builder*, which anyway attracted an up-market clientele (Brooks, 1981: esp. 89, 90). None of these directly competed for space in the same zone. So far as I can establish, no rivals are ever quoted, advertised or even condemned. This marks off the *London Journal* from other, usually less successful, penny weeklies which, as Chapter 2 showed, do refer to rivals at specific moments. Parergy, as manifested in the *Journal*, means constant awareness of rivals and refusal to acknowledge their existence, and an offer instead of mutant versions of higher-status, higher-cost cultural productions.

Familiarity Breeds Content: Brand-Names, Internationalism, Siblings and Rivals

Everyone to whom I have ever mentioned 'The London Journal' has claimed to know it. The title seems a natural one, always-already heard, familiar, one of the family almost. But how many of my interlocutors know *this London Journal*?

Here I shall first of all explore some of the reasons for, and implications of, the choice of title. Ever seeking to render visible the commodity's sleight of hand, I shall consider the title partly as a 'brand-name' *avant la lettre* and partly as a node in a personnel network, teasing out meanings available to different readers both amongst cultural producers and consumers.

A brand-name for today's marketing gurus has several components: it identifies the product, it differentiates it from rivals, it communicates messages to the consumer through associations and, finally, it is a legal property or 'trademark' (Keller, 1998). All these apply to 'The London Journal' as a periodical title. 'In a business environment ... the brand-name is usually the only variable that never changes' (Hankinson, 1993: 25). One thinks of how the chemical composition of same-name chocolate bars is varied over the world to suit perceived national tastes.

And a product can vary over time as well as space: the case of Coca-Cola is notorious. Stiff's magazine certainly did change: the product metamorphosed while the title remained immutable for almost four decades. It must by no means be thought that applying ideas derived from the modern-day study of branding smacks of the imposition of later 'scientific' marketing on a more 'primitive' market mentality. The selection of a periodical title for its specific associations in the consumer's mind was a practice sufficiently well established by 1861 for the first number of a twopenny weekly, *Robin Goodfellow*, to satirize it on its very first page, where it explores nine types of title aimed at different consumer populations.

As far as the title of Stiff's weekly is concerned, the defining part of the brand-name is clearly 'London'. 'Journal' on its own is too general and employed in too many contexts to be a distinctive feature. Similarly, numerous publications had used elements of the subtitle 'and Weekly Record of Literature, Science, and Art'. The *British Quarterly Review* (1859: 331-2) commented on this very one that 'the experienced public are not deceived by such labels' and indeed only the first issue of the *Journal* included (small) departments called 'Literature', 'Science' and 'The Fine Arts'. The subtitle functioned rather as a declaration that politics and theology would be excluded. Since 'London' is key then, the operation of the title needs to be analysed firstly through associations with preceding periodicals that use 'London' or 'London Journal' in their titles and with contemporary rivals in the field, and then through how the commodity redefines its brand-name through its practices.

The familiarity of 'The London Journal' as a collocation is due to a long history of use that runs at least from the 1720s to today. Examples include the *London Journal* (1720-34); the *Original Half-Penny London Journal* (1725); *Baldwin's London Journal, or British Chronicle* – an exceptionally long-lived weekly newspaper (1762-36); the *London Journal* (1975-). Boswell's famous *London Journal* (1762-63) was not, of course, a periodical, but adds to the familiar feel of the title. In summer 2002, *City: The London Journal* by Philip James was all over the London bookshops. No wonder people think they know exactly what I'm referring to.

In the decade or so before Stiff's *London Journal* there were numerous periodicals with similar titles which would have served to delimit its meanings even though they lay outside the cultural zone and product-type of the penny weekly miscellany. The *London Journal of Arts, Sciences and Manufactures* (1820-66) was an official monthly publication, conducted and published by W. Newton at the Office of Patents, devoted to publishing new patents. The *London Journal of Commerce* (1841-45) was a sixpenny weekly newspaper with a circulation of 2,000 in 1843 (see *London Journal of Commerce*, 8 June 1844). It was intended to supply updates on all news relevant 'to the Merchant and Man of Business'. The *London Sunday Journal* (7 March 1840 to 4 April 1860), while costing only 2d weekly and intended for 'heads of families, in the middle and humbler classes of society, as well as the youth of both sexes' (*London Sunday Journal*, 'Address', 7 March 1840: 1), was an attempt to redirect the title towards religion – its main feature was a sermon.

Yet the most famous of these early nineteenth-century 'London Journals' was and remains *Leigh Hunt's*. While it ran for less than two years (1834-35), Hunt claimed that his miscellany was still available at 'a good, steady price' on second-hand book-stalls, 'in request ... for sea voyages' in the late 1840s (Hunt, 1850: 428). Hunt had started his *London Journal* in opposition to what he saw as the dour, puritanical, non-fiction *Chambers's Edinburgh Journal*, providing for tastes 'a little more southern and literary'. Desirous of supplying 'the more ornamental part of utility', *Leigh Hunt's* put pleasure at the heart of utilitarianism, distancing itself from the 'business-oriented' *Chambers's* and the 'authoritative' *Penny Magazine* ('Address', *Leigh Hunt's London Journal*, 2 April 1834: 1). The use of 'Journal' in its title, as opposed to 'Magazine', no doubt attributable to the previous existence of the *London Magazine* for which Hunt had written, nonetheless indicates an equivalence between the two terms and a continuing distinction of both from the authoritative 'Reviews' that *Blackwood's Edinburgh Magazine* had earlier sought. While initially marketing itself as an 'English' literary weekly, in practice Leigh Hunt's *London Journal* is international in scope. It is also another form of what Edgecombe (1994) has called the Huntian 'rococo', an elaborate and intimate focus on the 'off-centre' pleasurable, here allied with a blithely confident, eighteenth-century-gentlemanly internationalism that can accommodate praise for *Legends and Scenes of the North of Scotland* and for Carlyle's translation of Goethe as well as poems on the virtuosity of Paganini and a series on classical authors. It does not belong to the satirical, risqué 'Spy' or 'Rambler' literature of the metropolis so common in the eighteenth century, but is rather an early bohemian textual version of the Grand Tour.

After identifying itself firstly with cheapness, the introductory 'Notice to Correspondents' in Stiff's *London Journal* allies itself with an internationality and an inclusivity covering both town and country which recall the Hunt.

> In future numbers of this journal Notices to Correspondents will constitute a prominent feature of our general plan, arrangements having been made with several writers, eminent in literature, science and art, to furnish replies to all queries that may be put to us relevant to these departments. A gentleman intimately acquainted with foreign literature is also retained to give any information which may be sought upon the subject, and, at an epoch when the writings of continental authors appear to excite so powerful a sensation, this is a *desideratum* which no Journal has until now undertaken to supply. The answers to our correspondents will invariably be given in the strictest spirit of impartiality; and no trouble or expense will be spared to afford information sought by parties either in town or country ...   (I: 16)

These are standard topoi for miscellany declarations of intent in the 1830s and 1840s, and, were it not for the brand-name's recollection of Leigh Hunt, I should not anchor them in his *Journal*. But besides the fact that Hunt is the first literary figure mentioned in Stiff's magazine (I: 11), there seems a reference to *Leigh Hunt's* in the tension between the pleasure of roving over as much geographical space as possible and the *local* significance of 'London', observable in Hunt's explicit opposition of 'London' to 'Edinburgh'. This opposition inserted his magazine into a history of struggle between 'North British' and London periodicals

THE LONDON JOURNAL.

WALLACE TOWER AT AYR.

Figure 3.5 'Wallace Tower at Ayr'
Source: I: 9.

which had erupted most spectacularly when the editor of *Blackwood's Edinburgh Magazine* had challenged the editor of the *London Magazine* to a duel in 1821 (Bauer, 1953: esp. 57, 62. Srebrnik, 1986: esp. 7-14). Rather than a national struggle based on ethnic lines (English versus Scottish), however, it should be recalled that the battle between Edinburgh and London was geographical, for Scottish intellectuals were at the heart of London print networks. The virulence had died down by the early 30s (Royle, 1980: 4, 147) – even the once anti-Cockney *Blackwood's* could by now make a point of praising Leigh Hunt's ([Wilson], 1834: 273) – and Hunt's reference to it was only a reflex prompted by the success of *Chambers's*.

I am suggesting that in its first issue Stiff's magazine took up this geo-cultural conflict in order to re-interpret — and dismiss it. This it achieved by publishing a large and rather grand illustration of the Wallace monument in Ayr on its 'second position' page along with an accompanying article (see Figure 3.5). It seems that peace was being made with Scotland by reflecting it back to itself. Yet at the same time, the country is reduced to no more than a tourist location. Through this latter tactic, the hero of Scottish resistance, Wallace, is assimilated into the ambit of pleasure and antiquarian interest, and ceases to be of much concern. The purpose of this initial alignment with Scotland was partly then a ritual of self-announcement in the field. It grants the *London Journal* a respectable genealogy while at the same time undermining that ancestry. More important, though, is that such an article announced that the *London Journal* was not local in its partialities. As the 'Address to Our Readers' in volume III concludes, as if aware that the title might indicate 'Londinocentrism':

It will have been observed that no portion of the United Kingdom has been neglected by us either in respect to illustration or to literature. We have devoted attention to topics, manners, places and legends, connected with the interests or linked with the sympathies of the inhabitants of England, Scotland, Ireland, and Wales. We seek to avoid all favouritism in these respects; we show no preference to one portion of the kingdom before another; but we study to render THE LONDON JOURNAL a publication of general interest in the most comprehensive point of view.   (III: 16)

Such protestations and indeed practices (for the *Journal* really did cover large parts of Britain) are particularly interesting for their contrast with what Feltes (1986) has seen as the interpellation of the metropolitan 'bourgeois' reader in *Pickwick*, his first example of a 'commodity text'. The *Journal* shows just how specific *Pickwick* was, for unlike its illustrious antecedent it was seeking an audience far beyond the metropolitan, and indeed beyond the 'bourgeois': its implied readership may have been urban, but it was national, indeed 'general ... most comprehensive'. 'Respectable', yes, but not necessarily 'bourgeois'.

In another sense, however, there *is* a definite and sustained geo-cultural preference, even if not for south-eastern England or London, that coincides with much of the periodical field at the time. By 1845, the axis of cultural involvement had turned from north-south (Edinburgh-London) to west-east. In 1841 *Punch*'s subtitle 'the London Charivari' had recalled and appropriated a Parisian model at a time when translations of Sue, Dumas and Paul Féval were selling well: the *London Journal* likewise preferred to look towards Paris.

The immediate cause of the *Journal*'s gaze in this direction was, I think, Reynolds's *Mysteries of London* which had been appearing in weekly instalments since October 1844, for it had been inspired by Eugène Sue's *Mystères de Paris*. The *Journal*'s association with 'London' would therefore also imply the labyrinthine metropolis of Sue's *Mystères*. This was a serial of exceptional influence that had redefined the cultural tour of urban space (ostensibly) as a vehicle for the delineation and denunciation of social injustice.[10] Both *The Mysteries of London* and the *London Journal* were published by George Vickers, both were written and edited by Reynolds, and both were owned by Stiff, so the three major figures in their production were identical. The choice of 'The London Journal' as a brand-name was therefore overdetermined, initially meant to suggest the social project, exposés and excitement of *The Mysteries of London* and at the same time, and contradictorily, Huntian aesthetic pleasure.

This tense hybridity was maintained until Reynolds left in the summer of 1846 when Ross asserted the aesthetic as the dominant mode. Very soon Stiff took up social and political exploration again by starting a newspaper. By January 1847, he must have had enough financial capital – or credit-worthiness – to begin the *Weekly Times*. This would eventually become one of the four high-circulation threepenny Sunday papers that dominated the mid-century middle-market for

---

[10] See Maxwell, 1992: 15-16 *et passim*; Humphreys, 1991. Denning (1998: ch. 6), although concentrating on its American developments, is nonetheless illuminating of the urban mysteries genre in general.

news, with *Reynolds's* [*Weekly*] *Newspaper* (1850-1923), *Lloyd's Weekly Newspaper* (1842-1918), and the *News of the World* (1843-1910).[11] Stamp returns suggest weekly circulations of 15,500 in the first year of the *Weekly Times*, rising to 62,000 in 1853 and 150,000 by 1865.[12] Not only was it an offshoot of the *London Journal* in that it precipitated out much of the magazine's political and social coverage into a separate publication, but it shared personnel and technology networks, being produced on the same premises and sharing writers. John Wilson Ross contributed 'Lives of the Prime Ministers of England' to the *Weekly Times*'s first volume; Edward Leman Blanchard, who had been writing anonymously for the *Journal* since 1846,[13] wrote a novel, *Confessions of a Page*, for the paper in 1847, and later wrote the drama column. Later still, Pierce Egan was to edit the *Weekly Times* for ten months 1859-60.

Three other periodicals were also closely related to Stiff's magazine in terms of personnel networks. Stiff had been head of the illustration department of the *ILN* and would certainly have been influenced by its particular marriage of knowledge with pleasure, news with illustration. He must have used his contacts to engage numerous illustrators and engravers. In the first years these included Stiff himself, Henry Anelay and, of course, John Gilbert. There seems also to have been a connection between Stiff and Landells, an engraver and one of the four founders of the *ILN* (Scott and Howard, 1891: 30), although I have found no unambiguous sign of Landells in the *London Journal*. Unsurprisingly, visual style and subject matter link the two magazines. In terms of the brand-name element 'London', the added association, derived from the *ILN*, would have been the idea of an illustrated weekly. In this hypothesis, 'London' would thus have functioned not only through reference to a vision or construction of the city or to previous periodicals, but as a signifier of visual elements within periodical discourse itself.

The *London Saturday Journal* (1839-42) was likewise related to Stiff's through personnel, but unlike the *ILN*, initially showed 'London' as uncomfortable with the conjunction of knowledge and pleasure. A twopenny weekly miscellany published by William Smith, with the secret backing of Bradbury and Evans (see p. 91 below), its Prospectus declares it yet another opponent of the SDUK, determined to concentrate on feelings, 'Christian principle and spirit' and social progress, as well as on facts. In practice though, feelings were sidelined, its first series concentrating on the serious, progressive and useful. James Grant (who would write for the *London Journal* in the 1860s) transformed its second series (1841) into something more similar to Stiff's magazine, introducing illustration and multi-part fiction. The final volumes (1842) were edited by no other than John Timbs, once of the

---

[11] Berridge, 1976 and 1978 remain the fullest accounts of this neglected field. She does not, unfortunately, address questions of the papers' ownership or production, and the *Weekly Times* is treated in far less detail than the other two papers she describes.

[12] See, for example, *British Parliamentary Papers* (1971), II: 206; Ellegård, 1957: 19-20; and see 'Revelations of the Newspaper Press', *Critic*, 1851: 49

[13] The only signed contribution by Blanchard in the *Journal* is an article on 'Meetings and Greetings', IX: 13-14. Interestingly, he was also a friend of Leigh Hunt's. On Blanchard, see Scott and Howard, 1891, I: 30, 60; II: 606.

Mirror and later editor of the *ILN*. He raised the amount of original matter, but this upped the costs and he was soon obliged to drop the illustrations (*London Saturday Journal*, 25 June 1842, n.s., no. 78: 1). Two months later the magazine closed. Frank Jay (1918-19: 1) believed this miscellany led to Stiff's *London Journal*. Given Stiff's and Timbs's work on the *ILN* (though at different times) and the general congruence of tone and format of the *London Saturday Journal*'s later volumes with the early years of the *London Journal*, this may well have been the case.

Finally, there was a third 'London Journal' that fed personnel into Stiff's, the 1½d *Chambers's London Journal* (5 June 1841 – 28 October 1843). This had nothing to do with the Chambers brothers, though initially it had similar educative aims in a concentration on non-fiction social issues. Hardly a parody of the *Edinburgh Journal*, it was more an English version of it that relied on the serious associations which the brand-name 'Chambers' had acquired. At first it was run by Edward Leman Blanchard (who contributed to both the *ILN* and the *Journal*), but none other than G.W.M. Reynolds took it over for the last ten months of its life. Like Grant and Timbs with their 'London Journal', Reynolds reoriented his magazine towards the literary, and started running fiction.[14]

In many ways Reynolds emerges as the centre of the literary/publishing side of Stiff's *London Journal* network. His French connections probably brought Galignani, of the famous bookshop and library in Paris, to act as joint publisher: this is suggested by how when Reynolds left to start up his *Miscellany* in 1847, Galignani soon followed him.[15] Stiff on the other hand was the centre of the engravers and artists. In this light, Stiff's *London Journal* appears as a reconfiguration of already existing networks of writers, artists, engravers and publishers who had experimented with and trained on previous 'London' weeklies of various kinds. It is possible that 'London' in the mid-1840s functioned internally to at least a sector of print-culture producers as a badge to indicate a personnel network that cut across individual periodicals, though this is unprovable with the paucity of information available. What is much more certain is that in the wake of

---

[14] See Baker in Sullivan, 1984, III: 64-9; James, 1963: 47-8. There are three other 'London Journals' that may have been related to Stiff's magazine, but what part they played I have been unable to determine. Although the first two are still listed in the BL catalogue, they have in fact been destroyed. I have located no copies of any of the following. a) *Kidd's London Journal* (1835). A 1½d weekly with the same title, also published by Berger, was advertised in *N&Q*, 31 January 1852, V: 19; b) *Grant's London Journal* (1840-41?), edited by James Grant (this does not appear to be a confusion with the *London Saturday Journal*), which Jay (1918-19: 42) believed was connected to Stiff's. c) Jay (1918-19: 1) also thought that a periodical called *Mayhew's London Journal* was published by Stiff in 1844 as the immediate precursor of the *London Journal*, although he admitted he had not seen a copy.

[15] Galignani disappears from the colophon of the *Journal* on 16 October 1847 and appears in the first issue of *Reynolds's Miscellany* dated 7 November of the same year. Galignani was also joint publisher of the *London Journal of Arts, Sciences and Manufactures*. This should not surprise as Galignani's involvement with the British market was immense (see Barber, 1961).

the success of both the *London Journal* and the *ILN*, the number of later 'London' periodicals considerably increases (see Waterloo, 1997, vol. IV).

The international inclusivity of the *London Journal* can be considered in several ways, not least as the product of a network within a social group defined by a characteristic habitus. In common with their fellow literary bohemians, many of its male writers were experienced travellers. Reynolds had lived and worked in France and even at one point had become a French citizen (Reynolds, 1839: ii). Ross was born in the Caribbean (*DNB*, XVII: 272-3). Both he and John Taylor Sinnett translated from French so I assume that both travelled at least in France. Later, John Dix, J.F. Smith, Charles Reade, Percy B. St. John and his brother Bayle, James Grant and Pierce Egan will have covered America, Europe and North Africa amongst them before they arrive at the *Journal*.[16] Watts Phillips, who contributed novels to the *Journal* in the 1860s and 1870s, studied at the Musée des Beaux Arts in Paris (like Thackeray) (Phillips, 1891: 19-23). In typical bohemian fashion, J.F. Smith sent instalments of a novel to Stiff from France (*Times*, 13 March 1856: 6). This determination to travel abroad is a sociological example of parergy, in that it is an emulation of the once aristocratic Grand Tour on the cheap, metamorphosed to bring back experience – cultural capital – instead of art treasures. Such confusion between aristocratic and literary mores is typical of bohemians and is the basis of Sala's 1854 article on that social group.[17] This particular form of cultural capital is then often transformed in the *Journal* into derivatives of the picaresque novel, which purchasers enjoy partly because they are enabled to experience a domesticated, moralized (but also emotionally heightened) Grand Tour in virtual form. While there are male exceptions to this *wanderlust* – Stiff himself and Thomas Miller in the late 1840s are notable – it nonetheless remains dominant until after the late 1870s when the commercial author became more thoroughly professionalized and *la vie de Bohème* was well on the way to becoming a major vehicle of middle mass-market nostalgia.

Another aspect of the *London Journal*'s internationalism is the major proportion of its fiction written by non-British citizens. After Reynolds's *Faust* (which ended in July 1846) it does not serialize any British novels for over two years. From the production point of view, the major advantage of non-British fiction was that it was cheap. Given the state of copyright in the 1840s, Stiff was not obliged to pay anything to Sue, Soulié, Dumas or Thiers. Although he would have had to pay Sinnett as translator of their works, rates would have been much lower than those of an original author: £25 was a standard price for translating a whole book (Reade, 1860: 300). In 1851 there was a new copyright agreement with France that made French work much more expensive (Reade, 1860). This, rather than a

---

[16] On Dix, see *DNB*, V: 1027; Bayle St. John: *DNB*: XVII: 617; Grant, *DNB*, VIII: 391-2; Egan, *DNB*, VI: 562-4. On Reade, on whom there is much more biographical material, the *DNB*, XVI: 797-801 is sufficient here.

[17] On the relation of what he calls 'cultural accreditation' and travel, see Buzard, 1993: 98-100, 110 and elsewhere. There were of course other reasons for bohemian travel, not least sexual exploit (itself part of the Grand Tour: see Buzard, 1993: 130-32). Edwards (1997) makes the seediness of bohemia very clear.

determination to save on translation costs, was a major reason the British mass-market turned to American writers. In the 1840s, however, translations operated according to the same economic logic as raiding, but were legally safer.

As Stiff and Reynolds well knew, French novelists were enormously popular before the *Journal* entered the lists. They were the territory which rival publishers struggled to conquer by publishing first, in a kind of literary colonization of the foreign. Cheap fiction magazines that failed to engage in this scramble for foreign fiction soon failed altogether.[18] The *London Journal*'s (effaced) relations to rivals in the zone were key to what material it ran. The big player in the mid-1840s, the *Family Herald*, had begun serializing Sue's extraordinarily popular *The Wandering Jew* the year before the *Journal* appeared. The *Journal* answered this with a restructured version, possibly by Reynolds, of a contemporary Parisian best seller, *The Mysteries of the Inquisition* by 'Victor de Féréal', the alias of a Madame Suberwick. The *Family Herald* countered with an attempt to offer something altogether different, serializing an Italian novel for the first and only time that I know in this zone, *The Challenge of Barletta* by 'Massimo d'Aseglio' [*sic*].[19] From mid-1846 to mid-1848, both magazines directly competed over the same ground with simultaneous translations of Sue's *Martin the Foundling* and *The Seven Deadly Sins*.

Another rival from late 1846, more bitter because closer to home, was *Reynolds's Miscellany*. Reynolds did not break with Stiff when he left the *London Journal*, as is usually thought. He kept writing *The Mysteries of London* for Stiff and used Vickers as publisher of his *Miscellany*, while John Wilson Ross took over as editor of the *Journal*. What occurred instead was an amicable separation that echoed the split between the social and political (*Weekly Times*) and the aesthetic (*London Journal*). *Reynolds's Miscellany* precipitated out Reynolds's particular brand of gothicism and 'labyrinthine' social exposé, while the *Journal* consolidated the aesthetic and replaced Reynolds's fiction with French novels. Even when *Reynolds's* changed publisher to John Dicks on 23 October 1847, Reynolds continued to write *The Mysteries* for Stiff and Vickers. As late as May 1848 he inserted an appreciative comment on the *Weekly Times* and its editor for publishing a letter in praise of the *Mysteries* (*Reynolds's*, 20 May 1848, III: 448).

The break with Stiff actually came in July 1848, when Reynolds announced a new, enlarged, second series of the *Miscellany*. He later published an account of

---

[18] See, for example, the lavishly produced twopenny *Illustrated Family Journal and Gazette of Variety* (8 March 1845 to 26 July 1845), or *Hunt's London Journal* (July 1844 to 28 December 1844), a magazine which came out just before Stiff's, was possibly meant to recall Leigh Hunt's – though its editor was called F.K. Hunt according to Waterloo, 1997, III: 2374.

[19] The original, *Ettore Fieramosca, ossia La disfida di Barletta*, was the first novel by Massimo d'Azeglio and written in the defiantly modern style of Manzoni (*Dizionario Biografico*, 1962, IV: 746-51). It apparently sold extremely well by Italian standards. Italy was, of course, neither politically and linguistically unified nor heavily industrialized at this time and had no major metropolitan centres. It therefore offered a much smaller potential consumer base for mass-market literary products than France, Britain or America, so it is logical that little should find its way into the British market.

what happened, instructive not least for what it tells us about the vital role that titles played in this market as well as about how the technological parts of the network operated.

> Number 1 of the New Series [of *Reynolds's*] was printed in good time, and many thousands were already worked off at the steam-press by Saturday evening, June 24th, the day of publication being Wednesday, June 28th; and on that same Saturday evening a considerable quantity of the impression was sent to Mr Vickers, the bookseller of Holywell Street, to be despatched to Scotland.
>
> On the Monday morning (June 26th) I was informed by a friend that Mr. Stiff, the proprietor of the *London Journal* (published by Mr. Vickers) had been to a printing-office to inquire whether he could have several pages of a new work printed there; and he stated that 'he intended to issue a publication in opposition to REYNOLDS'S MISCELLANY' ...
>
> On the Tuesday morning (June 27th) Mr Stiff issued Reynolds's Magazine, Mr Vickers being the publisher. This spurious work contained a wretched travestie of my tale 'The Coral Island', under the title of 'Corral Island,' – Coral being spelt with two r's. It likewise contained a portion of another translation of 'The History of the Girondists,' – these two features being introduced to mislead the public ... Even the 'Notices to Correspondents'... were travestied or parodied ... Mr Stiff moreover declared in the presence of witnesses that 'he would spend a thousand pounds to ruin me and the MISCELLANY.'
>
> But upon what pretence did Mr Stiff issue a work entitled Reynolds Magazine? He has a stoker in his employment of the name of Abraham Reynolds; and this man, who is perfectly illiterate, and who earns a pound or a guinea a-week, lent his name to the spurious publication! But that name has been withdrawn from the imprint of No. 2 of the said spurious publication ... law proceedings have been taken in this matter...
>
> ('Address to the Public', *Reynolds's Miscellany*, n.s. I: 48)

As I have suggested, it was common to play on well-established titles. The *Family Herald* complained that '[n]early a dozen periodicals ha[d] now adopted a portion of' theirs (*Herald*, VIII: 553, 29 December 1849). In the Reynolds passage we see not a leeching of cultural capital but a simulation of titles that possessed the economic authority of high sales figures. This indicates in turn that, even while the more consecrated zones were striving to create and maintain their ideal of a unified cultural field, whereby cultural and economic capitals coincided, the truly heteronomous already recognized that separate zones operated according to different laws, even while they were still looking up towards the high-status publications.

A gleefully detailed account of Reynolds's bankruptcy was published in the *Weekly Times* on 10 September, 1 October and 8 October 1848. This no doubt exacerbated the rift between Reynolds and Stiff, though a version of the quarrel published in *Reynolds's Miscellany* claims that the cause was a literary attack on *The Mysteries of London*. According to Reynolds, Stiff engaged Thomas Miller to write the third series of *The Mysteries*, made all the necessary legal agreements and printed the advertisements. When Stiff read the first number, however, he had a change of heart and sent his solicitor to talk with Reynolds's legal representative to enquire whether Reynolds would after all write the third series of *The Mysteries*. On 13 September, the day before the last number of Reynolds's second series was to be issued, Stiff and Reynolds met to discuss terms. Stiff offered £5 per number for the *Mysteries* and £10 a week 'for two years certain' for editing the *London Journal*. 'He added that he should unhesitatingly 'throw Miller overboard'' as he had just purchased the copyright of his *Godfrey Malvern* and thus 'had him completely in his power'. Similarly he would turn away Ross (implying that Ross and Reynolds had not got along). As Reynolds was in severe financial difficulties at the time, he might have interpreted this as a generous offer, but he refused and carried on with his *Miscellany*, because it was, as he put it, 'rising rapidly' ('To My Readers', *Reynolds's*, n.s. I: 304, 18 November 1848). We can only guess what effect Reynolds's publication of the affair had on Stiff's relations with Miller and Ross.

It cannot be denied that Miller at least was in a very vulnerable position at this time. His *Gideon Giles the Roper*, a story of English country life, had been appearing in the *Journal* since August. It was a reprint of a novel from 1841 that had been praised by the *Athenaeum* at a time when Miller was at the height of his fame. A basket-weaver who had been patronized by Lady Blessington, by 1848 Miller was well on his way down the literary ladder, his evocations of rural life passé (Cross, 1985: 133-41). He was always in straitened circumstances, and now more than ever, so Stiff probably purchased the copyright of his novels very cheaply – which would explain why an English novel suddenly appears after over two years of French. Miller was doubtless a temporary substitute for Eugène Sue, since Sue's productivity had been severely disrupted by the 1848 revolution (Bory, 1962: 319). The serial that that followed *Gideon Giles – Love, War and Adventure* – was a heavily compressed version of an 1846 triple-decker by the obscure Helen Harkness, and seems to fulfil the same function of cheap substitute. Nonetheless, its setting in Spain during the Peninsular War and picaresque narrative has much more in common with later *London Journal* serials than Miller's work. *Gideon Giles* remains anomalous, as Stiff seems to have realized. Nonetheless, a second novel by Miller, *Godfrey Malvern*, appeared in the spring and summer of 1849. A *roman à clef* concerning authorship and gender relations, set largely in London, it is very different from *Gideon Giles*, yet its juxtaposition of caricature, sentimentality, urban realism and broad country humour sticks out just as much.

Fortunately for Stiff, in 1849 he found not a replacement for, but an improvement on, Reynolds and Sue. J.F. Smith's *Stanfield Hall*, the first specially written serial for the *Journal* since Reynolds's *Faust* (1845-46), began only two months after *Godfrey*. The circulation, and Stiff's profits, now rose dramatically.

The Parergic Space

While much of this book is concerned with a metaphorics of space – the 'field', the 'zone' and so on – I shall deal now with an overlap between metaphorical and material that is as much part of the complex magic of the commodity as any other, but which is not often explored in studies of this sort. This particular mixture consists in what we might call a 'politography', or a writing on the polis in both major senses of 'on'. In the previous section I described some of the resonances of

'London' in the *Journal*'s title: other, more general, associations could certainly be adduced that do not depend upon a knowledge of the periodical field. London was the 'City of the World' as Haydon wrote in his 1841 *Autobiography* (quoted in Briggs, 1990: 311), and accordingly open to a vast range of contradictory meanings. This inclusivity was in fact one of its branding characteristics – it did not have the local and industrial specificity of Manchester, which in many ways was the 'shock city' of the 1840s, but offered instead associations with national and international trade and banking. This was accompanied by a whiff of danger and corruption enhanced not only by the Cobbettian trope of the 'Great Wen' and the more recent trope of labyrinthine mysteries (which offer refuge, terror or scope for sociological mapping as the case may be), but also by its proximity to the Continent, especially France. London was also, by the 1840s, the centripetal centre of information production and its centrifugal distribution point. It was the city of royalty, aristocracy and government, allowing anchorage in their authority and in the spectacle of their luxury, as well as in denunciation of their corruption and their sensational juxtaposition with the poor. All these the *London Journal* wrote on in the sense of 'wrote about'. Here, though, I am concerned to place the *Journal* through describing its principal publisher and thinking how the magazine made use of and 'wrote on' the very space of the city where it was produced and distributed from, exploiting and changing the meanings of metropolitan geography.

Politics is already written into politography, of course. As is well known, by the 1662 Printing Act, printers were compelled to operate within very restricted geographical areas in order that they might be policed more easily. Unsurprisingly, the space which print could be produced within and distributed from became freighted with enormous symbolic weight. In London, printers were concentrated in a small area between the City and Westminster. While in the nineteenth century the restrictions placed on printers were no longer in place, their geographical ghettoization still continued to a large extent, not least because of the expenses of moving and the profitability of maintaining contacts and contracts – indicating again the importance of the network in print media production. Celina Fox (1988: 27-8) has noted how by the 1830s a closely-knit community of Bewick-inspired wood-engravers had also come to be concentrated in the same area of London, both enabling and caused by the creation of illustrated magazines.

The nineteenth century also saw the separation of the printer from the publisher. As far as newspapers and periodicals were concerned, the publisher became 'the person appointed by the proprietor [of a newspaper or periodical], with more or less extensive powers of management, to dispose of their paper to the retail dealers, or newsagents' (Weir, 1841-44: 346). This implies a three-link chain of printer, publisher and retailer between writer, editor and reader. Here I shall be dealing only with the *London Journal*'s publisher, George Vickers: its printers and retailers will receive comment in the next chapter.

When the *Journal* began, Vickers was mainly a small-time printer and bookseller, with an office and shop at 28 Holywell Street, that published very few works so far as I can tell.[20] George Vickers himself died in 1846, a year after the *Journal*'s inception, but 'George Vickers', the name and concern, were carried on by his widow Anne and their sons George and Henry. They remained the publishers of the magazine through its various changes of ownership until 1884, with a break of eight years in the 1870s.[21]

As we know from the work of Lynda Nead (2000) and others, Holywell Street in the 1830s had been a hotbed of radical publications, but by the 1840s it was notorious for selling second-hand clothes and pornography. Vickers's office was in the midst of this. After a shop nearby was raided in 1857, George (the son) testified at the trial to the good character of its owner, William Dugdale, the erstwhile radical publisher.[22] While George's testimony had no effect, that he was called to give it suggests that by the mid-1850s he was considered respectable. While it has been said that Vickers published pornography, I have found no evidence of this, although it is true that most pornographic publications carry a false or no imprint, and Vickers may have published it in this way. What I have found under a Vickers imprint are a series of two-shilling yellow-backs which include the suggestive titles *Anonyma; or, Fair but Frail. A Romance of West-End Life, Manners and 'Captivating' People*; *'Left Her Alone'. A Tale of Female Life and Adventure in which the Fortunes and Misfortunes of a Charming Girl are Narrated*; *Annie, or the Life of a Lady's Maid*; *Skittles in Paris: a Biography of a Fascinating Woman*. These are dated 1864 or 1865, and, like Braddon's *Aurora Floyd*, exploit the topical interest in the West End demi-mondaine Catherine Walters, known also as 'Skittles' and 'Anonyma'. While the heroines of the Vickers novels happily lose their virtue – always off the page – they yet end up satisfactorily married either to their seducers or their childhood loves. Unillustrated apart from their racy but always decent covers, they are risqué but by no means explicitly pornographic in the way that, say, *My Secret Life*, is. Advertised on the back of *Anonyma* is Vickers's 'Shilling Volume Library', which includes novels by Sala (*The Ship Chandler*), Edmund Yates (*After Office Hours*) and two by *London Journal* authors, Emma Robinson (*Cynthia Thorold*), and Albany Fonblanque (*The Filibuster*, actually an unfinished novel started in the *Journal* in 1859). This suggests that the risqué novels should be regarded as a specialized sub-set of this series rather than as a separate 'pornographic' collection sold *sub rosa*. Their nature is nicely summed up in a publication that the BL catalogue attributes to Vickers in 1864, but which has no imprint or date: *Minnie Skittles and Hints of Life in London*. This is a sixteen-page pamphlet with a front-page illustration that

---

[20] For the little information already available on Vickers, see James, 1963: 47 and Neuberg, 1977: 157. Todd (1972: 200) lists an Albert Vickers at 28 Holywell Street who jointly owned a press with one Leakin Jones in the 1830s.
[21] See *London Journal* colophons. Publication was taken over by John Conway on 27 April 1872. While the colophon omits the name of the publisher from 15 May 1875 until 1880, the *Newspaper Press Directory* gives 'T. Connelly' for these years. I have identified no other publications by Conway or Connelly.
[22] Nead, 1997: 176. On Dugdale, see 'Mischievous Literature', *Bookseller*, no. CXXV, 1 July 1868: 449; McCalman, 1988: ch. 10.

suggests lubricious contents – a man-about-town accosts a hard-faced hussy – only to reveal very tame and general verbal warnings about where respectable people do not go in London, how to get on in the world, how to behave when married, and so on. Promised porn, the paranoid punter who has quickly concealed it about his person will open it at home to find the dullest of moral platitudes.

Vickers issued all these publications in the early 1860s. This was a particularly confident period for the firm when it published the largest number of books and expanded its periodical list: not only did it publish Percy B. St. John's new venture, the *London Herald*, but took over the publication of another apparent rival to the *Journal*, Vizetelly's *Welcome Guest*. This latter was accused of being 'fast', and it is a blend of the 'fast' and respectable rather than pornography that seems to have characterized Vickers as a firm. In the 1840s and early 1850s, this is confirmed by their then relatively few titles. These fell under five distinct classifications: a couple of plays (for example, *Oxberry's Budget of Plays*, 1844); a handful of Newgate works, amongst which figure *The Bermondsey Murder*, 1849; *Remarkable Trials*, 1851; a few parerga to more up-market novels (for instance, *The Adventures of Marmaduke Midge, the Pickwickian Legatee*, 1848); reprints in volume format of novels that had appeared in the *London Journal* (*Martin the Foundling*, 1846; Soulié's *Amelia*, 1846; Reynolds's *Faust*, 1847; Stowe's *Uncle Tom's Cabin*, 1852) and novels that are either associated with the magazine, like *The Mysteries of London*, or novels, often translations, that could well have appeared in it but did not, like Dumas's *The Three Musketeers* (1846); finally, the *London Journal* and, from January 1847, the *Weekly Times*. While making an independent profit, the latter two are also partially advertising vehicles for Vickers's other publications. As declared in the *Journal*'s initial 'Address to Readers' with which I began this chapter, Vickers is more interested in gaining profit from cheap mass sales than from expensive exclusivity, and this involved playing with the limits of the respectable.

This is not to say that some sides of the business were not definitely more respectable than others or that it was not important to separate them out. Besides indicating any necessity for larger premises, Vickers's changes of address as publisher of the *Journal* show this very well. Starting over the edge of respectability in Holywell Street, by number 32 the magazine's publication address has moved a few hundred metres west to 3 Catherine Street. This had recently been the address of J. Onwhyn's cheap and respectably avuncular miscellany, the *New Parley's Library*. In 1850 the eminently respectable *Household Words* would be conducted from next-door-but-one, where Catherine Street turned into the Strand, at number one. While Vickers maintained their Holywell Street base as a bookseller's, the *London Journal* moved out as soon as possible. Respectability of address was not the sole reason for the move – the *Journal*'s new printers were also based at the new address – but it is certainly a factor to consider in placing the magazine in a cultural field which is both geographically material and metaphysical.

If Catherine Street was more salubrious than Holywell Street, the Strand was where the magazine's two main models enjoyed frontages: George Biggs ran the *Family Herald* at number 421, and the *ILN* had its office at 198. It was also where the earnest, improving *Howitt's Journal* shared a house with a tea-dealer's at 171, next door to the more earthy *Bell's Life in London and Sporting Chronicle*, and only a few doors away from Chapman and Hall, the publishers of Dickens (at 186). It is worthwhile describing further who was producing and selling what in this particular metropolitan space since it looms so large in publishing history: the Strand in fact had the largest number of printers of any street in London, although since it is long it did not have the highest density (Todd, 1972: 234). Vickers will in fact move there in 1866 (Brown, 1982: 208; Boase, III: 1095).[23]

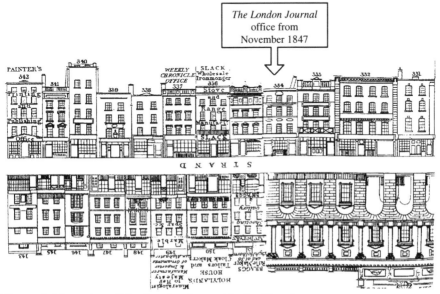

Figure 3.6 Location of the *London Journal* in the Strand
Source: Tallis, 1838: 93.

From the evidence of its colophons, the *London Journal* moved to 334 Strand on 20 November 1847. This had been the office of the *Satirist*, a disreputable sixpenny scandal and extortion sheet run by an unscrupulous editor-proprietor, Barnard Gregory (Gray, 1982: esp. 318. See also Vann, 1994: 278-90, esp. 278-79; McCalman 1988: 225-26), which now moved further from the main thoroughfare, to 12 Catherine Street. Started in 1831, by the 1840s it was in decline, ending as the *Literary Pioneer* in December 1848. The balconied Strand Hotel separated 334 from the rather grand office of the *Morning* and *Evening Chronicles* at 332, wider than anything in this area, with its commercial version of a *piano nobile* making a confident front against the imposing aristocratic façade of Somerset House opposite. The *Morning Chronicle* had been one of the principal Whig dailies on which Dickens and Thackeray had worked, while the *Evening Chronicle* was its

---

[23] Most of the information about the commercial premises on the Strand is derived from the 'Street Directories for 1847' in Tallis (1838).

afternoon reprint (Waterloo, 1997, III: 1802). In 1847 the *Chronicle* was embroiled in a cut-throat price war with its rival the *Daily News*, and indeed the *Evening Chronicle* had had to close in July.[24]

While William Cathrall's *London Mercury* at 335, next door to the *London Journal*, is proudly marked out in some versions of Tallis's *London Street Views*, it actually lasted less than a year before merging with the *Journal of Commerce* and moving in with it at 54 Gracechurch Street – nearer its main source of information, the Bank of England. The *Weekly Chronicle* office at 337 was owned and edited in the 1840s by Henry George Ward, the Radical MP for Sheffield. Of particular interest in this context is that it had been the model for the *ILN* (Jackson, 1885: 275, 284, 306), and is therefore a grandparent of sorts to the *Journal*. By the 1840s, like the *Satirist*, the *Weekly Chronicle* was in terminal decline in terms of circulation, but, unlike the scandal sheet, its opinions carried weight in literary circles (Rodolff, 1981). The side of the street between 300 and 350 into which the *London Journal* elbowed itself was a congeries of periodical offices, publishers and booksellers in the midst of an otherwise mixed but quite smart bag of retailers: 330 was a perfumer's, 336 a furnishing ironmonger's, 338 a watchmaker's, and so on.

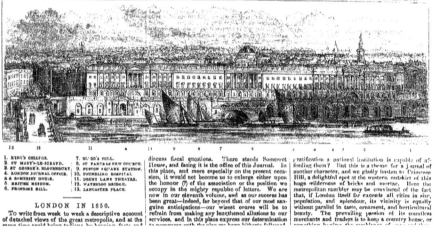

Figure 3.7 Location of the *London Journal* offices: Somerset House from the Thames
Source: XI: 153.

Unlike the grand premises of the *Morning Chronicle*, the *London Journal*'s offices at 334, with its shop-window, two doors and three floors is unremarkable apart from a wonky chimney (Figure 3.6). It seems rather overpowered opposite the grandeur of Somerset House, 'the central taxation depot' (XI: 153) and one of the sights of London (see Anon., 1845a: 36; Anon., 1845b: 68-9). The *Journal* commented on its spatial and fiscal relation to Somerset House a few years after its

---

[24] See Bostick, 1979: 57. Mayhew's famous reports on *London Labour and the London Poor* had yet to appear and must be seen as part of a wider strategy to regain lost circulation.

move, in its first extended paean to the metropolis, the series 'London in 1850', a 'progress up the Thames' (XI: 41), illustrated with views from the river. In the accompanying illustration (Figure 3.7), the *Journal*'s office is invisible behind Somerset House, even though its position is marked on the picture with a tiny number 4, itself hardly visible in the original and not visible in the reduced version reproduced here. It is as if the magazine is parading its subservience. The commentary collapses the language of spatial relations into cultural relations, rapidly moving from the literal into the figurative in the first few sentences – exactly the overlay of geographical and metaphysical I have described:

> There stands Somerset House, and facing it is the office of this Journal. In this place, it would not become us to enlarge either upon the honour (?) of the association or the position we occupy in the mighty republic of letters. We are now in our eleventh volume, and our success has been great ... when we sometimes gaze through our windows at its imposing front, we are forcibly reminded of the fact that, through its expeditious and scrupulously exacting machinery, we are some few thousands of pounds annually out of pocket. In one sense we have no reason to regret the abstraction, but we frequently feel inclined to be extremely positive that it cripples our usefulness, and prevents our undertaking many things we are often tempted to try, though we are so heavily burdened.
>
> (XI: 153)

This is but a momentary gripe, and the article passes on to Primrose Hill and the British Museum (called 'the repository of literature, science and art', a description that – as if by chance – associates that culturally consecrated place directly with the *London Journal*). Thence it moves to the Lyceum theatre (very near 332) and finally to the Strand itself, 'the most varied thoroughfare in the world' (XI: 154). The Strand, the communication channel between the City and Westminster, between commerce and politics, causes a burst of excitement, movement, energy and danger in a hymn to urban modernity, of the sort Marshall Berman (1983: esp. 89-98) detected in Marx's *Communist Manifesto* of two years earlier. It is as if communication, flow, circulation, metamorphosis were being lauded for their own sakes. The population of the street is constantly changing: servant girls, shopmen, policemen and tradesmen at 8am; shoppers, thieves and plainclothes police at mid-day. And it is during the evening that the hymn reaches its climax:

> Myriads of gas-lights illumine the whole roadway and splendid shops; the people are beginning to saunter instead of walk; and there is every indication of their having concluded the business of the day. The theatres open their inviting doors; the wandering minstrels of the metropolis are blowing some popular air; cigars glow in the mouth of almost every second man you meet; and all around, you see nothing but a mass of good-humoured contented people, who appear to have resolved to devote the remaining hours of the day to relaxation and amusement. (XI: 154)

By 1850, phantasmagoric, happy-consumer London and evening *flânerie* on the Strand, fastish respectability, mobility, mutability are what the *Journal* wishes to associate itself with, to project and to produce: a holiday crowd, so different from the mobs of 1842 and 1848 with their desire to penetrate and unmask the mysteries of the polis and politically reshape it. This joyous sauntering multitude, bent on pleasure, is the antidote to angry Chartists marching to reform. On the other hand, it is also the antithesis of the stultifying spatial occupancy and surveillance mechanisms of Somerset House. Typical of commercially 'radical' papers at this time (for example, Anon., 1851c), the suggestion that the *Journal* seems to be making is that its true 'usefulness' would lie in creating more of the happy crowd (and diminishing the marching mob), if Somerset House did not *stand in the way*.

Its ousting of a disreputable magazine lent the *Journal* a secure air. It did not really stand opposite to oppose 'the central taxation depot' so much as use this spatial proximity to announce its metaphorical closeness to, but difference from, authority. Rather than be simply overpowered and overlooked, the *Journal's* offices could feed off the fame of a London sight, becoming themselves something to point at. No doubt the *Journal* employed its façade as a billboard like other commercial ventures, perhaps announcing its vast circulation in bold lettering. The *ILN* certainly used its frontage in this way (Vries, 1995: 9; Sinnema, 1998: 191, 194; and cf. Figure 8.2 below). In this sense the *Journal's* publishing address became a spectacular and even tangible parergon. Its very location in the Strand involved a set of practices which comprised an appropriation of spatial capital that mirrored its textual parasitism of the cultural capital. Genre, title, network, space, all synergistically worked with each other in the *London Journal*, its politography neutralizing whatever potential it might have had for revolutionary politics, and rendering ever more enchanting its commodity magic.

Chapter Four

Cultural Numerology; or, Circulation, Demographics, Debits and Credits

Numbers Are Not Always Hard

In 1851 a hawker on Thames pleasure-boats reported to Mayhew that he sold what to us are annoyingly vague numbers of penny periodicals: 'Lloyd's and Reynold's [*sic*] pennies — fairish, both of them; so's the *Family Herald* and the *London Journal* — very fair' (Mayhew, 1851-62, I: 291).

In this chapter I shall look at the four remaining elements of periodicals, all numerical, that I did not cover in Chapter 3. First I shall examine circulation, the marker *par excellence* that defines the mass-market periodical as such, and next I shall consider how circulation relates to changes in the nature of the literate population – the 'demographics' of the consumer base – to create a feedback loop that affects contents. In the second section, I shall turn to costs, and finally to how these bear on profits (and again on contents). Since the amount of evidence available for all these elements is so small, I marshal into this chapter almost everything available for the time-span of this book.

While in Chapter 1 I made the distiction between hard data and speculation, here I have to stress that, in the absence of account books, all figures in this section are to some extent speculative. In any case, to consider any of these four quantitative elements as comprising an iconic map of reality, more real, 'harder', than the four qualitative discussed already, would be to place one's faith in a numerological magic. Even the 'numbers' on the *London Journal*'s headpiece are not 'hard' in the sense of refering directly and unproblematically to a material reality. The dates printed on the *Journal*'s front page are at least ten days ahead of actual publication and in its early years the magazine appeared on Wednesdays, not Saturdays as its headpiece claims. Its price for the consumer could rise or fall depending on the circumstances and exact point of sale: in the country it might cost 3d, whereas 1d bought four back numbers in Holywell Street (Ratcliffe, 1913; Thomas, 1913-14, VII: 221). If even these numerical anchors float away from their referents, therefore, the best one can hope for with the more obviously dubious circulation figures is an ideographic representation which does little more than amplify the vague comments of Mayhew's hawker.

Circulation and Demographics

Available circulation figures for the *London Journal*, as for most nineteenth-century periodicals, are all suspect for one reason or another: either they are part of the magazine's or the publisher's self-puffing or they partake in the cultural wars I described in Chapter 2. What they actually refer to is anyway complicated, since the *Journal*, like other penny fiction weeklies, was issued in a variety of formats: penny weekly numbers, a sixpenny monthly collection of four or five issues in a paper cover (the *Journal's* was beige or pink),[1] and half-yearly volumes. Furthermore, back numbers were being reprinted by 30 August 1845 ('An Inquirer', I: 432). A full-scale reprint, meaning that issues came out again in successive weeks starting with number 1, began on Wednesday, 3 March 1847 (see the repeated adverts from V: 16), compounding the confusion over what 'circulation' means. Early issues of the *Journal*, in which circulation figures were more freely broadcast, reveal something of the differences between these forms of sale. In June 1847, for example, circulation was supposed to be 'close upon 90,000', with back numbers, monthly parts and half-yearly volumes raising the figure to 140,000 of each number ('T.M.B.', III: 256). At other times, the difference between these various forms of publication is elided. A final confusion lies in how the distinction between readership and sales is sometimes made and sometimes not.

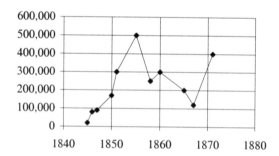

Figure 4.1 Selective Ideograph of the *London Journal*'s Circulation 1845-71
Sources: see Appendix.

The reasons for a periodical's sales are many and complex: state regulation, existence and attractions of rivals, advertising and distribution facilities, consumer knowledge of the product, user habits, production and purchase capacities, current events, and so on. In 1855, the *Journal* explained how the season affected sales: January, February, October and November regularly had the highest sales figures, whereas June to August had the lowest (XXX: 176). The same notice claims that

---

[1] In the 1840s, monthly parts comprising four issues cost 5d ('Notices to Readers and Trade', II: 16). By the early 1850s monthly parts cost 6d.

during 1854, 1,574 volumes of the *Journal* were loaned by Marylebone Free Library, 500 more than any other serial publication. I have found no other direct evidence that libraries subscribed to penny weeklies, and hence do not take them into account in my discussion of what follows, but it should not surprise that they did so. It has long been known that coffee shops subscribed to a large variety of periodicals, including the cheaper kind (Reach, 1844), and free libraries such as the Marylebone operated in more or less the same cultural zone. Obviously this suggests a larger number of readers per copy sold than direct purchase by consumers. However, in terms of sales libraries and coffee shops must have been insignificant for a periodical with sales in the hundreds of thousands.

In the remainder of this section I shall comment briefly on the relation of the *Journal*'s circulation (as shown by Table 4.1 and the Appendix) to its contents, to its rivals, and to the changing demographic.

The increases up to 1850 occur during the serializations of Reynolds's *Faust* (1845-46), the *Memoir* of Daniel O'Connell and of Sue's *Martin the Foundling* (1847). They also coincide with a marked drop in sales of the older and more earnest mass-market periodicals. *Chambers's* which had risen from an initial 25,000 average in 1832, its first year, to 86,750 in 1844, dipped only slightly in the year the *Journal* appeared to 86,192, but then lost 10,000 in 1846, and dropped to 64,000 in 1849 (Bennett, 1982: 206). In 1855 it had dipped further, to 35,000 monthly parts and 23,000 weekly (*Waterloo*, 1989, I: 259). The *Penny Magazine*, in decline since its triumphant entry in circulation tables at 213,241 in 1832, was down to 40,000 in 1845; 25,000 the following year finished it off (Bennett, 1982: 206). As mentioned in Chapter 2, Charles Knight believed this collapse was due to the *London Journal* and the *Family Herald*, but there were also many other new magazines in the same zone competing for attention, amongst them the lavishly illustrated 2d *Illustrated Family Journal and Gazette of Variety* (8 March 1845 to 26 July 1845), the *Illustrated Penny Novelist and Journal of Literature and Amusement* (29 October 1842 to 22 April 1843[2]), and the much longer-lived 1½d *Sharpe's London Magazine* (November 1845 to June 1848).

During J.F. Smith's serials in the early 1850s, circulation soars. To attribute this to Smith is tempting, especially when reprints of his works were successfully used to bolster circulation later in the century with different accompanying matter (Jay, 1918-19: 14; Francis, 1890). Yet simultaneously there were other reasons to buy the magazine, including in 1852 a series *gratis* of 'Ten Thousand Useful Receipts',[3] Stowe's *Uncle Tom's Cabin* and, in 1854, providing the double pleasures of charity and entertainment, a series of halfpenny benefit supplements whose profits went to an organization for widows and orphans of the Crimean war.[4] Thomas Burt, 'Pitman and Privy Councillor' (1837-1922) read the *London*

---

[2] The *Illustrated Penny Novelist* is undated, but an advertisement on p. 96 says no. 12 will be published on 14 January 1843, enabling the dating of the rest.
[3] The Bodleian possesses an imperfect copy of this supplement, which is lacking from the BL run of the *Journal*.
[4] Reported profits were suspiciously round, however, suggesting between 53,760 and 57,600 purchasers of the supplement (see XX: 80).

Journal when he was 14 (*c*. 1851-52), at the moment of the magazine's greatest popularity. He recalled enjoying the lurid tales, but it was *Uncle Tom* that had a profound influence on him, and recalls the power of Frederick Douglass's *Autobiography* (Burt, 1924: 9, 114-15). The *Journal* had serialized most of the latter in 1847 and, given the reprintings, it is possible that he could have read that version. Another documented reason to buy the magazine was for its prints. Thomas Fowke, a sculptor, claimed he bought it simply for the pictures, and never read a word of the stories (Thomas, 1913-14, VII: 221; cf. Page, 1914). Gilbert's illustrations were retained in the 1880s reserializations of Smith, so these too need to be considered for the rise in sales then. But there had already been a considerable rise in the number of publications before another, more general, factor that might also be relevant for the increases of the 1850s: the removal of the window tax in 1851, a tax that Dickens had seen as more of an obstacle to the spread of reading than the Taxes on Knowledge (Altick, 1998: 92).[5] Finally, there was a dramatic drop in prices for basic goods – bread, sugar, meat and fish – between 1848 and 1851 (Thompson and Yeo, 1971: 481-3) which would have increased the cash available for luxuries such as a weekly miscellany. I suspect that these factors, combined with the high sales of the three leading fiction papers, also influenced the Chartist turn to fiction at this time.

Particularly interesting is the absence (apart from one figure dating from 1866) of numerical evidence concerning the disastrous collapse in circulation under Mark Lemon's editorship (1857-9). All we have from the period is the comment in the *British Quarterly Review* (1859, XXIX: 345) that up to 40 tons of unsold *London Journals* were sold for waste paper. In 1849, the *Family Herald* (VII: 415) told a correspondent that its circulation of 140,000 used 'almost four tons of paper weekly' and using this figure as the basis for a calculation, 40 tons of the *London Journal* was the equivalent of about 1,500,000 copies. The stable high circulation figures advertised in the *Weekly Times* were certainly as inflated as those in Wilkie Collins's 'The Unknown Public'.

The high figure for 1864 is unconfirmed, but Braddon's *The Outcasts* may have contributed to a rise: in volume form at least it was one of Braddon's greatest financial successes (Wolff, 1979: 138). The figure from 1867 indicates a considerable slump, and this may be confirmed by the innovations the following year (a temporary increase in the number of pages from 16 to 20, the return of J.F. Smith, and 'Ladies Supplements'). As Reynolds suggests when inveighing against the *Daily News* (*Reynolds's*, III: 63-4), experiments signal anxiety about circulation. The *Journal's* lower sales may have been caused by new rivals on the scene, the *London Reader*, and especially *Bow Bells*, from which the *Journal* will borrow many of its 'improvements'. After 1868, circulation apparently rose once more, but beyond Ellegård's figure for 1870, I have found only a suspect claim in a trial for damages.

---

[5] Eliot (1995: 28-30) offers additional reasons for the increase in the number of publications in the 1840s and 1850s, including economic and political turbulence, the Oxford movement, the Great Exhibition and the death of Wellington.

Synchronous comparisons of the *Journal*'s circulation with those of other magazines have been readily available from Ellegård (1957) and elsewhere for over forty years (for example, Altick, 1998: 391-6). Instead of repeating them, I shall briefly consider the magazine's economic importance to Somerset House (and hence the state) before discussing some tables of *local* sales which indicate both its distribution in specific geographical areas and what the magazine meant to booksellers.

The 'central tax depot' of Somerset House extracted paper duties, not the Stamp Tax, from the *London Journal*, as the magazine ostensibly did not carry news. The paper duties were in fact more hated by the trade than the more noisily excoriated stamp. The *Weekly Times* (1 January 1854: 8) complained that it was paying 25 percent of its revenue in paper duties alone. Chapman (1852: 511) claimed the tax was 20 percent of the sales price of printed matter, but that excluded administrative costs. Since the tax depended on paper weight (it was 3d per pound on paper commonly used for printing), it is necessary to turn to other periodicals of similar quarto size and paper quality to guess what the *London Journal* was paying. In October 1849 the *Family Herald* (VII: 415) declared it was paying £54/13/9 weekly on the paper for its 140,000 circulation. This works out at a rate of roughly 13.5 percent on trade sales price. A circulation of 500,000 such as the *Journal* had in the early 1850s would have given almost £195 per week to Somerset House, or over £10,000 a year. With such amounts to be milked from mass-market periodicals, decisive intervention against them would have resulted in a considerable loss of revenue, even if the family papers had decided to adopt an explicitly radical stance. When we realise this, the intricacy of the *London Journal*'s complicity with authority is increased even further.

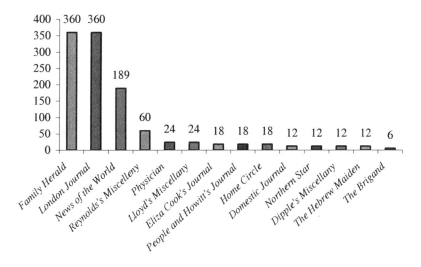

Figure 4.2 Mr Wilkins' Weekly Sales of Periodicals, Dowlais, *c.* 1850. *Source*: Ginswick, 1849-1851, II: 58

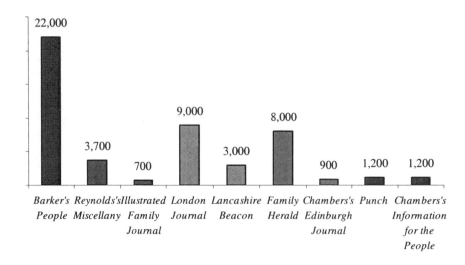

Figure 4.3 Abel Heywood's Weekly Sales of Periodicals, Manchester, c. 1850
Source: Ginswick, 1849-51, I: 63.

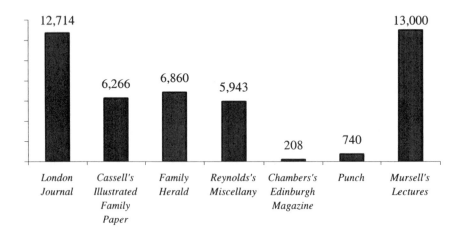

Figure 4.4 Abel Heywood's Weekly Sales of Periodicals, Manchester, 1860
Source: *Bookseller*, 26 February 1861, no. XXXVIII: 105.

Table 4.1 Agglomerated Sales of Booksellers, Leeds, May 1860
Source: Hole, 1863: 149-52.

Publication	Weekly	Monthly
All the Year Round	439	117
Annals of Leeds	1,011	
Beeton's Dictionary of Information		413
Beeton's Household Management		163
Boys' Own Magazine		331
British Controversialist		20
The Builder	51	
Cassell's Illustrated Family Paper	3,046	
Cassell's History of England	837	
Cassell's Natural History		237
Chambers's Journal	264	
Chambers's Encyclopedia	292	107
Companion for Youth		67
Cornhill		700
Dictionary of Daily Wants		654
Dictionary of Useful Knowledge		114
Englishwoman's Domestic Magazine		354
Family Economist	108	
Family Herald	2,834	62
Gardener's Weekly Magazine	33	
Home Magazine	567	
Ladies' Treasury		112
Leeds Herald		2,000
Leisure Hour	661	363
London Journal	4,234	
Macmillan's Magazine		106
Musical Times		140
Once a Week	194	43
part-issue novels, pub. Reynolds, Lea and Lloyd	2,234	39
Pastime		12
Popular Lecturer		9
The Reasoner	31	
Reynolds's Miscellany	2,809	
Welcome Guest	132	
Young England's Newspaper		71

Samuel Green recorded that 'penny publications of a low and vicious character' (he is writing of Reynolds, Cleave and Lloyd) were sold 13 – a publisher's dozen – for 8d or even 7½d, so booksellers made 38.5 percent or even 42 percent profit. The trade price for religious tracts was 9d the dozen, and the pernicious effect this had on what the booksellers promoted was clear to him (Green, 1850: 123-24; cf.

Report, 1851: 218). The *London Journal* persisted in selling at the latter price, however, perhaps because it could not afford the larger discount, although 8d for 13 was charged 'when 100 quires [14,400] of each number are taken'.[6] At those rates the bookseller Wilkins of Dowlais was making 9/- a week from the *London Journal* alone, the Leeds booksellers about £5/7/- between them, and Heywood in 1861 something in the region of £16 (see Figures 4.2, 4.3 and 4.4). John Parker in 1853 mentioned how sales of the *London Journal* paid the 10/- weekly rent of a bookseller in Seven Dials, which means he must have sold at least 390 a week (see Parker, 1853: 188-9). As for the special 100-quire rate, this could only have applied to the twelve or thirteen large distribution agents that operated in London (see Weir, 1841-44: 347), as not even Heywood could reach that target. With the large profits booksellers were making, the lower percentage they received nonetheless made it worthwhile to promote the *Journal*: despite the similarity of percentage profit with religious publications, the economics were actually in a different league.

While Figures 4.2 to 4.4 and Table 4.1 show the *London Journal*, the *Family Herald*, *Reynolds's Miscellany* and *Cassell's Illustrated Family Paper* consistently dominating the market, there is also the notable presence of the high sales of two other publications in the Heywood sales of Figures 4.2. and 4.3. Unlike the mass-market periodicals, these publications were both local. Joseph Barker's *People* was an unstamped penny 'ultra-democrat' weekly newspaper published in Wortley near Leeds. Its radical founder only claimed a circulation of 20,000 in his autobiography (see Barker, 1880: 288), and Heywood's figure probably represents virtually all its sales. The Rev. Arthur Mursell's *Lectures ... to Working Men* were printed versions of his 'rugged appeals to the hearts of the Masses', delivered between 1858 and 1864 in the Free Trade Hall, Manchester (see Mursell's *Lectures*, series I, 1858: iii). Then being published by Heywood's brother John as individual pamphlets and in volume format, it should not surprise that Abel promoted them. Again the numbers in Figures 4.2 and 4.3 probably represent total rather than a fraction of national sales.

Finally, it should be mentioned that the *London Journal* monthly supplements (like those of *Reynolds's Miscellany*) do not register in Table 4.1 probably because, although available through booksellers, they were also sold by subscription.

For almost two centuries it has been assumed that there were four or five readers per newspaper or periodical in the early and mid-nineteenth century (see 'A Layman', 1820: 52; Anderson, 1994: 3, note 4) and with this figure – at best speculative – it is possible to form an estimate of the cultural density of the *London Journal* and other magazines in the localities the tables refer to. Manchester and Leeds as large industrial towns both had very mixed populations and the figures make it impossible to deduce which sections of the population were purchasing what.[7] Dowlais on the other hand, was much smaller and unusually uniform in its

---

[6] See 'To the Trade', IV: 128; 'Notice to the Trade', V: 352. This was a common price for medium-to-low circulation, low-cost papers: see also Barker's *People*, 1848, I: 386.

[7] On Leeds, see Morgan, 1989: 46-71. Hewitt (1996: 23-65) stresses the social diversity of Manchester in the 1840s and 1850s.

social composition. In the early 1850s it was a growing part of the Welsh mining town of Myrthyr Tydfil whose total population in 1851 was 46,378. 'There are no men of middle station', an 1850 report claimed: there were only four masters, the rest comprising various grades of workmen (Carter and Wheatley, 1982: 8-9, quoting T.W. Rammel, *Report to the General Board of Health ... on the Town of Merthyr Tydfil*, 1850). Here we find the lowest density of sales per head of population in my researches. The people of Dowlais were only buying about 800 copies of fiction weeklies: perhaps 10 percent of the population of Merthyr would have read them, with under 5 percent reading the *London Journal*. This extremely low penetration contrasts markedly with the general situation in Britain. In the early to mid-1850s, the *Journal* may have had anywhere between 2,000,000 and 2,500,000 readers, or about 15 percent of the British population as a whole. Adding the sales of the *Family Herald*, *Cassell's Illustrated Family Paper* and *Reynolds's Miscellany* brings the total readership for these fiction magazines to an astonishing 50 percent.

There are several reasons for the low penetration of Dowlais. Firstly, language would have been an issue. The surrounding area was Welsh-speaking, and though by mid-century Dowlais was bilingual due to the large and always increasing number of immigrants from England (Pryce, 1988: 280), the proportion of English speakers would have been lower than in the other samples. Secondly, there is the problem of literacy: miners were the least literate of all industrial workers (Vincent, 1989: 97, 100).

It is generally agreed that literacy in the early and mid-nineteenth century was far higher than is often supposed. David Vincent and W.B. Stephens agree on almost 60 percent literacy in England by 1840. Patricia Anderson's (1994) and Teresa Gerrard's (1998) statistical studies of the correspondence pages of the *London Journal*, *Reynolds's Miscellany*, the *Family Herald* and *Cassell's Illustrated Family Paper* conclude that clerks, servants, artisans, school teachers, members of the armed forces and small shopkeepers comprised their main purchasers. This is hardly surprising as literacy rates were higher amongst them than amongst factory operatives, unskilled labourers and agricultural workers (see Kelly, 1993: 148; Vincent, 1989: 96-104; Stephens, 1987: 15-28). But, as I remarked in Chapter 1, 'class' alone is inadequate as a consumer descriptor. Gender and geography are two factors I want to consider here.

Both Vincent and Stephens remark striking differences in literacy between men and women, though the difference varied over time. Mayhew's periodicals hawker noted in 1851 that penny weeklies were bought almost exclusively by men. In the 1840s there was a decided preponderance of male literates, even though women outnumbered men by about 5 percent in the general population (Mitchell, 1962: 12). By 1864 women had become more literate than men in the southeast, and by 1884 this was the case for almost all of the south (see Vincent, 1989: 23-6). Growing female literacy would have suggested a corresponding market potential for material aimed at women and I suspect this was a strong contributory factor to the gradual reorientation of the *London Journal* towards women in the 1860s.

While it seems likely that the market for penny weeklies was much smaller in the country (confirmed by the lack of *Morning Chronicle* reports of sales from any country booksellers), this should by no means preclude consumption there (see Ratcliffe, 1913: 276). Later in the century especially, rural women's literacy greatly improved. Flora Thompson writes of how in the 1880s *Bow Bells*, the *Family Herald* and *Princess Novelettes* were avidly consumed and passed around by large numbers of women in a north Oxfordshire village (the *Journal* is not mentioned):

> Most of the younger women and some of the older ones were fond of what they called 'a bit of a read', and their mental fare consisted almost exclusively of the novelette. Several of the hamlet women took in one of these, weekly, as published, for the price was but one penny, and these were handed round until the pages were thin and frayed with use. Copies of others found their way there from neighbouring villages, or from daughters in service, and there was always quite a library of them in circulation.   (Thompson, 1945: 109)

The reference to one of the sources for such material as 'daughters in service' is interesting for its recollection of the trope of 'kitchen literature' at the moment when its currency was waning. Yet besides being a rhetorical trope, it could also refer to a material reality, for servant girls had greater employment opportunities if they were literate (Stephens, 1987: 21, 192; Vincent, 1989: 104). This was not the case with the mill girls whom, according to Vizetelly's influential account, J.F. Smith excited so much: industrial towns, and especially those in the north, returned very poor literacy rates for women. Leeds brides were twice as illiterate as their grooms in the later eighteenth century, and if in the first decades of the nineteenth the gap narrowed, it was because grooms became less literate, not brides more so. In the 1850s – Smith's heyday – their literacy did improve a little (Stephens, 1987: 5-6, 95; Vincent, 1989: 97), possibly as a result of the 1844 Factory Act which limited the hours women worked: Heywood certainly thought his sales rose because of it (Ginswick, 1849-51, I: 63). This notwithstanding, *pace* Vizetelly, it still seems unlikely that mill girls were Smith's biggest fans in the 1850s.

Debits and Credits

Speculation in the periodical press could produce vast profits. Anecdotal evidence suggests that the *London Journal* gave its owners profits of £10,000-£12,000 a year (see James, 1963: 45; Jay, 1918-19: 5; Thomas, 1913-14, VII: 122). Gibbons Merle (1829a: 223; 1829b: 480) had earlier reported that the weekly *Literary Gazette* was making a profit of £5,000 a year and the *Globe* and the *Courier* newspapers £7,000 each. Hetherington made £1,000 from the radical *London Dispatch* in 1837; the *Northern Star* gave a profit of no less than £13,000 in 1839 and £6,500 the following year (Curran, 1991: 19). According to the *London Journal* (I: 328), the *ILN* was making a net profit of £16,000 in 1845 – certainly a reason to adopt and adapt some of its characteristic features.

While for various reasons the accounts of the *Journal* do not survive, a partial breakdown of its analogous predecessor, the *London Saturday Journal*, is still available. Although undated, it seems to have been written towards the end of 1840 or early 1841, between its two series.[8] The following is a summary.

Table 4.2 Weekly Debits and Credits of the *London Saturday Journal* c. 1841

Debits

Composition and correction for each number, average	£8/15/0
Stereotyping	£2/14/0
Paper for 5,000, namely 10 reams at 23/3	£11/12/6
Working 10 reams at 6/6	£3/3/0
Folding at 1/3 per 1,000	£0/6/3
Total paper and print	**£26/10/9**
Annual salary for the editor: £200	= weekly about £3/16/9

Credits

Sales of 5,000 (77 dozen in each 1,000 copies, sold at 1/4 per dozen)
£25/13/4

With a circulation of 5,000, including the salary of the editor, but excluding any payment to contributors (none is stated), the *loss* was £4/10/2 per week.

Louis James (1963: 35-7) has criticized the estimates of Charles Knight for an imaginary penny weekly, and the *London Saturday Journal* accounts corroborate his rather than Knight's lower figures. Bennett's (1982: 239) figures for the *Penny Magazine* and *Chambers's*, though expressed in annual totals, also confirm the higher figures when broken down to weekly amounts. However, the *London Saturday Journal* trade discount at 38.5 percent of the retail price (13 copies cost 16d wholesale, 26d retail @ 2d each) was actually higher than that of the *London Journal* (13 copies cost 9d wholesale). James suggests 24/- per ream of paper (not Knight's 12/-) and composition at £8 (not £3). The *London Saturday Journal* was similar to the *London Journal* in so far as it was a sixteen-page miscellany of the same size. Paper costs did not vary much in the 1840s, so the relevant figures in theory apply to the *London Journal*. Extra expenses for Stiff would, however, have included woodcuts at perhaps 10/- each,[9] and unknown sums for contributors such as Ross and Sinnett. For monthly numbers, stitching and a coloured cover would

---

[8] See Bradbury and Evans Correspondence, Bodleian Library, MS.Eng.lett.d.398/2, 169-212, fol. 169. This is a printed sheet giving an account of the *London Saturday Journal* for Bradbury and Evans who, while backing the magazine financially, wished to remain anonymous. The *terminus post quem* is supplied by a reference to vol. IV (1840) of the magazine; the *terminus ante quem* is a postmark dated Kendall, 25 February 1841.

[9] The *Penny Magazine* claims the magazine spent £2,000 a year on woodcuts, suggesting a much higher cost per item ('Woodcutting and Type Founding', October 1833: 421). Cost obviously depended on the nature of the print and the status of the artist. Edmund Evans reports an artist earning 1/6 for a silhouette in *Punch* at mid-century (Evans, 1967: 11). Sinnema (1998: 53) mentions that Gilbert obtained 35/- for an *ILN* drawing in 1842. This must have been a particularly grand piece of work.

have had to be paid for, but this was passed on to the consumer, as the monthly number cost 6d, 1d or 2d more than the weekly numbers separately. Many covers of monthly numbers were plastered with advertisements which would have brought income. For the semi-annual volumes the extra expenses of boards and binding would have been involved, but again the cost was passed on, price increasing as circulation rose: the first two volumes were advertised at 3/6 each, volumes III to XIV at 4/- (the price of volumes I and II rose to the same price) and, from 1852, the time of highest circulation, at 4/6. This contrasts with the total of 2/2 (or 2/3 or 2/4 depending on how many weeks were included) that the equivalent in weekly numbers would have cost, or 3/- for six monthly numbers. The *London Journal* tells readers that cases for binding were about 1/3 if they wanted to get their copies bound themselves ('H.J.B.', II: 256; 'Henry', III: 80). This was a standard price (cf. *Reynolds's Miscellany*, III: 16, 32). One reader is told another, unspecified, method of binding would cost 4d or 6d ('J.F.B.', III: 128). Figures from a pamphlet published by the Society of Authors even 40 years later (Anon., 1889) to explain the costs of publishing to its members show that bulk binding could go as low as 4d per volume. Considerable profit could clearly be reaped from volume sales.

There is no sum given for advertisement in the *London Saturday Journal* accounts, but Knight proposed £2 when lumped in with stereotyping (which would have taken up the bulk of that sum). Chapman (1852: 517-18) suggests that 25 percent of the costs of *book* production and as much as 50 percent of *pamphlet* costs went on advertising. Forty years later, the Society of Authors guide (Anon., 1889) states that advertising was a fixed cost of either £20 or £30 depending on the type of publication, but it added that there was no real standard practice or price for this, as each publisher had their own promotional methods. I have traced very little advertising indeed for the *London Journal* outside the *Weekly Times*.[10] Presumably, like the *ILN*, the *Journal* relied on other forms of advertising such as sandwich boards and posters. An illustration from 1870 shows a wall in the background plastered with posters, amongst which is 'London Journal / New Story Fairfax Balfour', ironically self-reflexive since the novel being illustrated is Balfour's *Perdita* (LII: 8). Other prints from the 1860s and 1870s show street scenes with men carrying sandwich boards advertising the *Journal* (XLIII: 161; LVII: 125).

Reynolds was initially paid £3/10/- a week as editor (*WT*, 10 September 1848, I: 402-3), slightly less than the editor of the *London Saturday Journal*. This suggests a lower market value for his labour at this stage – *The Mysteries of London* had started publication only a few months previously and sales had probably not yet gained the 80,000 they are claimed as reaching.[11] At unspecified dates, Reynolds obtained £4 and then £5 a week for his editorial work on the *London Journal*. For writing *Faust* he was given £24 extra plus £40 for the copyright, which works out at less than £1/10 per instalment. His was a typical income: £200-£300 a year was

---

[10] For a rare example, see *ILN*, 12 July 1851: 240.

[11] On the circulation of *The Mysteries*, see 'A.B.C.', II: 400. In his introduction to Reynolds (1844-46: xi) Trefor Thomas claims only 40,000, following James (1963: 46) who quotes a figure from the *Journal* of several months earlier (I: 175). 'The Present State of Cheap Literature', *Liverpool Mercury*, 1 June 1847: 3 gives 60,000.

a common salary for newspaper editors, though a few earned as much as £1,000 (see Roberts, 1972a: 4; [Merle], 1829a: 223). The editor of the *Penny Magazine* had obtained £400 in 1833 (Bennett, 1982: 239). This was the sum that Trollope was earning when he married in 1844, and on that income, he wrote, 'many people would say that we were two fools to encounter such poverty together' (Trollope, 1883: 71). Such an income was by no means sufficient for Reynolds. Despite an extra £10 per week from writing *The Mysteries of London* and editing an unrelated newspaper (the *Weekly Dispatch*), he was still living above his means, at the more gentlemanly rate of £600-£700 a year (*Weekly Times*, 10 September 1848, I: 402-3). Dickens might have been able to afford this, but not Reynolds. It is no surprise that he was bankrupted in 1848.

Finally, no figure is given in the *London Saturday Journal* figures for essential overheads such as renting (or purchasing) premises, cleaning, heating and lighting. In the previous chapter, we read that Stiff employed a stoker for £1 a week who presumably kept the heating – or a steam press – working. I have therefore added an arbitrary 10 percent to the debit side to cover such necessary expenses.

Table 4.3 Hypothetical Debits and Credits of the *London Journal*, issue 1 (version 1)

Debits

Composition and correction of each weekly number about	£8/15/0
Stereotyping	£2/14/0
Paper for 20,000 (40 reams at 23/3)	£46/10/0
Working 40 reams at 6/6	£13/0/0
Folding at 1/3 per 1,000	£1/5/0
Original illustrations x 2 (others by Stiff or taken from stock)	£1/0/0
Total for paper and print	**£73/4/0**
Editor	£3/10/0
Overheads at *c*. 10% (adjusted up to make a round total)	£7/12/0
Total costs	**£85**

Credits

Sales of 20,000 at 9d per 13	**£56/15/2**

Extrapolating from the figures available, I conclude that the first number of the *London Journal* (sales 20,000) made a loss of about £25 to £30 (see Table 4.3), confirming Vizetelly's anecdote about the magazine's unprofitable start. Mitchell (1989: 4) claimed sales of 30,000 were necessary to break even in the penny weekly market, and James (1963: 36) pointed out that penny periodicals did not make nearly so much profit as Charles Knight claimed (£40 on sales of 40,000). Calculations based on the above estimates actually show that it is virtually impossible to make a profit whatever the sales, unless the extra income from sales of monthly numbers, semi-annual volumes and especially advertising space was considerable. The only way for the *Journal* to make a profit was to use cheaper paper and/or employ labour at well under the standard rates, as on Knight's imaginary magazine. This is what Cassell must have done to produce his temperance penny weekly the *Working Man's Friend* for £10 per number, as he sold them for 8d for 13 to the trade and ended up with a profit of £4/3/4 from each thousand he sold (*Report*, 1851: 213, 218-21). *London Journal* paper is in fact good quality down to 1871, so it was labour costs that were being kept down. It is clear that emphasis was placed on giving the consumer value for money – which meant labour exploitation and its concealment under the consumerly pleasures of the product.

A Commission of Inquiry Report (16 December 1845) reveals that, as compositors were paid according to the number of sheets they worked, the printers of the *Family Herald* and the *London Journal* (in the latter case Wilkinson's of Brydges Street, Drury Lane) exploited a loophole whereby the exact size of the sheet used was not specified (Howe, 1947: 254-58). They used sheets of 'demy' (of slightly different sizes) in order to get as many pages as possible out of the compositors. The printers thus paid for composition at what was basically half price. The Report declares:

> the necessity for laying down some plan whereby such works as the *London Journal* and *Family Herald* may not be imposed upon the trade as one sheet, when, in reality, they take up the space of two. The difference made upon many of them would be obvious, if they were publications [*sic*]; the 2s.6d. per sheet [payment to compositors] being doubled. Lloyd's works have scarcely a single extra [expense in comparison]; the alteration therefore would little affect them. The *Family Herald* and others must be made conformable to the rule; and but few fears may be entertained that acquiescence will follow a decision, in itself so reasonable and just.   (Howe, 1947: 258.)

I have been unable to determine whether Wilkinson ended up paying the rate demanded here or if Vickers and Stiff compensated him, but it may well be significant that the *Journal* went through five different printers in its first seven years, none reputable enough to be included in Todd (1972).[12] The evidence therefore strongly points towards confirmation of Knight's low costing of composition. The table of the *London Journal*'s production needs to be adjusted accordingly.

On the basis of Table 4.4, the *Journal* will lose on its first issue, but with sales of 100,000 (apparently achieved within six months) it makes a profit of at least £20. Thereafter, high profits would have been easier to make: as its popularity increased so more could be charged. Not only the price-rises of volumes reflect this: from 1852 back numbers older than a month increased in price from 1d to 1½d (see 'Notice to Trade', XV:16).

---

[12] Numbers 1-26 were printed by John Wortham, 313 Strand; nos. 27-111 by Wilkinson, who gives his address initially as 3 Catherine-Steet, Strand, and, from no. 76, as 'Bonner House' Printing Office, Seacoal Lane, Farringdon-Street; nos. 112-158 by John Fautley, also at 'Bonner House'; nos. 159-390 by Walter Sully also at 'Bonner House'; and nos. 391-406 by Robert Palmer of Brixton. On 11 December 1852, Vickers took over the printing until 31 May 1862, when the magazine was sold to W.S. Johnson.

Table 4.4 Hypothetical Debits and Credits of the *London Journal*, issue 1 (version 2)

Debits

Composition and correction of each weekly number	£5/0/0
Stereotyping	£2/14/0
Paper for 20,000 (10 reams at 23/3)	£46/10/0
Working 20 reams at 3/-	£3/0/0
Folding 20,000 at 1/- per 1,000	£1/0/0
Original illustrations x 2 (others by Stiff or taken from stock)	£1/0/0
Total for paper and print	*£59/4/0*
Editor	£3/10/0
Overheads at *c.* 10% (adjusted down to make round total)	£5/6/0
Total costs	**£68**

Credits

Sales of 20,000 at 9d per 13	*£56/15/2*

That same year, Vickers must have amassed sufficient capital to purchase machinery to take over the printing himself, and already from 1847 another significant reduction in production cost per item would have been caused by sharing office space and equipment with the *Weekly Times*.

In terms of income, advertisements on monthly covers when the circulation was high would have commanded a good price. The only information I have on charges for advertisements dates from early 1851, when a notice reveals the rate as 2/- a line plus 18d duty ('A Constant Reader' and 'J. Harris', XIV: 399). Whether there was a difference between advertisements on monthly covers and the very few the back page of weekly issues is not clear. Assuming the reference is to the latter, those on the same back page as the notice – one for the 'Absolute Sale!!' of clothes and another for *Tyburn Tree*, published in penny numbers by Purkess – would have brought in 18/- and 36/- respectively.

On the debit side, overheads would, however, have risen through rental of gradually more prestigious addresses, and from 1848 (when Thomas Miller was serialized), through payment to serial novelists rather than to a translator of French novels. Reynolds claimed that Stiff offered him £10 a week in 1848, but this may be Reynoldsian hyperbole. More certainly, J.F. Smith was getting £10 per weekly instalment of his serials by 1856 (*Times*, 13 March 1856: 10; 14 March 1856: 9). A further cost, which seems to be linked to Vickers's takeover of the printing in 1852, would have been the increase in page-size from 1853. Unsurprisingly, while readers were told that the *Journal* had undergone a 'Permanent Enlargement' 'to One-Fourth more than its original size' (XVII: 16), the increase from 8¼ inches/ 210mm x 11¼ inches/285mm to 8¾ inches/220mm x 12¼ inches/310mm hardly merits this claim.

Unfortunately, I have found no information about costs in the crucial period when the *Journal* was edited by Mark Lemon (1857-9), but they must have been very high from the exceptional number of named authors and the size and quality of the illustrations. Financial indicators do, however, survive from shortly after this period in a series of *Times* articles detailing Stiff's bankruptcy in 1861. The accounts cited, while not giving a detailed breakdown, reveal that the *Journal* was making a clear profit of £4,500 a year between 1859 and 1861 – about £86/10/4 per week. Calculations using a mean of the above figures and the average circulation of 313,000 that the auditor reported at the trial, suggest incomings of about £120 a week (excluding unknown sums from advertising). After deduction of the clear profit, roughly £33 would have been left for overheads and payment to the editor and contributors. By this time production costs would have been reduced, firstly by the removal of the paper tax in 1861 and the lower price of paper – caused mainly by the massive increase in child labour in the paper manufactories (Bennett, 1990: 170).

In the 1860s and 1870s, it seems W.S. Johnson, who had bought both the *London Journal* and the *Weekly Times* after Stiff's bankruptcy, regularly made £1,000 a month from the *Journal* alone (Downey, 1905: 30-32, 63). Such immense profits would not necessarily have needed as high a circulation as in the early 1850s. Not only had Johnson bought the magazine after the removal of paper duty, but he already owned the works he used to print his publications. This, no doubt, allowed the number of pages to increase temporarily in 1868, and contributed towards the extra expenses of importing fashion plates from Paris. Furthermore, paper prices were to drop even further with the widespread use of esparto from the late 1860s (Spicer, 1907: 89-91): the *Journal*'s paper quality markedly decreases from 1871.

On the debit side, the editor and main serial novelist at that time, Pierce Egan, was unlikely to have made less than £15 a week (a respectable £780 a year), since £10 had retained neither Reynolds nor J.F. Smith. The second-string novelist Mrs Gordon Smythies was paid eight guineas per weekly instalment in the early 1860s (Cross, 1985: 190). In 1863, the *Spectator* (1863: 1806)mentioned how 'a writer in one of the penny journals is said to be paid £25 a week for three or four pages of a continuous story. It is no uncommon thing for a tale to run through fifty-two numbers, – which would be at a cost of £1,300 for a novel – certainly not a bad price'. Mary Braddon, who wrote for the *Journal* in the 1860s, was at the same time commanding over £2,000 from Tinsley (Wolff, 1979: 134-37). In short, there was a considerable rise in the price of writers' labour in the *London Journal* zone.

To end this grossly material but necessary chapter, I want to compare the financial relationships of the American authors serialized in the *Journal* with their New York papers. In America, so valuable were star authors that regular contracts were the order of the day from the mid-1850s. Noel (1954: 88) suggests that '[i]t was like working for the civil service – fixed duties, a basic salary according to classification, security and periodic increments. Even pensions seem to have been provided for.' While I have been unable to confirm all of these points, good regular incomes were certainly common for the most popular American writers. E.D.E.N. Southworth was paid $40 a week when she joined the *New York Ledger* in 1857. In 1861 this was increased to $50 and by 1873 she was receiving $150 'plus extras'. At this time she is reckoned to have earned $6,000 a year (Dolesa, in Southworth, 1859: xx; Coulthorpe-McQuin, 1990, ch. 3). Beadle used to pay his authors much the same amounts, though for certain authors much more (Johannsen, 1950: 8). Harriet Lewis (over twenty of whose novels will be serialized in the *Journal* between 1869 and 1883) worked on a payment-per-novel basis in the early 1860s ($150-$250 dollars each) when she started writing for the *Ledger*. This rose to $3,000 for *The Girl Hermit* in 1870. Later again, she was earning $300 a week, indicative of how favoured she was by Robert Bonner, the proprietor of the *Ledger* (Robert Bonner Papers at NYPL, Lewis's letters to Bonner dated 19 November 1862; 26 June 1863; 16 October 1863; 15 July 1870). May Agnes Fleming enjoyed a similar relation, first with the Philadelphia *Saturday Night* ($2,000 for three novels annually from 1868) and later with the *New York Weekly* ($6,000 for three and later two novels per year). She also had a contract with the *London Journal* to supply advance sheets for £12 per instalment. Perhaps thirteen of her novels appeared in it between 1869 and 1882. Noel (1954: 89) claims that sick leave was also provided. Southworth applied to Bonner for it by forwarding a doctor's certificate, although when she was struck down by smallpox she suggested that either she dictate the end of her current novel from her sickbed or that the editor find someone else to finish it. The editor opted for the latter. When she was well, Southworth wrote to him to say how delighted she was with the result (Noel, 1954: 94-5).

Obviously, authors were treated well in order to increase productivity and, more pertinently, loyalty: their names were valuable commodities worth paying for. Rather than paternalistic benevolence for its own sake, what emerges is a picture of business professionalism in a demand-led economy of cultural production that offers to its most marketable producers financial security rather than cultural status. This is what seems to have happened in the British mass-market as well as the American from the mid-1850s, intensified from the 1860s on. The higher payments given to authors granted not only their financial safety, however. It coincided with a move away from the parergic into a more independent cultural system. While higher incomes for writers do not guarantee independence from higher-status models, I think all the factors I have described here – the size and nature of the potential markets, the nature and availability of the product and of potential producers as well as costs and profits – interact with one another in complex ways whose precise outcome I shall explore in later chapters.

For me, the most important lesson to be learnt from this descent into the materiality of Grub Street lies not in how vast profits could be made by proprietors, large sums by a few writers and small sums by most – a situation already well known – but in how the existence of mass-market reading and its concomitant pleasures were paid for not just by the penny demanded on the front page and by sales of advertising space, but also by the exploitation at different times of usually invisible labourers of literature. I have only evoked compositors and paper-makers here. No doubt other figures were exploited too, but they remain only as unperceived hands through which mass-market fantasy has been translated into the material I see on the table before me.

Chapter Five

1849-57. Moving from the Miscellany; or, J.F. Smith and After

[J.F. Smith] had a thousand readers where Dickens had ten or Thackeray one. He was the people's chosen author ... if his work was too slapdash to have literary merit, he never abused his influence and it is impossible to deny him the faculty of invention. Had he had more ambition he might have produced more lasting work; but he would have had far fewer readers ...

(*Athenaeum*, 15 March 1890: 343)

By June 1850, Stiff had a combined establishment of 80 working on the *Weekly Times* and the *London Journal* at 334 Strand. An account of the 'annual gathering of the establishment of George Stiff' appeared on 23 June 1850 in the *Weekly Times* (p. 453), revealing that Ross, having survived Reynolds's accusation that Stiff intended to sack him, was still the editor of the *Journal* and that Sinnett was also still engaged (in what capacity is not clear). Others on the outing mentioned by name include Edward Leman Blanchard, and a Mr St Leger (a contributor of tales, usually under the initials 'St.L.', in volumes X-XIII) and a Mr Ellis (who seems to be the editor of the *Weekly Times*). G.F. Sargent spoke on behalf of the artists and engravers. Neither of the *Journal*'s stars, J.F. Smith and John Gilbert, was present. Both had reputations as recluses. Gilbert used to work at home in Blackheath and does not seem to have come into contact with the novelists he illustrated (Thomas, 1913-14, VII: 221); certainly Charles Reade, whose novel he illustrated in the *Journal*, never met him (Reade, 1860: 166). Smith I shall discuss later in this chapter.

From the signatures in the *Journal*, other key members of the network included the almost certainly female contributor of witty articles and tales, 'E. O'H.' in volumes XII-XV, along with essays by 'E.C.' (XIV), and stories by 'M.A.B.' or 'Mrs Bird' (IX-XV). Charles Swain becomes the main *London Journal* poet of this period (especially in volumes XIII-XVIII), followed by Gerald Massey in the ensuing two volumes. Besides a large number of poems that appear also in his various collections, Swain's long and ambitious meditative poem *The Mind*, originally published 1831-32, is reprinted in full and proclaimed one of the greatest creations of the age. The signature of John Parsons Hall continues to appear and, towards the end of this period, Anne Marie Maillard (in volumes XVIII-XXVI) and 'J.C.' (in volumes XXI-XXVI) sign a large number of tales between them. There are also a great many tales and poems signed with initials and names that do not recur. While in the early volumes such signatures may mask pirated material, this seems unlikely from 1848 when the number of unidentifiable and unrepeated sets of initials considerably increased. By then, Notices to Correspondents had for several years printed replies to readers who had sent in material (and even applications for work on the magazine) and Ross had no doubt eventually decided to take advantage of their offers. From both the legal and economic points of view this made sense. Rather than raid already published material, readers could provide it just as cheaply.

Ross and Stiff had given even more importance to the visual in volume VII (1848) by exploiting their connections with *ILN*. Three artists then introduced all did work for the *ILN*: Harrison Weir, W.H. Prior and G.F. Sargent (from now by far the greatest contributor of signed illustrations to the *Journal*). The same link is perceptible in the engravers: W. Gorway, the mark of an atelier rather than a specific person (Engen, 1985: 103) and the commonest engraver's signature in the *Journal*, Thomas Bolton, J. Gelder and H. White. The last named, a pupil of the great Bewick himself, was a notably skilled engraver and had initiated the fashion for 'sketchy crosshatching' which is such a feature of *London Journal* prints (Engen, 1985: 280-81). There are even a couple of cuts signed by the *ILN*'s most prestigious engravers, Dalziel and Greenaway & Wright. These *ILN* connections would have been expensive, a sign of achieved profits and a bid for yet more.

If 1848 was important for developments in illustration, the major innovation that justifies the following year as the start of a new period was the introduction of J.F. Smith as a novelist. As Frank Jay found in 1918, less than thirty years after Smith's death, information about him is very hard to find. What little that does survive is mainly anecdotal, most of it depending on just two sources.[1] One is 'Penny Novels' in *Macmillan's Magazine* (Anon., 1866); this both set the fashion for treating the name 'J.F. Smith' as a sociological phenomenon rather than as a literary corpus, and provided the biographical information that has been the basis for most twentieth-century references. The second is the passage in Vizetelly's *Glances Back* quoted at the beginning of Chapter 2. Again Vizetelly proves unreliable, mixing the verifiable with the exigencies of a good story. The unfinished novel Vizetelly referred to there is *Masks and Faces* (1856). From a notice in *Cassell's Illustrated Family Paper* (I: 386) I can confirm his assertion that Smith wrote only the first twelve chapters – but there is no sinking of a Mississippi steamer in the published version, and the novel was actually continued by Emma Robinson not Pierce Egan. Robinson later published a triple-decker version of *Masks and Faces* as *The City Banker* with Routledge, replacing all the chapters by Smith and changing all the names of characters he had introduced (suggesting that, unlike Smith and Reynolds, she had retained the copyright of her work). Smith's sudden defection to Cassell is, in fact, less amusing than Vizetelly makes it. Several sources confirm his remark that Smith left the *Journal* for

---

[1] Curiously, the only major act of vandalism now visible in the entire run of the BL *London Journal* is the removal of Smith's biography and portrait ('Portrait Supplement' no. 8, n.s. XIII, 7 June 1890). Advertisements in the *Journal* claim 'exclusive information' about him. I have not found another copy, though Jay (1918-19), hitherto neglected as a source for Smith's life, includes information found nowhere else which may well derive from this supplement.

financial reasons: from Cassell, Smith obtained £10-£15 a week, whereas from Stiff he got only £10. But *Masks and Faces* did not appear until 23 June 1855, while Smith's *Soldier of Fortune* had begun in *Cassell's* on 14 April and continued until 29 December. The dating implies not the sudden decision that Vizetelly describes, but complicated negotiations between Smith and two publishers.

Cassell's Illustrated Family Paper had appeared on 31 December 1853.[2] It was designed to look like a version of the *ILN*, comprising the same newspaper-sized page, the same extravagant size of illustrations on its front pages, and over 400 large illustrations a year (as opposed to about 210 in the equivalent two volumes of the *Journal*). Unlike the *ILN*, however, *Cassell's Illustrated Family Paper* had only eight pages, carried mainly fiction and, crucially, it cost only a penny. The circulation of the *Cassell's* rose with exceptional rapidity, reaching 300,000 by the beginning of 1858 (Brougham, [1858]:11). Apart from size and visuals, its main differentiating factor from the *London Journal* was an insistent topicality. Its first serial was Percy B. St John's *The Arctic Crusoe: a Tale of the Polar Seas*, clearly designed to promote and profit from interest in the mystery of Franklin's Arctic Expedition which had recently filled the newspapers: the *Morning Chronicle* devoted over 180 column inches to the affair over just two days in October 1853 alone (Riffenburgh, 1994: 27-30). Later, during the Crimean War, *Cassell's* reported and depicted events earlier than the *Journal*, with larger cuts and even *ILN*-type supplements. The *Journal* reported the Battle of the Alma in the Crimea, for example, on 25 November, with a lack-lustre picture, while the *Cassell's* version had come out a fortnight earlier with a splendid illustration. The prints in *Cassell's* recall the urgent sense of immediacy characteristic of *ILN* much more successfully than the *Journal*'s new attempts at the same. Cassell had secured several *ILN* artists, including the two *London Journal* stalwarts Gilbert and Sargent even while they were still drawing pictures for the rival magazine. Gilbert even designed the headpiece of Cassell's new venture (Houfe, 1981: 73-4). In several ways, therefore, *Cassell's* was encroaching on the *Journal*'s territory in the mid-1850s.

By the time *Masks and Faces* appeared in the *Journal* in June 1855, Smith had already been working for several months not just on an isolated novel but on what would be a series of novels for *Cassell's* without break until November 1858. In January 1856, Cassell prosecuted Stiff for lifting illustrations from the French weekly *L'Illustration* to which Cassell claimed he had owned exclusive rights in Britain since 1852. In an echo of the case brought against Vickers by Bentley in 1847, the judge accepted Cassell's case without even listening to Stiff's defence (*Times*, 25 January 1856: 8). Two months later, in a clear *quid pro quo*, Stiff tried to prosecute Cassell for Smith's defection, but, yet again disliked by the law, Stiff was made to pay costs and his case dismissed. The *Times* version of this second case (13 March 1856: 10; 14 March 1856: 9) carried details of Stiff's arrangements with Smith. On 22 February 1855, Stiff had offered him an agreement for two

---

[2] On Cassell in general, see Nowell-Smith (1958) and the Smilesian hagiography by Pike (1894).

tales, 'the titles hereafter to be agreed upon', for £10 per instalment, each of which was to be as long as the instalments of Smith's most recent serial *Temptation* (1854-55). The first number was to be submitted by 23 April 1855. This in turn implies that Stiff had already thought of pirating the American E.D.E.N. Southworth's *True And False Heiress* which he had started to publish on 3 March. Smith got round to signing the agreement only the day before that. About seven weeks after *Masks and Faces* had started to appear, Smith went to Paris, from where he sent a portion of the manuscript in which his novel 'was brought to an abrupt conclusion' says *The Times*. Since Smith's characters had not left their English village by the time Emma Robinson took over, a considerable amount of Smith's work must have been jettisoned if he had brought his characters to the Mississippi to drown them as Vizetelly claimed.

The second amusing anecdote derived from Vizetelly concerns how Smith would turn up at the *London Journal* office just before copy was due, lock himself away with a bottle of port and emerge hours later with the requisite number of words. He would then disappear until the following week. There is contradictory evidence concerning this. Against it is Smith's long relationship with Cassell who had very strong temperance views. Simon Nowell-Smith mentions a teetotal party at Cassell's house with Cruikshank, the Howitts, Mrs Gordon Smythies and her father, and J.F. Smith and his son.[3] Tea and coffee were served; Mrs Gordon Smythies played her own composition on the piano, Cruikshank sang a song and Smith recited a poem he had written (Nowell-Smith, 1958: 54-5). The anonymous writer of a *TLS* article (25 December 1930: 1104), who seems to have known Smith, explicitly dismisses Vizetelly's anecdote about the port. On the other hand, another acquaintance confirms it, even adding a new one where port proves an essential ingredient to Smith's writing (see 'J.F. McR.', 1890). What is interesting is not whether Vizetelly's anecdote linking drink and Smith's writing is true or not – it may well be both depending on Smith's time of life – but how it gets repeated over and again so as to become one of the definitions of Smith's life. It derives its vitality from two closely related commonplaces, the first linking popular reading with narcotics or drink and the second associating journalist and alcoholic. Both were common tropes in the nineteenth century, the latter especially concerning bohemians writing of themselves, its very repetition lending it the air of 'truth'.

Beyond Vizetelly and the anecdotal, what I been able to dig up of J.F. Smith's life is skeletal, and much of that derives from Jay (1918-19). Even the year of Smith's birth is uncertain, various sources giving either 1803 or 1804. I prefer the former as he died in late February 1890, 'aged 86' according to the *Star* (4 March 1890: 1) and the *Speaker* (8 March 1890: 254): assuming he was born in 1804 gives a window of two months for his birthday, as opposed to ten months if we presume 1803. He was the son of George Smith, the manager of the Norwich theatre circuit. Jay (1918-19: 9) claims a wealthy uncle cast off his father when he got involved with the theatre, a story that puts Smith in the category of disinherited

---

[3] This reference is the only allusion to the possibility that Smith was married (he would be unlikely to take an illegitimate child to Cassell's). In no other source is there reference to either wife or children.

gentility. Even though lost inheritance is the theme of all his *London Journal* novels, I have found nothing else to sustain this story. Smith visited Russia with a relative (an experience recalled in his second novel for the *Journal*, *Amy Lawrence*), and then rebelled against his strict education by a Jesuit, following his father into the theatre. Aged 29 (c. 1832-33), he travelled to Rome where he spent several years. Rome was extremely volatile during the early 1830s, the Pope in need of foreign allies and his administration undergoing intense reform. It seems that Gregory XVI conferred on Smith the Order of Saint Gregory. This was a not especially prestigious medal created in 1832 by Gregory XVI for both military and civil action in three grades (Dorling, 1983: 317-18). One article signed by Smith in the *Journal* claims that Cardinal Fesch (the brother of Napoleon) showed him his picture gallery. The same piece claims that, disguised in the soutain of a friend at the English College Rome, Smith was also able to observe Napoleon's mother both alive in church and, later, dead ('The Mother and Uncle of Napoleon', IX: 341-42). I have been unable to establish whether this article forms the basis of the twentieth-century hypotheses that he may have been a Jesuit and an agent in the pay of Cardinal Fesch. What is clear is that the account is highly elaborated and fictionalized, even if based on fact.

According to Jay (1918-19: 10), after Rome Smith then wandered in Germany writing plays and libretti, and returned to England, only to leave once more to teach English at the University of Paris.[4] Evidence from his publications of the 1830s and 1840s confirms a peripatetic life – the dedication to the lead actress of *Sir Roger de Coverly* (*sic*), a 'Domestic Drama in Three Acts' put on at the Adelphi in October 1836, is dated 'Rome, November 16th, 1836' and apologizes that the author was not in London to see the production. The dedication of a later burletta, *The Court of Old Fritz*, is marked 'Albany Terrace, February 7th, 1839', showing that Smith was at least temporarily in London then. While Germany does not figure in his *London Journal* novels, opera and theatre several times play major parts. *The Will and the Way* (1852-53) uses Rome as a setting for the hero's adventures, and an audience with the Pope forms a climactic scene. Typical for his social group, Smith was translating experience – cultural capital – into financial capital.

Again typical is Smith's career, a form of the cultural descent narrative. Smith's earliest traceable publication dates from 1832, the lyrics of a song cycle set to music by C.H. Mueller, a Norfolk composer. The difficulty for both singer and pianist of *Songs of the Ocean* leaves no doubt as to its High Art pretensions – a kind of Anglicized cross of Schubert and *bel canto*. The verses recall Mrs Hemans (whose status was then high). There soon followed a triple-decker, *The Jesuit* (1832), brought out by the reputable firm of Saunders and Otley, the publishers of Bulwer Lytton. Thereafter came a handful of plays which always made the West End theatres (the Adelphi, the Olympic, the Surrey), and, the same year as his guide to the Seine, a second novel appeared, *The Prelate* (1840). But this time, the

---

[4] *A Handbook up the Seine* (1840) appears under the signature of Smith, adding on the title page that he was 'Professor of the Royal College of Bayeux, Officer of the University of France'.

novel comprised two, not the more valuable three, volumes and was published by the grasping and roguish Newby – a decided move down-market from auspicious beginnings.[5] Nonetheless, *The Prelate* still received a review in *The Athenaeum* (1840), even if a lukewarm one. Thereafter, on the rare occasion when Smith was noticed in the high-status press, his name was treated as sociological phenomenon; never again would his work be treated as *literary*.

In 1848 Smith's libretto *Robin Goodfellow* was set to music by Edward James Loder and put on at the Princess's Theatre, London, where Loder was then music director. The production was reviewed favourably in *The Times* (11 December 1848: 8) both for its music and for its words. But their author remained anonymous. When D'Almaine published songs from the work in an undated publication only Loder gets mentioned. Smith's authorship is apparent only from a reference appended to Smith's signature in the *Journal* (IX: 412).

Despite his invisibility in print, it was probably the success of *Robin Goodfellow* that made Smith an attractive option for Stiff. In May 1849 Smith's *Stanfield Hall* began, the first of what would turn out to be probably the most famous *London Journal* novels of all and amongst the most widely read fiction of the nineteenth century. Despite Smith's recent success in the theatre, it seems to me that *Stanfield Hall* did not start out as a serial novel but rather as a short serial tale, since for the first few episodes it gives the impression that it could stop at any point. It feels as though Stiff were testing Smith, and only when the story proved successful did he engage him to continue the work as a full-scale serial. Thereafter, Smith published an uninterrupted series of works in the *Journal* until 1855: six serial novels, poems and the fictionalized *Lives of the Queens of England*, which would later inspire Cassell to ask him to write the *Illustrated History of England* (1857).

At £10 per instalment and lasting about a year, the novels that raised circulation to half a million earned Smith about £500 each. This was a reasonable sum, though hardly spectacular considering the profits that could be made by authors like Dickens, Bulwer or, later, Braddon who had good business sense and bankable names. Whether Smith actually edited the *Journal* and therefore earned more is not clear. In any case, John Wilson Ross continued to sign essays in the magazine until early 1851.

It is curious to compare the deployment of 'J.F. Smith' as a star name with contemporary transatlantic practice. American periodicals had already started to pay authors vast sums and to advertise their names in proportion. Over 1855 to 1856 Robert Bonner of the *New York Ledger* – the American analogue of the *London Journal* – broadcast the amount he paid as part of his advertising campaign: each of the columns written by 'Fanny Fern' in the *Ledger* cost $100. His reasoning was that by publicizing the price, people could calculate exactly how much each article by the writer cost and value their work accordingly. This logic apparently worked (Noel, 1954: 64; Fern, 'Introduction' by Belasco Smith, 1997: xv-xvi). While Fanny Fern's immense profits were reported in the *Weekly Times* (29 April 1855: 262), the *Journal* remained reticent about its most characteristic

---

[5] In 1860, after Smith had already achieved fame, *The Prelate* was re-issued by Ward and Lock as part of their shilling Railway Library.

author: only three major works were to carry Smith's signature. Over the nineteen months when *Lives of the Queens* ran in the *Journal* simultaneously with his novels (1852-4), Smith was writing almost half of the magazine each week, although this density is masked by the curious anonymity of the novels and by a term – 'by-lines' – whose meaning I shall narrow more closely than is usual for lack of alternative terminology. When I use it 'by-lines', it means not the usual authorial signature but 'By the author of ...'. Very often in Smith's case such 'by-lines' are without any sign of his name. Only a few advertisements in the *Weekly Times* suggest him as the author of his later serials and even then his name is not emphasized, again the naked by-line being preferred.[6] In 1842, Malcolm Rymer, himself a very successful popular author, had written of what he called the 'star system' of author's names. The idea had been borrowed from the theatrical world, he claimed, and had started in earnest with Walter Scott. Now Scott had withheld his name for many years, a practice that effectively fetishized it all the more by creating a mystery around it. Nonetheless I do not believe Stiff was hoping to achieve the same effect by playing peek-a-boo with "J.F. Smith". The other star, Gilbert, did not sign his work as a matter of course, even for the *ILN*. I suspect that Stiff, taking advantage of an indifference to signature felt by both Smith and Gilbert, sought to make the magazine itself the 'star', the origin and anchor of the novels it carried.

However, that does not exhaust the possible reasons for Smith's relative invisibility as a name. Another reason that might explain his anonymity concerns the nature of his relation to the printed version of what he had written. On hearing of Smith's death in 1890 through the paper, a correspondent ('J.F. McR.') wrote to the *Speaker* that Smith's handwriting was so illegible that the corrector of proofs and the compositors 'had been able to decipher barely one quarter [of *Minnigrey*] ... had "fudged for" another quarter, while the remaining half was entirely the fruit of the said corrector's own ingenious vamping'. Smith's surviving autograph letters to Robert Bonner from 1870-88 are written with elaborate flourishes which require attention but are by no means illegible. Bonner must have complained about his writing, however, for Smith soon promised to simplify it (letter to Bonner, 25 December 1870, NYPL). Even allowing for wild exaggeration, perhaps Stiff or the *London Journal* compositors objected to a signature that claimed a single origin when they had to 'fudge for' so much. Whatever the reason, Smith's anonymity increased the longer he wrote for the *Journal*. When he moved to *Cassell's Illustrated Family Paper* on the other hand, his stardom was not only trumpeted but he was even granted a front-page portrait, the only picture of him now available (see Figure 5.1).

With the arrival of Smith arrived in 1849, the *London Journal* gradually changed its identity, shifting its position in the literary field, and indeed altering the nature of the field. It transformed its relationship to authoritative texts. Its principal attractions turned away from (but did not altogether abjure) miscellany compilation and the parergic towards original matter. Specially written for the discursive space

---

[6] See, for example, the advertisement in the *Weekly Times*, 5 November 1854: 712, where *Temptation* is cited only as 'By the author of "Minnigrey"'.

of the magazine, Smith's novels were clearly written to 'fit' there, both recalling and redefining previous serials and harmonizing with other departments. In so doing they formulated the periodical as more of an enclosed, autonomous world with a distinct identity, a magical space whose value is legitimated by its self-consistency. And when Smith's novels did react to texts outside the *Journal*, they dialogued with or absorbed facets of them rather than parergically mutated or raided the authoritative.

Figure 5.1 Portrait of J.F. Smith
Source:*Cassell's Illustrated Family Paper*, n.s. I: 385, 22 May 1858.

The title of Smith's first novel for the magazine, *Stanfield Hall* (1849-50), referred to a widely reported trial, 'The Stanfield-Hall Murders' as it was headlined in the contemporary press.[7] Its protagonist was executed the very week the serial appeared (though the *Journal* issue was, of course, dated a fortnight later). While never actually mentioning the murders themselves, the novel implicitly sought to 'explain' them by offering a history of where they took place, starting with just before the Norman conquest. The novel thus appropriated the notoriety of a topical event rather than a cultural authority. Such practice is related to, but different from, execution broadsheets and chapbooks, publications that had enormous sales well into the 1840s: James (1976: 257) prints a 'lamentation' by the Stanfield Hall murderer and there is an excellent website that offers a wealth of other material connected to the crime.[8]

But if *Stanfield Hall* played on the oral tradition of which the broadsheet is a printed manifestation, it also has a foot in the more literary. Book III recycles characters and plot devices from Smith's own play *The Protector! or, The Rebel's Gauntlet!* which had played the Royal Surrey Theatre in autumn 1844. More significantly, in several ways Smith maintained the London–Paris axis. This same part exploits the central idea of Soulié's *Les Deux cadavres* (1832 and partially translated in the *Journal* in 1846) that Cromwell's and Charles I's corpses were exchanged for one another. The structure of *Stanfield Hall*, a division into several 'books' each telling a different tale, maintained that of the immediately preceding novel by Eugène Sue in the *Journal*, *The Seven Cardinal Sins* (1847-48). Furthermore, by taking the history of a family through the centuries from an originary invasion as the figure for the nation, Smith arrived at the same idea as Sue's *Mystères du peuple*, which came out in Paris later the same year. Smith had, of course, lived in Paris and would return there, but what part he played in networks of French writers remains uncertain. What is important in political terms is how the novel resignifies the murders at Stanfield Hall by draining them of social causes – not least their relation to more general unrest in Norfolk – and by mythologizing them (in a quite strict Barthesian sense) into the result of a family curse. In so doing, *Stanfield Hall* was moving the *London Journal* more firmly into the pleasurable politography of the Strand, offering now less parergy than reference to a generalized mass-market cultural lexicon detached from its sources: the familiar in new contexts.

Smith's second novel, *Amy Lawrence* (1850-51) is less concerned with continuing diachronic links with earlier stories in the magazine. While its title echoes the most recent Sue novel in the *Journal*, *Mary Lawson* (1850), the major axis of reference swings around to Manchester and to another contemporary Mary, *Mary Barton* (1848). In more thoroughly melodramatic and denunciatory mode than Gaskell's negotiations of sympathy and condemnation, Smith's Manchester novel is concerned with corruption and the economics of everyday life, obsessively

---

[7] See, for example, *Morning Herald*, 4 December 1848: 3; *Weekly Times*, 14 January 1849: 102; *Northern Star*, 31 March 1849: 1; *ILN*, XIV, index.

[8] See http://stanfield.und.ac.za/saga00.html, part of the extremely comprehensive Jermy family website, http://stanfield.und.ac.za/jmainscr.html.

using the language of sale and barter. Dickens seems to hover outside the frame at times not only in the work's extreme thematic control but also in its mixture of comic, sentimental and quasi-realist modes. These links might suggest parergic links to higher-status British fiction, yet an important false imprisonment for madness of a key witness maintains a link with France by recalling Dumas's *Monte Christo* (serialized in the *Journal* 1846-47) and by the evocation of Sue rather than Dickens or Gaskell in the low-life episodes. The second half of the novel pursues parallel plots, the heroine subject to sexual temptation in London while the hero has adventures in St Petersburg. These latter perhaps not only recall Smith's own experiences in Russia but also take their cue from Ernest Jones's recent Chartist novel *The Romance of the People* (1847) whose hero likewise fights on the side of the 'people' (Smith's in the 1830 French Revolution; Jones's in Poland). In its defusing of potentially politically inflammatory material, *Amy Lawrence* continues the mythologizing of *Stanfield Hall*. Besides connecting to established narrative tropes, elements of the novel chime in with the rest of the magazine synchronically, notably with the advice meted out to readers in Notices to Correspondents. This comprises a 'practical morality', a fundamentally liberal model of conduct that accepts an ideal of behaviour as an aim, but also recognizes its frequent impossibility – a facet of the periodical I will have more to say about in Chapter 9. In *Amy Lawrence* the poor heroine marries a rich old man out of gratitude for saving her virtue, and only marries the hero after her husband's convenient death in a French riot: there is no need for her to marry her true beloved as the virgin we might expect from more consecrated fiction at this time.

If circulation had already risen significantly with Smith's first two novels, *Minnigrey* (1851-52) was by all accounts the real breakthrough in terms of sales. Set in the Peninsular War, it rewrites an earlier *London Journal* serial, *Love, War and Adventure*, by sending its active, virtuous and tempting Spanish heroine into a convent instead of into marriage with the hero, who eventually pairs with his English childhood love. Importantly, *Minnigrey* altered the direction of plagiarism: rather than the *London Journal* raiding high-status texts, now the cheap East End theatres raid the *London Journal*. According to Nicoll (1959, V: 719), there were four anonymous stage adaptations of *Minnigrey*, plus another by S. Davis who also adapted three more Smith novels for the Newcastle stage in 1856. There was also a much later version of *Minnigrey* by Henry Young and G. Roberts put on at the Elephant and Castle Theatre in 1886 to coincide with the reserialization of the novel in the new series of the *Journal*. The *Weekly Times* (18 April 1852) reviewed one of the earlier anonymous versions when it was put on at the Standard especially for the Easter holiday crowds. It was, apparently, very well received by a 'bumper house'. The *London Journal* was indeed enabling the existence of a happy-consumer holiday crowd.

Even greater sales and more theatrical adaptations were achieved by Smith's next two novels *The Will and the Way* (1852-3) and *Woman and her Master* (1853-54), such that for one admirer it was difficult to separate out the printed from the theatrical versions (Rogers, 1913: 10).[9] Picaresque romances like *Minnigrey*, these are motivated by lost inheritances and genealogies, beginning and ending in paradisal English countryside with a few adventures in a labyrinthine London and many more abroad. In this they follow the pattern of Smith's very first novel, *The Jesuit*. While that had been set just before the French Revolution, the *London Journal* trio are all set ostensibly in the 1810s and 1820s. In the same way that *Stanfield Hall* had encouraged the reader to enmesh the past into the present, in these too topicality was always implied. Contemporaneously with social upheaval in Naples (in 1852), *The Will and the Way* sends its hero to Italy; in *Woman and her Master*, the hero goes to America during the simultaneous serialization of *Uncle Tom's Cabin* in the same magazine, and confronts similar issues.

The trio of *Minnigrey*, *The Will and the Way* and *Woman and her Master* came to typify *London Journal* stories both for readers (see Anon., 1866: 103; Hitchman, 1881: 391; and cf. Wright, 1883: 285-6) and, it seems, for *London Journal* novelists themselves. Obvious connections with Paris are severed to create a more self-enclosed world. While a clear antecedent of these novels is Smollett, rendered less comic, more genteel and heroic, one cannot call this relationship parergic as Smollett is never violently raided and the reference is only available to the reader who already knows eighteenth-century codes. To others the stories are simply fast-moving quest narratives. With Smith the parergic loses force. The *London Journal* effectively separates itself further from contemporary authoritative texts on the way to developing its own cultural ecosystem, a universe that will never be hermetically sealed off from high-status texts but which, importantly, will no longer look towards them with such resentful anxiety. *London Journal* redefines its brand name yet again, rendering it a more easily identifiable product with a unique selling point. In ideological terms, it is particularly striking how all of Smith's novels so far are concerned to resignify the social and civic in terms of the patriarchal reproductive family. Anticipating soap-operas, the political in other words is reduced to the personal, becoming easier to comprehend and, at least in fantasy, to control.

Temptation (1854-55), Smith's last completed novel for the *Journal* in this period, though in some respects recalling the dark realist moments of *Amy Lawrence*, is very different from its predecessors. It may have achieved a lesser popularity, for I have found no references to reading it or to theatrical adaptations. Furthermore, when Stiff reserialized it in another periodical, the *London Reader*, in 1866, he placed it internally with no illustrations. It suggests that the balance between the familiar and the original was a difficult one to maintain. Straight away, the novel sets itself up as different, the pastoral opening of Smith's central trio darkened by discussion of antique punishment methods and by the immediate death of the hero's beloved friend. Most of the novel takes place in a claustrophobic, labyrinthine London where murderous men pursue a small girl.

---

[9] Nicoll (1946, II: 282, 559, 610, 768) lists eight adaptations of *The Will and the Way*. A late version was put on by J.H. McCarthy at the Arena Theatre, May 1890 (Mullin, 1987: 412). *Woman and her Master* was less popular on the stage: Nicoll (1946, II: 610) lists one version and Mullin (1987: 410) another.

While the hunt through the metropolis derives from Sue's *Mystères* – and the title in fact repeats that of another Sue novel – *Temptation* is by no means a return to Parisian popular modes. Its central concern, the overlay of the feminine with the maternal, has nothing to do with the usual 'mysteries' novel: the girl is passed along a chain of no fewer than five substitute mothers, each of whom is very different from the others, yet always positive and strong.

Masks and Faces (1855-56), which I shall comment on at some length in Chapter 9, initially returns to familiar but exceptionally dull ground, as if an unwilling Smith had been asked to return to his successful formula after the experiments of *Temptation*. When Emma Robinson intervened, she instantly enlivened the story with a strong dose of picaresque, adding a strong proto-feminist agenda borrowed from contemporary American women writers. At the same time she continued the emphasis on strong women begun by *Temptation* but removed the emphasis on the maternal. Robinson then started another novel for the *Journal*, *The Star in the Dark*, but, curiously, only a few episodes were run and it was omitted from the magazine's semi-annual index. *The Star in the Dark* is even further from the picaresque *London Journal* novel than *Temptation*. Consisting almost entirely of dialogue on social issues, in formal terms it imitates the quasi-modernist innovations of Fanny Fern's remarkable *Ruth Hall*. Perhaps Stiff felt it inappropriate and threw Robinson over as Reynolds claimed he had threatened to do with Miller.

Further redefinition of the *London Journal* as brand-name now occurred. Smith was eventually replaced by a combination of pirated stories from American women novelists and a British male author poached from *Cassell's Illustrated Family Paper*, Percy B. St John, who evidently was willing to write to the appropriate formula: his second novel, *Quadroona*, was so successful the by-lines for his later *London Journal* novels would always recall it. E.D.E.N. Southworth and Caroline Lee Hentz had proved immensely popular in America from the early 1850s.[10] While the huge sales of Susan Warner's *Wide, Wide World* and Stowe's *Uncle Tom's Cabin* had already directed attention to American women as a source for fiction, it was 1855 that marked the beginning of over two decades during which the *London Journal* would be identified by an almost equal distribution of American women and British male writers. That year Oliphant realized the potency of American fiction in the 'sensation' market,[11] yet the influence of American fiction in Britain has been vastly underestimated in the twentieth century. Mary Noel (1954: 25) is virtually alone in pointing out that the two popular markets are actually inextricable from one another. As she remarks, stories from the *London Journal*, the *Family Herald* and *Reynolds's Miscellany* were widely pirated in America. The *Journal* had an agent in New York from this date so it was readily available there (see, for example, the advertisement in the *Weekly Times*, 9

---

[10] Tebbel, 1972-81, I: 247; on Hentz, see Baym, 1993: 130-39. More work has been done on Southworth: see Mullane, 1990 for a selection.

[11] [Oliphant], 1855: 562. Oliphant applies the term 'sensation' to the novels of Hawthorne, and later in the same article to Wilkie Collins, and, by implication, to Reade's *Christie Johnson* and *Peg Woffington*.

December 1855: 7). It was actually Southworth's success when pirated in the *Journal* that caused Robert Bonner to engage her for the *New York Ledger*. This in turn caused the *Ledger*'s sales to rise ever higher and the *Journal* to pirate its serials in turn. Yet Southworth's initial import into the *Journal* had almost certainly been a response to the *Family Herald*'s pirating of Fanny Fern's *Ruth Hall* from the *New York Ledger*.

Based on a New York–London axis, this system is thus a complex exchange where each magazine both learns and steals from the successes of the other. One cannot now talk of a parergic system that looks *de bas en haut* or which scrambles for translations from French. That had been a one-way system that did not expect to influence what it raided, whether the culturally up-market or the culture across the Channel. The transatlantic system, by contrast, is dialogic.

The Anglo-male/American-female redefinition of the *London Journal* did not appear as a solution to the loss of Smith at the time, but only emerged in retrospect, for Stiff was still looking for alternative attractions. Now able to mobilize vast profits, in 1856 he approached no less an authority than Bulwer-Lytton, offering him a contract 'on any terms he cared to name'. Bulwer-Lytton declined, but by chance his young friend Miles Gerald Keon, leader writer for the *Morning Post*, who had never before written a novel, was in the room when Stiff called. On the spur of the moment Bulwer-Lytton suggested him. Stiff accepted, terms were duly negotiated, and the result was the short serial *Harding the Moneyspinner* ('Preface', Keon, 1879: ix-xi).

The anonymous *Madame de Marke* took over as front-page attraction several numbers before *Harding* had concluded. Keon evidently did not provide satisfaction, and Stiff now looked elsewhere. By the time *Harding* was being serialized, negotiations had probably already started with Charles Reade. A letter from Reade appeared in the *Journal* on 7 March 1857 (XXV: 16) asking that a note be printed to refute a libel in the *Sunday Times*. Typically for Reade's hot head, a retraction had to be printed a month later (XXV: 96). Reade had finally gained commercial success with *Peg Woffington* and *It Is Never Too Late to Mend* (Burns, 1961: 176) and Stiff no doubt considered that he was now taking on someone tried and tested, unlike Keon. Reade wrote *White Lies* for the *London Journal* (July – December 1857), basing it on his version of a French play by a collaborator of Dumas, Auguste Maquet, *Le Château de Grantier*, the British rights to which Reade had bought for £40 in 1852. As Reade explained, he thought that he had found an opportunity to profit from this material after failing to do so in dramatic form (Reade, 1860: 166-71; see also Coleman, 1903: 230). It is possible he believed that the *Journal*'s reference axis was still London-Paris: always aware of the American market for his own goods, he was perhaps less conscious of the mass-market zone's interest in American imports. He demanded huge sums from the American publisher of *White Lies*, assuring him that 'I am [not] writing beneath my mark, because I happen to be writing in the London Journal. Quite the contrary ... It shall be my best story out and out ...' (quoted in Burns, 1961: 176). A letter from Reade to Bentley on his work for the *Journal* indicates how he felt about it:

It is I am aware the general opinion that a story published in a penny journal is exhausted – I do not think so. I am a great believer in rascally bad type – I believe there is a public that only reads what comes in a readable form. I may be wrong – we shall see: if I am right the London journal [*sic*] will do little more than advertise my story to Public No. 2.

(quoted in Sutherland, 1976: 38)

From this it seems that the story was written with a double market in mind and that Reade considered 'Public No. 2', the up-market one of Bentley, to be his principal target. The *London Journal* was only to act as an advertisement. Quite how this was to be achieved is not clear. Was Reade implying that Bentley's public read the magazine or that they would be attracted by the advertising the *Journal* presumably ran for his story? In any case, his belief in the 'readable form' of *White Lies* was unfounded. While his 1887 hagiography claimed that the novel quadrupled the *Journal*'s readership (Reade and Reade, 1887, II: 42-3), Reade himself was forced to admit privately that it was a disaster — at which point he claimed he'd written it with his left hand (Burns, 1961: 176, and cf. Stevenson, 1888: 33; Anon., 1866: 103; Edwards, 1900: 46-7). The following year (1857, he launched it more specifically at 'Public No. 2' in three-volume format with Trübner – though at his own risk. The critics hated it. It was 'probably the most French novel ever written in English by an Englishman' (Anon., 1862: 148). Later still (1867), Reade reworked it again as a play, stealing the title from the Southworth novel that had run contemporaneously with it in the *Journal*, *The Double Marriage*. Even though Ellen Terry came out of retirement to perform in the drama, it was a resounding flop. The audience burst into laughter at what was supposed to be the pathetic climactic scene (Coleman, 1903: 241-45). Not only East End theatres were now stealing from the *Journal*: Reade took Southworth's title for later editions of his novel as well as for its theatrical incarnation.

Robert Louis Stevenson recalled that *White Lies* 'almost wrecked' the *Journal* (quoted in Mitchell, 1977: 36) and another writer suggested that Reade's 'was not the sort of writing that had any chance with the readers of the *London Journal*' (Anon., 1866: 103). Clearly Stiff was not fully conscious of his consumer profile and, 'in despair at finding any one who could succeed like ... Smith, [Stiff] sold the periodical to Mr Herbert Ingram' (Anon., 1866: 103). Ingram was the proprietor of the *ILN*. The *London Journal* was returning to its origins.

Chapter Six

1857-62. When is a Journal not Itself? or, Mark Lemon and his Successors

> We need not repeat, what is now so generally acknowledged, that our circulation far exceeds that of any of our contemporaries, and that amongst all classes – at the artizan's fireside, as well as in the lady's boudoir – the JOURNAL is a weekly and a welcome guest ... We do not assume the severe aspect of a Public Instructor, but not the less do we seek to render our readers familiar with all that, in English History and English Literature, most concerns them. And above all, it is our pride and our consolation under those occasional discouragements, inseparable from our position – that there is not a line, not a word, in the columns of THE LONDON JOURNAL which unfits it for the perusal of the young and innocent.
>
> ('Preface', XXIX)

In September 1857 Ingram bought the *Weekly Times* and the *London Journal* together for around £30,000.[1] Since a literary property was usually valued at three years' returns (Tuchman, 1989: 169), £30,000 suggests an annual return of £10,000 per year, confirming the anecdotal evidence of its worth. Once again hiding their speculations in the mass market, Bradbury and Evans, the publishers of *Punch* (and now Dickens), entered into a secret partnership with Ingram in the purchase (see Bodleian MS, Eng.Litt.D/398/2, fols. 151-2, 14 June 1859). This zone was evidently not respectable enough for them publicly to be connected with it.

The purchasers placed Mark Lemon, long editor of *Punch*, in charge of their new property (Adrian, 1966: 94-5; Burnand, 1904, II: 168). He tried to rebrand the *London Journal* through a variety of new marketing strategies, chief amongst which was the serialization of three novels by Walter Scott. As mentioned previously, it was a disaster in terms of circulation. Prefaces were usually a space for unabashed self-promotion, but that quoted above, while still claiming the highest circulation of all magazines, was nonetheless forced to admit 'occasional discouragements'. The new owners managed to sell in July 1859, and Lemon retired to *Punch*, bruised by the experience outside his preferred zone.

I am going to argue that Lemon's rebranding and the resulting decline in circulation constituted a misreading of the literary field, caused partly by the new editor's and writers' positions within it. Rather than follow the narrative logic of

---

[1] The exact sum is disputed. In Vizetelly, 1893, II: 10-11 it is £24,000; £20,000 in the *Bookseller* 18, 25 June 1859: 1004-5; when prosecuted by Ingram in 1859 Stiff claimed both £30,000 and £31,500 (*Times*, 8 April 1862: 12). I prefer the version given by *The Times*, since that is when Stiff's accounts are most fully revealed. *The Times* (4 June 1859: 11) assigns the sale to September 1857.

cultural descent that I outlined in previous chapters and so end with a parergic product, or pursue the development of a separate cultural ecosystem that had started with Smith, Lemon sought instead to redefine the *London Journal* by assimilating it into the cultural positions he and his network already wrote from and for. In other words, although in many respects bohemian, he was too unequivocally caught within the cultural desire to unify the field. His failure to achieve his aim is pivotal not only for the *Journal* but, as I suggested in Chapter 2, for the general conceptualization of the entire field by the field itself.

Networks, Names and 'Books'

The first perceptible sign in the *London Journal* of its change in ownership is the introduction of John Hutton into the colophon dated 17 October 1857. I have been able to discover nothing about Hutton, the BL catalogue yielding only three very small titles and his name not appearing in indexes of publishers. His connection with the *Journal* lasted only 32 numbers, to 22 May 1858, though he kept publishing the *Weekly Times* until 1884. Other early modifications included a partial return of a visual aesthetic reminiscent of Ross's, perhaps due initially to the Christmas season: between 7 November and 26 December there was an exceptionally high concentration of art reproduction.

In the 5 December issue more radical changes took place and, although the sale occurred in September, for two reasons I suspect that this issue marked the actual exchange of the magazine between Stiff and Ingram. Firstly, personnel differences were marked. Three signatures appeared for the first time: Mark Lemon's, Charles Smith Cheltnam's (who would only write for the *Journal* under Lemon) and Pierce Egan's, whose first novel for the *Journal* began here. Secondly, there were two exceptional inclusions: an unusually large print of a picture by Gilbert loaned to the Manchester Exhibition, and a reference to Stiff as the picture's owner in the accompanying article. Nowhere was Stiff's relation to the *Journal* stated, though Gilbert is mentioned as being a prolific contributor. If members of the production network could read this combination of reference and signature as greeting Lemon while saying farewell to Stiff, readers outside the network may well have noticed nothing. There is, in fact, no other public announcement of a new proprietor or editor than these oblique signs.

Such a double address is not unusual in this or indeed any zone (see King, 2000) but in retrospect it shows a misunderstanding of what constituted a star name here. For what was the meaning of Lemon's signature for workaday consumers of the *Journal*? While they would certainly have known what the *ILN* or *Punch* stood for in broad outline, they were unlikely to recognize 'Mark Lemon' as a star name. They could never have discovered from the pages of the *Journal* alone that Lemon was editor: the name was always that of one contributor amongst many. When 'Hipparchia' queried the identity of the editor she was wryly refused (Notices to Correspondents, XXVII: 400). The simple appearance of his name at the end of an article or poem, which is where it would always appear, could not establish it as a star name with the same efficacy that heading a front-page novel would, accompanied at least by an advertisement that he was editor of *Punch*.

A more spectacular misreading of the zone lay in Lemon's mishandling of the names 'John Gilbert' and 'Pierce Egan'. Gilbert almost never signed his illustrations and before the casual mention of his name in the 'handover' issue, the only reference to him within the *London Journal* as its illustrator had been in the spring of 1857, in a small notice 'To Our Readers' (XXV: 112) that had mentioned his drawings for the anonymous serial *Madame de Marke*. In fact, until Lemon, the only name to appear regularly on Gilbert's illustrations for the *Journal* was 'W. Gorway', a name on *London Journal* prints for over forty years. Readers were more likely to think 'Gorway' the artist, rather than the atelier of engravers it actually was (I certainly did before my researches). Only a constant reader with a very good memory would remember the couple of casual references to Gilbert. It is true that Gilbert had by the late 1850s gained a reputation in art galleries for his history paintings and, much less publicly since he did not regularly sign his illustrations, in the *ILN*. Readers of *Macmillan's Magazine* in 1859 were assumed to know who he was:

> [Gilbert's] designs for the long-winded tales [are] published in penny periodicals. We need hardly call attention to the spirit and vigour of Mr Gilbert's designs, or point them out as an instance of the power of life-like art to attract an immense audience, to remunerate the publishers, and extend the artist's fame.   ([Stephens], 1859: 49)

Following the logic of chapter 2, we realize that *Macmillan's* readers were located in a zone more likely to go to galleries and buy pictures than the *Journal*'s. Stephens's assumption that Gilbert was spreading his 'fame' – and therefore his name – by illustrating penny periodicals simply ignores the priorities and knowledges of actual readers of such publications: yet another example of the narcissistic epistemological problems I described in Chapter 1. Readers of the *Journal* on the contrary may well have had only a vague idea what 'Gilbert' signified. Almost certainly they would not have known his relation to their magazine.

Readers in the *Journal*'s zone of the field were far more likely to know what kind of product the name 'Egan' was associated with. Egan had provided illustrations for the *ILN* in 1842 (*Times*, 8 July 1880: 10), and, while this is perhaps how he came to find a place in Ingram's new purchase, it would hardly have guaranteed product recognition. However, there are numerous reasons for him to be regarded as already a minor luminary in the penny fiction zone, a star in the making whose brightness could easily have been magnified by appropriate handling. First, he belonged to a dynasty of journalists. His father was the Pierce Egan who had run his own newspapers (*DNB*, VI: 560-62) and written *Tom and Jerry* in 1821, which was so famous it became a catchword (see Mackay, 1852: 628). Second, Pierce Egan the younger had published sixteen novels since 1839, some in penny parts illustrated by himself, and others in *Reynolds's Miscellany* (Summers, [1940]: 39-40; *DNB*, VI: 562-64). Thirdly, he had been a named illustrator of numerous penny plays, such as the version of *Oliver Twist* by George

Almar (1840). Finally, he had been editor of a minor rival to the *London Journal,* W.S. Johnson's *Home Circle* (1849-54 – see *Times,* 8 July 1880: 10). 'Egan' was therefore already established as a name in a zone proximate to the *Journal*'s when not indeed overlapping with it. Yet when his first novel is announced by Lemon in the *Journal* in November 1857, it is granted little space in the advertisement and his name is not given. All that is said is that arrangements have been made with 'A POPULAR AUTHOR' for 'A NEW AND INTERESTING TALE' (XXVI: 176, 192, 208). Lemon curiously did not capitalize on 'Egan' as a name at this stage.

This sidelining of the unconsecrated name in favour of the more up-market artist was not unequivocal, however. 'Egan' *was* granted considerable typographical prominence in advertisements for his second novel, *The Snake in the Grass,* while Gilbert's name is smaller. Furthermore, the frame to this advert was very elaborate (see XXVII: 160). Such apparent acceptance of the power of Egan's name in the zone did not last, for immediately after *The Snake* Egan was let go. He was not consonant with Lemon's project to rebrand the magazine. An envoi to the last episode of *The Snake,* dated 27 November 1858, 'respectfully craves leave of absence for a brief period'.

[The author] wishes [his readers] to understand that he parts with them as one who leaves relatives and dear friends only for a short time, that he may recruit health and strength, as well as replenish his mental resources, so that he may come back to the magazine with re-invigorated powers ...   (XXVIII: 239)

If this excuse sounds remarkably like the public reason why today's soap-stars leave when really they are eased out because they no longer fit the soap's profile, the *DNB* (VI: 563) explains that Egan was 'dispensed with ... to encourage a higher taste among the purchasers of penny miscellanies'. His removal must have been a crucial decision in the story of Lemon's failure, for Egan's two novels with their feisty heroines in risqué situations were recognizable *London Journal* types. They had taken on board the lessons of Smith on the high-tension picaresque, and of Robinson and the American women authors on the centrality of women characters. Not least, they continued the 'practical morality' that emphasized Christian charity and making the best of a bad job. The icy aristocratic heroine of *The Flower* appears to be the mother of an illegitimate child until the last episode, when she and we learn that she was legally married after all. Before this at no point are we to condemn her, the appropriate response being modelled by the contrasted sempstress heroine who assists her spiritually, emotionally, financially and physically in an inversion of the usual beneficent *grande dame* trope. It was precisely this kind of liberal practical morality, a kind evidenced in the illuminating work of Barret-Ducrocq (1991) on Coram's Fields Foundling Hospital – 'it's unfortunate, dear, and you shouldn't, but it'll be alright if we help one another' – that Lemon was determined to eradicate. After Egan, high, pure, absolute moral principles return *en masse.*

The promotion of the up-market name 'Gilbert' was by no means unique. In his determination to raise the level of taste, Lemon insistently promoted many names and practices from his own zone. He proudly advertised that the illustrations to

Scott's *Fortunes of Nigel* were *legally* reproduced from the Abbotsford edition (XXVII: 416), as if readers in the penny fiction zone would perforce care. From February 1859, the names of the *Journal*'s artists were printed prominently on the monthly covers as well as in a contents list Lemon introduced on the front page of each weekly issue. 'Gilbert' was highlighted (as one would now expect), along with T.H. Wilson; new were E. Weedon, Julian Portch, Percival Skelton and ten other artists and engravers. Many contributed to the *ILN*, unsurprisingly strengthening the connection between the two periodicals. Retained from Stiff's management was the artist Frederick Skill, but White and Sargent, once mainstays, no longer appeared. Amongst the many writers whose names now studded the *Journal* were Lemon's brother-in-law Frank Romer, Dudley and Louisa Costello, Albany Fonblanque, and Marguerite Power. All wrote for the quarterlies and reviews or other up-market publications. The poetry now included works not only by Charles Smith Cheltnam but also by J.E. Carpenter, William Allingham, Mrs Hemans, Charles Kingsley, and so on. If some, like James MacFarlan or Sir Edward James Reed are today unknown, like all the other poets under Lemon they nonetheless had a presence within the prestige zones of publishing. It is comparatively easy to find out information connected to them – itself an indicator of their status. But they are names that are either unknown in the mass-market zone or they carry *too much cultural weight*.

It is instructive to compare the poetry in previous volumes of the *Journal* with that under Lemon. Under Stiff a great deal of it, if not indeed the overall majority, had been written by readers. It had been included both within Notices to Correspondents, where its location makes its origin clear, and 'inside' the magazine at various points to fill up column space. In this second form it looks the same as the poetry from established poets the *Journal* also printed, such as Charles Swain. Divorced from any association with Notices to Correspondents, such a position lends the reader's poem an authoritative air: the only way we can tell the poem is not by a 'professional' writer is by carefully tracking the migrations of the poets' names between Notices to Correspondents and the rest of the magazine over considerable periods (a tedious occupation unlikely for most *London Journal* readers). The status so offered must have been very attractive, as some poets sent in poems for many years: one such was 'L.M. Thornton' whose many contributions began in 1855. While by no means all readers' offerings were accepted, they were least refused politely with sometimes learned admonitions to write more 'modern' verse (a slippery instruction, which in the quotation below meant less erotic):

> Rusticus. Well written, but too Anacreontic for modern taste. Some of Moore's best lyrics are only read by a few of the morally educated in the present day. Consider our remarks in the light of a suggestion to try something more applicable.   (XXV: 272)

This tone was continued under Lemon for a few months, until suddenly contributions received firm yet casual rejection, insultingly cold and unhelpful:

> James Onions, James Goodrich, and Batey (Harpertown). – There is nothing new or remarkable in your lines that we should insert them.   (XXVII: 112)

From then on poetry came from poetic *vates* with established credentials, 'fine taste' and 'lofty genius' – criteria of excellence set down in a review, under Lemon, of E.J. Trelawney's *Recollections of the Last Days of Shelley and Byron* (XXVII: 127). As the epigraph to this chapter put it, '[w]e do not assume the severe aspect of a Public Instructor, but not the less do we seek to render our readers familiar with all that, in English History and English Literature, most concerns them'. A special department, 'Songs and Ballads of England', was set up 'to furnish our readers with the best songs and ballads of our best English poets, appending explanatory notes and brief biographical data when necessary, so that they may enter with enjoyment upon the study of a more delightful portion of English literature' (XXVIII: 63). In fact, this department effectively excluded reader-contributors: 'L.M. Thornton' found nothing accepted under Lemon.

   Despite (or because of?) this commitment to established poets, Lemon continued to publish his own poetry: contributions by his editorial assistant W.H. Davenport Adams by far outnumbered those of any other one writer over the whole 'Lemon period':

Love and Reason – 'tis told
By the minstrels of old –
One eve went a-roaming, a-roaming;
Tho' Reason avow'd
There was fate in the cloud,
And ominous, too, was the gloaming.
On, on thro' the dells,
Where chime blossom-bells,
And o'er the green moorland they wander'd,
And down by the stream –
Love all in a dream,
While Reason grave theorems ponder'd!   ('Love and Reason', W.H.D.A., XXVIII: 127)

Two stanzas later Love leaped into the stream in a fit of enthusiasm and was swept away. The moral is directed to 'maidens' to 'take heed'.

   Reader-contributors had the cultural capital to match this. What they did not have were Adams's or Lemon's access to print or social capital. And the magazine, for all its supposed educative aims, now ensured that they did not get them. Readers were deprived of models that seemed to be produced by themselves (whether these models really were all produced by readers is unimportant for my argument here). Instead, they were either given models with so much symbolic capital that they could not hope to compete, or were kept out by Adams and Lemon's self-satisfaction in the value of their own products. This is what I meant when I referred above to names in the *London Journal* now carrying 'too much weight'. Lemon refused to acknowledge the cultural validity of production in zones other than where he felt he himself belonged.

   Granting readers the magic of symbolic capital by allowing their works and names to appear in print had been one of the functions of *London Journal* poetry. Now reader-contributors were increasingly confined to two other places in the magazine with very little status indeed. Firstly, they were kept within Notices to

Correspondents where editorial replies were printed and their own voices very rarely materialized. Secondly, they now started to send in enigmas for the new department, 'The Sphynx'. Whereas sixteen names appeared under puzzles in 'The Sphynx' within just the twelve issues in which it appears in volume XXVII, there were only twelve poems signed by reader-contributors in the entire volume. In volume XXVIII there were nine. Besides contributors of riddles, there was now a profusion of names of readers who sent in the correct answers. There is a definite pleasure in seeing your name or pseudonym in print for solving or formulating a riddle. But it is not as powerful as becoming a Printed Poet.

I suggest that there had been an intertwined complex of fantasies operating in readers' contribution of poetry (and tales) under Stiff that Lemon completely misunderstood. Firstly, readers had been offered the idea that they were part of a community of writers (not just readers). They were able to occupy print space proximate to star names, and were thus offered a fantasy of social capital: they could produce as well as consume the text in a dream of artisanal co-operative production, where alienation between the impersonal mass-produced commodity and the consumer was overcome. A second strand, which will require longer unravelling, involves the parergic in so far as the latter means that consecration should constantly be aspired to yet never quite reached. To reach it in reality would mean that reader-purchasers themselves would have to change habitus, which would make them unfitted for and alienated from the places they occupy in the wider fields of social hierarchization and political power. This transformation of society is what in effect Lemon was trying to do, but with rather different intended results. His vision was, no doubt, that workers would absorb his culture and learn their places, rather than feel alienated from his product.

Here I want to introduce the concept of 'ownership' of the magazine which opens out the previous paragraph to readers more generally. By 'ownership' here I do not refer to its legal or commercial senses – ownership of the production process and product – but the even more fantastic process of 'ownership' of a text during reading. This process of reader 'ownership' operates in several different ways and to varying degrees of relationship to the name. At the simplest level, before the 'Lemon period', a good deal of the *Journal*'s contents, words and pictures, had been either completely anonymous, signed only with mysterious initials or by-lines, or raided from elsewhere. Rarely was the origin of texts heavily marked. The very act of raiding, even when it was acknowledged, undermined an unequivocal authority of origins. Anonymity set images free to be anchored elsewhere, such as in the texts they illustrated, not in the name of the artist, as individual art objects traditionally have been ('a Raphael', 'a Gilbert'). Readers could themselves fill the void left by anonymity and thus themselves 'own' the magazine. Lemon on the other hand anchored the *London Journal* with a profusion of names in all possible places, including the new contents lists on the front pages (see Figures 6.3, 6.4 below).

Secondly, anonymity could hide the manufacture of the magazine (with its implications of division of labour, management, alienation, commercialism). In place of multiple industrial sources, a reader could imagine a single unified origin. Mayhew (1851-62, I: 25) reported precisely this belief amongst costermongers:

"Don't the cove as did that know a deal?' for they fancy – at least many do – that one man writes a whole periodical, or a whole newspaper ...'. Charles Mackay (1877, II: 67) reported the same even of *ILN* readers. This is a nostalgic fantasy of unalienated artisanal production related to overcoming the consumer-producer alienation I mentioned above.

Even when star names were used, if reader-contributors could see themselves sharing print space with them, their names were emptied to some extent of alienating individuality and symbolic power. Furthermore, by the Lemon period many star names operated as indicators of product-types, not authorial ownership. 'J.F. Smith' or the 'Bulwer-Lytton', whom Stiff had tried to obtain for the *Journal*, were brand names for kinds of literary experience in this zone, like 'Stephen King' or 'Jackie Collins' today. Later in the century, Smith was regarded as the founder of a '*London Journal* school of fiction', his name transferred from a particular work onto a sub-genre. This is confirmed in the frequency of the by-line which lists other works associated with the name: Smith's *The Will and the Way* is by 'the Author of "The Jesuit", "The Prelate", "Minnigrey", &c.'. In a gesture meant to advertize the name's other works, the by-line effectively defined the name as a category of fictional experience, rather than as the creator-owner of an individual work. And, of course, in a legal sense, many authors in this zone, including Smith, never 'owned' their works, instead selling the copyright to a publisher. This again only encourages a generic approach to writing: it was more important to reproduce the generic house style rather than try to stamp a text with a personal identity.

A third aspect follows on from this and concerns the apparent 'sources' of *London Journal* novels. I want to argue that the habitus Mark Lemon tried to impose took the part of literacy in the nineteenth-century battle between it and oral culture. The habitus of reader-purchasers of Stiff's *London Journal* were, on the other hand, closer to the latter. While it seems an absurdity to claim that a printed artefact is 'oral', I propose that under Stiff the *Journal* nonetheless took into account 'the continuing vitality of oral modes of entertainment and the prevailing weakness of the new tools of literacy' (Vincent, 1989: 219). I have already referred to how Smith's novels took on board the oral elements of broadsheet tradition, but I think an even more important relationship resides in how, in the nineteenth century as today, mass-market tales are bricolages of narrative *objets trouvés*. This relates directly to their lack of author-ownership. Such stories do not have the clearly personal and coherent voice that writers rich in symbolic capital have usually sought to achieve in the prestige novel (or which has been read into what has become the prestige novel). In this sense mid-nineteenth-century mass-market tales approach oral folk tales such as the *Odyssey,* where the tale-teller is not an originating author but a relayer or medium of variations on the narrative (cf. Ong, 1982: 20-30). In this zone there is no construction of a 'George Eliot' who, in complex ways and however ironically, will act as a guarantor and source of the work's uniqueness. *London Journal* tales are, in this sense, anonymous *even when they are attributed authors.* Wilkie Collins was right when he wrote that the novels in the different penny weeklies could have been written by the same person. In writing that he meant to ridicule them, for the cliché-ridden text is scandalous to the low-circulation/high-prestige zone, partly because the lack of a unique vatic source written into the textual fabric undermines the idea of the originating Genius. This the high-prestige market had for some time been promoting as an eternal verity through its various forms of advertising (including, of course, criticism). The cliché – which we should rename as formula (*pace* Feltes, 1986) following students of oral narrative – is the basis of a market in which the iterability of a written text is of less importance than momentum from one weekly episode to another. That is, it is less important to be able to reread a novel in this market and to recall its details, than to find out what happens next. This is exactly Dutch Debbie's point in *Children of the Ghetto*: she is able to reread only because she forgets.

While the surviving copies of the *London Journal* are in volume format, and hence tempt book-like attentive reading, their rarity is important. This is not only because of a systematic neglect or destruction by prestige culture as I suggested in Chapter 1. Weekly issues of the *Journal*, stripped to essentials and open to the elements, present a stark contrast to the clothed book. The covers, the title-page, the frontispiece and endpapers all protect the volume against time and the external world. Such technological life jackets were available to bind collections of issues, but only as optional extras: through the economic investment of a penny for the title page and volume index, and the cost of binding the volume, reader-purchasers could raise the symbolic value of what they have already invested in. The rarity of the volumes suggests that most readers did not consider the *Journal* worth the investment: its symbolic capital was both too low to invest in financially and/or the economic outlay was not easily available. As a book, whether bought in volume format or bound into one by purchasers, the *London Journal* was expensive for most of its target audience. At 4/6 for a ready-bound volume in the late 1850s it was actually 2/- more expensive than a volume of *Household Words*. In a *London Journal* Christmas article on books for children, printed under Lemon, most books reviewed cost between 1/6 and 3/6 (XXVIII: 300-301), and even these would have been prohibitively expensive for readers on £100 a year or less. In an essay on 'Books' in 1851, a major point is that weekly issues of the magazine *are* affordable, even to those on ten shillings a week, whereas 'books' were not (XIV: 218-19). From the economic point of view, then, a bound volume of the *London Journal* was in excess of its cultural value as a book. The place where economic and cultural values intersected lay in the *Journal*'s status as a periodical, with the ephemerality that that implies, as opposed to the potential for longevity the book always carries within itself. The successful formula novel took account of this ephemerality and of forgetting. Even in rereading, the nature of the *London Journal* was to be less iterable than disposable.

Reading aloud to groups engaged in other activities (as in Zangwill's novel) comprised a large part of the popular consumption of the printed word. Webb (1955: 34) notes how one worker read aloud in the workplace while listeners carried on with their work and did his task for him. The headpiece of the *Illustrated Family Journal* (Figure 6.1), like the better-known one of *Cassell's Illustrated Family Paper* (Figure 5.1), presents a model of the ideal reading situation in the form of a family where the father is reading, the women are sewing while a female servant is standing in the background ready to assist. Reading aloud in a family certainly went on in circles where the prestige text demanded and was given dutiful and disciplined attention: in a letter to Scott from 1814, Maria Edgeworth writes of reading his *Waverley* in this way (Hayden, 1970: 75-78).

Figure 6.1 Headpiece from the *Illustrated Family Journal*, 8 March 1845

But what we know of audience behaviour amongst other social groups suggests a more disrespectful and vocal involvement. At the least, reading aloud in groups which do not respectfully fetishize the text means being interrupted by children asking what words mean and adults commenting on the story or the way it is being read, all while other tasks are being carried out. Rose (2001: 87-8) tells of one family where the mother read out serials from the *Family Reader* and discussed them with the grandmother, while every few minutes the father would interject items from the newspaper he was reading. The formulaic nature of the novels under Stiff means that the text does not impose its authority by demanding careful attention. But even when it was read in solitude, there was probably little time to reread an episode before the next came out the following week. Besides the pressure of work, several readers would pass one copy between them as in Lark Rise (cf. Vizetelly, 1893, II: 12). This implies little time in which to reread or even read carefully. Formulaic phrases and plots assist readers to cover the gaps, allowing them more easily to 'grasp' the text. Certainly this is what I and several of my students have discovered when trying to recreate such reading practices both in and out of class.

The final aspect of 'ownership' I want to consider here returns to the practice of raiding. Under Lemon, explicit raids are much reduced, not only from *Punch* but also from other magazines. The number of acknowledged raids from *Punch* drops from 128 in volume XVII, and 170 in volume XXI (both under Stiff) to a mere 14 in volume XXVII, the first volume under Lemon's editorship. There are none (at least acknowledged) after that. On Stiff's repurchase, the number immediately rises again: volume XXX, in which Stiff is in control after the first two issues, offers 75, none of which occur in the issues under Lemon. Unsurprisingly, Lemon will not have the magazine he most closely identifies with dismembered to feed another. He has a more respectful attitude to the *producers'* ownership of the text and to the copyright laws that prioritize that. Readers, on the other hand, unable to know (because uninformed) that the editor of *Punch* was now the editor of the *London Journal*, would only have noticed that they were no longer allowed the complex pleasures of raiding.

As I have already commented, the cultural direction of raiding is not properly reversible. While the down-market East End theatres may have come to raid the *London Journal*, *Punch*, as more up-market, cannot do so. When the latter appears in *Punch* in 1863, several years after Lemon had departed from the *Journal*, it is in the form of a caricature, *Mokeanna*. The author of the latter was an educated upper-middle-class young man set on making his name in the *Punch* zone, Francis Burnand. Forty years after the event, having been *Punch*'s editor for over twenty years, he set down an account of his first success. But he confused the *London Journal*, *Reynolds's Miscellany* and the *Family Herald* – the last was what Bradbury and Evans were actually publishing at the time. Such lack of accuracy is instructive of the ways the penny periodical zone was regarded.

Burnand had the idea of writing a burlesque of penny fiction as a way of gaining notoriety in *Fun* or *Punch*:

> Gilbert's dashing illustrations to some story caught my eye in the window of the office where the current number of *Reynolds'* was sold, and, after supplying myself with sufficient material, I took it home with me to Richmond and at once started upon it ...
>
> (Burnand, 1904, I: 410)

Burnand was able to meet Lemon, who was delighted at the idea.

> 'Bravo!' [said Lemon] and then as if struck by a brilliant idea (as it was), he cried in his rich husky voice, and in the most jovial manner, 'We'll have it illustrated! I'll get the artists to burlesque themselves! ... We'll have it set up at once- and,' ... here he became excessively confidential, as beaming with the brilliancy of the notion, he said to [Burnand] in a confidential tone, 'We'll have it set up as a facsimile of *The London Journal* or *Reynolds'*!! Mum! Not a word to a soul ...   (Burnand, 1904, I: 420)

Although *Mokeanna* was to cause a sensation, it almost never reached distribution. Bradbury, the senior partner of *Punch*'s publishers, had been unable to attend the office.

> [O]n receiving his early copy of *Punch* on the Sunday previous to its date of issue, [Bradbury] was utterly horrified, on opening it, to see, as he thought, the first page of *The London Journal* (or of *Reynolds'* I forget which it was) appearing as the first page of *Punch*! The error was just possible, as *The London Journal* (or *Reynolds'*) was at that time printed by Messrs. Bradbury & Evans.   (Burnand, 1904, I: 421)

Bradbury was furious and wanted to stop the issue, thinking it 'a risky departure from the beaten track', but he was persuaded otherwise by Lemon and Evans. By the second number he had accepted that the serial 'had made a decided hit' (Burnand, 1904, I: 421).

Pace Burnand, Bradbury and Evans were no longer printing or publishing the *Journal* in 1863, but the point of the anecdote remains that Lemon's apparent delight with *Mokeanna* confirms his refusal of the literary dynamics of the the the *London Journal* zone. He had failed to appreciate that in the hands of readers who are distant from the market of the auratic named and owned Art Object, the great advantage of an assemblage of formulae is that it can more easily be appropriated. It is interesting that readers of *Punch* were expected to have only a vague knowledge of the zone: from the second episode *Mokeanna* moves to works that *Punch*'s readers were more likely to have been acquainted with, Wilkie Collins, Mrs Henry Wood and Mary Braddon's triple-decker sensation fiction.

MOKEANNA,
OR THE WHITE WITNESS*.
A TALE OF THE TIMES.

Dramatically divided into Parts, by the Author of 'Matringa', ''Ollow Arts', 'Geronimo the Gipsy,' 'The Dark Girl', 'Dustman of Destiny,' &c. &c.

PART I.– THE OVERTURE IN THE ORCHESTRA.

CHAP. I

'For oh! it was a grölling night.'
RARE OLD SONG.

The clock on the old Church Tower had scarcely sounded the last stroke of one A.M., when the little fishing village of Rederring, on the coast of Rutlandshire, was shaken to its very foundations by the fierce wind that dashed the towering and hissing billows against the red-beetling crags of the white-cliffed shore.

'A nasty night,' growled the Coast-guardsman, who, according to ancient custom, was sitting on the highest point of land with his feet in hot water; 'but I must keep my watch, silently, silently!' Then singing in a lusty voice the old Norse ditty:–

'With a hey, with a ho!
When the wind does blow!'

He cautiously lay down among the rank and damp herbage. A small boat battling with the waves came towards the shore. Not a soul was within it. Onward, onward, until at length, with a fearful lurch, it was hurled upon the shingle.

PART II. – THE PIT.
CHAP. I.

'Slay him'
FOL. DE BOLLO THE ROVA, B.I.C.2

Two dark forms crept from beneath the keel.

'England at last,' said the taller of the two, in a gruff whisper.

'Is it?' inquired the other. The speaker was a short, stout, hunchbacked man, about six feet three in height, enveloped in a light P-jacket loosely thrown over his shoulder …

---

* The Author begs to inform everybody, including his friends, that he has protected the dramatic right in this thrillingly sensational novel, by having caused several versions of the same to be made for Farces, Burlesques, Melodramas and Operas, respectively. A reduction on taking a quantity …   (*Punch*, XLIV: 71; see Figure 6.2)

Figure 6.2 'Night Flight of the White Witness o'er the Dismal Wold', [Francis Burnand], opening of *Mokeanna*
Source: Punch, XLIV: 71, 21 February 1863.

While parody can always be regarded as in some sense a compliment to the object parodied (and it is the authority of financial rewards that is implicitly acknowledged here), this is of less concern to me than exactly what is being mocked. The success of many *London Journal* novels in theatrical versions is directly alluded to, its refusal of the values of the autonomous side of the field spotlighted by the warning footnote and its ready-for-dramatization division into 'Parts'. In stylistic terms, the longwinded mixes with the laconic, successions of clichés with geographical gaffs and invented authorities for epigraphs (J.F. Smith used to invent poetic epigraphs from imaginary sources with auratic titles, the commonest being 'The Heir of the Sept.'). Most of the comedy derives from the illogicality of the prose, which depends on self-contradiction. In any assemblage of formulae that prioritizes narrative momentum over narrative unity, one cliché may well contradict another. I want to rename these unintentional contradictions 'contrascriptions' because they assume importance only when read from a place where textual coherence is prioritized; that is, where a text is taken to mean an iterable written document from which producers can erase inconsistencies before the reader receives the text, and which the reader can scan backwards to look both for connections to make a unity (considered as ideal) and for inconsistencies which reveal fragmentation (considered as a flaw). Abjection of the contrascriptory can exist only in a place where economic and cultural capitals and their concretizations in the form of artificial heat and light, time and mental energy permit the scrutiny of texts. Even when, like George Eliot's *Romola*, it is serialized in a magazine, the high-status novel aims for the ejection of the contrascriptory, assuming a reader with the cultural and economic capitals to identify and condemn it.

Contrascriptions are, at least in theory, intolerable in the high-status sector. They are scandalous because they are associated with the non-literate lower classes who are excluded and exclude themselves from the reading spaces and practices of the culturally and economically powerful. They are scandalous because they are associated with the venal side of the field at a time when Art was usually presented by critics as beyond economics. They deny the fixity of knowledge and stability of viewpoint that Ong and Couturier after him see as encouraged by printing (Ong, 1982: 135; Couturier, 1991: vii-viii). Finally, contrascriptions are 'fraud' in that they reveal that the producers have not laboured sufficiently to remove them: texts which are contrascriptory are shoddy goods and do not give value for money (cf. Anon. (1859) discussed in Chapter 2 above). It is no surprise therefore that unity should be a sign of 'distinction' in the sense given it by Bourdieu (1984), with the result that in prestige zones the formula novels of the penny press are only permissible as parody or, as in so much of Chapter 2, as exotic objects of study.

Ivanhoe in the *London Journal*: National and Gender Cleansing

Of all Lemon's changes to the *London Journal* his serialization of three Scott novels became the paradigmatic example. *Ivanhoe*, the last of these after *Kenilworth* and *The Fortunes of Nigel* was run between March and November 1859. In July, however, the *Journal* was resold to Stiff. I shall deal in this subsection almost exclusively with the serialization of *Ivanhoe* under Lemon (to 23 July 1859), as under Stiff it loses its illustrations and is relegated to an insignificant position.

Scott's success as a novelist from 1814 with the publication of *Waverley* is well known. He is often regarded as 'popular' until the 1880s (Hayden, 1970: 16-17; DeGategno, 1994: 12). In 1824, even the hostile Hazlitt had to admit that Scott was the most 'popular' writer of the age. *Blackwood's* still regarded him as an irresistible force in 1858: '[reading Scott] we are carried on, if not with the force of a torrent, yet with the swift unpausing current of a strong river' ([Smith], 1858: 59). Around 1847, Scott's publisher Cadell was worth around £121,000 (Millgate, 1987: 51), largely due to the sale of 60,000 volumes of Scott's work over a twenty-year period (Jeffrey, 1849: 523, note). While such sales are of course low for the penny fiction market, the profits were not. Scott remained an expensive luxury. 'Popular' he may have been amongst the book-buying public; 'mass-market' he was not. As the *Journal* announced soon after it began serializing *Kenilworth* in April 1858:

> Scott has been placed in the hands of the peer, the merchant, the scholar, and the wealthy trader, in a hundred shapes. He will now, for the first time, be introduced to the PEOPLE in the pages of The London Journal, and at a merely nominal price!   (XXVII: 174)

While Scott arrived in the *London Journal* carrying a great deal of vatic weight, there are two more aspects of the name that the *Journal* wraps it in: Scott's image as a patriarch and as an 'English' classic. Both were directly related to the perception of British popular reading-matter both as 'feminine' and, increasingly, as 'non-British'.

Tuchman (1989) has argued that men invaded the novel between 1840 and 1880, resulting in a split between the male up-market and feminine mass-market. One can see how this trend is acted out in the *Journal*. During the Crimean War, the number of female signatures in the *Journal* had undergone a remarkable increase, not only amongst the serial novelists but amongst the one-episode tales and articles written by authors who attributed themselves feminine markers within the text, such as 'J.C.', and Anne Marie Maillard. None of these survived Ingram's take-over. Neither did those male writers sympathetic to women such as John Parsons Hall. All regular women writers disappeared apart from Marguerite Power, the niece of the Countess of Blessington and editor of the extremely up-market (and by the mid-1850s old-fashioned) annual, *The Keepsake*. Power contributed one novel, *Too Late* (1858–59). A few well-established women such as Adelaide Ann Proctor (XXVII: 303, 343) had short poems reprinted, but on the whole Lemon purged the *Journal* of women. This is not to say that women readers were *altogether* neglected or rejected. There was in fact a sudden but thinly-spread efflorescence of material aimed specifically at them between August to December 1858: 'On the Cultivation of the Voice', 'A Gossip about the Hair' and 'The Piano' between them offer a total of eleven items on feminine pursuits over five months. It is unlikely, however, that most women readers of the *Journal* were training their voices (and if so would perform the tedious exercises offered), were fascinated by ancient Roman hairstyles or were delighting in dry reviews of piano music. The attempts to interest them were hopelessly inappropriate as well as half-hearted.

Women novelists were replaced by two male ones, Egan and Scott. As stated, Egan lasted for only two novels. Even though his work lacks blatant contrascription and alludes readily to respectable texts (for example, the opening of *The Flower of the Flock* inverts *Bleak House*'s initial paragraph, turning fog into ironic sunshine), it was no doubt too 'feminine' in its heavy concentration on the subjectivity of the heroines. Scott, by contrast, was robustly masculine. In a two-part biography printed in the *Journal* in May 1858, he is described as 'Manly' [*sic*] and as a 'gladiator' (XXVII: 174), a construction in line with other criticism of the time. Carlyle (1838: 342-3) had described him as 'a brave proud man of the world

... a proud strong man, he girt himself to the Hercules' task ... to his Hercules' task like a very man ...'. A famous article insistently defined Scott as 'vigorous' with 'a strong sense and genial mind', most of whose work 'suit[s] the occupied man of genial middle life' (Bagehot, 1858: 445, 446, 447, 450, 459). Even though *Ivanhoe* was one of those works 'addressed to a simpler sort of imagination, – to that kind of boyish fancy which idolizes mediaeval society as the 'fighting time'' (Bagehot, 1858: 460), it was still regarded as a masculine book. It came to the *London Journal* with a reputation as a work by a writer suitable for middle-aged patriarchs and as peculiarly appropriate for their sons. This in turn suggests that Lemon, like Hawthorne in America, regarded readers in the mass market as children who needed weaning from the trashy maternal pap of the 'd—d mob of scribbling women' specializing in sensation.

In replacing women novelists with Scott, Lemon was also cleansing the magazine of un-'Englishness'. For Stowe, Hentz, Fanny Fern and Southworth were all, of course, American. To suggest that 'Scott' be treated as an 'English' antidote to them may cause surprise given his national origin. But despite the appearance in the illustrated advertisement for *Kenilworth* of two ambiguous icons of Scottishness – possibly a plaid draped over a Celtic harp (XXVII: 96, 112, 128) – only Scott's 'English' novels were selected for serialization in the *Journal*. Although a previous article had identified Abbotsford, Scott's residence, as on the Tweed (XXVII: 174), a description of it does not actually say where it was. The only national adjective in the entire article is 'English' (XXVII: 285). In an earlier biography, Scott is associated with 'English literature' and its most potent modern representative:

> As long as English literature endures, as long as men reverence the power of genius, the name of Scott will be a 'household word'. No writer, except Shakspeare, has contributed so largely to the amusement and edification of the world... Scott, indeed, in many things resembled Shakspeare ...   (XXVII: 157)

The biography rapidly skims over his Scottish novels while enthusing about the English ones at much greater length. His use of Scottish dialect and customs is reduced to the two phrases 'his quaint and peculiar research' (XXVII: 157) and 'auld nick-nackets' (XXVII: 174) – a touristic reduction of Scott's engagement with Scottish culture very similar to what we saw in the *Journal*'s first issue. Under Lemon, though, the appropriation of Scott for England is part of a larger politographic restriction that contradicts the *Journal*'s original complaisant roving. Numerous series that emphasize English heritage start up: 'Homes of English Worthies', 'Songs and Ballads of England', 'English Novelists', 'London in the Olden Time', 'Stories from the Old Dramatists', 'Sketches in the English Lake District', 'Castles on the Coast' and so on. In many ways too the *Journal* becomes more geographically anchored in London. Series on 'The Benevolent Institutions Of London', 'London In The Olden Time', 'Inside London' and one called 'Days Out' address inhabitants of the capital. There is also a series for the residents of northern industrial towns, 'Away North', and 'Castles on the Coast' ranges over Britain, but between them they offer a total of only eleven parts over thirteen months. This suggests a preference for the metropolitan (and indeed 'bourgeois') that Feltes (1986) rightly saw in Dickens: after all, Lemon and Dickens were part of the same cultural zone, and might be expected to invoke similar readerships.

Figure 6.3 'Cedric the Saxon – Drawn by John Gilbert', Walter Scott, *Ivanhoe*
Source: XXIX: 177.

In short, the constellation American-women-sensation was replaced by another: English/London-men-history. This was more consonant with *Punch*'s misogyny, its anti-Americanism and its anti-sensation novel stance, rather than with actual currents in the penny fiction magazine zone.[2] There topicality was the order of the

---

[2] On Lemon's misogyny, see Fisher, 1988. For examples of attitudes to women in *Punch*, see XXXV: 181 (30 October 1858); XXXV: 192 (6 November 1858); XXXVI: 117 (19

day. *Reynolds's Miscellany* was running *The Sepoys: or, Highland Jessie. A Tale of the Present English Revolt* by 'M.J. Errym'; *Cassell's Illustrated Family Paper* was serializing J.F. Smith's *Smiles and Tears; A Tale of Our Own Times* and running numerous prints and articles on the Indian uprising. Lemon was not keeping an eye on rivals in the appropriate zone or indeed in trends in any zone. Historical novels had been losing popularity in the upper end of the market since the end of the 1840s (Simmons, 1973: 55, 60) and contemporary settings had overtaken the historical in the penny weekly zone too. Gilbert's elaborate prints in the style of historical anecdote pictures would only have served to stress the magazine's backward-looking gaze. Lemon seems to have realized this when he replaced the words of *Ivanhoe* on the front page with the sensation novel *Violet Davenant; or, the Red Hand* by Bayle St John.

Scott's *Kenilworth* and *The Fortunes of Nigel* had been kept in second position behind Pierce Egan's romances; *Ivanhoe* by contrast was projected as the *Journal*'s lead novel on its front page. Its first illustration is the usual size for *London Journal* front pages (roughly 12cm x 19cm), but the second initiates a new look, the size of the illustration increased by a half (roughly 18cm x 19cm) (Figure 6.3). This new glamour is clearly a bid to attract purchasers, and, if Reynolds's logic followed, should be interpreted as a reaction to having already lost many.

Gilbert and his engravers clearly worked carefully over these new-style prints, and, apart from those for *Faust* in 1846, they are closer to his historical anecdote paintings than to his previous *London Journal* illustrations. One characteristic they share with the grand historical anecdote genre is how they position viewers below their subjects. This well-known visual rhetoric is intended to overwhelm and impress viewers with the idea that the subject is more important – higher – than them. Such diminution of the viewer, however, also invites opposition and resistance, unlike the parity of viewer and subject in the more usual serial illustrations. As much as this constituted a misunderstanding of mass-market pleasures, these illustrations also committed a much graver error for they began to infringe the well-established practice of treating the illustration as advertisement.

The way *Ivanhoe* was dismembered and attached to illustrations means that after the third episode the illustration no longer referred to events described in the episode actually printed in the issue. Previously it had been the norm for the illustration to be decoded by words a few pages inside the magazine, usually on page 2 or 3 (King, 2000). But the words that anchor the fourth illustration to *Ivanhoe*, 'Prince John and the Jew', do not occur until the second page of the following week's issue. Such pictorial anticipation of words by one week continued for seven more issues, until the eleventh illustration, 'Front de Boeuf and the Jew', when *Violet Davenant* appeared underneath the *Ivanhoe* illustration on the front page (Figure 6.4.). The caption explains 'See page 325'. But although next episode of *Ivanhoe* indeed started on that page, the picture actually referred forward to words printed not on that page, nor on immediately succeeding pages,

---

March 1859); 138 (2 April 1859). Altick (1997: 510-17) offers a more comfortable view of *Punch* on women. For mockery of America, see *Punch*, XXXV: 125 (25 September 1858), XXXVII: 92 (27 August 1859).

nor even in the next issue of the magazine, but in the next issue but one – on page 358. The serial organization of the words was thus completely disrupted by the serial organization of the illustrations. Rather than whet the appetite for the verbal text, the illustration remains unanchored for a fortnight.

As we know from our own reading practices, illustrations distant from the relevant text in a book may be irritating but does not matter that much. In a book we can look forward and back; but we cannot do this if we buy *The London Journal* week by week and do not save and assemble each issue into a book.

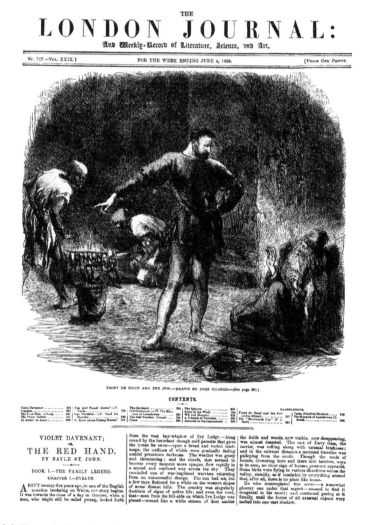

Figure 6.4 'Front de Boeuf and the Jew – Drawn by John Gilbert – (See page 325)' [*sic*], illustration to Walter Scott, *Ivanhoe*, above *Violet Davenant* by Bayle St John
Source: XXIX: 321.

Yet another implicit contract between reader-purchaser and the product that had been maintained for almost fifteen years was thus ruptured. Such lack of care over the contract tells readers that what they are buying does not love them: it is unfaithful, skittish, unreliable, a male *flirt* of the kind Notices to Correspondents has no mercy for. Such a practice is an insult, a further creation of distance between the magazine and its readers. In terms of production, it indicates a refusal to place oneself in the position of the consumer, to think of the desires of the target market segment, to speculate appropriately.

Finally, Lemon's project to raise the level of taste by running Scott was flawed at a basic level, for there was also the question of the fitness of Scott's novels for serialization. Although Trollope (1883: 41) delighted in *Ivanhoe*, he also pointed out how Scott did not serialize well:

> The production of novels in serial form forces upon the author the conviction that he should not allow himself to be tedious in any single part... the writer when he embarks on such a business should feel that he cannot afford to have many pages skipped out of the few which are to meet the reader's eye at the same time. Who can imagine the first half of the first volume of *Waverley* coming out in shilling numbers?   (Trollope, 1883: 143-4)

It is true that *Ivanhoe* had been issued successfully in sixteen-page parts by Cadell 1848. But it had been published in that form not as a serial, but as sections of a book and indeed part of a series of volumes. Cadell's *Ivanhoe* was continuing the practice begun in the eighteenth century of the part-issue of already commercially successful fiction, and exploited the movement for collected editions which had begun in the 1830s. Such publication in parts meant that works were available at an economically more manageable rate than the complete book or set: literally a payment on instalment plan. But we must be careful here as always not to conflate separate market segments. Even the cheaper end of the respectable new book market was expensive: monthly parts of 32 pages each usually cost a shilling (Tillotson, 1954: 25; Sutherland, 1976: 21). Regular purchase of luxury items such as this was well beyond the means of much of the population. While Stiff's *London Journal* had aspired in some ways to the prestige of the book (it was after all available in volume format, complete with index), it had never lost sight of its basis in the ephemeral periodical. Its most characteristic serial fiction took this into account, fulfilling all the criteria that Butt and Tillotson (1957: 15; Tillotson, 1954: 32) outlined for successful serial fiction. Within each episode incident and interest were to be evenly spread, and chapters balanced both in length and effect. Each had to lead to either a climax or a point of repose and, of course, it was also necessary to take into account somehow the interruptions in reading from issue to issue: to recapitulate where necessary and to use formulae.

One can see how some attempt was made to break the narrative of *Ivanhoe* at exciting points. The instalment for 14 May 1859 (XXIX: 273-5) begins at chapter XII with the second day of the tournament at Ashby. Ivanhoe is rescued by the appearance of *Le Noir Fainéant* and his identity is uncovered in a grand climax (illustrated the previous week). Chapter XIII is started where Prince John invites Cedric and Rowena to a banquet (of which there is an illustration, even though the banquet is described the following week). The episode ends halfway though the chapter with John's reading the letter that announces '*Take heed to yourself, for the devil is unchained*'. As it stands, this is good serialization as far as the words are concerned. We do not yet know who the 'devil' or *Le Noir Fainéant* are (though we can probably guess) and we will be tempted to buy next week's number. The second tournament and discovery of Ivanhoe constitute a very exciting chapter, followed by the more relaxed conversation between John and his men, wherein a new twist is introduced: John intends to marry Rowena to De Bracy. The sudden arrival of the letter is an effective close. But this episode is unusual, and, anyway, the illustration cuts across the episodes. The following week is more typical (XXIX: 289-92). Chapter XIII is continued, and the archery contest won by Locksley is detailed. Then comes the lengthy description of the feast, rich in archaeological observation, that had been illustrated the previous week. Despite Cedric's defiance of the Norman yoke, these are hardly exciting, and the climactic moment of the number, Locksley's victory, comes too early in it. The following week is worse, as there is no action at all (XXIX: 305-7). The first chapter of this instalment comprises the conversation between De Bracy and Fitzurse about the plan to capture Rowena, and the second (ch. XVI) describes the arrival of *Le Noir Fainéant* at the hermitage, breaking off with his asseveration that 'the fat buck which furnished this venison had been running on foot within the week' (XXIX: 7), a scandal unlikely to thrill most metropolitan readers brought up on (literary) raiding. Only the De Bracy plot looks forward to future episodes. The following instalment is similar in its flatness (XXIX: 325-7), the only events being the singing competition of *Le Noir Fainéant* and the hermit, and the Saxons' journey home to Rotherwood. The episode stops before the plot by De Bracy to waylay Rowena and the other Saxons is put into action. That comes the following week (ch. XIX, XXIX: 341, on the issue's fifth page), far too long after the conversation in which it was planned. Meanwhile, the grand illustrations of course have no relation to events in the issue in which they appear. They present themselves as Art, collectible for their own sake, visible rejections of ephemerality.

Lemon's *Ivanhoe* assumes book-like reading practices and neglects the nature of the *London Journal* as a periodical. Lemon again is stuck in the habitus of his own zone.

1859-62. Title v. Practice: Incorporating the *Guide*

The most significant of Lemon's changes to the *Journal* took place in April 1858, after its offices moved across the Strand to 141, to a narrow frontage facing Catherine Street. Until then, there must have been an arrangement with Stiff to allow the offices to remain at 334. Almost immediately after the move, Stiff started the *Guide*, published by 'John Smith' – surely a facetious pseudonym – on 1 May 'at the office of THE WEEKLY TIMES, 334, Strand'. The *Guide* cost a penny, or sixpence in monthly parts, or 4/6 per six-monthly volume with title-page and index. It comprised sixteen pages that gave reader-purchasers two serial novels, balaams, short fiction, biographies, 'Science', 'Facetiae', 'Statistics', 'Household

Receipts', a poem, 'Gems of Thought' and Notices to Correspondents. It looked like the *London Journal* under Stiff, cost the same and ran the same type of material. It was, as *The Times* (4 July 1859: 11) was later to put it, 'in every respect similar to the *London Journal*'. A glance at Figure 6.5 will show how true this was.

The episode of the *Guide* in the *Journal*'s history dramatically highlights the elements that chapter 3 proposed as constitutive of a periodical's identity. As far as practices were concerned, the *Guide* was now 'The London Journal'. Lemon tried to perform a total rebranding exercise and so altered the *London Journal* that only its title remained the same. Even the *Guide*'s network of authors was the same as Stiff's *London Journal*. Percy B. St John's *Photographs of the Heart* began on the first front page and his *Alice Leslie* started later in the volume. Anne Marie Maillard (= 'A.M.M.') contributed tales, articles and a novel (*A Woman's Secret*). 'J.C.' wrote six tales, and 'M.A.B.' five poems. Gelder, Sargent, Hartshorn, and Bolton were the illustrators and engravers.

Figure 6.5 'The Birth of Capitola', [E.D.E.N. Southworth], *The Masked Mother; or, the Hidden Hand*
Source: *Guide*, II: 257, 19 February 1859.

An enormous coup must have been the anonymous *Masked Mother* (see Figure 6.5). It is, in fact, E.D.E.N. Southworth's *The Hidden Hand*, her best-selling novel of all, and one of the most popular novels of the nineteenth century (Habegger, 1981; Ings, 1996: 131; the Introductions to Dolesa's and Baym's editions of Southworth, 1859). Stiff was alive to what the zone wanted and gave it Southworth's novel a mere week after it had finished in the *New York Ledger*. Southworth published a letter in the *Ledger* (10 March 1860) complaining about being plagiarized in Britain (Boyle, 1939: 40) and it was no doubt Stiff's reprinting that brought the importance of British markets to her notice. There were at least three stage versions of the novel in London, and when Southworth arrived there in 1860 – perhaps invited by Stiff – she found hats, suits and even riverboats all named after her heroine (Boyle, 1939: 39). Egan's absence from the *London Journal* would only have allowed *The Masked Mother* to shine brighter in the zone.

The Times reports a complaint that letters to Ingram's *London Journal* had been delivered to 334 Strand after it had moved to number 141 (see also 'Notice', XXVII: 336). Stiff was obviously keeping and using the letters. But there is also evidence that readers as well as writers actively migrated from the *Journal* to the *Guide*, the reader-contributor 'Fred', rejected by Lemon, being but one example. Already by June there was a flood of contributions offered by readers (see, for example, *Guide*, I: 128, 144). 'W. Paterson' was told not to send his manuscript as 'we are overwhelmed with literary contributions' (*Guide*, I: 160).

While the *Guide*'s introductory 'To Our Readers' comprised the usual platitudes of miscellany introductions that in theory harmonized well with Lemon's project (literature 'of the purest description' will 'provide entertainment and instruction at the same moment' so that 'that earthly paradise – the English Home' will be safeguarded), it differentiated itself from Lemon's *London Journal* in several respects. First, the *Guide* stressed that it was offering an *original* novel 'by an author of celebrity, to be illustrated by one of the first artists of the day'. Second, in 'keep[ing] pace with the extraordinary progress of the age', it claimed it would 'afford the fullest information on the improved manufactures and industry of the age' (*Guide*, I: 16). Whereas the *Journal* was now backward-looking and historical, the *Guide*, like other publications in its zone, offered contemporaneity and a gateway into the future. This is perceptible even in its attitude to poetry. One correspondent to the *Guide* had compositions rejected 'not from their want of merit, but as being rather out of date' ('Nitor', *Guide*, II: 336) – a practice very unlike the contemporary *Journal* with its poetry by established *vates*. Furthermore, the *Guide* was clearly managed well throughout and kept its contract with readers: there were no confusions as there had been with the *Ivanhoe* illustrations.

In little more than a year, the *Guide* would be incorporated with – or would incorporate – the *London Journal*. While in terms of the title the *London Journal* incorporated the *Guide*, it was the practices of the *Guide*, which had been those of the pre-Lemon *London Journal*, that the *London Journal* would now follow.

The story of the incorporation is curious. On 1 June 1859 Stiff published a newspaper called the *Daily London Journal*, of which three numbers were printed. Immediately the title appeared, Ingram took out an injunction to stop Stiff using it, even though the paper looked nothing like Ingram's *London Journal* and its contents were very different. Summing up at the trial, the judge declared that the *Daily London Journal* and the *Guide* were not plagiarizing the *London Journal*, thereby infringing copyright, but were actual 'frauds' (*Times*, 4 July 1859: 11; *Bookseller*, 25 June 1859, no. XVIII: 1004-5). Further prosecution was halted by Stiff's purchase of the *London Journal* for £18,500, plus £15,000 for the *Weekly Times* (*Bookseller*, 25 July 1859, no. XIX: 1072). To raise the capital he had to borrow £17,000 from a certain Mr McMurray in order to pay the £33,500 total. Now, considering the *Journal*'s massive fall in circulation, paying £3,500 more than he sold for seems ridiculous. There are two rational possibilities that might explain it. First, as the *Bookseller* suggests, Stiff might have lost less by buying the magazine back, even at an inflated price, and settling out of court than seeing the legal case through. The second possibility, which by no means excludes the first, is that the *Guide* had been doing so well that a lowered *Journal* circulation did not matter if the two were combined.

Figure 6.6 'The Fatal Peril Averted', E.D.E.N. Southworth, *Brandon of Brandon*. The front page of the *London Journal* on Stiff's repurchase
Source: XXX: 33.

I have been unable to find any data at all regarding the circulation of the *Guide*, but some indication of relative sales may be gauged by the decision to reprint stories originally serialized there in the *London Journal* 'Supplementary Volumes'. These comprised a set, published during the mid-1860s, presumably to meet demand for specific stories. Knowledge of this set, however, comes solely from advertisements on some of the monthly covers of the second series of the *Guide*. There the novels are placed in order and granted various degrees of typographical prominence. The most prominent (and the best selling?) were printed originally in the *Journal* itself. Unsurprisingly, they comprise J.F. Smith's novels, the first being *Minnigrey*, but four *Guide* novels are also reprinted: Percy B. St John's *Photographs of the Heart* and *Quicksands and Whirlpools*, the former also reserialized in the second series of the *Guide* (1865-66), E.D.E.N. Southworth's *The Twin Beauties* and *Lost Jewels*. The run-of-the-mill typographical status of these four novels in the advertisement suggests a fair, if not outstanding, amount of success. If we may extend this status to the entire periodical, one is still left wondering if the *Guide*'s profits would have counterbalanced the £3,500 extra: as so often, information is lacking in this zone.

Immediately on his purchase of the *Journal*, Stiff returned it to its former practices (and address at 334) by introducing a version of another Southworth tale, *Brandon of Brandon*. Figure 6.6 shows the front page of the *London Journal* looking like its former self – or like the *Guide*. Stiff also put a novelist experienced in popular publishing in the editor's chair, Percy B. St John (*Bookseller*, XLIV: 522, 26 September 1861). St John had proved his loyalty to Stiff not only by defecting from *Cassell's Illustrated Family Paper* to write for the *Journal* in 1856 but also by writing for the *Guide*. Faithful reader-contributors returned, including the 'L.M. Thornton' and 'James Onions' whose poems had been unceremoniously refused under Lemon. When in 1862 Stiff introduced poetry by Sheldon Chadwick, who wrote poems 'expressly [professionally] for the *London Journal*', the work of reader-poets was nonetheless still included both in Notices to Correspondents and in the body of the magazine. Stiff, however, did continue one aspect of Lemon's *London Journal*: emphasis on the star system of authorial names. Unlike in the case of 'J.F. Smith' in the early 1850s, Stiff now aggressively marketed names that were known to sell, a lesson perhaps learnt not only from Lemon but also from Cassell who was advertising Smith's name at every opportunity.

'E.D.E.N. Southworth' was Stiff's special star. In 1860 he ran two of her serials simultaneously, *Love's Labour Won* and *Laura Etheridge*. This is a density of authorship comparable only to the period when Smith's novels and his *Lives of the Queens of England* were running together. In both cases, one work is masked by anonymity, however. This is particularly revealing of complexities of ownership I remarked earlier, the interplay between the authorial name and the generic 'anonymous', ownerless tale. Clearly Stiff felt he needed to juggle the two.

If before his sale to Ingram and Bradbury and Evans his experiments show an uncertainty of the nature of market demand, by now Stiff had evidently established what his zone wanted: the type of stories produced by women writers for the analogous American zone. His realization was perhaps helped by Lemon's blunders, but also encouraged by Southworth's presence in London between 1859 and 1862 (Boyle, 1939: 39). During those years she wrote at least one serial especially for the *Journal*, *Captain Rock's Pet*. *Eudora*, her novel that preceded it, seems to me also to have been written originally for the *Journal*, and sold later to the *New York Ledger*. Not only did it appear in the *Journal* before its publication in the *Ledger* (29 June 1861 to 12 October 1861, as opposed to 20 July 1861 to 6 November 1861), but it had an English setting in its American version, when, as Boyle (1939: 41) points out, Southworth otherwise set her novels in America.

Pierce Egan, meanwhile, had been made editor of the *Weekly Times* and soon became editor of the *London Journal*. It is likely Egan succeeded St John after leaving the *Weekly Times* in April 1860.[3] By the middle of 1861, St John was conducting his own *London Herald* (*Bookseller*, 26 September 1861, no. XLVII: 522). Although its combination of the titles of the *London Journal* and the *Family Herald* suggests direct rivalry with them, I do not think this was the case. Published by Vickers, like the *Journal*, St John's magazine was only a halfpenny eight-page weekly and seems rather a venture in a cheaper market that plays on and with the distinctive elements of famous brand names. Although the *London Herald* lasted until 1866, St John conducted only the first two volumes (to June 1863) while it was being published by Vickers. Its publication was taken over by Berger upon which the magazine did become a direct rival to the *London Journal*, with a format that looked as similar as possible to it, its price upped to a penny, and its number of pages to sixteen. It was still clearly unsuccessful, however, since it changed publisher and printers several times before it finally collapsed.

Stiff started up a second series of the *Guide* to carry reprints of the most popular novels from both the first series of the *Guide* and from the *Journal*.[4] But these moves did not help him avoid bankruptcy in March 1862. He had obtained his loan of £17,000 by mortgaging the *Weekly Times*, the *Guide* and the *London Journal*. His lender McMurray now called in the loan and immediately resold the publications, on 12 March, to the theatrical printer William Spencer Johnson for £18,000. Stiff was ruined and imprisoned for debt until December.[5]

In many accounts – not only Vizetelly's – Stiff comes out badly. Mrs Gordon Smythies complained to the Royal Literary Fund that Stiff failed to pay her for a

---

[3] See *Weekly Times*, 19 June 1859 to 22 April 1860 for repeated announcements concerning his editorship at the head of each leading article.

[4] *Guide*, second series, 27 July 1861 to 11 May 1867, when it was reincorporated into the *London Journal*. See changes in the *Guide*'s colophon 12 April 1862 and 31 May 1862, the time of Stiff's bankruptcy and Johnson's purchase of the *Journal*. The final issue of the *Guide* (VII: 48, 18 May 1867) claims that 'Next Saturday, May 11, [it] will be incorporated with *The London Journal* which will contain the continuation of the popular story "Winning Her Way"'. There is no mention of the incorporation in the *Journal*, although May 18 1867 is a double number, 32 pages for the usual 1d. The *Guide* had obviously been labouring under difficulties, having gone up to 1d a week and 16 pages, and moved from a beige to a redesigned blue monthly cover.

[5] On Stiff's bankruptcy, see *Times*, 12 March 1862: 11; 8 April 1862: 12; 10 April 1862: 11; 12 May 1862: 11; 25 July 1862: 11; 21 August 1862: 11, 5 November 1862: 11; 4 December 1862: 9. As always, the exact sum paid for the *Journal* is disputed: the *Bookseller* (LII, 30 April 1862: 248) asserts Johnson paid £18,500 for it.

novel he had commissioned and that she had delivered to him as agreed. He had also secreted her manuscript and destroyed the plates: as Cross (1985: 190) sympathetically comments, this was every writer's nightmare. In court, judges seem ill disposed towards Stiff: he quickly lost all cases. Dix (1854: 287) called him 'a Shylock sort, an ignorant fellow who treated authors as though they were his inferiors'. While Cassell, for example, was part of the same network and social status as Ingram – both had been on the Committee for the Repeal of the Taxes on Advertisements in 1849 (Collet, 1899: 105) – Stiff had far less social capital. He had been an employee on the *ILN*, not an employer. Perhaps, unlike Cassell, Ingram, Bentley, Johnson, or even Reynolds, he was not a 'gentleman'. In Bourdieu's terms, he possessed low degrees of social, symbolic and cultural capitals: he was not supported by a large network, he had little reputation for honour, and slight intellectual or educational 'distinction'.

Another and perhaps more important reason for his bankruptcy may have been that he was unable to handle the immense profits and the complicated accounting procedures necessary for running a family of periodicals in the increasingly crowded market of the 1860s. In other words, the fourth of Bourdieu's types of capital –economic – escaped him as well as the other three. This can be seen in his bankruptcy trial, not so much from the exaggerated sums he initially adduces regarding the worth of *Journal* (this is almost certainly a ploy to stave off his creditors), nor from his declaration that he did not keep a cash-book (he may well have destroyed what records he had to cover evidence of his losses), but from the way that he did not seem to understand how the figures worked to put him in debt. The accounts adduced on 25 July 1862 by the legal clerk Joseph Hart show a profit from the *Journal*, after all deductions, of about £4,500 a year – to be precise, £19,264/4/9 between July 1859 and March 1862. This was an income that placed Stiff easily amongst the top 200 payers of income tax in Britain, in the category of 'upper-class gentleman' (for this classification, see Baxter, 1869: 105-6). Despite the frequency of bankruptcy and imprisonment for debt amongst cultural producers (see Cross, 1985), his financial potency perhaps made him feel inviolably wealthy. Confusing types of capital, perhaps he even saw himself as the 'gentleman' that others failed to recognize in him. While Stiff's personal expenditure during the same period of 32 months was over £9,400 ('Enormous' gasps the judge), yet his profits from the *Journal* alone would easily have covered it. Where he sustained huge losses was in his other and newer publishing ventures: the *Weekly Magazine* and *Everybody's Journal*.[6] He had also reduced the price of the *Weekly Times* to a penny from twopence. While at the latter price it had been making a profit of £1,800 a year, at a penny it made a decided loss.[7] He had also purchased, probably

---

[6] According to Waterloo (Phase I, 1976: 1119), the *Weekly Magazine* was a penny illustrated weekly published by Vickers in 1860. The magazine is omitted from Waterloo (1997) and I have not traced a copy. *Everybody's Journal of News, Literature, Art and Science* was a twopenny monthly published by Houlston & Co and edited by Lemon's associate on the *London Journal*, W.H. Davenport Adams (Waterloo, 1997, III: 1823). I have not seen any issues: the BL copy is destroyed and I have not located another.

[7] Cf. the accounts in Chapter 4 on the tight margins of the cheap press. The *Weekly Times*

in 1861, the *Morning Chronicle*, the venerable newspaper at 332 Strand, at a time when it was already losing money.[8] Charles Mackay is damning about Stiff's management of the *Chronicle*, not even deigning to name him:

> [T]he copyright of the *Chronicle* was sold to a person unskilled in newspaper management, who damaged its character by selling its columns for a subsidy from a foreign potentate. From his possession, after a short and not very brilliant struggle to keep it standing on this rotten foundation, it passed into the hands of a speculative American ...
>
> (Mackay, 1877, II: 164).[9]

It seems to me that Stiff ran his business as though it were a small concern, a Bohemian boom and bust model of publishing, with stress on a good finished product and relations with the reader in the immediate and short term. What he needed was an impersonal industrial method of running the magazine with sophisticated methods of debit and credit, and, since there were more opportunities now for authors to sell their wares to rival magazines, attention to their needs too. This latter is what the magazine's new purchaser, W.S. Johnson, clearly understood. For a long time he had been part of the culture industry both as the owner of the large Nassau Steam Press in St Martin's Lane, and as manager of the City Theatre. Located in the poor area of Cripplegate, his theatre specialized in melodrama (Booth, 1991: 4): a version of *Minnigrey* had been put on there in 1853 (*Lloyd's Weekly London Newspaper*, 18 April 1853: 8). Johnson already had experience of the mass-market weekly, too, for he had published the *Home Circle* between 1849 and 1854, edited by Pierce Egan next door to Johnson's printing works. What I have gleaned about Johnson's dealings with his employees suggests care to maintain good relations as and when necessary. The same compositors' report from 1845 that provided a glimpse into the printing of the *London Journal* also shows Johnson's insistent and ruthless charm. He successfully resisted paying

---

was reduced to 1d on 12 October 1861, after the repeal of the paper duty, having already been reduced from 3d to 2d at the repeal of the Stamp Tax in 1855. Advertisements in the *Journal* (October-December 186) claimed the *Weekly Times* had a circulation of 350,000 and then 370,000. This cannot have been true for a sustained period or the paper would not have made such a loss.

[8] Advertisements for the *Morning Chronicle* start to appear in the *Journal*, 30 March 1861 (XXXIII: 208) suggesting the date of Stiff's purchase.

[9] Waterloo (1997, IV: 3308-9) records uncertainty about both Stiff's ownership and the end of the *Chronicle*: while listing 19 March 1862 as its termination, it also suggests it may have continued until 1865. The latter is true. Contrary to the obituary of Stiff in the *Bookseller* (1 December 1874: 1109), the paper did not quite 'die' under him: the last issue to bear his name was 19 March 1862 and the newspaper appeared – for eight issues over three years – in a new format under a new owner (see *Morning Chronicle*, 24 March 1862: 2) until 2 March 1865. These eight numbers were published from 30 Red Lion Square by Harry Price Charlton and printed at 60 St Martin's Lane. The latter was where W.S. Johnson had his *London Journal* printing works. The name of the new owner was not specified, but it may have been McMurray. I have found nothing that confirms the accusation of selling column space to a foreign potentate.

overtime, night work or Sunday rates to his printing staff but maintained good relations with them (Howe, 1947: 254).

Stiff's bankruptcy, measured against the success of Johnson's methods, can be read as an example of the gradual breakdown of the older small-scale methods of business, already transitional between the artizanal and the professional, before the triumph of rationalizing commercial staff and consumer management that was taking place throughout the second half of the nineteenth century. Usually this transformation is described as a shift from 'gentlemanly publishing' to impersonal organizational structures (Feltes, 1986; Coulthorpe-McQuin, 1990; Johannings-meier, 1997; Law, 2000). But what happened here seems rather, I think, to be a crushing of an ungentlemanly entrepreneur who possessed low amounts of capital of all the four types Bourdieu describes – social, symbolic, cultural and economic – and the takeover by a man who, enjoying all four capitals in higher degree, prefigured the industrial impersonality of the later nineteenth century while masking it with gentlemanly charm.

Chapter Seven

1862-83. The Secret of Success; or, American Women and British Men

L'Elisir d'amore: an Authorial Stable and a Fixed Format

The remaining years of the *London Journal*'s first series are all under Johnson's ownership.[1] In 1862, after taking over the printing of both the *Journal* and the *Weekly Times*, he moved their offices to the former building of the *Morning Chronicle* at 332 Strand. This was a structure with one of the most impressive frontages on the north of this part of the street. In 1877 Charles Mackay (II: 73) referred to the building as notable for its association with the *Chronicle*, remarking only incidentally that it was the present home of the *Journal* and *Weekly Times*. As late as 1891, 332 Strand was still remembered as the offices of the *Chronicle*, and the present residents, by now the *Weekly Times* and the *Echo*, are mentioned only as representatives of how times have changed (Wheatley, 1891, III: 324).

Meanwhile, back in 1862, Stiff, had set up the *7 [sic] Days' Journal*, another almost exact look-alike of the *London Journal*, while still in debtor's goal. It opened with reruns of Smith's *The Will and the Way*, of Southworth's *The Hidden Hand* (retitled *Capitola*) and a newish novel, her *Astraea*. It operated out of 13 Catherine Street, where Stiff had secured his faithful engraver J. Gelder as publisher. He was released from prison in early December (*Times*, 4 December 1862: 9) and on the twentieth of that month, at the same time as the *London Journal* moved to 332 Strand, he transferred his new magazine into his old haunt, 334 (*7 Days' Journal*, colophon, I: 248). The following year the *7 Days' Journal* was renamed the *London Reader*.

The *London Journal* seems to have so successfully redefined the signifier 'London' in the context of periodicals that it now stood for penny weekly fiction magazines in general: it is 'The London Journal' as a metonym for the whole genre that features in novels of the 1860s, as discussed in Chapter 2. But Stiff could not now colonize the space that the *Journal* had once occupied as he had once done by starting the *Guide*. Firstly and most importantly, Johnson maintained and extended the very practices that Stiff had initiated, and managed to keep most of the authors he had assembled. Secondly, not having Johnson's capital in any sense, Stiff was forced to prowl around what was once his cultural empire, trying to poach writers

---

[1] Johnson initially owned it jointly with a certain Thomas Wilson, according to Tinsley (1900: 343-4; see also *Times*, 20 November 1863: 8-9). I have been unable to establish any details about this partnership: perhaps Wilson is 'T.H. Wilson', the *Journal* artist.

while having the means only to steal less well-known names. One such was Anne Marie Maillard. Under her initials 'A.M.M.', she had regularly contributed one-episode tales for Stiff's *London Journal* and *Guide* since 1854. A short novel appeared under her full name a month after Johnson's purchase of the *Journal*. Only two tales by Maillard were printed in the *Journal* after this until 1867-68, when a couple more appeared. When she moved from Johnson's camp to Stiff's at the end of that year she was upgraded to principal novelist.[2] Of particular interest are reprints in Stiff's new magazine of J.F. Smith's *London Journal* novels. Stiff had presumably managed to retain the copyrights.[3] But Johnson would soon be printing them in *London Journal* Supplementary Volumes: presumably he had been able to purchase them from Stiff.

Besides possessing greater financial capital, Johnson had also more social capital in that, unlike Stiff, he was part of the network that included newer popular publishers. According to Edmund Downey, who worked for William Tinsley, Johnson was charming, immensely wealthy, and always perfectly in control:

> a lightly-built, dapper, sprightly man. As he walked briskly through the streets, swinging his arms, he was always humming. His favourite perch at Catherine Street [Tinsley's office] was the counter. He would spring lightly upon this with an air which said: 'What do you think of that for an old grey-beard?... (Downey, 1905: 61)

Some time between 1879 and 1884, Johnson wanted to get rid of the *Journal*,

> either growing tired of his property or becoming anxious about it. He proposed to sell it and Tinsley was to find a syndicate to purchase it. I was to manage the Journal. Johnson allowed me to have a view of his private ledgers for the purpose of arranging the deal, and I found some of the figures amazing. For a considerable time the circulation had remained in the neighbourhood of half a million copies, and it can break no confidence to say that Johnson used to draw regularly £1,000 a month out of it. It must be borne in mind that it was a penny publication, relying solely on its circulation; it printed no advertisements – nowadays the backbone of cheap publication.[4] At the time I was investigating it, the circulation (and of course the profits) had dropped heavily. Johnson's idea of the value of the property was about £30,000. One morning Mr Tinsley informed me, gleefully, that he had got his syndicate together. During the same week the negotiations fell through, the purchase price being the difficulty. (Downey, 1905: 62-3)

Johnson's desire to sell his properties may have been triggered by the death in 1880 of Pierce Egan. The pair formed the nucleus of the production network and had been in contact for over thirty years since their first magazine together, the *Home Circle*.

---

[2] See *Loving and Being Loved* (1863), started in the *7 Days' Journal* and finished in the *London Rea*der. The front page *Cloud and the Coronet*, printed anonymously in 1863 and again spanning the two titles, was also hers (Jay, 1918-19: 25).

[3] *The Will and the Way* (1862-63, over *7 Days' Journal* and *London Reader*); *Woman and her Master* (*London Reader*, 1863-65).

[4] Note the same *ubi sunt* topos as in Vizetelly (see Chapter 2 above). The *Journal* did of course carry advertising on its monthly covers, and a few on the last page of each issue.

Unlike Stiff, Johnson was open about the accounts and put them at Downey's disposal, suggesting a grasp not only of the necessity for keeping account books but the potential profitability of business transparency. However, at this stage Johnson grossly overvalued his magazine. £30,000 meant that the magazine should have brought in £10,000 a year at a time when it almost certainly did not. Perhaps he felt the title itself was sufficiently redolent of commercial success to warrant such a price. After all, as today's marketing specialists know well, a brand name comprises past and future values, however imagined or re-imagined, as well as the nitty-gritty of present-day cash-flows and market position. As in 1857, it was assumed that only a syndicate could afford to purchase such a magazine: few individuals had Johnson's combination of wealth and interest in this cultural zone.

For Anglophone literary history in the early twenty-first century, probably the most striking thing about the entire *London Journal* is the publication of four Mary Braddon novels, all under Johnson, including her two most famous, *Lady Audley's Secret* (1863) and *Aurora Floyd* (1865-66). While she originally published these elsewhere, she also wrote two novels especially for the magazine, *The Outcasts* (1863-64) and *Diavola* (1866-67), both of which Braddon later rewrote for the triple-decker market, as Charles Reade and Emma Robinson had done before her. Before it appeared in the *Journal*, Braddon had published *Lady Audley's Secret* with Tinsley in volume form, and it was almost certainly through him that she became part of the *London Journal* network. '[B]y no means a star of the first magnitude in the world of the penny journals' (Anon., 1866: 97), Braddon remained marginal to the central names of Southworth and Egan. She was marginal to a pair of even more obscure names: Mrs Gordon Smythies, whom Johnson brought back to the *Journal* after her quarrel with Stiff, and a new arrival, the playwright-cum-popular novelist, Watts Phillips, who wrote mainly under the pseudonym 'Fairfax Balfour'.[5]

These four formed the core of *London Journal* serial writers for this first period, joined in 1864 by Percy B. St John. After his failure at the *London Herald*, St John had written *Violetta* as lead serial for Stiff's *London Reader* (1863), but presumably Johnson offered better pay: after that there is nothing signed by St John in the *Reader*. He instead remained a faithful contributor of tales and novels to the *Journal* even into the New Series in 1883.[6] A later new arrival (in 1865) was the novelist James Grant, whose very successful *Romance of War* had been published 1846-7.[7] Another whose work appeared over several years was the 'working-class' poet, Sheldon Chadwick, who contributed on average four or five

---

[5] Watts Phillips used his pseudonym from 1862 which he derived from his step-son by his second wife, Caroline Huskisson. My thanks to his relative John Phillips for this information.

[6] Johannsenn (1950, II: 252) comments that he 'died of psoriasis in a low lodging house in London, 15 March 1889, after he had lost his money in a publishing venture'.

[7] Cross (1985: 5) comments that between 1856 and 1882 *The Romance of War* sold 100,000 copies. This is not, incidentally, the James Grant familiar to press historians as the author of *The Newspaper Press, its Origin, Progress and Present Position* (1871-1872).

poems per volume until 1877,[8] and to some extent he took over the *London Journal* laureateship that Charles Swain had held in the late 1840s and early 1850s. Other faithfuls included 'T.E.S.', who wrote tales from 1864 to 1870, and 'L.G.', who wrote poetry and tales between 1862 and 1866. Johnson and Egan thus gradually assembled old and well-tried *London Journal* names, judiciously bolstered with old and well-tried ones from nearby zones, while lesser writers were reduced to initials and fenced into poems and tales like reader-contributors. If Stiff had experimented with many authors, several of whom had left in stormy circumstances, Egan and Johnson formed a loyal stable of *London Journal* writers.

Johnson was not able to retain his star artist, however. Gilbert left in 1863, possibly, it has been suggested, because of a 'sentimental attachment' to Stiff (Clayton, 1911: 522). But Gilbert virtually abandoned drawing for the press after 1863, painting mainly for his own pleasure: his withdrawal was part of a more general retirement from the high-pressure world of design on demand. Although it should not, in theory, be difficult to detect his exact date of departure from a change of style in the illustrations, this is not the case. While he certainly drew at least twenty-eight illustrations for Egan's *The Poor Girl*, which finished 5 September 1863,[9] it seems that his replacement (according to Anon., 1866: 103, his brother) was instructed to imitate his style. Of course, there are no signatures to help us.

In 1864, the *Guide* advertised re-issues of the *Journal*'s most successful novels as illustrated by Gilbert. By this time his name was clearly famous enough in the zone to function as an attraction, although it is still not given the emphasis of the stars Smith and Southworth. There still seemed to be the assumption that even if 'Gilbert' had low recognition value, 'Southworth' and 'Smith' would carry the advertsiement. Its status still uncertain, if 'Gilbert' was now more famous than under Lemon, this had probably been caused by Lemon's insistent advertising: Lemon had the misfortune only to start its promotion in this zone and was not long enough in the field to benefit from his efforts. Yet it is also true that his promotion was only part of an increased general cultural penetration of 'Gilbert' throughout the century (cf. Thomas, 1913-14: 122). By 1894 'Gilbert' had almost eclipsed 'J.F. Smith' in the new zone in which the *London Journal* was then operating: when *Stanfield Hall* was reserialized in volume XXI of the *Journal*'s new series, 'Illustrated by SIR JOHN GILBERT, R.A.' appeared every week in large letters. By the 1920s 'Gilbert' had become the great attraction: the last incarnation of the *London Journal* regularly placed an illustration by Gilbert on its front page, divorced from any novel.

Just as a more-or-less stable group of professionals as well as amateurs was maintained by Egan and Johnson, so the format of the *Journal* became much more

---

[8] Chadwick may have been a friend of Egan's (see XXXIX: 79). On his perceived working-class origins, see the reviews at the back of Chadwick (1875): his father was actually a city missionary in Manchester (see 'Dedication', Chadwick, 1875).

[9] See Thomas, 1913-14: 181-5. Before his death, Gilbert donated to the Guildhall Library two books of cuttings from the *Journal* of his illustrations. This is not a complete collection, as Thomas (1913-14: 144) realized, but includes those for *The Poor Girl*.

firmly fixed. It gradually metamorphosed into that of a fiction magazine where each serial novel had a place in a hierarchy formed by the structure of the weekly issue, all the while retaining some compilative miscellany elements: the balaams and departments of 'Science', 'Gems of Thought', 'Household Receipts' and 'Miscellaneous'. These occupied less space than formerly and did not parade their status as cuttings. Early on, the *Journal* had had the potential to become a fiction magazine. Already in 1846 two novels were being run simultaneously, Reynolds's *Faust* and Soulié's *It Was Time*. A clear hierarchy existed between them, the Reynolds prominent with a half-page illustration on the front page and the Soulié moved around inside each weekly issue where much smaller illustrations identified its position (when there was an illustration at all). By late 1849, three novels were running at the same time: Thomas Miller's *Godfrey Malvern*, J.F. Smith's *Stanfield Hall* and Dumas's *The Thousand and One Phantoms*. Here the hierarchy was marked by Smith's place on the front page, Miller's on page 9 (with an illustration), and the Dumas at various places in the second half of each issue, unillustrated. From this we can appreciate how the illustrations served not only to illustrate the text but function as *punctuation* – signposts telling the reader where its most important divisions are.

During the Johnson-Egan period, four or sometimes five novels ran simultaneously. The format congealed and with it the hierarchization of its elements and the formulae for its narratives: the recipe for making itself loved by consumers had been discovered – precisely, *L'Elisir d'amore*. While a reference to Italian opera may seem well outside the zone of the *Journal*, we should not be misled by its exclusivity today. J.F. Smith and numerous later novelists grant it a prominent place in their fiction, and the *Journal* regularly offered portraits and biographies of opera singers. The idea of opera was certainly more firmly fixed in the *Journal*'s lexicon than the penny gaff. Donizetti's comic opera was regularly given close to the *Journal*'s office, not only at Covent Garden but also at the Lyceum (Rosenthal, 1958) and as in the Donizetti, the *Journal*'s recipe (or, indeed, 'receipt') for the elixir of love was hardly complex, its effect depending entirely on its fantasmatic investment by the consumer. Prime importance was given to the front-page novel. Physically closest to the magazine's title, it most powerfully defined the *Journal*'s projected image and identity. Second position in the hierarchy was that of the novel that started on page 9 of each issue, the right-hand centre page of each weekly number. That likewise had an illustration which headed it, above its title. It could easily be turned to by simply opening the issue at its centre page and bending the centrefold back. Third position novels had an illustration on page 8 of each issue, facing that of the 'second position' novel, while its instalment started several pages *before* the illustration, usually on page 5. The beginning of each episode was thus less prominent, which is why, even though it is second in order of page numbers, I regard it as third in the hierarchy. Its illustration still draws attention to it, while 'fourth' and 'fifth position' novels are almost always unillustrated. These have extremely variable positions, clearly being fitted around the pillars of the main three. From 1872 Harriet Lewis's novels become fixed in 'fourth position', occupying pages 12-14 of each issue, while the 'fifth position' novel, where there is one, is inserted wherever it will fit.

There was a passage through the hierarchy that a front-page novel came to take under Johnson and Egan. When a new novel was placed on the front page, the novel already there migrated to second position. The demoted novel usually stayed there until yet another new one was placed on the front page, when the previous front-page novel would push it down the hierarchy. As serials continue, their usefulness as bait for a next purchase diminishes. Accordingly, the last instalment of any novel is virtually always in the lowest possible position.

Not every novel followed this gradual demotion, and actually this hierarchy is more interesting for when its ideal form varies, for it is then that it can tell us about the market status of each novel and the struggles between them to win the consumer's love. *Fair Lilias* by Pierce Egan began in first position (14 January 1865) and retained it for an exceptional period until October when Southworth's *The Manhater* pushed it into second. There Egan's novel stayed until only its last two instalments when it dropped to third position and finally to bottom, unstressed and unillustrated, on the fourth to sixth pages. Meanwhile the success of *Fair Lilias* made new novels contravene the rule of beginning on the front page: in April Gordon Smythies' *The Sleepwalker* started in second position where it stayed until James Grant's *Moreley Ashton* began and it was relegated to third. Soon Grant's and Smythies' novels were alternating in second and third positions, until Grant's won out.

While I think it a strong factor, I am not suggesting that movement down the hierarchy was predicated on popularity alone. While *Lady Audley's Secret* took second place in 1862 to Pierce Egan's *The Poor Girl*, I think the criterion of novelty was in play: before its appearance in the *Journal*, Braddon's novel had already appeared in three forms, in volume format as well as twice serialized in magazines (see King, 2002). Furthermore, *The Poor Girl* turned out to be Egan's most popular novel (*DNB*, VI: 563): remarkable in that even its last episode was placed on the front page, it also resulted in a spin-off, *The Poor Boy*, a few years later. When Braddon's *The Outcasts* ceded first place to Egan's *Such is Life*, on the other hand, this may show the logic of the superiority of the new rather than an assumption that Egan's selling power outweighed Braddon's. *The Outcasts* was, after all, the greatest financial success of a very successful writer (Wolff, 1979: 138). At the same time, a more specifically producerly criterion may be in play here, as with all of Egan's novels, in that, as editor, Egan may have been determined to place his creatures in the most prominent position with less than usual regard for their commercial attractiveness compared with that of other novels in the same issues.

Another criterion determining position may concern the origins of the serial. This, I suspect, is the reason why Harriet Lewis's novels were consistently in fourth position from 1872. Like Southworth, Lewis was contracted exclusively to the *New York Ledger*, but had secretly supplied advance sheets to the *Journal*. For a long time this had kept them in second or third position and illustrated. Yet after the *Ledger's* proprietor discovered what was happening, the *London Journal* versions dropped to the less visible fourth position where they stayed. Simultaneously, the previous blazon to each of her novels – 'The only edition in this country sanctioned by this celebrated American authoress' – was dropped.

In other cases, such as that of *Uncle Tom's Cabin* – which never occupied a prominent site in the *Journal* when it appeared in 1852-53 – a combination of factors may have operated. Not only was it pirated, like virtually all other British editions of the novel at that time, but another serialization was already available very close in the zone, in *Reynolds's Miscellany*. Hildreth (1976: 8-12) lists about fifty editions in Britain in 1852 alone, including two by Vickers, one in six penny numbers of sixteen pages each, and the other in volume format.[10]

If the *Journal's* practices invite linkage with the arch knowingness of Italian comic opera, its system of seduction based on hierarchical organization of 'departments' also begs comparison with the scientific cellularization of the 'department store' (the *grand magasin*) that was arising at the same time and which Zola lovingly details in *Au Bonheur des Dames*. What is particularly striking is how the *London Journal* reverses the trends of the department store, gradually decreasing the number of its departments, simplifying in place of complicating its cellular structure. By 1883 the number of departments will have dwindled to fiction, 'Miscellaneous', 'Household Hints', 'Facetiae' and Notices to Correspondents (which will have itself been transformed from a space where magazine and reader interacted into one where readers communicated with each other – marriage advertisements now occupied most of the space). The earlier miscellany format was actually much closer to the sales architecture of the department store. Not only were there were many more departments, but there were frequent capricious changes in a department's location. As Zola makes clear, department stores came to be organized and re-organized so that customers had to wander through departments they would not otherwise have visited (a practice we are all too familiar with in today's supermarkets with their constantly mutating geographies of consumption). So the *Journal's* earlier variable layout had the corollary of encouraging the reading of texts that otherwise might be ignored – a kind of walking the pages or readerly *flânerie*. While from Stiff's repurchase in 1859 the front page was exclusively occupied by an illustrated serial novel, before that only 'Notices to Correspondents', 'Facetiae' and 'Miscellaneous' had been nailed in place on the last three pages. Each of these departments comprised short paragraphs that could be added to or cut in order to accommodate previous text lengths. They thus function as giant balaams. While technological issues of production thus provide an origin for the fixity of these three departments, in the bifocal vision of the commodity fetish, more relevant is how the magazine *as a whole* was being sold over time, not the dominant of an established hierarchy of departments and pleasures. While before 1859, and especially before the arrival of J.F. Smith, serial novels were mainly placed on the front page and can therefore be said to be particularly identified with the *London Journal*, this was by no means always the case. The magazine's capriciosity of format destabilized too fixed a hierarchization and stabilization of desires. The *Journal* was trying to be loved by as many different kinds of people as feasible. What was discovered under Stiff and

---

[10] Hildreth remarks neither the *London Journal* serialization (2 October 1852 to 15 January 1853) nor that in *Reynolds's Miscellany* (18 September 1852 to 15 January 1853).

refined under Johnson, on the other hand, was a greater market specificity, even while the old rhetoric of literature for 'the Million' was still being used. The *London Journal* was no longer a miscellany but a magazine of serial fiction. The pathways of desire were more tightly directed: no longer the pleasures of casual *flânerie* but a trip to the theatre with a predefined programme.

From Parergy to Performance: The Artiste in the City

Although Cross (1985: ch. 6) has suggested that improvements in the conditions of British writers had to wait until the 1880s, I strongly suspect that the American practices I outlined in Chapter 4 helped increase rates of pay in Britain as early as the 1860s, at least as far as the stars of the mass-market magazines were concerned. No longer pining for symbolic capital with the same intensity, writers in its zone were compensated by high economic rewards. This partially explains why traces of parergic *ressentiment* and aggression attenuated. This is not to say that the parergic evaporated altogether. Traces remain, for example, in the clunky style of *The Woman in Black* and *The Man in Grey* by Mrs Gordon Smythies, but emptied of the urgent and multi-faceted frustration of the 1840s, with its raids on *Bentley's* and other high-status publications. Indeed, raiding ostensibly ceased. That word 'ostensibly' is important as what happened from the mid-1860s was that the sources of the balaams, 'Facetiae' and the 'Miscellaneous' departments were very rarely given. The magazine no longer paraded its depredations on the high. Relations between the cultural zones still existed – the ecosystems were never entirely sealed off from one another – but in a gentler form. The titles of the two Smythies novels I mentioned above may formally recall Wilkie Collins's *The Woman in White*, but in fact her serials have little to do with Collins's novel: they want to be associated with its commercial success rather than with tropes lifted from Collins. Similarly, when Clementine Montagu took from *Villette* the surname 'de Bassompierre' for the heroine of *The Double Vow* (1879-80), it seems due merely to a memory of the name, voided of specific reference, rather than a raid or even a significant reference as such.

The polymorphous traces of resentment that once characterized the parergic had on the whole moved out of the *London Journal* to zones that are beneath it both economically and culturally. *Mokeanna* in 1863 does not accurately model the *Journal's* current front-page fiction but an idea of it created in a different zone. What *Punch* was mocking was in fact more common in the zones below *The London Journal*: examples include Braddon's very early serial *The Black Band*, serialized in the *Halfpenny Journal* (1861-62), or Bracebridge Hemyng's *The Bondage of Brandon*, serialized (anonymously) in the *London Reader* two years later.[11] Hemyng seems to have despised his penny fiction readers (Mitchell, 1989: 148). Characteristic of *The Bondage* is heavily stylized writing comprising staccato

---

[11] *London Reader*, 9 April 1864 to 5 November 1864. Its authorship is given in its triple-decker format (1884). *Pace* Sutherland, 1988: 290, there is no identifiable work by Hemyng in the *London Journal*.

jabs and shocks, emphatic lack of psychological realism and treatment of the reader as so stupid as to require constant reminding of the current situation and the general plot, even though both are always formulaic. When the wicked Lady Brandon lies dying in the final pages of Hemyng's novel (she has just fallen out of a window), she is nonetheless able to speak perfectly formed and reasonable sentences:

> At twelve o'clock that night, Lady Blanche Brandon died, but before she died, she was able to say a few words to her husband, who had been summoned by telegraph to her bedside. He bent over her with tender solicitude. All he could see was a mass of linen bandages, with a hole in the centre, indicating the position of the mouth.
> 'Forgive me, Reginald,' she murmured. 'You were too good for me. I should have married Sir Lawrence Allingford. I might have lived happily with him. You have so much to forgive me for. Will you forgive me before I die?'
> 'I do – God knows how fully – forgive you.'
> 'Thank you for that. There is one more subject I wish to allude to. Our child is not Earl of Brandon, but – but you will love him; will you not, Reginald? Do love him. Love him for my sake, will you dear – dear Reginald? Whatever may have been my crime, he has done you no injury. He has been guilty of no harm. Will you love him, dearest? My own Reginald, say you will love him. It would smooth my passage to – to – would, I could say to, heaven [*sic*]; but God is good, and I will hope, for I truly repent me of my sins …'
> (Hemyng, *The Bondage of Brandon, London Reader*, III: 816)

Lady Brandon promptly dies and the novel ends two paragraphs later. This is the zone to which a transformed parergic moved. No longer basing itself on works of higher symbolic capital (George Eliot, for example, at this period), it raided genres that yielded instead high economic capital. While *London Journal* novels also raided, and formed part of, the same corpus, what characterized the lower zone was that aggression and resentment remained prominent. The style, casually mixing registers, at once telegraphic and long-winded, formal written and colloquial spoken, is a symptom of this: the writers could not be bothered to – did not *want* to at some level – 'write well'. As before, a reader can derive considerable pleasure from this simultaneous complicity with and resistance to authority, when not indeed reading it as parody, a mode which most readers of academic texts today will no doubt prefer.

Throughout Egan's reign as editor (1860-80), the *London Journal* delivered much more obviously 'polished' fiction than this, far less liable to contrascription and what nineteenth-century critics might call 'faults of style'. It is impossible to give examples brief enough for citation to demonstrate what I mean, but one has only to compare Braddon's famous novels with the passage above. *London Journal* novels on the whole respect a reader familiar with the conventions of sensation, adventure and romance plots. Developing the narrative strategies of J.F. Smith, novelists now openly play with the economically authoritative conventions they have inherited. The reader is consistently unable to predict quite how the established generic outcome will be reached. Even Braddon's *The Outcasts*, which in some places reads as distinctly parergic, is notable for a new kind of crime, whereby readers are tantalized by the possibility that a murderer may have taken on the identity of the murdered man. My main point is that the novelists in this zone perform like musical virtuosi or circus artistes (a metaphor familiar from *Hard Times* and Figure 7.1): we know that such performers will end with a perfect cadence, an exit or the resolution of mysteries, but we do not know how they will get there or what tricks or routines they will execute or how they will vary them. Theatrical performance is a frequent metaphor for authorship now, having assumed validity as a justification for and in itself. In the article in *The Mask* that accompanies the famous image below, it is Braddon's extemporized storytelling to her family that is claimed to have started her on her literary vocation, a metonym of her short-lived career on the stage which is not otherwise mentioned.

Figure 7.1   Mary Braddon as equestrian artiste, leaping through hoops held by John Maxwell
Source: *The Mask*, I: 139, June 1868.

As performers, authors are not 'artists' in this zone. They are 'artistes'. As at the massively popular equestrian shows in the Lyceum close to the *London Journal* offices or at concerts by the musical pyrotechnicians whom the *Journal* promotes, one delightedly gasps at the risks taken, measuring the technical skill of the artiste in a knowing awareness of the rules of the game.

It is the gasp that is the sensation. Reading *London Journal* novels of the 1860s and 1870s, we can verbalize it as the question and exclamation, 'How is the author to solve *this* problem in the narrative while using the conventions? Surely s/he will fail and fall!'. We know what the routines are – how well are they executed? And the performers know we know and perform with seductive irony and reflexivity: precisely, that knowingness we associate with the music hall and indeed with its sunny analogue, Italian comic opera.

As Simon Frith (1995-96: vi-vii) remarks on performativity in late twentieth-century popular culture, audiences want to pay for 'performance as labour'. In other words, they want a display of cultural capital in the form of technical skill. Together with audience satisfaction, skill is a constant criterion for evaluating performance in *London Journal* accounts of stars of the stage. In its novels, successful resolution of the problem set up by a plot within the formulae – the rules of the game, the routines of the genre – confirms the labour value of the commodity. Unless they are comical, as in many pages of Egan's *Such is Life* (1863-64), novels that offer magical, gothic, non-realist, solutions do not give value for money (a rule which is subverted in the lower zones of fiction which resistively or parergically parade their casual assembly).

There is a second, more difficult explanation of the audience's gasp – that the spectacle of technique they have paid for is also a spectacle of performed otherness. As such, its function can in turn bifurcate, depending on whether it is successful or not. A successful performance confirms the superiority of the artiste over spectators and so keeps the latter in their (social) places by reminding them that they are inferior; the difference between self and a superior other remains intact. In this sense the function of the performance is socially conservative and liable to fall into Lemon's exclusionary practices. But part of a spectator/reader's pleasure in the performative lies in the possibility of the artiste's technical failure. The performer risks collapse into the fallible, into the 'like us', into the disappointment of 'we could have done that', or worse, 'we could have done better'. The gasp is the sign of the affect that marks the switch in the tracks leading to vilification, to identification or to acknowledgement of superiority.

There is also a possibility that leads simultaneously to identification and awareness of superiority. This double destination results in emulation of the star who remains unfallen. Such emulation encourages readers to contribute poems and tales. Readers contributed in substantial numbers from 1848, and while the collapse of the reader/writer distinction was not new to the Johnson-Egan period, it became even more emphatic. From Stiff's repurchase, reader-contributors, especially poets, had become more faithful, repeatedly sending in their works. Tracing the position of their contributions between Notices to Correspondents and 'inside the magazine' makes it possible to determine the status of each contributor with a little more certainty than in the case of the isolated appearances of unidentifiable initials only 'within' the magazine. The mobility of, say, 'A.C.' in volumes XLII-XLV and 'Erato' over volumes XXXVIII-LXVIII suggests that they were primarily readers. Others, however, blur this already fuzzy distinction even more. The status of 'A.H.B.' who contributed from 1868 to 1882, is very unclear. While poems with this signature are found in Notices to Correspondents, most tales and poems with it are 'inside' the magazine. In one number towards the end of a period during which a large number of works have carried the signature, 'A.H.B.' appears both after a tale 'inside' and after a poem on the correspondence page (LXVII: 213-15, 224). In the 1870 Christmas supplement a tale is signed 'Astley H. Baldwin' which may fill out the name. Since Christmas supplement writers were from the centre of the *London Journal* network, 'A.H.B.' may therefore have been primarily a paid contributor. Might the appearances of this signature in Notices to Correspondents mean a professional's invasion of readers' space rather than a reader's invasion of the professionals'? There is, of course, no reason why 'A.H.B.', 'Erato' and others may have been paid or not at different times. As one journalist wrote, reflecting on his beginnings in the trade:

> Soon after I came to London, I commenced writing articles for newspapers and periodicals, some of which were inserted and others were not; and some of those which were inserted were paid for, and others were not.   (Edwards, 1906: 19-20)

Isabella Fyvie Mayo (1910), who wrote for the *Family Herald*, tells a similar story. Such uncertainty of status between professional and amateur does not detract from the point I am making here. Rather such confusion of the difference between them only encourages emulative identification. That said, the confusion has quite clear boundaries, for it occurs almost entirely with one-episode tales and poems. Despite the possibility of a few exceptions (perhaps some of the unsigned novels), readers do not contribute lengthy serials. The serial is the arena where professional artistes perform, marking out the difficulty of the genre and their technical superiority. The difference between the two kinds of space is that between the songs the *Journal* occasionally published to be played and sung at home, and the coloratura that the professionals performed and the *Journal* praised. If readers could become writers, they were nonetheless kept as amateurs, fillers of space between the four or five serial pillars.

If the parergic lost ground to the performative, the politography of 'London' was also redefined. Johnson continued the national and international rovings that Stiff had initiated and returned to after Lemon's distinctly metropolitan stance. While there were numerous articles on various aspects of the metropolis, there continued a greater proportion on places and events outside it. Volume LXIX (1879), for example, had twenty-nine 'General Articles', of which nine were concerned with places in London; volume XLV (1866) twenty-one, of which three were concerned with locations in the capital. Modernity continued to be the predominant light that London was presented in, with stress on urban spectacle and possibilities for entertainment: 'London Railways' (XLIII: 141), 'Alexandra Palace' (LVI: 56), 'Regent's Park Zoo' (LVI: 4), 'The Latest Additions to the Crystal Palace' (LVIII:133), 'The Thames Embankment' LIX: 37-8), 'Her Majesty's [newly rebuilt] Theatre' (LXV:267-8), 'The New Savoy Theatre' (LXXIV: 285-6). From the early 1870s a substantial piece on the Oxford and Cambridge Boat Race became a regular annual feature. While the event was reported and depicted in the *ILN* too, the *Journal*'s articles do not constitute continued parergy – there is no trace of metamorphic resentment – but rather exploitation of a spectacle available to the masses. Even though it reappears sometimes in the 1860s (for example, in *Such is Life*), by the 1870s the *Journal*'s 'London' had almost entirely lost its dark, labyrinthine, potentially radical status; associations with commerce, the law and entertainment dominated instead. 'London' had become a conglomerate of luxurious mansions and shops, opera boxes, receptions and novelties of all kinds. Figure 7.2 shows how the spectacle of the boat-race was less important than the kind of dress to be worn at it: not only are the women's clothes more prominent than the race but the woman on the left stages the reader's desirous gaze towards the fashionable belles on the right.

[THE UNIVERSITY BOAT RACE.—THE FINISH.]

Figure 7.2 'The University Boat-Race: The Finish' (1872)
Source: LVII: 248.

Many novels reinforce the idea of a metropolitan consumer utopia in their oscillation between a glittering, social London and an isolated, quiet and primitive countryside where, contrary to the 'mysteries' novels of the 1840s, abduction, murder and illegal imprisonment are now more likely than in town – almost a reversion to eighteenth-century ideas about the city and the country. This reconfiguration is closely related to the realignment of London with Paris from 1868. Even while the fiction axis remains London-New York, in the 'Ladies Supplements' now introduced, London becomes a Paris *manqué*, mediator and distributor of the newest consumer items in clothes. The garrulous reverence for the chic that characterizes 'London' in the 1870s is very different from the years when London raided Paris for the socio-political novel. It deserves a chapter to itself (see Chapter 10).

Over the Johnson-Egan years, the 'London' of the *London Journal* consolidated its position in the Strand. It was happy not just amongst the perfumers and its fellow periodical offices but amongst the theatres. Its published words and images were again congruent with the geographical point they were assembled in and distributed from – a politography of feminized consumer desire that offered a skillful performance at little cost. The 'holiday crowd', excitedly walking along the 'home of the theatres' (Dickens, 1879: 243), pleasure its only aim, was completely victorious, its connections to consumerism locked into place, its political potential emasculated: an ideological stance echoed by the *Journal*'s new premises in the grander 332 Strand, with its commercial version of a *piano nobile*.

1868-80. The Ladies' Supplement and the Transatlantic Exchange

Where will you find an ANGEL
OF INNOCENCE?
Seek 12,5,67
Is there to be found
An Angel of Innocence?
YES!
Where would you look for
An Angel of Innocence?
Strange but true!
An Angel of Innocence
Is Coming among you.
Maidens
Welcome the
Angel of Innocence!
Bachelors
Salute the
Angel of Innocence!

THE WHITE WIDOW!!
WHO IS THE WHITE WIDOW?
HAVE YOU SEEN THE WHITE
WIDOW?
NO, I HAVE NOT SEEN THE
WHITE WIDOW.
Do you wish to know who is
the White Widow?
YES! – READ the NEW NOVEL
in THE LONDON JOURNAL
Written by a popular Author.
The most exciting of all
modern Romances EVER
WRITTEN!

Figure 7.3 Typical wording of notices advertising forthcoming serials in the late 1860s
Sources: *Weekly Times*, XXI, 21 April 1867: 7. *Weekly Times*, XXII, 22 March 1868:7

1867-69 seems to have been a difficult period for older periodicals in the penny weekly zone. *Cassell's Illustrated Family Paper* changed its name and became a more up-market monthly in March 1867. In 1869 *Reynolds's Miscellany* folded. There were various attempts to revive the *London Journal*'s circulation. By 1870 the *Journal* was advertising its worldwide consumption on its revamped monthly covers. New kinds of strident advertisement were appearing in the *Weekly Times* perhaps inspired by American models (cf. Figure 7.3 with several adverts in Johannsen, 1950). From 1867, there were sixteen-page 'Christmas Supplements' at a penny extra. After an initial experiment of four separate stories, the Christmas Supplement regularly comprised a garland of tales set in a frame narrative. In terms of production, it seems to have had a double function for the first few years. Not only directed outwards as an attraction for readers, it may also have served to consolidate and mark out the centre of the *London Journal* network. James Grant,

Pierce Egan and Fairfax Balfour continued to be central for the first three years, joined in 1869 by John Parsons Hall, who now returned, having left just before Lemon took over. The supplement for 1870 added Mrs Gordon Smythies (and Astley H. Baldwin). Thereafter, most Christmas Supplements were anonymous or signed by Egan alone. In 1878, summer Holiday Supplements began, connected with the increase in the number of Bank Holidays in the 1870s. They are less helpful in identifying networks, as Clementine Montagu alone signed the first, and the remainder are by unidentified authors.

Other alterations were made to the *Journal* at this time. The number of pages of each weekly issue was temporarily upped to twenty at the beginning of 1868. This only lasted four months and led, in April 1868, into the most visually striking innovation of the entire first series, the fortnightly Ladies' Supplements and the monthly hand-coloured fashion plate. The latter cost a penny extra, and must have produced an amazing shock of colour to readers used only to black and white engravings in the magazine — they certainly amazed me when I saw them for the first time. The plate was a steel engraving, roughly 18cm x 30cm (usually slightly smaller than a *London Journal* page, though this may well be due to the librarian's knife). For many years it was water-coloured by hand: for other publications it is documented that armies of women were employed to do this (see Ginsburg, 1982: 10; Steele, 1988, ch.7). In October 1876 a chromolithograph of 'The Beautiful Georgiane' was given away with the monthly part, and from May 1878 it is clear that the colours were laid on by machine, possibly encouraged by the increasing use of chromolithography in American magazines such as *Frank Leslie's Popular Monthly*.

Initially these changes were almost certainly in imitation of a new penny illustrated fiction weekly, *Bow Bells*. *Bow Bells* appears to have been connected in some way to the *Journal*'s one-time arch-rival, *Reynolds's Miscellany*, at least through its publisher, John Dicks, and possibly though Reynolds (Lloyd-Jones, 1952: 526). From 1864 both *Bow Bells* and *Reynolds's* shared the same publishing address, in the Strand of course, at number 313.[12] In terms of networks, *Bow Bells* was thus a descendant of the *Journal*. It began to compete with its forebear on 12 November 1862, no doubt encouraged by the repeal of the paper duties the previous year. Strahan (1870: 449) would later class it with the *Journal* and the *Family Herald*, and, noting its especial appeal to women readers, that it added 'music and work-patterns'. Mitchell (1989: 146) described it in terms of 'commercial slickness'.

The second series of *Bow Bells* (from 1864) had broken new ground in two main ways. Firstly, it increased its number of pages from the hitherto standard sixteen to twenty-four, offering more value for money. Secondly, it aimed sections explicitly

---

[12] The publishing history of *Bow Bells*, like that of so many cheap periodicals, needs clarification. The magazine first came out 12 November 1862. Its new series started 3 August 1864 and lasted until 28 December 1887. It was then transformed into *Bow Bells Weekly: A Journal of Fiction, Society Gossip, and Fashion*, which carried on until 12 February 1897. An attempted continuation, *Bow Bells: a Journal for the Home*, had only two issues, dated 15 and 22 February 1897.

at women with some spare income and pretensions to gentility. Its main distinguishing feature was a piano or piano-and-voice piece on the last page of each number, but it also carried fashion plates, imported from Paris, according to the usual practice of the time. They were etched by the famous French engraver Carraché and printed by the firm of Moine et Falconier, a well-known syndicated printing house specifically for the magazine.

Since at least the 1790s, the fashionplate had formed part of the expensive ladies' magazines such as the *Lady's Museum* and the *Magazine of Female Fashions of London and Paris*, and there were several long-running costly periodicals which carried them in the nineteenth century. But *Bow Bells* seems to have been the first penny weekly to introduce them, possibly inspired by the success of the Beetons' *English Woman's Domestic Magazine* which, at twopence a month from 1852, had created a different market from its more expensive predecessors (Beetham, 1996). Besides the fashion plate, *Bow Bells* also ran a Ladies' Page by 'Madame Elise', a signature repeated until the 1880s. The Ladies' Page in fact usually covered around three pages of text, its border with the rest of the magazine difficult to discern. There seems little attempt to corral 'Ladies' into one section of the magazine. Where the 'family' section starts again and the Ladies' Page ends is impossible to pin down, though the start of the Ladies' Page is always made clear with a heading.

In this new format *Bow Bells* was very successful: the preface to volume I claims a circulation of half a million. Even if this figure is a gross exaggeration, it is almost certain that it would have bitten into the *London Journal*'s sales. What is strange is how slowly the *Journal* reacts given its quick responses to earlier combatants in circulation wars. There may have been several reasons for this. When *Bow Bells* first came out, Stiff was publishing the second series of the *Guide*. The latter had started life on 27 July 1861 at 334 Strand, at the same time as the repeal of the paper duties. It initially cost a halfpenny and comprised eight pages of recycled serials, articles and prints from earlier volumes of the *Journal*: its first serial was *Minnigrey*, with the original prints by Gilbert. It was aimed at a cheaper market than the *Journal*'s and one that was treated as less discriminating in its demand for the new. When Johnson took over, he was more concerned to bring out a series of Supplementary Volumes of reprints. These two reprinting moves were not so much intended to increase profits through raising circulation of the primary product (and so fending off a new rival) as with invading other markets – the halfpenny and the volume – with the same material.

It took four years, until after the *Guide* had been reincorporated, for the *London Journal* to engage *Bow Bells* in direct combat. The former's Ladies' Supplement was clearly modelled on its rival's Ladies' Page in its inclusion of small patterns and comments on fashions, but more significantly the engravers of the plate included Carraché, and its printers were Moine et Falconier. Moine et Falconier continued at this time to be the printers of *Bow Bells* plates, though since the beginning of 1868 *Bow Bell*'s engraver had been A. Lacouvrière and its artist the notable chief designer of *Le Petit Courier des Dames*, François-Claudin Comte-Calix. After a few issues, however, the *Journal* managed to gain more prestige by using as its main artist E. Mille, known as one of the best later artists of the famous up-market French fashion magazine *Le Follet*. Presumably all this was successful: not only did the *Journal*'s claimed circulation increase but Stiff's *London Reader* engaged in related practices in October 1870 by adding a page of piano music and a monthly clothing pattern.[13]

The *London Journal* fashion plate was only available with the monthly number. The latter had always offered the purchaser a more unfavourable exchange rate between price and quantity of contents compared to the weekly issues. The appeal of the monthly part could not have been 'value for money' in any simple sense. As we saw in Chapter 4, monthly parts were often bought by post, and one could conceivably opt for this if one lived remote from a stationer's. But one of the reasons the monthly number sold must have been precisely because it was more expensive: it *distinguished* the monthly purchasers from the weekly, indicating their greater financial resources. A further distinction was introduced with the monthly fashion plate. Like that of *Bow Bells*, it cost a penny extra on top of the extra tuppence for the monthly part, and this further option sub-divides the two main classes of *London Journal* reader, the weekly and the monthly, into those who cannot afford the fashion plate and those who can.

The advertising on the monthly covers – exemplified in Figure 7.4 – is clearly directed to a social group with some spare cash for Slack's Silver-Plated Cutlery, the Excelsior Knife Cleaner, T. Venables' Carpet, Furniture and Upholstery Shop in Whitechapel, Oezman & Co.'s Furnishing Catalogue, John Goswell's Cherry Toothpaste, Mrs S.A. Allen's Hair Restorer, Bond's Permanent Marking Ink, Dr Locock's Pulmonic Wafers, Parr's Life Pills, Lamplough's Pyretic Saline & Concentrated Lime Juice, and a variety of sewing machines.[14] Taken together, the advertisements suggest a reader who has the purchasing power (or potential for it) to achieve a certain domestic gentility, and whose priorities are family health and, interestingly to a lesser extent, appearance. This reader profile is mainly gendered feminine, an aspiring 'lady' who may well desire to shop in the Strand (Slack's was only a few doors from the *Journal* office). There are also a few advertisements directed to men: overcoats, White's Moc-main Lever Truss and Kinahan's LL Whisky. More gender neutral, there was also extensive advertisement of the *Journal*'s 'Supplementary Volumes' and of novels by Pierce Egan, now in book-form and published by Johnson. And in case cash in hand did not quite stretch to the advertised commodities, notice is constantly given of a moneylender in Fleet Street ready to help out.

If for the first time colour flashed in the *London Journal*, equally striking changes were taking place amongst the authors. Besides Smith's re-emergence in 1868 (including a reprint of his first tale for the *Journal*, 'Mariamne', now anonymous but illustrated, in 1870), Emma Robinson briefly returned after an absence of over ten years with a two-part tale. Given the brief and unexpected re-appearances of John Wilson Ross and 'E.O'H.' during the end of Stiff's ownership

---

[13] In the BL run, the *London Reader* patterns only last over vol. XVI: it is not clear whether the patterns were dropped thereafter or whether the BL failed to bind them in.

[14] These commodities and others in the paragraph are advertised repeatedly in the monthly parts of vol. XLVII (1868).

in 1862, and the reversion in the last numbers of Lemon's reign to the format which he first experimented with, a curious rule seems to be that revenants must oversee a critical transition from one stage to another. This will also be the case with the surprising second return of J.F. Smith in 1880 at the death of Pierce Egan, not with a reprint, but with a 'New and Original Story', *The Lost Wife*.

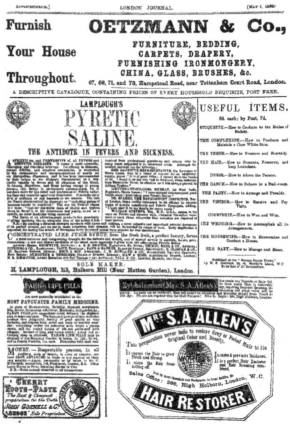

Figure 7.5 Page of advertisements from monthly cover
Source: XLVII, May 1868.

Despite a misleading announcement in the *Weekly Times* (10 November 1867: 7) that he was 'exclusively engaged to the *London Journal*', J.F. Smith was never part of Johnson's stable. Why he never became so remains obscure. In 1863 Smith had taken out an injunction to stop Johnson (and his then partner Thomas Wilson) republishing *Stanfield Hall* in a *London Journal* supplement, maintaining that he had retained copyright. The vice-chancellor adjudicated in his favour (*Times*, 20 November 1863: 8-9). Publication nevertheless continued, and it can be inferred that Johnson bought the copyright, along with the copyright to Smith's other novels that Stiff had held. Johnson seems to have wanted a monopoly of Smith's name, for in 1871 he paid Cassell £1,200 for all the copyrights of his stories that had been published in *Cassell's Illustrated Family Paper*. This was a worthwhile purchase: if Johnson's claims in the *Times* can be credited, when the *Cassell's* stories were republished in the *Journal* under different titles, circulation, having dropped alarmingly, rose back up to 400,000. [15]

Smith's relationship with the *Journal* in the 1860s and after is less clear than in the 1850s. He went to America, probably in late 1869, and contacted Robert Bonner, the proprietor of the *New York Ledger*. His first surviving letter to Bonner is unfortunately opaque, relying as it does on allusions only Bonner would have understood:

> I quitted New York last Friday night. Circumstances led me to remain longer than I intended. I had accepted an absurd position and felt bound to fight the battle to the bitter end. Bound by a tie no one can understand better than Robert Bonner – Honour.
> By remaining I succeeded in saving very nearly a thousand pounds out of the wreck for Mr Johnson.
>
> (J.F. Smith letter, dated Toronto, 27 April 1870, Robert Bonner Papers, NYPL)

Perhaps his presence was meant to secure Johnson's copyrights in the face of American pirating; perhaps he was negotiating for more tales directly with Bonner's contractee, Southworth. Either would explain these remarks. Thereafter, while his serials were being rerun in the *Journal* with great success, and at least one novel was pirated in Canada,[16] Smith was to remain in an isolated part of upstate New York where he pursued a downward-spiralling career writing for the *New York Ledger* and other papers for medium to small sums. He wrote fifteen novels for the *Ledger* between 1871 and 1885 at a rate that varied between $1,200 for *The Last Move in the Game* (1871; $100 per episode), to only $500 for *The Reign of Terror* (1878), a reworking of the third book of *Stanfield Hall*.[17] He died a pauper in February 1890, presumably in West Chazy where he had lived on and off for almost twenty years. His last letter to Bonner (3 December 1888), almost illegible with the spidery hand of the aged and ill, begs for a loan of $100 to cover the costs of 'a doctor, medecine [*sic*] and fire in [his] room'. In the event of his death he promises that a brother in India will pay the debt. Typically for his generation in this literary zone, he had not kept his copyrights; nor did Noel's idea of old-age pensions for *Ledger* authors apply to him.

Meanwhile, so successful was the reserialization of his novels in the *Journal* that at least one was pirated in England and provoked a prosecution. In 1871 a novel called *Dick Tarleton* was being printed in a provincial weekly newspaper, the *Conservative Standard*. *Dick Tarleton* had been its original title in *Cassell's Illustrated Family Paper*: in the *London Journal* it was renamed *Girls and Wives*.

---

[15] See *Times*, 4 August 1871: 11, 'Johnson v. Lister'; see also *TLS*, 1930: 1104, which claims the sum as £1,000.
[16] *Minnigrey* was serialized under the title *The Hidden Ring*, in the *Montreal Daily Star* in 1881 (my thanks to Toni Johnson-Woods for informing me of this).
[17] See Bonner letters dated Weldon House, St Albans, Vermont, 12 July 1871; West Chazy, Clinton County, 6 November 1876, 20 November 1876, 26 November 1877 in NYPL.

The circulation of the *Standard* was only 3,000 to 5,000 a week, yet both Johnson and Egan, appearing as witnesses for the prosecution, demanded 'considerable damages', since sales of the *Journal* had, they claimed, been seriously cut as a result of the piracy. The jury at first decided to award £125 compensation, but on appeal this was reduced to a risible £5. It was considered that the *Journal* had in reality lost only 800 purchasers – the sales of the *Standard* which bore Smith's novel (*Times*, 18 August 1871: 9).

The return of Smith notwithstanding, the biggest change during the last twenty years of the *Journal*'s first series fiction occurred with the introduction of Harriet Lewis in 1869. After Lewis's entrance on 24 July with *The Double Life* there is not a single number of the *Journal* without one of her serials until 8 February 1879, a succession of tales halted only by her death. She took over the position as doyenne American serialist from Southworth, eventually totalling no fewer than twenty-two novels in the *Journal*, a number of serials second only to Pierce Egan's twenty-four (Johnson-Woods, 2000: 356). The same year she appeared, the Canadian May Agnes Fleming began her contribution of possibly thirteen novels.[18] From 1872 the unidentified Clementine Montagu contributed sixteen. Meanwhile, Pierce Egan continued writing, alone exceeding Lewis not just in number of novels but in density of appearance. Percy B. St John, Fairfax Balfour, James Grant, and Mrs Gordon Smythies were published more sporadically, along with a newcomer, 'Ernest Brent', the pseudonym of Henry Emmett, who wrote for the *Journal* between 1871 and 1875.[19] Also in 1871, John Parsons Hall marked his return with a series on 'Whom to Marry, When to Marry and How to be Married', picking up his earlier essays from the 1850s on 'Courtship and Marriage Etiquette'. Thereafter he regularly contributed articles on social topics (and especially on the roles of women in society), as well as a few tales to the end of 1876 (only two more pieces appear after that). The following year, Edith Stewart Drewry, two of whose novels had already been published in the *Family Herald*, became a regular serialist, although she was only ever identified through by-lines.

Two difficulties now arise: the identity of an untraceable major *Journal* writer and whether and in what sense the works by identifiable American women were pirated. The unidentified writer I refer to is 'Clementine Montagu'.[20] While there is no sign of this name in biographical dictionaries, in the separate volume market, in analogous periodicals or the literary reminiscences I have read, it is broadcast immediately, and the fact that she is included in the Christmas supplements, like Mrs Gordon Smythies before her, suggests that she belonged to the centre of the network. It is possible that 'Clementine Montagu', was a pseudonym that a writer known in more up-market fields used only for work that appeared in the penny

---

[18] The *Journal* attributes thirteen novels to Fleming. I have uncovered two more, but I have not been able to confirm some of those the *Journal* assigns her. MacFarlane (1895) lists her novels, warning that Fleming wrote 'hundreds' of others and that she was so popular that her name was attached to works not written by her at all.

[19] My thanks to several members of the Bloods and Dimes on-line discussion group for identifying Emmett for me.

[20] Two spellings of this author's name are used, one with final 'e' and one without.

fiction zone, but it could also be a generic name, invented by the *London Journal* network covering the work of a 'serial factory', or of several different writers either pirated (with titles altered) or paid for. There are known examples of such practices, including a 'dime novel factory' in New York later in the century, where the stages of writing were split between groups of employees: some read the daily and weekly press to find articles of interest; managers chose from the selection; another group made story outlines before the chief manager sent them out to appropriate writers for elaboration (Denning, 1998: 17-18; Palmer, 1991: 6). Closer in terms of date and transatlantic interaction is a complicated case of pirating and then appropriation of a name recorded by Noel (1954: 187-8, 190) and Denning (1998: 23-4). Late in 1876, the *New York Weekly* took a serial from the *Family Herald*, *Wife in Name Only*, 'by the author of *Dora Thorne, Redeemed by Love, Love Works Wonders*, etc'. At the end of the serial, the American weekly found the initials 'C.M.B.' and made up the name 'Caroline M. Barton' for a subsequent story with similar English background and tone. Later, for a third serial, they used the same initials in reverse, filled out as 'Bertha M. Clay'. In fact, the *Family Herald* author was Charlotte May Brame. She died in 1884, while 'Bertha M. Clay' continued as a signature in the *New York Weekly* up to the 1920s.

It is similarly difficult to determine whether the stories by North American women were pirated, for the decision depends partly on the definition of the term 'pirating' and partly on information that is lacking. While Stiff still owned the *Journal*, there is no doubt that *Uncle Tom's Cabin* was pirated in the same way that novels by Sue and Dumas were. But later works present complications, showing the complex effects of transatlantic interaction that differ from local or French raids.

Although May Agnes Fleming's first two novels in the *Journal* were pirated in a quite straightforward sense, this surprisingly worked to her advantage. In 1868, Fleming had signed an exclusive contract with the Philadelphia *Saturday Night*. The following year the *Journal* took from it a novel originally called *The Heiress of Glengower*, renaming it *The Sister's Crime* and publishing it anonymously. Several papers in America pirated it in return, unaware that it was already copyright in America. It was so popular that when it was legally stopped in the American papers, a 'bidding war' for the author resulted. The outcome was victory for Fleming: she transferred to the *New York Weekly* where she immediately tripled her income, later signed a contract that gave her 15 percent royalties on the sales of her novels in volume format, and, from 1872, contracted an arrangement to send the *London Journal* advance sheets for £12 per instalment. Altogether this gave her an income of $10,000 a year (McMullen, 1992: 68-9).[21]

Southworth's relations with the *London Journal* were even more complicated. After *Captain Rock's Pet*, none of her novels appear in it for two years, suggesting that Bonner may have found out that, despite her public protestations to the contrary, she really was selling her products to the *Journal*, and/or that she herself felt uneasy about breaking her exclusive contract with him. The next Southworth

---

[21] Joan Hall Hovey offers a brief but fascinating biography of Fleming (1840-80) at http://www.angelfire.com/ca3/joanhallhovey/mayagnesfleming.html (accessed 19/5/2003).

novel in the *Journal*, *Sylvia* (1864), may well have been pirated without her permission, as it is a version of *Hickory Hall*, a serial that had appeared in the *Era* in 1850. But such is impossible in the case of Southworth's next novels in the *Journal*, *Left Alone*, *The Manhater* and *The Malediction*. With the usual caveats about the unreliability of dating, these all appear either a week before or a week after they are printed in the *New York Ledger*.[22] Southworth's last novel in the *London Journal*, *Married in Haste* (1869), is a version of another *National Era* serial from twenty years previously, which again suggests piracy. Perhaps Bonner prevented Southworth from sending more advance sheets. Boyle (1939: 43) notes that she wrote a particularly strong declaration of loyalty to Bonner dated 12 January 1869, which we may read as protesting too much. It is probably because of problems with Southworth that Egan and Johnson turned to that other and younger *Ledger* staple, also under supposedly exclusive contract to Bonner, Harriet Lewis.

There is virtually no recent work on either Harriet Lewis or her husband Leon, also a novelist, though of their centrality to the nineteenth-century Anglophone mass-market there can be no doubt.[23] An insight into their relations with the *Journal* is available from the copious letters from them in the Robert Bonner files in NYPL. Leon blusteringly carried on the business writing in both his and Harriet's names. The following letter, which I give in full, is particularly interesting for its revelations of the *Journal* and the scramble for foreign fiction – as presented by Leon's exceedingly messy, extravagant scrawl and even more overblown imagination.

9 April 1873

Dear Mr Bonner

We hasten to return by first mail the London letter and to reply to the question with which you accompany it.

You refused us the proofs 4 years ago, saying (in substance) to Mrs L. that if she were to have them she would be likely to give undue prominence to the thought as to how the stories would suit over there, etc. (which, by the way, was a mistaken estimate of her character).

We or you or all of us have consequently had some $1500 or $2000 yearly less income during the period named than we might have had. Mr Johnson, of the London Journal, and others have repeatedly written to us to this effect, but we never replied to more than one in ten, and then only to say (you having refused us proofs) that they were not at our disposal, etc.

The next thing in order of course were [sic] offers for original stories – i.e. for manuscripts – but a like answer was returned, although the offers made exceeded any sums that had ever been paid anywhere by anybody for anything in the line of stories.

---

[22] Only Southworth's *Winning Her Way* does not display this temporal proximity at this time: in the *Ledger* 22 December 1866 to 5 October 1867; and in the *Journal* 18 May to 7 December 1867.

[23] Moore (1992) comprises a description of the Lewis letters to Bonner; Johannsen (1950, II: 183-86) gives an account of Leon's romantic life. Johnson-Woods (2000) ranks them top in the global popularity stakes.

And under this state of things it became a question with Sunday English publishers as to which of them would derive the most benefit from republishing from the regular Monday Ledger Mrs L.'s stories.

That is a race of printers of which we do not propose to constitute ourselves the time-keepers. We can do no less, however, than except Mr. Johnson, of the Journal, from the general condemnation. True, he reprinted the stories without authority and without paying for them – (since he could'nt [sic] have them for pay) – but he has done so under certain conditions which command attention from their rarity:

1st – He has given the name of Mrs L. and even given her a standing qualification of 'celebrated American authoress'

2nd – The London Journal is of ten times more literary importance and pecuniary value than all the rest of the story papers of the British E̶m̶p̶i̶r̶e̶ kingdom [sic] put together. The sum of $3,750,000 (£750,000) has been vainly offered for it to our own certain knowledge. [Here an unidentified extract from a book or magazine is pasted into the letter claiming the excellence of *The London Journal*.]

3rd – During our stay in London in '71, (as we must have told you upon our return) Mr Johnson called upon us at Morley's [Hotel in Charing Cross], offered us every civility, private boxes at theatres, invitations and introductions, etc. and upon the last day of our stay pressed upon Mrs. L a roll of bank [sic] of England notes, as an acknowledgement of the good he had derived from the stories, even in the face of sharing them with everybody else and under all the adverse circumstances – at which time he renewed his offers for proofs, as also for stories written expressly for him.

And now is this Mr Fiske[24] more to you than we are that you should 'aid and abet' him with the proofs you have so expressly refused to us, and so drag our names into a wretched squawk of a paper that could not possibly last three months, and during this period exist only in obscene contempt? After all you have been to us and we to you – after all we know of your heart and brain – we shall require your written declaration of preference in favor of Mr. F. before we will believe it!

Excuse scratches. We write in haste to catch the mail.

Ever yours,

Leon and Harriet Lewis

For all Leon's protestations, the *Journal* must have been supplied with advance copy of Harriet's novels since 1869, when Leon made the first of his many requests for proofs. Even more consistently than Southworth's novels, Harriet's appear in the *New York Ledger* and the *London Journal* at the distance of only a few weeks. Furthermore, all her novels until *Edda's Birthright* (1873) carry the notice that the *Journal*'s is '[t]he only edition in this country sanctioned by this celebrated American authoress'. This was no doubt prompted in the first instance by the appearance of Lewis novels in the *London Reader*, which, we recall, Stiff was publishing next door to the *Journal*. While almost all *London Reader* serials were anonymous, novels with Leon's signature had appeared there in 1866 and 1867, followed by one with Harriet's. More immediately, *The Hampton Mystery*, a version of Harriet's first novel in the *Journal*, *The Double Life; Or, The Hampton Mystery* had come out in Stiff's magazine only a fortnight before the *Journal*'s. Since the original had been published in America at exactly the same date as in the

---

[24] Amos Kidder Fiske (1842-1921), the editor of the American fiction paper, the *Boston Globe*, between 1874 and 1877.

Reader, Stiff could only have obtained a copy and put it into print by means of advance sheets: even given the unreliability of the printed dates, the sequencing of each number forecloses any other possibility. Perhaps he obtained the novel through a mistake in the address (as had happened under Lemon). Quite possibly, he was continuing the underhand practices he had already exercised with Reynolds. Later, Harriet's *Tressilian Court* (1871) would likewise appear in the *London Reader* a week before the *Journal* version, and *Lady Chetwynd's Spectre* (1873) at exactly the same time.

Yet there is another possibility. It is clear from the Bonner letters that Leon was a spendthrift and a gambler. After Harriet had procured fame and a good deal of money for them both since first appearing in the *Ledger* in 1862 (aged fifteen and already married to Leon), he had got very deeply into debt. Bonner, who was clearly very fond of Harriet, kept lending them money which she would pay back by writing several serials simultaneously for him under both her own and Leon's names (romances under hers, adventures under his): eighty-one numbers spread over five novels managed to pay off $6,075 at half rates. It seems to me very likely that the Lewises sent Johnson (and quite possibly Stiff – and others?) advance copy to increase their already huge but always insufficient income. Leon boasts their house cost $9,000, their carriage $3,000 and their horses $5,500 (letter to Bonner, 29 September 1874). A letter from Harriet (12 September 1877) reveals that Leon's debts were enormous: they had mortgaged their home for $36,000 to Bonner, sold 'books, diamonds, etc' but still owed between $6,000 and $7,000. This is the letter where Harriet confesses to having written Leon's stories: she wanted a five-year contract and a five-year extension of their mortgage. She needed to prove that she, at least, was reliable.

In such cases, one cannot talk of 'piracy' in the sense familiar from Dickens and elsewhere of robbing an author, or even of raiding a work owned by the publisher (as in the case of the *Journal*'s printing of extracts from the novel by Bulwer-Lytton, whose copyright was owned by Bentley). Here there is collusion between author (or author's husband) and a foreign publisher. Despite his protest, Bonner was not legally able to stop the Lewises sending copy to London, as there was no copyright agreement with America.

Although the notice that the *Journal*'s were the 'only sanctioned editions' in Britain was dropped after Bonner's complaint and her novels were now hidden away, unillustrated, in 'fourth position', the chain of Harriet's serials remained unbroken until her death from a botched gynaecological operation five years later.[25] Suggestive of quite how popular she was, it is the name 'Harriet Lewis' that was chosen to save the *London Journal* from Zola in 1883, just as 'E.D.E.N. Southworth' had saved it from Scott in 1859.

---

[25] See the letter to Bonner dated Rochester, May 1878, that he would only get in the event of Harriet's death – she was to undergo a 'painful and perilous' operation the next day. See also obituaries in *New York Times*, 21 May 1878: 1; *New York Herald*, 21 May 1878: 5; and a particularly affectionate one by Bonner in the *Ledger*, 15 June 1878: 4.

1880-83. Pierce Egan III and the Failure of the First Series

Pierce Egan died on 6 July 1880. Unlike most bohemians, he left £1,000 secured on his life assurance to his wife, and his valuable copyrights, furniture and effects, including his bound volumes of the *London Journal*, to his son and to his daughter Kate Watson. He had evidently been a Mason, as he left his cup and jewels to his son-in-law, but what part the Masonic network played in the *Journal*, if any, I have been unable to establish.[26]

After his death, numerous changes took place. Indeed, the set of practices and the network that had defined the magazine were radically altered. After eight years of publication by John Conway and later by T. Connelly, on 10 July 1880 Vickers again returned to the role. The editor's chair was taken over by Egan's son, also called Pierce, though there are signs that he had been editing the magazine for some time before his father's death.[27] Like Ross in the 1840s, Pierce Egan III was an editor unable to write serials and, according to Jay (1918-19: 17), was unhappy in his inherited position. Percy B. St John came out of semi-retirement to provide the necessary material: in 1878 he suddenly contributed two novels after years of writing perhaps only one short novel or a tale or two a year. In 1880 the density of tales with his signature increased and, with the exception of one volume, stayed at this level until the end of the series. By now he identified himself only through initials or the by-line 'the author of *Quadroona*' (his second serial for the *Journal*, signed only with initials, in 1856). As the only survivor of the first generation of *Journal* authors, perhaps he was called on to support and advise as well as provide copy.

Notwithstanding the presumed help from St John, the serialization of *Is He The Man?*, by the Sampson and Low author W.A. Russell, evinced bad management, the like of which had not been seen since Mark Lemon's time. On 6 December 1879 it suddenly ceased, only to be completed six months later in a series of free supplements. In February 1879 a further series of monthly supplements had started up: 'Complete Novels', each twelve pages long. By August 1881 these were being issued irregularly after there had already been confusion about when they actually came out. On 13 March 1880, four months before Pierce Egan II's death and the week after his last novel ended, a new feature had been introduced that attempted to break the grip of the serial novel within the body of the magazine. Again the term 'Complete Novels' was used but now it referred to stories seven pages long which occupied the front pages of the main magazine. Both kinds of 'Complete Novels' were clearly an attempt to move into the 'novelette' market patronized by the women of Lark Rise. But those in the magazine itself lasted only until a few weeks before Egan II's death: on 3 July 1880, the serial *Nellie Raymond: A*

---

[26] For details of Egan's will. see *Times*, 3 September 1880: 8. Obituaries are printed in *Times*, 8 July 1880: 10; *Weekly Times*, 11 July 1880: 5, *Athenaeum*, 10 July 1880: 49-50. His death is announced in the *Journal*, LXXII: 95.

[27] See, for example, the repeated advert for the Christmas supplement 'with stories by Clementine Montague [*sic*], Pierce Egan, Percy B. St John, and the Editor' (LXXV: 16, 32, 48, et seq.).

Romance of Regent Street by Watts Phillips's sister Emma was promoted to the front page after a fortnight in second position.

Holiday and Christmas supplements continued, but the only one that may indicate the centre of the *Journal* network is that of summer 1882. This included writing by C.H. Ross, E. Owens Blackburn, M. Byrnes and Alice Gunter, but only the latter two fill out initials that appear elsewhere in this period – the prolific tale-writer between volumes LXXII and LXXVIII, 'A.G.', and the commentator on social subjects and the female stage, 'M.B.' (LXXVI-LXXVIII). New authors from 1880 comprised mainly those who, even when a name can be found, remain unidentified and whose precise relationship with the *Journal* is unknown: apart from 'A.G. and 'M.B.', others include 'Mrs. Lodge', 'Cosmo Cumming', 'Annie M. Watson' and, in the Ladies' Supplements, 'Beatrice', 'Louise' and the 'Special Paris Correspondent', 'Hélène de St. Ange'. Of British writers only Emma Watts Phillips is identifiable, though like her brother she wrote under a pseudonym ('Annabelle Grey') or by-lines. Nonetheless, there seems continued use of the star name wherever possible.

The surprising return of J.F. Smith in 1880 with one 'New and Original' serial, *The Lost Wife*, was announced through relatively muted advertising, its typography indicating the virtual equivalence of Smith with Egan and Grant. Even in these advertisements confused management is evident: the advertised Egan novel never appeared and the Grant not for eight months. Smith's new story was followed by the arrival of the American actor-author Howard Paul with *Sylvia's Treachery*. I have been unable to determine Paul's exact relations with the *Journal*, but the suggestion that he was editor in 1854 is definitely a mistake (cf. Myerson, 1983). While Edith Stewart Drewry and St John continued to write, the network that had defined the *London Journal*'s character in the late 1860s and 1870s had on the whole broken up or died. New solutions were needed to carry the magazine forward.

For today's readers, by far the most important event in the *London Journal* since Braddon's two famous novels is the first British translation of a work by Zola, *The Ladies' Paradise*, 'TRANSLATED UNDER THE DIRECTION OF THE AUTHOR *Expressly for the London Journal*' as each instalment claimed. Originally serialized in 75 parts by the Parisian daily, *Gil Blas*, between 17 December 1882 and 1 March 1883, as *Au Bonheur des dames*, *The Ladies' Paradise* started to appear only six weeks later. Even though the *Journal* has the honour of publishing the first Zola translation in Britain, unsurprisingly, given the general observance of the zoning of the literary market, it has hitherto been hidden from bibliographers and critics. It has been known for some time that a translation had been published *en feuilleton* in Britain, but not where. The massively researched edition of Zola's letters had come across a reference by Vizetelly to its magazine serialization, but Vizetelly had erroneously assigned it to the *London Reader*. Not finding it there, the researcher had come to a halt (Zola, 1978-95: IV: 341). There is no trace in the *Journal* of who the translator was, but two sources enable his discovery. First, the *London Journal* translation is very similar to the first one in book form, by 'Frank Belmont', which came out in November 1883 as a triple-decker from the Tinsley Brothers. Second, while amongst Zola's correspondence there is no mention of a

'Frank Belmont', letters do survive from and to a 'Frank Turner'. These date from September 1882 to January 1883 – and concern the translation of *Au Bonheur des Dames*. Turner unfortunately never mentions the names of the two British 'grandes maisons' to whom he is offering his translation (and Zola never asks) but the upshot is that Zola provides him with a manuscript of the novel in three parts for 1,750 francs, plus 500 francs for an advance summary of the plot, so that the publishing houses can decide whether to accept the entire product (Zola, 1978-95, IV: 340-41).

Figure 7.4 'An Anxious Time for Denise', Zola, *The Ladies' Paradise*
Source: XXVII: 65.

Edmund Downey provides further information about the publication of the Tinsley translation. He never connects it to the *Journal*, although the fact that Tinsley and Johnson were good friends is surely as significant as in the case of the passage of *Lady Audley's Secret* between them: they certainly constitute Turner's two 'grandes maisons'. Downey's account focuses on the multiple authorship of the translation and the absurdity of censorship. He tells of how, although not finding *The Ladies' Paradise* an offensive novel even as it reached him, Tinsley had him work it over to produce something no more scandalous than '*Adam Bede* or *David Copperfield*' (Downey, 1905: 268). But then at the last moment Tinsley excized even more, desperately worried that the circulating libraries might not buy it. His surgery was in vain. The very name 'Zola' frightened them off and sales were disastrous.

Apart from the *Journal*'s omission of the last third of the novel (on which see Chapter 11 below) differences between the Tinsley and the *Journal* versions are slight: what are certainly misreadings of the manuscript by compositors ignorant of French names are returned to the original French version (for example, 'Bandu' in the *Journal* returns to 'Baudu', 'Deforges', to 'Desforges', and, curiously, the *Journal*'s 'Decker' to the original 'Hartmann'). There are also some slight changes in the prices of items and rare vocabulary substitutions. Given the reaction of the circulating libraries, the suppression of Turner's name in the *Journal* (and his eventual use of the pseudonym 'Belmont') may well stem from an anticipation of shame. It is unlikely the thought of prosecution was a worry: Vizetelly was to start publishing Zola the following year and would not be jailed for it until 1888 (Vizetelly, 1904).

Besides claiming Zola's authorization, the *Journal* also points out to readers who Zola was: the 'Author of "L'Assommoir"'. *L'Assommoir* had been repeatedly denounced in the British press as grossly immoral since 1877 (Baguley, 1976: 4), so we can assume that the *Journal* must have wanted to generate the thrill of transgressive reading. Not only was this going to be a French novel – and therefore wicked by definition – but by one of the most wicked of all writers. Its inclusion cannot, however, be seen as a move by Pierce Egan III towards a new market and the exclusive minority culture of avant-garde naturalism. As Bourdieu (1996: 116) points out, Zola's relationship to the avant-garde had been 'compromised' through his high sales: *L'Assommoir* had been one of his greatest commercial successes in France, making him a rich man. *Nana* (1880) had caused even more notoriety than *L'Assommoir*, but is discreetly not mentioned. Egan's commercial considerations are visible not only in his checking of the plot in advance but also in a request for Zola's permission to alter the text transmitted through Turner. Zola's reply cleverly negotiated economic and cultural capital, writing that there were certain things an author would put up with but not 'authorize' (Zola, 1978-95, IV: 348). At least he would get paid for this version, unlike for the completely unauthorized American translations that were currently available in the British market. As in the case of Scott in the *Journal*, however, *The Ladies' Paradise* flopped. In France, too, *Au Bonheur des Dames* continued the sharp decline in Zola's popularity after the preceding novel *Pot-Bouille* had failed to do as well as *Nana* (Schom, 1987: 105).

There are several ways we can deduce the novel's lack of success in the *Journal*. Firstly and most importantly, the *Journal* version is severely truncated, ending on 5 May 1883 after fifteen episodes. The explanation for the precise size of the abridgement lies partly no doubt in how Zola sent the translation in three parts. Instead of printing the last third, the *Journal* version ends with a condensed and rewritten adaptation of what in the modern Gallimard edition comprises only its last three pages. While serial novels in the magazine had, in general, become much shorter than they were in the 1850s (most in the 1880s last for around fifteen episodes or less), novels of twenty or more episodes were also printed. The complete *Ladies' Paradise* would not have been impossibly long therefore. Secondly, the translation is demoted from the front page to second position after only three episodes, replaced by *A Terrible Suitor*, with the tried and tested signature of 'Harriet Lewis'. The next week, *The Ladies' Paradise* falls to third position, where it stays for six weeks before spending the rest of its life in unillustrated bottom place. Lewis had died in 1878, so *A Terrible Suitor*, although not having appeared before in the *Journal*, must have either been recycled and renamed from an earlier and unidentified serial or been written by a different hand (or hands) and Lewis's name attached to it for promotional purposes. *A Terrible Suitor* will remain in first position until the anonymous *Fairest of All* pushes it to second position for its last three episodes. Even in its very last episode when its usefulness has been exhausted, *A Terrible Suitor* does not move down the hierarchy: *The Ladies' Paradise* is still occupying the bottom place.

The *London Journal* was by now definitely a women's fiction magazine. The *Weekly Times* advertised what it kept calling its 'charming' stories, *The Ladies' Paradise* amongst them (p. 7 of each issue, 7 January 1883 to 22 July 1883). In *May's British Press Guide* (1883: 269) the *London Journal* was included in an advertisement for Mather & Co. who now handled the advertising in its monthly parts. All the other magazines mentioned in the advertisement were women's fashion magazines: *Le Follet*; the *World of Fashion*; *London and Paris: the Ladies' Magazine of Fashion*. Over the first three months of 1883 twice as many feminine as masculine signatures appeared in the *Journal*'s Notices to Correspondents, even though the page had been turned over largely to marriage advertisements. Perhaps it was thought that a French novel about shopgirls and shopping would appeal to its readership. The novel after all maintained the axis with Paris that the Ladies Supplements had reintroduced in 1868. But this was by no means the only factor involved in success in 1880s mass-market fiction. Three decades earlier, the *Journal* had affected the conceptualization of the field, but it no longer enjoyed anything like such power, its smaller circulation and the enlargement of the field having massively reduced its market share. When the emblematic *Tit-Bits* had exploded onto the scene on 31 October 1881, fiction magazines had been directly competing with the *Journal* for some time. These likewise had become orientated towards women readers. The *Family Herald* was now 'the inseparable familiar and vade mecum of young ladies' (Waite, 1887: 73). After Fanny Fern's two novels in the 1850s, it had preferred to run English serials, several by 'S.S.' and at least one by Mrs Bird (a former *London Journal* author) in the 1860s. In the 1870s and early 1880s, Charlotte May Brame and Howard Markham were the mainstays, both writing romantic fiction. In his survey of the field, Hitchman (1881) mentioned other long-standing papers: the *London Reader* and *Bow Bells* of course, and, newer and less successful, the *Family Reader* (from 1871), the *Illustrated Family Novelist* (1879-1897), the *Illustrated London Novelette* (1880-1893), the *Family Novelette* (1880) and the *Ladies' Own Novelist* (1880). Newspapers had been carrying serial fiction since 1840 (James 1963: 39), but weekly supplements which carried fiction as well as news were now being issued by provincial dailies such as the *Manchester Courier* and the *Leeds Mercury*. Tillotson's Fiction Bureau (1873-1935) was busily securing serial rights from authors to sell on to these papers (Jones, 1984; Law, 2000). And, as I have suggested, cheap volume-format novels were becoming more and more accessible.

In this crowded fiction market the serialization of Zola appears as a failed attempt to differentiate the *London Journal* from its rivals. Soon other ways would be found. Just as Lemon had tried to attract purchasers by striking visual means in the last months of his editorship, so in the first week of 1884 the *Journal* underwent a radical redesign in a new series with a new graphic style and layout. Later that year Johnson succeeded in selling it to the printers C.W. Bradley of 12 and 13 Fetter Lane (issues from 11 October bear their imprint). I have no information about whether they formed part of a syndicate of the kind Tinsley tried to assemble. The *Weekly Times*, though, was sold to the radical journalist, politician and cultural philanthropist, John Passmore Edwards. He kept it at its old address of 332 Strand to which his most famous and profitable paper, the halfpenny *Echo*, now moved. The new series of the *London Journal* underwent several transformations, the new design clearly failing. From 1885 it reserialized novels by J.F. Smith and Pierce Egan in an apparently successful attempt to raise circulation. J.C. Francis in the *Star* (13 March 1890: 1) claimed circulation had doubled since the reprint of Smith's stories and Hitchman (1890: 164) declared that Smith's stories kept the *Journal* alive (see also Jay, 1918-19: 14, 17).

From 1890 a friend of Pierce Egan III, Herbert J. Allingham – the father of Margery Allingham the famous 'Golden Age' detective novelist and himself a mass-market fiction writer – edited the *Journal* (Thorogood, 1991: 8-15). In 1906 he relaunched the magazine as the *New London Journal*, with yet another run of Smith's *Minnigrey*. He removed the fashion plates and turned it into a general interest magazine, indeterminate in its gender address, in an attempt to combine the newer practices of Newnes, Pearson and Harmsworth with what was by now a traditional format. The magazine's offices were at 185 Fleet Street, from which Margery remembered watching the Lord Mayor's procession (Thorogood, 1991: 13). Three years later the redesigned weekly was still losing money and Allingham gave up the editorship: the title reverted to the *London Journal*. In three more years it ceased to exist as a separate publication.

C.W. Bradley incorporated it into *Spare Moments*, a fiction weekly started in 1888 which Allingham had also edited. The joint title was now *Spare Moments and the London Journal* (3 February 1912 to 10 March 1928). In 1919 this was sold to F.A. Wickhart, a printer that, according to the London Post Office Directories of 1925-8, shared its offices with several other printers and the *United Service Gazette* in an alley off Fleet Street. Included with the magazine were the copyrights of all *London Journal* stories (Anon., 1918; Jay, 1918-19: 33). The *London Journal* was now printed as a four-page supplement to *Spare Moments*: together they sold at 1½d per week or 8d for the monthly part. The joint magazine was explicitly designed to appeal to older readers who wished to revisit the fiction of their youth, and opened with 'Peeps into the Past', an invaluable but hitherto neglected history of penny fiction magazines by Frank Jay. Although a mere supplement, the *Journal* was still granted its own cumulative page numbers and seriation, and lugged around its history since 1 March 1845: 'NS 422 OS 3123' was printed in the headpiece of the last number. Gilbert's illustrations to J.F. Smith's novels adorned the front page of the monthly covers of *Spare Moments*, torn out of context. One of his illustrations to *Stanfield Hall* posed melodramatically on the cover and Egan's *The Flower of the Flock* was in mid-flow when the magazine abruptly ended on 10 March 1928, and Wickhart disappeared from the Post Office Directory.

Part 3

Periodical Gender; or,
The Metastases of the Reader

Chapter Eight

1845-55. Gender and the Implied Reader; or, the Re-Gendering of News

Gender Issues

In 1994, Slavoj Žižek published a volume provocatively entitled *Metastases of Enjoyment* in which he discussed, from a Lacanian perspective, the intermixture of politics and gender. His basic contention was that the local and temporary dissolution of identity that is orgasmic *jouissance* is particularly associated with femininity, but appropriated, transformed, and spread wide in war and racism, *metastasized* like cancer, by masculinity into the violence of everyday life. Part 3 does not continue what I see as the problematically essentializing procedures of Žižek's form of analysis. It does, however, negotiate the labyrinth of gender, violence, appropriation and transformation by means of the thread of metastasis and the murky light of psychoanalysis.

Žižek never defines exactly what he means by 'metastasis'. When I use it I wish to combine several of its senses. In classical rhetoric, it means a transition from one point to another in an argument. Its commonest usage today is in medicine, however, where it means the movement of a disease from one site to another, especially when a cancer moves to another part of the body and is transformed in the process. Metastasis, as I use it then, refers to relocation in a field that is also a transformation in rhetoric, which in Part 3 concentrates on the rhetorics of gender. The present chapter charts the metastases of the gendered implied reader over the first ten years of the *London Journal*'s existence.

When we talk of the 'gender' of a media text, or indeed of a commodity in general, it is curious that most of the time we define it in terms of its projected consumer. A 'lads' mag' is aimed at a certain kind of man, a 'women's novel' at women, and so on, irrespective of the sex or gender of the producer. Though we may retrospectively imagine origins, the gender of a commodity is arrived at through destination. We conceptualize gender in this case not through the producer or the material but through the imagined lover, not the seducer but the seduced, almost as if the commodity were the consumer's fault. But perhaps the seducer has in some sense to become the seduced, charming him or her with an image of themselves: a peculiar magic of the commodity fetish that underlies Part 3 as a whole but which will receive most direct treatment in Chapter 11.

The derivation of the gender of a commodity text from its imagined consumer has an important implication. For, based on the split between producer and consumer, there may be conceptualized a split between the text's content and its use. This division is to some extent arbitrary as I shall use it here – for what external evidence do we have of the real consumer's usage of the text at hand? Rather, compelled to deal with the implied reader, I have to search out traces of 'use' encouraged or permitted by the text, and hence to some extent written into it: I have to derive use from content. Nonetheless, as I hope my examples will make clear, the distinction I am making here is a tactically valuable one, especially in charting what I shall be describing as the gender masquerade of the *Journal*'s first decade, when content and use, producer and consumer, masculinity and femininity, messily seeping each into the other, do not correspond in any neat way to either side of a set of binaries.

In historical terms, the Crimean War proved a critical moment for transformations in the media, above all for the practical abolition of the Stamp Tax and the consequent explosion in cheap newspaper publication. Key to this explosion was a desire for 'news'. I shall in fact take a quite specific tack here, concentrating on how the war opened up the gender exclusivity of 'news'. 'News' was one of the major signifiers of the gender of the implied reader and one that the *London Journal*, as a cheap domestic *men's* magazine, had to negotiate in its early years. Later chapters will take up the story as the *Journal* slowly and unsurely metamorphoses into a space where women feel at home.

News and the Gender of the Domestic Miscellany

As I argued in Chapter 3, the *Journal* started by echoing generic miscellany practices of the 1820s and 1830s. This included its peculiar gendering of its implied reader. As one of the miscellanies put it: 'in each number ... [these] aim[ed] at variety ... be[ing] learned with the learned, didactic with the student, grave with the serious, jocose with the mirthful ...' (*Hughes' Weekly Miscellany and New Parthenon*, 8 July 1837: 1). A few explicitly addressed every member of the family: in the initial 'Editor's Address to his Readers', *Chambers's Edinburgh Journal* (4 February 1832, I: 1) divided its readers into no fewer than ten categories, including 'ladies' of the 'new' and 'old' schools. But most miscellanies only claimed to have something for everyone while in practice addressing men almost entirely. In its drive to provide a Church of England alternative to the utilitarian *Penny Magazine* and, more urgently, 'infidel' publications, the *Saturday Magazine* was ostensibly trying to include all possible categories of reader. Yet when it came to list them, all were men: the 'man of literature', the 'scientific man', the 'lover of Nature' (whose sex is indicated by the pronoun 'his'), 'the agriculturalist, the manufacturer, the mechanic, and even the intelligent operative' ('To Our Readers' of the *Saturday Magazine*, XIX). The *New Parley's Library* contained a 'Lady's Page' on Paris fashions but was otherwise entirely androcentric. Margaret Beetham remarked that when 'artisan magazines of the 1850s such as *Eliza Cook's Journal* and the *Family Economist* ... aimed at a class dialogue centred around the shared values of self-improvement and domestic virtue', they blurred the boundaries between 'women's magazines' and those for the unenfranchised respectable male (Ballaster, 1991: 84). Murphy (1994: 130) made a similar point about Chartist magazines. Nonetheless, we should not overstress this inclusive address. I maintain that, while the miscellany did not construct one subject position from which to read the entire text, the implied reader was nonetheless predominantly masculine.

The *Journal* constructs its early versions of the reader along similar lines. Apart from a few articles under Mark Lemon in the late 1850s, there was never anything directly intended for children and very little obviously addressed to women in its first fifteen and more years. While series such as 'Etiquette for the Millions' and 'Courtship and Marriage Etiquette' (1849-50) have sections directly addressing young women, and departments such as 'General' and 'Miscellaneous' have the occasional piece directed towards women, by far the most common addressee is masculine.

However, the *Journal*'s masculinity was always compromised. When its first issue declares its respectability, it uses terms that place it in the refined domestic space:

> Those who may purchase this journal ... may rest assured that they will not have given their suffrage and countenance in favour of a publication which will ever raise a blush upon the cheek of chastity, offend with political bias, or interfere with domestic tranquillity ...   (I: 16)

This recalls the aims of Thomas Bowdler, who, in his Preface to *The Family Shakspeare* of 1807, emphasised that

> it is to be hoped that the present publication will be approved by those who wish to make the young reader acquainted with the various beauties of [Shakespeare], unmixed with any thing that can raise a blush on the cheek of modesty... (Bowdler, 1807, I: vii)

In the 1861 edition Bowdler added that '[i]t is certainly my wish, and it has been my study, to exclude from this publication whatever is unfit to be read aloud by a gentleman to a company of ladies' (Bowdler, 'Preface', 1861, n.p.). Bowdler has taken on and improved the role of the family patriarch, policing in advance the reading and knowledge of women and children in the domestic space. By excising passages potentially offensive or embarrassing – those that disturb the fine balance of the patriarch's power over discourse – Bowdler allowed *The Family Shakspeare* to pass, in theory, directly into the hands of the family. To achieve this he has assumed that all language was controlled by and appropriate for men. Bowdlerization was therefore a sub-set of men's language made 'gentle' and available to non-men. In that sense, it was the common linguistic ground where genders could meet but men remained in control. It was masculine speech feminized.

This exactly mirrors the way women were not expected to buy magazines such as the *Journal* but only to be involved with their reception: men remained the gatekeepers of the flow of printed language. Hence the irregular inclusion of a women's version of 'useful knowledge' – instructions about food and keeping clothes clean, for example – that relates only to what was perceptible by men in the home. There is nothing in the *Journal* that relates to those essential areas of women's lives that tended to be invisible to men, such as details on childcare (found in Mrs Beeton's *Book of Household Management* of 1861) or the complex management of female networks necessary for domestic maintenance. This contrasts with the wealth of material on the management of men's relations with other men under the rubrics 'business' and 'politics': there are essays on 'How to Make Money', 'Monopoly in Trade', 'Individual and National Independence', and so on.

Figure 8.1 'Discussing the War, in a coffee-house, at Copenhagen – sketched by E.T. Dolby'
Source: ILN, XXV: 196, 26 August 1854.

The full title of *The London Journal: and Weekly Record of Literature, Science, and Art* played a key role in its self-presentation. 'Literature, Science and Art' was a standard collocation with a pedigree in miscellanies and was the part of the title that immediately told the reader that the magazine did not carry news – a key point, as periodicals that did were liable to a penny tax on each issue. This tax, the Stamp Duty, had been inaugurated at a time of concern for political turbulence and was intended largely to police the dissemination of news: it kept the initial sales price of newspapers high, in theory delaying (if not stopping) the spread of news to those who could not afford it. Underlying the tax was the notion that news implied participation – desired, potential or actual – in the political public sphere. While a clause advocating the voting rights of women had been included in the first draft of the People's Charter of 1837, it was quickly dropped. Support for women's suffrage continued to be sporadic and it was not until 1867 that the question was to reach Parliament (see Seymour, 1915: 475-6; Clark, 1996). Unlike women, most men could *in theory* vote, since property was the main qualification (this is not to suggest that most men actually were property owners and could vote, only that according to the law they could). Unsurprisingly, then, news was regarded as masculine, read and used by men for homosocial bonding in, for instance, the exclusively male geography of the barber's, irrespective of whether they could actually vote.[1] Another aspect, less closely related to enfranchisement than to crime reporting, was that news did not come ready prepared by Bowdler and was potentially improper for ladies to read. A *paterfamilias* might have actively to censor some items when he read the newspaper out loud to his household (Flint, 1993: 120-1, 129). Figure 8.1 provides a clear visual example where the only woman present amongst men discussing news is a serving maid. While the scene takes place outside Britain, the silent assumption is that this is the normal state of things. Figure 8.2 depicts only men clamouring for news of the 1848 French revolution. The official exclusion of news from the *Journal* therefore denied it access to one of the most important markers of masculinity in the periodical field.

Figure 8.2 'Rush for the Daily Newspapers', by Birket Foster
Source: ILN, XII: 155, 4 March 1848 (issue in which the 1848 French Revolution is first reported).

---

[1] On the gendering of the Habermasian notion of 'public sphere', see Clery (1991) and cf. Clark (1996) and Rogers (2000). See [Wright] (1867: 220, and 193-4, 219) for comments on where working-class men read newspapers.

If its gendering was more or less clear, what exactly news comprised was difficult to define, however. Most contemporary writers assumed that meaning and its uses inhered in the text, and thought that news too must be contained, indeed 'carried', within words. John Timm, the Solicitor to the Board of the Inland Revenue, declared that the legal identity of a newspaper lay in what was inside it — its contents — not in whether it had simply been registered as a newspaper (*Report*, 1851: 18). The latter would have been a purely legal fiction rather than a definition that based the legal on the inherent. In more general terms the commonplace, described in Chapter 2 above, that writing was like some kind of food or poison supported the notion that print carried substances from producer to consumer. Victorian linguistics itself was in general concerned less with how meanings might be produced than with philology and etymology, and these were aspects of content in the sense that the history of a sememe was considered to lie 'within' it (see Aarsleff, 1983). Such a conception of meaning clearly prioritises the sender of the message as the one responsible for – authorizing – the meaning. In terms of media history, this resulted in the prosecutions of the owners and printers of unstamped publications that were accused of 'carrying news'. In short, a definition of a text type based on content was linked to producers. It may seem that there was little appreciation that whether a text was 'news' or not might depend on how the text was read. In other words, 'news' was not considered as a 'mode of reading', an interpretative activity engaged in by consumers, but as determined by producers. This is the very opposite of the gender definition of a commodity text that I remarked on earlier.

The legal anomalies of 'class publications', which were officially exempt from the Stamp Duty yet did often 'carry' political news, severely tested the definition based on content: Collet (1899) is especially amusing on the contradictions. 'Class publications' were aimed at specific classes of readers: their definition was informed by their imagined consumers rather than just by their producers. And there were numerous comments on the intention- and production-led definition of publications and indeed of 'news' that did recognize the role of the reader. The following is typically ironic, and is useful also for its succinct explanation of the legal relation of 'news' to a subjective and *consumerly* relation to time:

> news [comprises] events of recent recurrence [*sic*], as what is recent is relative; i.e. relates to people's means of information; so that without going so far as to suggest, with some wag, that to ignorant persons Rollin's Ancient History might be news – it is obvious that the idea of what is recent is uncertain, and the definition of it must be arbitrary ...
>
> [According to the law] a newspaper is defined to be any paper containing public news, intelligence, or occurrences to be dispersed and made public, however old the news may be, unless the 'intelligence' consist only or principally of advertisements, in which case they cease to be news after twenty-six days: but on the other hand, if there be, without any news at all, any remarks or observations on any public intelligence or occurrences, the 'paper' is a 'newspaper' unless twenty-six days shall elapse between each number, or unless the size exceed two sheets, or the price exceed sixpence.
>
> (Mitchell's *Newspaper Press Directory*, 1851: 40)

Here we find an idea that we are more familiar with than the purely juridico-political definition of news which depends on the producer: news is defined by what is new for the consumer. This double definition allowed the *Journal*, like its major rival penny weeklies, room to manoeuvre. They were, I think, well aware of how news might be considered a mode of reading as well as a producer's intention, as 'use' as well as 'content'. As a result, these publications used techniques derived from their gender-ambiguous alliance with the miscellany and with domestic bowdlerization that encouraged or at least allowed its readers to use certain contents as 'news' or news-related, even while the contents might also be defined as non-news according to the juridico-political definition. By these means mass-market penny weeklies were able to bolster their gender identity as masculine.

I want to test this hypothesis by somewhat perversely examining the taxonomy provided by the *Journal*'s subtitle, 'Literature, Science and Art' – the very words that supposedly evacuated the periodical of news.

Literatures, Arts and Sciences

'Literature' is a comparatively simple case. The two modes I shall discuss, fictional and historical, provide a quite clear way of allowing in a news-like reading. Since in chapter 3 I discussed the *Journal*'s relation to the 'Mysteries of London' project, whereby political readings of society were made available unstamped through the assumption of fictional form, I want to say little about fiction here other than to note the importance both of how easily Sue's novelistic explorations and denunciations of French society could also be applied to British, and how the many topical references in Smith's historical novels could have encouraged typological readings, whereby events depicted in the past prefigured the present. The typological mode of understanding narrative, which Denning (1998) convincingly sees as key to American dime novels throughout the nineteenth century, would have been heard every Sunday by large numbers of readers in sermons, where it was a standard way of relating the Old Testament to the New, and the Bible in general to everyday life (cf. Wheeler, 1994: esp. 17-19; Joyce, 1996: 187).

The 'historical' side of 'Literature' requires treatment for two reasons. Firstly, in his report to the 1851 Stamp Committee, Abel Heywood identified the *Journal* by its 'large proportion of historical matter' (*Report*, 1851: 216). Secondly, the concept of history was in one sense the defining opposite of news, as Mitchell's *Newspaper Press Directory* explained above. Nonetheless, one of the commonest ways the *Journal* encouraged a news-like mode of reading was through what I shall call 'topical history', closely related to the typological mode of reading fiction. Thus from April 1848, just after the revolution in France, an account of the 1830 French Revolution was run. In the preceding March, just before the Chartist petition was presented, an article on the Birmingham Chartist riots of May 1839 headed a series on 'Narratives of Popular Outbreaks'. Not 'news' in the sense of reportage of very recent events, such pieces comprise 'news' in the sense I have defined earlier, through its implicit invitation to discuss current political events in the barber's, pub or coffee shop.

At other times, the *Journal*'s 'historical matter' was of a kind that during the 1840s was being colonized by women: biographies and memoirs (Maitzen, 1995). These also allowed the distinction between history and fiction to blur. When an account of the Irish politician Daniel O'Connell was serialized on the occasion of his death in 1847, it was called a *Memoir* and was run only a few weeks after the end of Sue's long serial novel, *Memoirs of Martin the Foundling*. At the outset it was claimed that politics would be eschewed from the O'Connell *Memoir* (V: 121), and the same claim was repeated at the end:

> We have simply chronicled the rise and progress of a great movement in the progress of intellectual freedom by the removal of those conscience restraints by which the refusal of political rights to Roman Catholics bound millions of our countrymen. It was a victory which we, bound by no party ties or political prejudices, may rightfully celebrate with acclamation.
> (VI: 40)

What is apparent in passages such as these is a sleight of hand whereby politics is redefined so narrowly as 'party politics' that it leaves the field open for information and debate about social issues. In other places in the O'Connell *Memoirs*, equivocation and melodrama veil a narrative that actually inserts readers into the public sphere. The 'story of her wrongs' (Ireland's) at the hands of English 'oppression and cruelty' (V: 286) is told in detail, playing on the trope of the wronged Irish maid (a common figure in mass-market fiction that appears both in Sue's *Mary Lawson* and, later, in Robinson's *Masks and Faces*). Extracts from O'Connell's speeches are reproduced at length (see, for example, V: 301, 307, 308) accompanied by a disingenuous and ambiguous comment that he was a 'political agitator' (V: 301). Thus, under various literary disguises, 'news' becomes part and parcel of the reader's relation to the *Journal*.

'Art' suggested news in similar ways. The many topographical sketches that populate the first ten years of the magazine are important in this respect. While some follow the pattern I described in Chapter 3 where a picturesque print and topographical description lead into an associated tale, others mask political commentary or news of parliamentary proceedings. Volumes III and IV carry a series openly called 'Political Sketches' *in the volume indexes*. Appearing at six monthly intervals, longer than the twenty-six-day period that defined a newspaper, the volumes were not subject to the restrictions on carrying news. In the individual numbers, the illustrated articles that make up the series appear as isolated pieces. The first, in May 1846, under a picturesque print (Figure 8.3), begins, like the memoir of O'Connell, with a disclaimer that '[w]e are not about to inflict upon you a political article', and goes on to give a sympathetic account of Robert Peel and reasons why the Corn Laws should be opposed, mixed with information about the importance of corn in the diet. This was extremely topical: the Corn Laws would be repealed in June after several months' discussion in Parliament (III: 165-7). The standard model for these 'topographical' articles, hidden away on inside pages, comprised a picturesque drawing of the relevant politician's country seat, followed by a biography and/or other information, interlarded with political commentary from a mildly radical perspective.

THE LONDON JOURNAL. 165

[DRAYTON MANOR, THE SEAT OF SIR ROBERT PEEL.]

SIR ROBERT PEEL AND HIS FREE-TRADE MEASURES.

START not, reader! We are not about to inflict upon you a political article, nor to attempt by the aid of our immense circulation, to encourage the

tion, and gradually becomes quicker and quicker in his utterance.

Now he has entered upon his career;—and mark how breathless is the attention around! He speaks on the Irish famine—he is deeply tragic in his language, mien, and gesture. He now repudiates un-

Barley is, next to wheat, the most important of all the cereal grains which are now cultivated in Great Britain. Its use as bread-corn has very much diminished of late years in this country. We read in Turner's History, that the monks of St. Edmund in the eighth century, ate barley bread, because the

Figure 8.3 'Sir Robert Peel and his Free-Trade Measures', with picturesque print of 'Drayton Manor, the Seat of Sir Robert Peel'
Source: III: 165.

Nunn (1987: 5-8) has remarked on the association of the picturesque sketch with the genteelly feminine, and the *Journal* seemed to be seeking through the picturesque print to maintain the appearance of a miscellany's domestic respectability. It also seems to be exploiting its marginal cultural value – the notion that it was of such indifferent status that it would not be carefully read by the periodical police at Somerset House. It assumes that respectable dress was enough to cover potential infractions of the law, especially as almost all are placed on inside pages. If in Chapter 3 I described the *Journal*'s politographic relation to Somerset House, in terms of gender the *Journal* does not so much attack Somerset House directly as skirt around it with virtually transparent masquerades and nonchalant, barely-concealed hypocrisy.

Readers versed in the 'Old Corruption' trope were sometimes offered a view of the splendours in which their political masters lived. This was especially the case with 'The Sale at Stowe', a series resembling a commercial catalogue minutely detailing the sale by the ruined Duke of Buckingham and Chandos of his ancestral treasures in late 1848 (VIII). Whereas other periodicals such as the *ILN* and *The Times* tried to tie down with commentaries the meanings of this media event, the *Journal* simply listed and depicted the bankrupt's goods. No direct commentary was needed to allow consumers to read in a politically critical way: such was the melodramatic fate corrupt 'harristrocrats' would necessarily come to. Yet at the same time such bare accounts easily allowed delight in the aesthetic 'ornamental' qualities of the art objects depicted, a particular bifurcation of interpretative possibilities that confirms a point in Chapter 3.

The 'picturesque political' had unsurprisingly started under Reynolds, as a variant of the quasi-sociological 'Mysteries of London' project, and it continued under Ross's editorship. The latter was still in control when the 1848 spring revolutions broke out. News erupted onto the front page in ways that the *ILN* was exploring and that we are more used to now, accustomed to thinking of news in terms of the immediate (see Figure 8.4). There was a string of articles on events in France, accompanied by the historical series on the revolution of 1830. The first piece on the 1848 revolution was careful to start with a variant on the usual disclaimer that the *Journal* was not carrying news, this time distancing the events reported from the present and suggesting the conservative outcome of what might have proved truly radical:

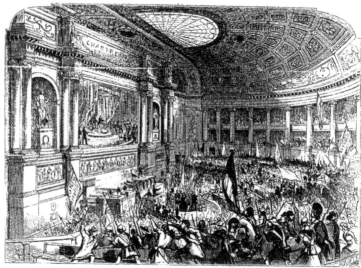

Figure 8.4 'The Chamber of Deputies' (1848)
Source: VII: 113.

At the time we are now writing, and probably at the time when this number of THE LONDON JOURNAL will be published, the agitation which has long prevailed in Paris has subsided, and tranquillity has been restored to a wonderful degree...   (VII: 33)

If the words implicitly claimed the piece was dealing with history, the illustrative style recalled the action pictures of the *ILN*. Figure 8.4, dated 29 April 1848, depicted the dramatic invasion of the Chamber of Deputies on 24 February. The *ILN* had reported and depicted the same scene on 4 March, so the image for all its sensational shock of the now, referred to a historical event older than the arbitrary twenty-six days imposed by law. Buried on the third page of the article was a paragraph on French hopes for the Chartist petition planned for 9 April, narrated as a future event and thus taking on the tense system of a political advertisement. But by the time this number was published, 9 April had passed, a flop, safely over, and effectively 'history', even if well within the twenty-six-day window of news. While I want to stress yet again that in the 1840s the relation of news with the 'now' was not as strong as we in the twenty-first century experience it, the *London Journal* was careful that its most noticeable content be defined as 'history'. It offered there the 'nearly news'.

Like 'Literature' and 'Art', 'Science' could refer both to a type of content and be co-opted into a gendered politics through readers' use of that content. The term occurs in departments variously called 'Scientific and Useful' and 'Science, New Inventions, etc.'. Even in terms of content, it had unstable boundaries, the 'and' and 'etc.' of the department headings allowing in a wide variety of topics: import and export figures for the month from the board of trade (XVII: 204); admission prices to the Great Exhibition (XIII: 28); the novelty of iron-cladding on houses and of an improved pump (XIV: 282); the digestive value of cheese after dinner (XIII: 12); how to make good butter in winter (XIII: 362). Such breadth – which importantly includes household hints – suggests that the term be treated as a metonym of an extended kind of 'useful knowledge' which slides smoothly into what we call 'consumer affairs' today. *London Journal* 'Science' is certainly not 'high science', the experimental and theoretical knowledge that distinguished the gentleman amateur and linked him to august official institutions such as the Royal Society. It is much more closely related to what Susan Sheets-Pyenson (1985) has called 'low science', a form of experiential, inductive, democratic knowledge which flourished from the 1820s to the 1860s in magazines such as the *London Mechanics Register* (1824-26) or the *Penny Mechanic, a Journal of the Arts and Sciences* (1836-37). It is important to note that the *Journal* also exhibits signs of what Sheets-Pyenson calls 'popular science', a divulgation and simplification of high science that she regards as appearing only from the 1860s (the relevance of the parergic metamorphosis of the high is evident here).

The low-science periodicals Sheets-Pyenson discusses were all non-political in the sense that they were explicitly intended to quell passions for revolution. In 1836 the *Penny Mechanic* (I: 305) wanted 'to substitute placid trains of feeling for those which are too apt to be awakened by the contending interests of men in society or the imperfect government of our own passions'. A flyer for the

Mechanic's Organ, or Journal for Young Men and Women bound in with the BL copy of the magazine actually defined its 'Politics' as 'Temperance, Frugality and Cleanliness, Early Rising and Industry, Education and Progress, Honesty and Self-Reliance' – yet another redefinition of 'politics'. Such refusal to be involved in the public sphere of enfranchisement actually put everyone on the same level, women included. The *Mechanic's Organ* declared as much in its title, and set up a department especially addressed to women called 'Our Sisterhood' that decried the gender exclusivity of Mechanics Institutes. As I pointed out in Chapter 3, one of the defining practices of the cheap illustrated miscellany was the inclusion of 'Useful Domestic Hints', a department whose links to 'low science' more deeply seem to tinge the latter with femininity. Curiously, then, it is 'Science' and not 'Art' or 'Literature' – and certainly not 'history' – that seems the defining opposite of 'news', its content consisting in a domesticated discourse intended to displace 'news' in the periodical press. While it would be possible to render the *Journal's* 'Science' political through allegorical decoding practices, very little obviously encourages this.

But, as I have suggested, domestic hints in the *Journal* are almost entirely concerned with the household as a service area for men that facilitates the effective running of their relationships with other men. The *Mechanic's Organ* was exactly the same in this for its department addressed to women comprised household hints, that sought to render women more efficient in the service of their men. 'Science', for all its supposed gender ambiguity, was as fundamentally masculine as bowdlerization. Unlike 'Art' or 'Literature', 'Science' did not lend itself to, nor need, the masculinization of 'news'.

Before continuing further, three more issues need to be addressed, all interconnected: the politics of reading 'news' into an unstamped periodical like the *Journal*, the function of 'Woman' as a discursive object in the *London Journal*, and the double question of whether women read it and what pleasures they might have derived from it.

Firstly, I want to state that in making the claim that the *Journal* offered news, I am not trying to heroize it with the suggestion that it was a crypto-seditious publication. While news reading in the *Journal* encouraged a mildly radical viewpoint under both its early editors Reynolds and Ross, it was always ambiguous, and its quantity should not be exaggerated. Even Reynolds's own publications, although not as radical as is sometimes claimed, are more politically definite. What underlies news in the *Journal* is less sedition than an intermittent effort to project a commonality between its declaredly masculine producers and its readers through the resentful creation of a more powerful Other (the Government) who seeks to control them both, and whom they both resist: a paranoid gender identity, dependent upon an us and them. The inclusion of news under the cover of domesticity is thus related to resentful parergy (even if news and parergy do not exactly overlap). What is important is that 'news' recuperates the gender ambiguity of domesticity for masculinity. While a fantasy of heroic struggle underlies them, the *Journal's* market strategy can only in a very problematic sense be called 'heroic' in terms meaningful today. As John Tosh (1999) has argued, the domestic ideal was both a sign of masculinity and, being associated with the feminine, a threat to it. The *London Journal* was seeking to resolve a similar aporia by presenting its domesticity as only a mask that 'real masculinity', identified with the heroic homosocial political, wore because it had to.

In order to achieve this goal, femininity had to be kept in its place. A pervasive strategy comprised treating the figure of 'Woman' as a discursive object that required endless definition and discussion between men. Significantly, the very first 'Essay' was concerned with it (I: 53). Almost all the considerable amount of non-fiction material on it in these early years refers to women in the third person and, in common with most nineteenth-century writing, almost exclusively in the abstract singular form 'Woman' (cf. Palmegiano, 1976: 5). Although speaking generally with pseudo-scientific detachment and authority, such pieces remain indifferent to enquiry into women's actual situation, despite the use of gendered sociological investigation since at least the Commission that led to the 1844 Factory Act (Rendall, 1990:57). The very lack of referentiality in the discourse on Woman is indicated by how static and circumscribed it is, as if the first essay set the agenda for non-fiction accounts of Woman for the next forty years and longer. Woman's province is the home and her 'prime duty' is to make a man 'ambitious to stay' there. Woman is religious, imaginative but not capable of true learning, tender-hearted and so unsuitable for public office, and so on. There is nothing in this formulation of Woman that will astonish students of Victorian culture. The only possible surprise simply confirms the discourse's lack of referentiality, the conflation of Woman with 'lady' that was supposedly a characteristic of publications from higher market zones (cf. Beetham, 1996, esp. ch. 2): 'Why, the very appellation in common use – lady – confounds a duke's child with a tailor's daughter' announces the first Essay in pseudo-levelling and aspirational tones (I: 53). Series such as 'Etiquette for the Millions' (1845), numerous balaams and instructions in Notices to Correspondents indicate how lady-like behaviour in women was supposed to be an important ideal for readers. Perkin (1993) has pointed out that, although widely promulgated, the ideal was actually possible for very few women indeed. Non-fiction pieces may ignore the gap between the ideal and reality, but readers' numerous failures to live up to the ideal in Notices to Correspondents amply confirm the difference between the two. This disjunction between prescription and reality was advantageous for the print market in that it constituted a problem that could not be solved, thus providing endless material for verbal bridges between producers and consumers. In this sense, 'the Woman Question' in the early *London Journal* is a communicative act that is concerned less with women than with consolidating homosocial relations between men.

Another way figures of women, especially in fiction, could be shared between men was through reading them allegorically. This was extremely common, from Britannia on the penny coin to Liberty, Justice and Truth (Warner, 1985). As several historians have pointed out, there was a tradition that stretched from the 1790s to at least the 1840s of reading the victimized woman of melodrama politically, as an allegory of class oppression in general (Gallagher, 1985; 127-9; Clark, 1986: 47-70; Walkowitz, 1992: 86-7; Joyce, 1996; Rogers, 2000). This opened the way for the insertion of the discourse of the 'lady' into politics – the victimized woman is as much a 'lady' as her upper-class sisters and deserves similar treatment. It simultaneously wrote real women out of political representation since in that context the figure of 'Woman' would really mean 'Disenfranchized Working Men'.

Finally, it is important to add that, while I am stressing the male homosocial, I do not at all intend to suggest that real women never bought the *Journal* in its early years, enjoyed reading it, or listening to it being read. While the implied reader was fundamentally masculine and the little evidence there is suggests that men were the main purchasers, there is a huge gulf between implied and real readerships. It might be argued that Notices to Correspondents tend to show a predominantly masculine readership in the 1840s, but this does not indicate that women did not read the magazine, only that writing to Notices was perceived as mainly a masculine activity. Furthermore, as Laura Mulvey (1989: 33) remarked some time ago, 'trans-sex identification' is a 'habit' for women in the west. The prescriptive masculine construction of the 'lady' might have functioned for women as a pleasurable fantasy of 'trans-class' identification in the way that today periodicals with social category 'C' readers allow imaginative participation in 'A/B' lifestyles (Ballaster, 1991: 11; Hermes, 1995: 39). As a discipline of life or askesis, the rules that make a 'lady' could generate pleasure as the ideal of the 'gentleman' could for men. There are also pleasures in resisting and mocking discursive constructions, ironically remarking the gap between the read ideal and the lived real; bitter, perhaps masochistic, pleasures that do not prevent repeated consumption of the mocked text.

The Art of the Crimean War

The Crimean War was critical in the metastasis of the implied reader of the *London Journal*, for it widened the fissure between the domestic masquerade and male readers. Key here was the repeal of the Stamp Tax, linked to almost volcanic eruptions in the periodical field before and after it. What is especially important in this context is that news became an even more important factor in the cheap periodicals market than before: between October and December 1854 large numbers of penny papers were set up in the wake of reports of the battles outside Sebastopol, causing complaints from the established provincial weekly press and prohibitive action by government (see Collet, 1899: II, esp. 6-8; Anderson, 1967: 172-4). At the same time, extraordinary developments in information technology were taking place. The telegraph had linked Britain and France in 1851; by spring 1855 it would connect London to the Crimean front. Coincident with changing dynamics in literacy, which I referred to in Chapter 4, the result was a redefinition and re-gendering of the notion of news.

The war generated desire for a kind of reading that was not covered by the political definition of news. Addressees suddenly wanted messages that had as recently as possible been emitted from senders — the 'now' of 'news'. Newspapers filled with eyewitness accounts from their 'Special Correspondents', with letters and sketches sent them by soldiers and seamen at the front. Letters from combatants were forwarded to the press by their families and printed.[2] The conception of sensational-immediate news sprang into prominence.

Figure 8.5 'Publication of a War "Gazette" Extraordinary, at the office, St. Martin's Lane'
Source: *ILN*, XXV: 564.

The Times's 'Own Correspondent' late in the war was accused of reporting merely 'gossip' (*Saturday Review*, 1855: 44-6) – a very gendered description of discourse designed to play down Russell's political effects (he actually contributed to bringing down the government). Figure 8.5 shows more women clamouring for news than men, women from social groups in which men were not enfranchised either. Women were perceived as wanting to buy newspapers more than ever before. According to the *ILN* (XXV: 562) the crowd gathered outside the *Gazette* office wanted to know whether their loved ones were dead or alive. News as politics suddenly became rivalled by desire for the latest news about a loved one at the front and became entwined with it. The definition of 'news' was thus infiltrated by 'news of a family member', a resignification into the personal and private that opened the gendering of the concept to include women.

The *London Journal* could not respond unambiguously to these changes in the field for three reasons: firstly, because of the Stamp Tax, which was not to be made optional until 1 July 1855; secondly, beyond fears of prosecution, because it might lose its identity as a fiction miscellany if it printed news too obviously; thirdly and,

---

[2] See especially *The Times* for letters (for example, 10 October 1854: 6-8; 13 October 1854: 7; 16 October 1854: 9; 20 October 1854: 6-8), though the *ILN* prints them too. For sketches sent to the latter, see, for instance, XXV: 336.

I suspect, most importantly, because such a transformation might cut into the circulation and profits of its brother newspaper, the *Weekly Times*. However, it could offer a sense of the urgently up to date, the affect of the now. Following the *ILN* and *Cassell's Illustrated Family Paper*, it did this through Art.

Striking kinds of illustration, new to the *Journal*, appeared. In volumes XIX-XX the topographic print (of a kind that the *ILN* denominated a 'picturesque map') became far more common than formerly. Ethnographic images appeared in unusual concentration, as did panoramic pictures spread across two pages. Although picturesque scenes remained the commonest type of non-fiction illustration, sensational-immediate scenes (such as Figure 8.6), diagrams and other *ILN*-type images were printed with a frequency far greater than even during the 1848 revolution, especially after the *Journal* had reported the Battle of the Alma. As before, but much more intensely, illustrations coupled news and 'history'. The Battle of 'Sulina' (7 July) was reported and illustrated two months after it occurred (XXV: 104) and over a month after *ILN* had reported 'Sulineh'. When the Battle of the Alma was depicted on 25 November 1854, the *Journal* offered an action scene (XIX: 185) that, suggesting news from its apparently being taken from life, was (so it seems to me) a composite of two scenes taken from the *ILN* of the previous month (cf. *ILN*, XXV: 377, 425). The verbal text was as much concerned with military history as the details of the battle. By the date of the *Journal*'s report, *The Times* and *Weekly Times* had both long ceased to regard the Alma as news, the former having declared it history with a formal Latin epitaph and an English poem (24 October 1854: 9), the latter simply ceasing to comment on it. They had already reported both Balaclava, with its disastrous Charge of the Light Brigade, and Inkerman, 'the most terrible encounter in the history of the British army' (Lalumia, 1984: 59). The *ILN* had even printed a sketch of Balaclava on 18 November (XXV: 517).

With these new kinds of illustration, the *London Journal* was again offering 'history' in the guise of 'news', its constant oscillation between the two no longer really serving its original purpose of keeping it safe from prosecution, but rather continuing as a habitual reflex which had become a defining characteristic, a practice that constituted its identity.

And yet none of these types of illustration survived the end of the Crimean War in the *Journal*. Even when the Stamp was no longer a legal requirement, the *Journal* chose not to include much political 'news'. Rather, the Crimean War had other, more subtle effects on the gendering of 'news'. Again Art was where these were most evident.

After *Stanfield Hall*, J.F. Smith's most famous novels had all been set ostensibly in the teens and twenties of the nineteenth century, although temporal markers are vague and sometimes contrascriptory. In Gilbert's illustrations markers of period are often likewise imprecise except in one area: clothes. Sometimes, it is true, costume was so vague as to render dating impossible, but usually costume of the appropriate period was depicted. Gilbert's attention to accurate sartorial detail had in fact been mentioned in a discussion of a 'Print for the People' he had executed for the *Journal* (VII: 170). Increasingly, however, contemporary clothes invaded Gilbert's illustrations.

Figure 8.6 'Scene in Sebastopol', Action Picture of the Crimean War, with Flying Bombs
Source: XX: 377.

In Figure 8.7, the first illustration to Smith's *Temptation* (1854), a historical *bildungsroman* beginning in 1800 and reaching the early 1830s, the tricorne hat flaunts its antiquarianism. Soon, however, the illustrations relocated the novel decisively into the 1850s even while the words maintained a setting in the past. In Figure 8.8, for example, the gas lamp could in theory date from the 1820s, but the soldiers' caps or 'Albert pots' had been introduced only in 1844. The woman's skirt, too full for the 1820s, fits better into the 1850s, and the small bonnet set back on her head was fashionable from about 1853.[3] In Figure 8.9, the four flounces, low tight bodice, and skirt filled out with petticoats mark Madame Garacchi's luxurious gown as the height of fashion for 1853-54 (cf. Cunnington, 1937: 178-179, 181). While the narrative incident may recall the famous wax model scene in chapter XXVI of *The Mysteries of Udolfo* of sixty years earlier, fashion dates the picture as defiantly modern. Meanwhile, in the verbal text, George IV is still on the throne.

As I have suggested, there were many decoding strategies available that encouraged readings of past events in terms of the present. In *Temptation* the hero is a soldier in the previous European war that Britain had been involved in (parallels between the Crimean War and the Peninsula War were common at the time – see, for example, XIX: 105-6), while the figure of Madame Garacchi, a famous opera singer, suggests the star Giulia Grisi who was making her farewell

---

[3] For information on the uniforms, see Barnes (1957: 189-90 and plates 31, 34, 36). On the bonnets, see Foster (1984: 13).

performances in 1854 (see the portraits and articles in XIX: 213 and *ILN*, XXV: 16). Be that as it may, the *Journal*'s illustrations bring its novels up to date more explicitly and insistently through a discursive system that was increasingly seen as what Margaret Beetham (1996: 91-6) has seen as an aspect of 'feminine news': fashion.

[OLD MIKE AND THE TRAVELLER AT THE STOCKS.]

Figure 8.7 'Old Mike and the Traveller at the Stocks', J.F. Smith, *Temptation*
Source: XX: 1.

Still remaining well within the masculine version of the domestic, during the Crimean War the *London Journal* seems marked by awareness of a new market sector. While men continued to produce the magazine, for the first time, women were considered as possible sustained consumers of it: these are the first signs of the *Journal*'s slow metastasis of the feminine from the excluded third person to a second-person addressee, and hence its own Tiresian metamorphosis of gender from domesticated Rebecca Rioter to women's fashion magazine. Developments in the American mass market, where women authors critically writing about women's places in a male-dominated society were gaining the greatest sales, no doubt bolstered this trend, yet the re-gendering of 'news' is key, even if it can only be claimed as a temporary effect. As a heteronomous commodity that had to make itself repeatedly desired, the *Journal* was concerned to maintain relations with the categories of person perceived as its major consumers. In the final analysis, then, the *London Journal*'s relationship to and construction of gender are effects of its particular relation to the market, defined by the commercial and communicative exchanges that it existed in and through.

Figure 8.8 'The Attack upon Sally Carroll', J.F. Smith, *Temptation*
Source: XX: 161.

Figure 8.9 'The Cabinet in the Banker's Bed-Room', J.F. Smith, *Temptation*
Source: XX: 193.

If the present chapter concluded that the *Journal*'s complicated textual cross-dressing was by no means 'heroically' oppositional or even alternative, the next chapter is concerned to see what happens when what is today considered a key text 'subversive' of gender norms is read in the mass market. If this text is truly 'subversive', how may its construction of gender be the result of massive consumer demand and willing producer supply?

Chapter Nine

1863. Lady Audley's Secret Zone; or, Is Subversion Subversive?

Why Sympathy and not Subversion?

Lady Audley's Secret has received a good deal of comment since the late 1970s. The influence of Showalter (1977) on readings of the novel as a protest text is enormous, from Miller (1986) to Tilley (1995) and beyond. Within the last dozen years or so, paperback editions by David Skilton and, more recently, by Jenny Bourne Taylor have made it easily available for study on university English courses. It has come to be regarded as a paradigmatic protest text against women's carceral position in Victorian society. This is an interpretation validated through 'oppositional' criteria derived from feminism and supported by the novel's provocation of scandal for its supposed subversion of gender-roles. This chapter tries to see how the meanings available to readers of *Lady Audley's Secret* metastasize when the novel is relocated from its volume formats, be they triple-decker or modern-day paperback, back into the *London Journal*.

While by no means repudiating the gender politics through which many readings of *Lady Audley's Secret* have been constructed, or the possibility that such readings were made in the 1860s, it is important to point out the extremely limited cultural zones in which definitions of Lady Audley as 'subversive' are generally anchored. There may be constant repetition of how a contemporary described Braddon as passing between the kitchen and the drawing room, yet the novel has been situated historically through the drawing-room responses of a very limited range of reviewers in the high-status press, a social category that a mid-Victorian critic emically described as 'inspectors of the literary market' who 'keep a keen watch on … dealers in second-hand truths' ([Ainger], 1859: 113). Reading *Lady Audley's Secret* through these 'inspectors' – whom Lessing might call the judges of the 'horserace mentality' – begs the subversion many critics now find within it. We have neglected the way the hostile attitudes of these reviewers comprise a decided minority. It is, rather, vital to keep in mind the ambiguity of a novel that delighted not only Henry James and Tennyson but continues to enthrall modern-day students.[1] Such semiotic openness must be part of what Iser (1978) would have called the 'conditioning force' of this text. It precludes any simple decision about

---

[1] See Wolff (1979: 6, 9-15) for the popularity of *Lady Audley's Secret* amongst the nineteenth-century élite. On its popularity today, see the Braddon discussion list: http://www.onelist.com/Braddon.

what our attitudes to Lady Audley and Robert are supposed to be, or whether, as one critic puts it, Robert's 'subtextual' homosocial/ homoerotic attachment to George really reveals Braddon as a covert 'feminist' who 'forces the reader to recognize the way in which a patriarchal society depends on repression and denial for its very existence' (Nemesvari, 1995). Is subversion therefore subversive? – to reword a question once famously asked by Elisabeth Wilson (1993). If this is the case and if *Lady Audley's Secret* is a mass-market text, then why do not all readers rise up against patriarchy? Does subversion lie at the core of the mass market? Certainly, labelling a text as subversive is useful in marketing it for both publishers and teachers – perhaps to students convinced that the Victorian novel is dull – just as celebration of unconventional meanings in canonical texts has political value in claiming a space for oppressed groups within the academy. This chapter, I repeat, does not seek to undermine the gender politics of such a reading, but the fact remains that condemnation by high-status reviewers is not a sufficient reason for arguing that a text *in itself* is or was 'subversive of patriarchy'. That we saw in Chapter 8 when apparent 'content' alone was an insufficient descriptor. I question the value of simply adding glamorous tags to works in order to promote them. For me academic criticism is not simply advertisement but, though sometimes speculative, it involves careful and always political investigation.

My attempt to determine meanings available to readers of *Lady Audley's Secret* in the *London Journal* does not, on the other hand, claim to be a heroic isolated enterprise, for it continues the work of Linda Hughes (1991), Laurel Brake (2001), Mark Turner (2000), Deborah Wynne (2001) and others in imaginatively engaging with the notion that the medium changes if not the message and its meanings, then at least the parameters within which meanings might be made.

The complicated publishing history of *Lady Audley's Secret* is well known. It appeared first in *Robin Goodfellow* for twelve issues before the magazine collapsed. From the format of the one issue I have seen,[2] *Robin Goodfellow* was an unillustrated twopenny weekly consisting of 32 pages, the size, look and price of *All the Year Round*, with which it was, no doubt, supposed to compete. This seems to confirm something that is regularly suggested, that *Lady Audley's Secret* invites a cross-reading with *The Woman in White* which had appeared in Dickens's magazine. Only the first chapter appears in the issue, leading me to suspect that only the first twelve actually appeared there. It is known that Braddon considered abandoning the tale but was persuaded to continue by the enthusiasm of her readers. As a result, it appeared complete in twelve monthly parts between January and December 1862 in the *Sixpenny Magazine*, not in single-chapter chunks but in monthly instalments of three, four or five chapters each. The *Sixpenny* was more up-market than *Robin Goodfellow*: the 'Preface' to volume III (in which *Lady Audley's Secret* is started) trumpets its 'independence from the despotism of great Names' that by implication the more famous shilling monthlies were subject to, yet

---

[2] 6 July 1861, the first issue of the magazine. The catalogue of the BL persists in claiming it has 12 issues in its collection (6 July to 28 September 1861) whereas in fact all its copies were destroyed in World War II. The copy of number one now in the BL was acquired as a replacement in 1947. My thanks to Reader Services for informing me of this.

at the same time its format and other declarations direct the readers to see it as a shilling monthly at half price. While it would be erroneous to consider *Lady Audley's Secret* in the *Sixpenny* as in the same market as *Romola* (serialized in the *Cornhill* July 1862 to August 1863), it is nevertheless in one that looks towards that market. In October, the publisher Tinsley brought out *Lady Audley's Secret* as a triple-decker, in a form which the 'literary inspectors' would see and indeed review it. The following year, the novel was, however, serialized in the *London Journal*, almost certainly because Tinsley was a good friend of Johnson.

Now, while Braddon crossed the boundaries between zones, she did not occupy the same position throughout the field. Hugely successful in volume format, Braddon was only moderately so in the *Journal*, as a writer in *Macmillan's* makes clear, explaining too that it was her moral ambiguity that was the problem:

> The writers of these stories [in the *London Journal* and the *Family Herald*] are a class by themselves, and it is seldom that their productions find their way into our circulating libraries. We know Miss Braddon, but that lady is by no means a star of the first magnitude in the world of the penny journals ... We suspect that Miss Braddon does not moralise enough to suit the taste of the penny people ...
>
> The honest beer-swilling Briton of the lower orders loves to make moral reflections when he finds himself in doubtful company. He is thus about a hundred years behind the more educated Briton; for we must repeat, that in order to find anything like the moralising of the penny novels in fictions we have to go back to Richardson ... they want ... to have the story well washed with moral sentiment ...   (Anon., 1866: 97, 101)

The limits to Braddon's success in the *Journal* can be determined in several ways. On the negative side she seems a substitute when Southworth novels are not available. *Lady Audley's Secret* indeed seems a substitute for a substitute, since it occupies a place between novels by Mrs Gordon Smythies, herself probably brought in to replace Southworth – Smythies' first novel for the *Journal*, *Our Mary; Or Murder Will Out*, starts in the issue that Southworth's *The Gypsy's Prophecy* finishes. Secondly, following procedures I outlined in Chapter 7, Braddon's position in the hierarchy of authors can be gauged by tracing where her novels appeared in the magazine. *Lady Audley's Secret* was published initially in 'second position', while Pierce Egan's *The Poor Girl* was the main attraction at the front. After nine instalments (out of twenty-two), *Lady Audley* migrated to third position where it stayed, demoted in favour of Fairfax Balfour's *Ida Lee*. By contrast, Braddon's next novel for the *Journal* (*The Outcasts*, 1863-64) remained on the front page until supeceded by Egan's *Such is Life*. *Aurora Floyd* (1865-66) was placed on the front page for only its first episode before it was pushed into second place by *The Light of Love; Or, The Diamond and the Snowdrop*, again by Egan. Braddon's fourth and last serial for the *Journal*, *Diavola; or, the Woman's Battle* (1866-67) thrust Percy B. St John's *Engaged in Secret* off the front page and kept its place for sixteen weeks until the anonymous *A Woman with a Vengeance*. While Braddon's two novels especially written for the *Journal* are therefore given quite high visibility (though kept subservient to the editor's), her two reprints are distinctly second- or third-string. Presumably they had already penetrated the market to the extent where those most interested had already read them: after initial advertising flourishes, they were now accompanying Egan's serials as extras. Arriving as no more special than the productions of the low long-forgotten editor, *Lady Audley's Secret* must be regarded as but a run-of-the-mill *London Journal* serial.

Magazines like the *Journal* offer particular resources to the establishment of semiotic parameters within which a serial was read. First, and most obviously, there are the replies to correspondents' queries. But they does not help with any specificity: a few may tell us what readers wanted to read – there are some queries about what issue particular serials started in – but, *pace* Teresa Gerrard (1998), they tell us very little about *how* readers read: content prioritized over use again. During *Lady Audley's Secret* there are several queries about the law of divorce, separation and legitimacy which suggest that that fiction raised issues connected to readers' own lives – an unsurprising conclusion (cf. also Zboray, 1997: esp. 164). On the other hand, since these questions are not exclusive to the time-frame of its serialization they only indicate that Notices to Correspondents was considered a space where such matters could be aired.

Only very slightly more useful are the twenty-two illustrations to *Lady Audley's Secret*, which can be read as offering their own readings of the verbal text. They are remarkable for their exceptional inconsistency over the moral nature of the characters, indicating how difficult the artist found it to depict them. Cumulatively, they fail to suggest the clear-cut moral manichaeism of the illustrations to serials running contemporaneously, with their instantly identifiable ethical situations and characters.[3]

The extract from *Macmillan's* I quoted above pointed to the eighteenth-century culture of sensibility, which, together with recurrent features in the figuration of narrators and audiences in *London Journal* novels, suggests a focus on 'sympathy' as the mode in which to read *Lady Audley's Secret*. Sympathy is redefined and fought over in the *Journal* in several ways, but one of its stable characteristics is how it remains a sign of accessible nobility and refinement. In this sense it acts in the same way as prints of the genteel picturesque or Parnassian poetry, offering consumers the cross-class pleasures of simulated, well-established, élite culture. While the nature of sympathy is altered by its relocation into the *Journal*, this is not an example of parergy. On the contrary, sympathy *undoes* parergy through its denial of resentment as a valid relation. Such a mode is, however, perfectly consistent with the aspects of the performative, as defined in Chapter 7, in its insistence on identification with the Other who exhibits or performs the signs of suffering.

A key work that had wide ramifications and influence in the culture of sensibility, Adam Smith's *Theory of Moral Sentiments* (1759), had separated sympathy from competitive economism and made it into the fundamental moral feeling that binds society together. Sympathy is 'beyond gold', echoed J.F. Smith's *Minnigrey* in 1851 (XIV: 225, and see XIV: 260). In virtually all *London Journal* novels from Sue to Southworth, sympathy between teller and audience is strongest

---

[3] For reproductions and discussion of several of the illustrations, see King (2002).

when the story is personal: self-narration to a sympathetic listener is consistently represented as the deepest form of social bond. When enemies share stories, they do so on the deathbed of one of them, annulling their enmity in so doing. Such confession is the mark of reconciliation, the return of the criminal to within the confines of the law and of redemption before God. Readers thus come *in theory* to sympathize with all those who perform and tell their tale. Even when the term 'sympathy' is absent, the mode of reception remains. Helen, the principal heroine of Egan's *The Flower of the Flock* (1857-58), confesses to the sempstress who has rescued her from suicide that she is pregnant and unmarried. The narrator explains the listener's reaction and so suggests that of the reader: 'A woman's error out of woman's love, oh! it was not unpardonable, least of all in the eyes of a woman with a young and loving heart' (XXVI: 356).

Richardson had explored the moral aspects of sympathetic audiences in *Clarissa* (1747), suggesting the difficulty of reconciling guilt with a sympathetic stance. The heroine, reflecting on Lovelace's behaviour, writes to her friend Miss Howe that 'there would hardly be a guilty person in the world, were each *suspected* or *accused* person to tell his or her own story, and be allowed any degree of credit' (1747: 172). Essential too to sympathy are a suspension of disbelief when someone tells their life-story. Narratives to the sympathetic become transparent and non-conflictual in the sense that they mean what they say. Even when allegory or typology come into play, the second level narratives will not conflict with or question the first. In effect, this forecloses resistive reading. *Clarissa* had also related sympathy to Christianity and brought to bear the authority of religion. A sympathetic response is a sign of closeness to heaven and the redemptive divine law of the New Testament, as opposed to the retributive law of man and the Old Testament. In sum, then, sympathy in some sense atones for a narrator's guilt by encouraging the listener/ reader to stand in the place of and 'suffer with' the teller of the tale, an antitype of the redemptive sufferings of Christ, and a very different interpretation of what later theorists might well call 'identification'.[4]

I want to explore some corollaries of a 'sympathetic reading' of *Lady Audley's Secret* as a run-of-the-mill serial in the *London Journal*, concentrating on what the high-status reviewers saw as the 'guilty' character, Lady Audley. She is associated with many semes that encourage a sympathetic response (her confession and the way we are shown her mental suffering, for example), but I shall concentrate on specific aspects of her supposed subversiveness that would have been familiar tropes in the *London Journal* and its zone: she is a mad woman whose abandonment by a man forces her into crime and who is eventually imprisoned.

The Pleasures of Sympathy: Women's Crimes and Madness

Mad women are very common in *London Journal* fiction from J.F. Smith onwards, and, as in the Braddon, always connected with crime and some form of

---

[4] On Clarissa as a figure for Christ, see Ross's 'Introduction' to Richardson (1747: 25).

incarceration. In Southworth's *The True and False Heiress* (1855) one of the central characters, Norah, goes mad and ends up in an asylum after taking revenge on an overly stern judge who had condemned her son to death for a murder that everyone (apart from the judge) realizes he did not commit. Just as he took her child away from her, she steals his, with the significant difference that she ensures the stolen child is brought up as well as possible. Her theft is presented not as a crime against him, but against his long-suffering wife who had begged for the condemned man's life: there is little question that the judge deserves to suffer as a child murderer, a 'barbarian' criminal to whom, according to Adam Smith, no sympathy could extend (Smith, 1759: 163, 342-3). In J.F. Smith's *The Will and the Way* (1852-53), Lady Mowbray, the hero's mother, goes mad after murdering a man who had tried to rape her. She too is put into an asylum and later confines herself in a convent. As in the case of Norah and Lady Audley, Lady Mowbray's crime, madness and incarceration are caused by masculine outrage. While the women are guilty according to earthly law, according to the rules of sympathy they are not. Their madness indicates an aporia caused by two forms of justice, stern earthly and the sympathetic divine. Only when one law, that of sympathy, wins out do the madwomen recover their sanity.

There is a common variant whereby madness in a victim is induced by drugs or caused by false imprisonment. In this case there is no question of the victim's innocence. In the first episode of J.F. Smith's *Woman and her Master* (1853-54), Clara Stanley's brother tries to have her removed as an unknown madwoman when she returns home widowed, sick and accompanied by a child. She only foils his attempt to have her put away by dying before he can do so. Later in the novel, Lord Moretown and the equally wicked Ned Cantor unjustly lock up their virtuous wives in parallel plots at either end of the social scale. Moretown causes his wife to go mad through administering drugs (XXVIII: 131-2). In Southworth's *The Hidden Hand* (1859), one of the most widely read novels of the nineteenth century and serialized in Stiff's *Guide*, the heroine's mother is falsely incarcerated in a madhouse run by a Frenchman, so that she may not enjoy the inheritance that is rightfully hers.

But it is in the best-selling *Ruth Hall* (1855) by Fanny Fern that false incarceration for madness seems to me to reverberate most powerfully in the mid-century mass market.[5] Although appearing in the rival *Family Herald* (10 February 1855 to 17 March 1855), I have argued above that it has a major impact on the *London Journal* (see Chapter 5 above). Particularly striking is how the widowed heroine remains happily unmarried at the end, having become financially secure through her own labour, and even having found a male friend who is not related to her by either family or sexual ties, but only by intellectual and commercial. In a Christian death and resurrection narrative whose structure of itself suggests the priority of divine law over earthly, the heroine quickly gains happiness and

---

[5] *Ruth Hall* was originally published in 1855 in volume form by the Mason Brothers of New York, selling 70,000 within a year of its appearance. On *Ruth Hall*, see the introduction to Fern (1855) by Susan Belasco Smith; Warren (1993); Kelley (1984); Reynolds (1988: esp. 402-7).

children in marriage, only for one of her children and her husband to die. She sinks lower and lower in wretched poverty before she discovers that she can earn money by writing. Forming the nadir of the story, a visit to hell and coming immediately before the glimmerings of her (economic) resurrection, the heroine chances by an 'Insane Hospital' where she hears of the death of her friend Mary Leon (*Family Herald*, XII: 692-3, 3 March 1855). In the laconic style that characterizes the novel, Mr Tibbetts the Superintendent tells Ruth that Mary 'was hopelessly crazy, refused food entirely, so that we were obliged to force it. Her husband, who is an intimate friend of mine, left her under my care, and went to the Continent. A very fine man, Mr. Leon' (*Family Herald*, XII: 692). On her way to see Mary's body, Ruth hears the screams of a woman who, the matron tells her, went mad after losing the legal case against her husband for custody of their child when he deserted her. Finally, Ruth is presented with a scribbled letter that the matron found under Mary's pillow: 'I am not crazy, Ruth – no, no; but I shall be; the air of this place stifles me; I grow weaker – weaker. I cannot die here; for the love of Heaven, dear Ruth, come and take me away' (*Family Herald,* XII: 693). Much less ambiguously than anything in *Lady Audley's Secret*, the reader is asked to interrogate the meaning of the collocation 'Insane Hospital': is it for keeping the insane inside or is it itself part of an insane system which labels women mad who are inconvenient to men?

Lady Audley's incarceration in the *maison de santé* and her rapid death from a *maladie de langueur* would have arrived to readers in the mass-market zone as a glyph for a whole series of imprisonments of women that demand a sympathetic response. Before leaving this list of precendents, it is important to remark two formidable, blonde and beautiful figures from Eugène Sue. In romantic vein there is the St. Simonian, horn-playing *femme libre*, Adrienne de Renneport, in *The Wandering Jew* (1845-46) who is locked up by Jesuits to keep her from her inheritance, and who is eventually killed by them with her lover, her cousin, the equally beautiful Indian Prince Djalma.[6] Even more shocking to 'inspectors' would have been the angelically blonde Basquine in Sue's *Martin the Foundling* (*London Journal*, 1846-47), a figure who amply demonstrates that Lady Audley was by no means the first 'fair-haired demon' in the guise of 'the daintiest, softest, prettiest of blonde creatures' (Oliphant, 1867: 263). Still a child, Basquine is raped by one of her keepers and, escaping with her male child-lover (also the victim of explicit sexual abuse), is eventually locked up in a seraglio of young girls for the pleasure of a duke. From there she escapes into adult prostitution and acting. She works to exact vengeance on those who hurt her and at last commits suicide when reunited with her childhood love after he has been condemned to death. In case we are

---

[6] *The Wandering Jew* was issued 1845-46 by at least seven English publishers and serialized in two periodicals, *The Mirror* and the penny weekly *New Parley's Library*: see James, 1963: 225-26. *Martin* was also published by Vickers in penny weekly numbers and 5d or 6in monthly parts at 5d or 6d, as well as in volume format, 'beautifully illustrated', price: 3/9. It was later re-issued in *London Journal* Supplementary Volume VIII. Another penny-number translation was published by B.D. Cousins, London in 1847. A version was also serialized in the *London Pioneer,* 1846 and in *The Family Herald,* 1846-47.

unsure how to react to her, we are explicitly instructed both by numerous footnotes added by the translator and by passages within the text such as the following (emphasis in the original):

> Reader, whatever this little child may do hereafter, remember that manner in which she was torn from her home; and be assured that her history is the sad history of thousands of other poor girls, *who err because they are pushed unwillingly into the gulf of crime, whence there is no escape for the repentant.*   (IV: 117)

Finally, there are Lady Audley's exact contemporaries in the *Journal*, Floret and Ida in Pierce Egan's *The Poor Girl*, who are locked up and drugged so that they can be raped and forced into a brothel.

In a clear Gothic inheritance, virtually all female imprisonments are unjust in the *London Journal*, virtually all caused by male wickedness. According to the moral binarism that prevails, Robert Audley should therefore be cast in the role of villain, especially as he is the 'motor of the plot' as we follow him in his investigations.[7] That he is not a villain in any unequivocal way suggests a collision of the novel with the narrative and affective conventions firmly established in the penny-fiction zone. This conflict indeed may well have led to the unusually ambiguous iconography of the illustrations.

Virtually all of us will have felt sympathy for Lady Audley, but this is because the liberal reading strategies promoted by Sue, Smith, Southworth and others have won out. Yet sympathy does not necessarily imply that its object is subversive of patriarchy. Just because G.H. Lewes (1863: 133) dismissed the novel as not calling forth 'healthy sympathies' need not support the idea that the novel is transgressive. As I argued at length in Chapter 2, we need to be conscious not only of the work criticized but also of the criticism. For it can be contended that Lewes was recognizing that in the low-status market the proairetics of Lady Audley were associated with the mode of sympathy characteristic of that zone, while he, and George Eliot, were keen to redefine and reappropriate the concept for the consecrated works of art they were currently creating and sanctifying. A perception that a novel is crossing market boundaries does not make it subversive. Subversion I regard as leading to social or political action against established authority. There is no evidence that a sympathetic response to *Lady Audley* ever achieved this.

Adam Smith had made the difference between social action and sympathy abundantly clear in *The Theory of Moral Sentiments*. Action for the public good rarely stems from sympathy, he says, but from 'love of system', 'regard to the beauty of order, of art and contrivance'. There exist

> men of the greatest public spirit, who have shown themselves in other respects not very sensible to the feelings of humanity. And on the other hand, there have been men of the greatest humanity, who seem to have been entirely devoid of public spirit.
>
> (Smith, 1757: 185-6)

---

[7] On the villain as always providing the action of melodrama, see Brooks (1976: 34).

Sympathy can only too easily function as conservative containment, a feeling that is circulated between men (and women) that maintains them in superior positions over the victim they feel for by validating inaction through moral condescension and other pleasures. Whatever the validation, this function is plainly visible in the practical morality of the marital advice offered to women in Notices to Correspondents. When an 'Unhappy Wife' seems to be about to leave her husband, she is told, quite kindly, that it is in her interest to stay with her husband as 'Society will not pardon what [she is] contemplating' (XXXVII: 400); 'One in distress' is told that her conduct is 'blameless' but she must return to her husband (XXXVIII: 208).

> Hopeless Polly. – It is a sad case, but the old story of a drunken husband and a patient, meek, and enduring wife. Make another effort, and if that fails, another, and another after that.   (XXXIX: 16)

Sympathy and Social Transformation

Elisabeth Wilson (1993) had ended her critique of the radical claims of the 'transgressive' with a plea for replacing transgression with social transformation. And in fact it would be false to confine sympathetic reading of the *London Journal* unequivocally to conservative pleasures divorced from social reform. Conservative sympathy had already been challenged in *London Journal* novels for well over a decade before *Lady Audley's Secret* appeared. While the political projects of Sue and Reynolds in the 1840s, for all their ambiguity, tended towards the radical and relied often on sympathetic responses, Braddon's novel had different generic alliances which dated from the 1850s and which made rather different uses of sympathetic responses. The sympathetic that I wish to discuss took two main forms, neither of which is taken up by *Lady Audley's Secret*. The first was through the educated quadroon woman. Brought up in luxury as white but then sold as a slave, this figure appears prominently in several novels as the locus for debates about slavery and sympathy. While I do not want to posit a singular origin, Cassy in *Uncle Tom's Cabin* has many features that reappear as standard later on: separation from her child, desire to free slaves, education, polyglossia, beauty, seduction by a wicked slave-owner, and a loving nature. A second form of social protest makes use of the conflict or debate between a stern husband and a sympathetic wife, with final conversion of the husband to his wife's point of view. This is also found in *Uncle Tom,* in chapter IX, a point which I think confirms the immense influence of this novel not only on American but also on British fiction.

In Emma Robinson's *Masks and Faces* (1855-56), one of the principal characters, the quadroon Oriana, is first presented sitting on an ottoman, learned and regally beautiful, splendidly attired but chained to the floor, a captured odalisque queen (XXII: 308). She is literally a commodity on sale, yet is seething with rebellion and already plotting her escape. She has no trace of the madness that has been taken as a necessary metaphor for women's anger in more up-market fiction (see Gilbert and Gubar, 1979). She freely expresses it, intending to return to

Madagascar and educate her people so that they can revolt against their white masters (XXII: 322). The last words of the novel concentrate on her triumph as 'one of the first women of the age' (XXII: 452). Independent as Ruth Hall, both anglicized and empowered through the myth of (Gl)Oriana, the Virgin Queen, she is disdainful of sympathy, explicitly preferring concrete action and reform. The debate is continued in Percy B. St. John's *Quadroona* (1856-57), which both re-inscribes the quadroon into sympathetic slavery and redirects the trope's semantic force. Whereas Oriana only offered an implied comparison with British women, Quadroona rails against their position to the hero, Willy:

> Women with you are painted dolls or slaves – slaves to conventionality or custom. You love to see the graceful dance, the rounded limb, the elegant form – but it must be ... of hirelings and foreigners. You encase your wives, sisters, daughters in coats of mail, and long, hideous skirts that prevent all motion ...   (XXIV: 130)

Willy replies that women in England and North America are, on the contrary, fortunate. The narrator agrees, while, typically for the producer of a commodity that tries to cater for as many desires as possible, adding the rider that 'we are far from perfect'. But St. John is just as much concerned to redirect the associations of slavery from women to the British working classes in general. When Quadroona later tells her life-story to the inevitably sympathetic Willy, she starts by making America a parallel universe with England (XXIV: 194), comparing England's 'mechanics' and America's slaves and emphasizing the worse conditions of the latter in a rhetoric that encourages political quietism for the British worker (XXIV: 195). A standard trope for much of the nineteenth century, American authors had already made the connection between slaves and the working classes (see Denning, 1998: 107; Hall, 1992: esp. 205-54). After Robinson, it is significant that St. John wants to keep the allegory within the older political tradition, even if it is reworked to harmonize with the happy consuming crowd and no longer with the politicized mob. The *London Journal*'s male producers are not yet willing to cede meanings entirely to the Woman Reader even if they feel her pull.

Sympathy was also debated as a struggle between husband and wife in a domestic encapsulation of the conflict between divine and earthly laws. Contradicting Adam Smith's formulation, sympathy in this mode was associated with acts of charity and social reform – by women. It thereby provided women with a role and status in society and could act not as a container but as empowerment. There is ample evidence that *Uncle Tom's Cabin* empowered women in this mode, including Emmeline Pankhurst (Flint, 1993: 245).

Southworth's novels are particularly concerned with promoting sympathy in this socially active form. Her *True and False Heiress* is entirely concerned with it. While Norah's son was an adult when he was executed, he is insistently presented as her child, and the novel uses the parent-child relationship to argue against the death penalty, in what amounts to a politicization of motherhood. We are all a mother's child: hence all murders and executions are infanticide, and their perpetrators, if not beyond sympathy, are at least villains that require reform. Other novels explicitly discuss patriarchy. *Captain Rock's Pet* (1861-62) inserts the language of law and crime into a lay and comic context. Mrs Rock, the embodiment of socially active sympathy, rebels against her husband's refusal to care for a relative. The result is that the 'captain was a dethroned despot, and so everybody took sides against him' (XXXIV: 395). When the pet of the title tries to cheer him up, he justifies his actions with the same kind of appeal to 'justice' as the arrogant judge in *The True and False Heiress*:

> 'Never you mind, Uncle Harry. S'pose you were naughty, you've got the same right to be naughty that other people have, I s'pose, and so don't you feel cut up about it!'
>   'But I've not been naughty, Elf,' would be the captain's answer, almost meekly; 'I only wanted justice – what was in the bond, you know!'
>   'Never mind, unky – never mind whether you have or not! You've got as much right to tell fibs about it as the murderers have to plead "not guilty".'   (XXXIV: 395)

Men's rigid adherence to earthly law always brings disaster in cautionary tales of masculine adherence to earthly law. Through the sufferings men bring on themselves and others, they are eventually converted to the woman's sympathetic perspective. Feminine sympathy wins out, translated into social action and validated through appeal to the New Testament. This is also the case with Egan's *The Poor Girl*, which occupied the front pages of the *Journal* while *Lady Audley's Secret* was running. It trumpets the triumph of feminine sympathy and social action by giving the novel's last words to Floret, the heroine, as she moralizes to her new husband. The very punctuation refuses the termination of a full-stop, the dash instead opening the novel out into the world of the reader:

> There are many Florets in the world … let us seek them out, and remember, dearest, while we mingle with them, how sorely I needed a friend, so that we might be to them friends and helpers –   (XXXVIII: 149)

Lady Audley's Secret flies in the face of feminine sympathy triumphant, for the mad woman's opposite, the lawyer Robert, learns not sympathy but to be stern and unyielding: he becomes more and more integrated into the world of earthly law to end a 'rising man upon the home circuit' who 'has distinguished himself in the great breach of promise case of Hobbs v. Nobbs' (p. 445[8]). When he accuses Lady Audley of the murder of her husband, he is 'transform[ed] into another creature – a pitiless embodiment of justice, a cruel instrument of retribution' (p. 271). 'Vengeance', decried consistently in *London Journal* novels of sympathy, is what Clara Talboys calls on Robert to enact. His decision is couched in language that recalls not the New but the Old Testament: "Heaven help those who stand between me and the secret,' he thought, 'for they will be sacrificed to the memory of George Talboys" (p. 202). The novel's last paragraph, with its overemphatic

---

[8] Bound by what my readers can easily access, I refer to Skilton's (1987) edition rather than to the *Journal*'s. The texts are virtually the same apart from some minor alterations (a proper name for a pronoun) that the *Journal* makes to facilitate reading in instalments.

labelling of the good, seems to be addressing the domestic battle of sympathy in its unusual appeal to the authority of the Old Testament patriarch King David:

> I hope no one will take objection to my story because the end of it leaves the good people all happy and at peace. If my experience of life has not been very long, it has at least been manifold; and I can safely subscribe to that which a mighty king and a great philosopher declared, when he said that neither the experience of his youth nor of his age had ever shown him 'the righteous forsaken, nor his seed begging their bread.'
>
> (Braddon, [1862] 1987: 446-7)

Aware perhaps that the triumph of the lawyer Robert did not follow the divine law of sympathy, it is as if Braddon felt she had to justify her story through reference to an alternative divine authority in the Old Testament. Only in the *Journal*'s zone would this anxiety have been noted. In the higher-status zones, Robert's triumph is perhaps more in line with reader expectations of the naturalness of patriarchy.

Homoerotic is not a Synonym for 'Subversive'

A similar ill fit with *London Journal* conventions is observable in the homosocial/ homosexual relations that Cvetkovich and Nemesvari have rightly seen as central to the plot (Cvetkovich, 1992: esp. 56-68; Nemesvari, 1995). I have already commented on how 'Woman' is an object of discussion between men in the *Journal*. Taking her cue from Sedgwick's *Between Men*, Cvetkovich posits a variation on an 'erotic triangle' in which two men form their relation by passing a woman between them: Lady Audley links Robert with his uncle, as with George. Later, Clara, who physically resembles her brother George, will link Robert to his friend even more closely, enabling the final *ménage* of two men and a woman. Both Cvetkovich and Nemesvari emphasize this as well as the potentially homoerotic nature of Robert's relation to George.

I am going to argue that *Lady Audley's Secret* can be read in the *London Journal* as picking up and developing a trope, established by J.F. Smith's novels from 1849, of the homosocial male couple as one of a series of erotic attachments that lead eventually to marriage and the reproductive family. The links with Smith are especially evident in the way George, Robert and an unnamed friend suddenly go to St Petersburg for no apparent reason[9]. It seems a curious memory of Smith's *Amy Lawrence* in which the hero's friend delays his marriage in order to travel to St Petersburg, where the hero is doing business, simply to tell him he has inherited vast wealth (XIII: 275-6). This enthusiasm, when a letter would surely have sufficed, is typical of the strong affections between the hero and his friend in

---

[9] According to the chronology of the novel, they go about eighteen months after the end of the Crimean War with Russia. Although something could have been made of this, it is never referred to. Similarly never mentioned is how, according to the chronology, George left the army and deserted Lucy when the Crimean War was just about to start and already discussed in the press, suggesting a double desertion of wife and country – and yet further moral complications that Braddon perhaps wished to avoid.

Smith. The end of Smith's four central novels offers the vision of a socially solid universe resting on an erotic quadrilateral between two male and two female friends, bound by the sympathies of both the homosocial and the heterosexual. On the way, the hero works through a series of erotic attachments after the manner of ancient Greek romance, such as Longus's *Daphnis and Chloe*: with older women (no less than Napoleon's sister, Pauline Borghese in *The Will and the Way*), with foreign women (for example, the Spanish Agnes in *Minnigrey)* and, most relevant to my argument here, with his special male friend.

Woman and her Master offers not only Fred and Dick, but also a master and servant couple familiar from Smollettian picaresque, Frank and Willie, the latter of whom professes undying loyalty to his master, in strong terms for a servant: 'Married or single, at home or abroad, it's all one to me – so that I am near the only friend I ever found in the world!' (XIX: 88). In *The Will and the Way* Henry and Walter behave in very similar ways to what Cvetkovich notes in *Lady Audley's Secret* when Robert acts as nurse to George: sickness justifies physical contact between men. In similar manner, Blue Peter encounters the hero Gus in *Minnigrey* for the first time, just after the latter has been press-ganged, in a passage that may stand for all such in Smith's novels:

Accustomed as he was to scenes of violence [Bing, the surgeon] could not but feel an interest in the poor boy [Gus], whose appearance indicated that he belonged to a superior class of society to those who generally came under his care. Stopping down, he carefully examined the wound, first cutting off the dark curls on the temple, which were thickly clotted with gore. The sailor [Blue Peter] carefully gathered them up.

'What are you going to do with them?' demanded the surgeon.

'Nothing, sir.'

'Why keep them, then?'

The young fellow coloured as he replied:

'A foolish thought – perhaps you will laugh at me; but it struck me that he might have a mother or a sister who love him, and who might be glad to have them.'...

'Where am I?' demanded Gus looking round with astonishment.

'On board his Majesty's tender the Firefly,' said Blue Peter, pressing his hand; 'where all are not such devils as you suppose...'

'We may leave him now,' observed Bing...

'Leave him!' repeated the sailor. 'If I do, may I never go afloat again...'   (XIV: 212)

Later, alone on a boat together, Gus and Blue Peter 'mutually embraced, and vowed a friendship which neither time or distance should destroy' (XIV: 227). Feminine blushes, tender physical contact and declarations of undying friendship open up homoerotic spaces for those who wish them: the narrative can be appropriated and fantastically taken off by the reader in any number of directions in the same way as the eroticized descriptions of Quadroona or of Lotte the sempstress in *The Flower of the Flock*. Exactly as with the endless discussions of Woman, such relations between men put women very much in second place, usually as a memory or even a supposition that the men share in order to justify, consolidate and maintain their own relations.

Such homosocial/homoerotic relations are, if not the norm, nonetheless very common in Smith's *London Journal* novels between 1849 and 1855, echoing the general strategy of the magazine. For during that period, the *Journal* is concerned to attract as large a (masculine) clientele as possible (King, 1999): almost all desires can be suggested as long as the proprieties are maintained in the end. *Lady Audley's Secret*, however, makes the relation between Robert and George into the primary motivation for the plot. This is not so much a return to Smith as an exaggeration, for in Smith the central search is always for the identity of the self; the homoerotic is only incidental. In place of Smith's final erotic quadrilateral, *Lady Audley's Secret* concludes with a (Sedgwickian) *ménage à trois* that recalls, if anything, the household of the wicked Lord Moretown, his mistress and his wife in *Woman and her Master*.

Intense relations between men had not appeared in the *Journal* for some time before *Lady Audley's Secret*. Smith had immediately killed off the hero's beloved friend in *Temptation*, his last novel for the *Journal*, and one where relations between women had figured much more centrally than those between men. Indeed, it is possible that Smith was attempting to answer what was perceived as a problem in the nature of Woman that had been raised by the mass-market American women novelists, by re-inscribing the idea into a multi-faceted 'maternality' (as opposed to 'maternity'). That is, he is trying to show that the nature of Woman is maternal irrespective of whether she has actually had a child. She may be an opera star, a circus artiste, a country-girl, or an oppressed daughter of a criminal miser, but it is her nature to care for the needy that defines her – and saves the day.

Emma Robinson's continuation of *Masks and Faces* proved again a decisive turning point by directly addressing the issue of the masculine homosocial. Smith had returned to more familiar tropes in his opening chapters and what Robinson offered looks like a deliberate overturning of the cosy homosocial and the sharing of Woman that he had set up. Smith had duly presented a male couple, the foundling Fred and his beloved Augustus Pophly. They plan to travel together, until the picaresque possibilities of this are dashed by Fred's decision to enter a counting house in the last of the chapters that Smith wrote. Robinson immediately turned the friendship on its head. In the first instalment that she contributed, Augustus – now become 'Gus', an inversion or parody of the hero from Smith's *Minnigrey* – suddenly turns out to be a dissembling seducer and murderer. Fred is attributed the blame for both seduction and murder, and is forced to flee. And so the plot is finally jerked into action, after Smith seems to have done his best to close down all possibility of plot development. To make the story exciting Robinson certainly needed to introduce new elements, but her choice of severing this particular bond through the violence of one of the male pair against a woman is significant, especially in view of the later appearance of Oriana, the quadroon who prefers action to sympathy. Robinson gives Woman a more definite subjectivity that resists the homosocial, and in passing the blame for seduction between men, criminalizes the passage of Woman between them in a much less ambiguous way than *Lady Audley's Secret*. Mirroring its appeals to the woman reader through the contemporaneity of fashion, *London Journal* novels now no longer work through homoerotic attachments, and the primary affective links on the way to reproductive marriage are narrowed to the heterosexual or those between parents and children.

The history of the trope of the male couple is particularly interesting for a reading of *Lady Audley's Secret* in which it has been discussed as though it were new and isolated and 'subversive of patriarchy'. But this forgets that power (of which patriarchy is but one structuration) is in constant metamorphosis: what is subversive for 1990s middle America would not necessarily have shocked 1860s London. For a Constant Reader of the *London Journal*, Robert's attachment to George would have seemed less subversive than old-fashioned. *Lady Audley's Secret* in these respects was revisiting the imaginative universe of the early 1850s, of the proto-sensation author she significantly names 'Sigismund Smith' in her triple-decker *The Doctor's Wife*. The *Journal*, however, had been offering figures of women triumphant in sympathy for almost a decade, suggesting an increased awareness of a market for women who wanted imaginative spaces of their own. If 'subversion of patriarchy' is to be found in any *London Journal* novels, it can more readily, if always ambiguously, be located in those.

A final return to Adam Smith: sympathy for victims, even when textually linked to restitutive action, need not lead inevitably to material change. The *London Journal*, always 'economic literature', sold utopian pleasures characteristic of commodity consumption, not agendas for reform. The question to be asked rather is who controlled those pleasures.

Chapter Ten

1868-83. Dress, Address and the Vote; or, the Gender of Performance

The Science of Life and the Girl of the Period

What Dress is to Women

Dress and address comprise the science of life, especially for women. They form that indispensable social science whose practical influences pervade daily life. A woman's duty does not by any means end with her appearance, but it certainly begins there. Mrs. Madison's rule – to remember yourself in the dressing-room and forget yourself in the drawing room – is a condensation of the ethics of the toilet. It is indeed a woman's duty to be beautiful if she can, and pleasing if she cannot be beautiful. Nor is it altogether a matter beyond control. Care in the toilet, thoughtfulness about the effects of costume, is far more determining than the original endowments of nature. No woman need give herself up as a hopeless case. Health is the first requisite. Good taste and care do the rest.

(LXXVIII: 159)

Jenny Taylor (Introduction to Braddon [1862] 1998: xiii) has noted Lady Audley's consummate shopping skills and many of the illustrations in the *London Journal* bear this out. Lady Audley is carefully dressed in the height of fashion to fit her role, moving amongst tasteful surroundings. By 1883 the *Journal* had moved from a 'penny family weekly' into what was recognizably a 'woman's magazine' through an intensification of the pleasures of 'Lady Audley' both as a novel and as a character. 'Art' had metastasized into a mixture of fiction and fashion, with an illustrated Ladies' Supplement and monthly coloured fashion plate. 'Literature' comprised romances with sensational elements, which focused on the heroine. 'Science', once earthed in masculinity, had morphed into what the epigraph describes as 'the science of life' – 'dress' and 'address' – consisting in occasional series such as 'The Ladies' Alphabet of Love', 'Our Working Girls' and into the women's news of fashion.

The *Journal* was not alone in its migration to women consumers: other 'family miscellanies' and even newspapers were also moving in this direction (Law, 2000: 141) and the resulting competition with rivals, combined with changing demography were almost certainly determinant in the *Journal*'s transformation. Furthermore, it may well have introjected and acted out its description by high-status texts as a magazine for female servants. The most immediate trigger for the introduction of the Ladies' Supplement in April 1868, however, seems a media event that itself had multiple causes: the furore over a short, vitriolic and anonymous article that had appeared in the *Saturday Review* the previous month, the 'Girl of the Period' (actually by the journalist Eliza Lynne Linton). The piece had launched out against the sartorial confusion of the once respectable English girl with the prostitute and against her calculated sale of her own body in marriage.

What the demi-monde does in its frantic efforts to excite attention, [the Girl of the Period] also does in imitation. If some fashionable *dévergondée en evidence* is reported to have come out with her dress below her shoulder-blades, and a gold strap for all the sleeve thought necessary, the girl of the period follows suit next day; and then wonders that men sometimes mistake her for her prototype. ([Linton], 1868: 340)

The article's notoriety was overdetermined by a constellation of issues revolving around the conjuncture of fashion and women's control over their sexuality and lives in general. The clothing trade was a vital part of women's economy, with nearly a quarter of women employed in it (Thomis and Grimmett, 1982: 19). Mass-market novels had been presenting heroines who took charge of their identities through altering their appearance since at least the cross-dressing Eliza of Reynolds's *Mysteries of London*, and the three-volume sensation novel had been insisting on it since the beginning of the 1860s.[1] The Contagious Diseases Acts of 1864 and 1866 had made the visible, and hence partly sartorial, distinction between the respectable woman and the prostitute highly contentious. Well before this, prostitutes themselves had become objects of debate and, indeed, had appeared in their own voices in newspapers even before Mayhew's 1861 additions to *London Labour*. 'Skittles', the mistress of Lord Hartington, brought the trade to new levels of visibility by riding openly in Hyde Park in the early 1860s: Landseer even exhibited her portrait.[2] Finally, a sense of the growing disproportion of women to men (see, for example, Greg, 1862), together with the rise of the women's movement and fears of the invasion of the professions and politics by women, only added to the sense of femininity in crisis (see Levine, 1987, esp. ch. 3 on suffrage societies of the mid-1860s).

The outcome of the controversy was not what Linton had intended. As Rinehart explains:

'Girl of the Period' caricatures and farces appeared, and the phrase itself, often abbreviated as G.O.P., became a catchword in serious as well as popular publications. Indeed, Mrs Linton might regret that she could not copyright her title. A *Girl of the Period Almanack* sold extremely well, as did a *Girl of the Period Miscellany* which appeared monthly for a year. The predecessors of modern T-shirt manufacturers launched 'Girl of the Period' parasols and articles of clothing ... (Rinehart, 1980: 4)

G.O.P. became a commercial phenomenon. In the *London Journal*, the result was a still firmer reinterpretation of 'economic literature' as 'consumer reading'. The Ladies' Supplements started in the very issue after a piece appeared on '*The*

---

[1] See Pykett (1994) on the relation of the 'Girl of the Period' to the sensation novel.

[2] On the representation of prostitutes, see Nead (1988); Kent (1987). Fisher (1997) reproduces many of the relevant documents. Pearl (1955: esp. ch. III and pp. 58-68) remains informative on the visibility of prostitutes in the press.

Saturday Review and the Women' (XLVII: 307-8), which itself appeared a month after Linton's article (indeed sooner, given the practice of advance dating). Admitting that the description applied to a few girls 'possibly ... in the neighbourhood of St John's Wood' – a suburb noted by Pearl (1955: 5) as a 'seraglio for mistresses and harlots' – the *Journal* strenuously denied that it applied to the 'discreet and wise daughters of the gentlemen of England' who made up the majority of women (and its consumers). It went on to note how the writer of G.O.P. had refused to acknowledge the existence of 'sensibility', 'rational esteem' and – key term – 'sympathetic sentiment' in the 'Girl of the Period'. She was, instead, subject only to her material appetites, 'a mere animal – without a mind qualified to feel and enjoy any of the charms and intellectual refinements of civilised life': so unlike the girls the writer knew.

In the autumn, the *Journal* began a whole series of articles entitled 'Girls of the Period', the first a deliberately provocative choice, the 'Flower Girl' (XLVIII: 236-8). 'Born in a garret and reared anyhow', coarse and crude, 'she is not a being cast in the sentimental mould'. But she has a useful function as

> an agent, scattering and circulating beneficial influence, for the sight of flowers, fresh and fragrant, is always humanizing ... [She is] a missionary, who brings home to worldly habits and feelings the eternal love of the beautiful.   (XLVIII: 237)

Beauty and consumerism, the targets of Linton's article, are rewritten as a religious duty so as to harmonize with what Cynthia White (1970: 271) has wittily called the 'Kinde, Küche, Kleider' formula of the nineteenth-century women's press. As we shall see in the next chapter, the *Kleider* overlays but does not altogether efface the *Kirche* of the original expression. Later the *London Journal* 'Girls of the Period' add Linton's other theme, the control of women's sexuality, in variants from the extreme discipline of the 'Sister of Charity', to the saucy but sensible 'Sewing Machine Girl' (XLIX: 76-8) who, as Sally Mitchell (1989: 158-9) has observed, marries the man with whom she can live as a business partner not a subservient wife. Finally, there is the story of the dressmaker on the brink of seduction, saved by the candid advice of her overseer at work. This is a tale in which the *Journal*'s practical morality is much in evidence:

> Calmly, like a true woman of the world – a lady of the period, as she was, every bit of her – she unfolded to Mary's horrified and awakened sense of duty the exact nature of the snare that had been set up for her undoing, and instead of upbraiding the girl for her almost silly confidence in a stranger, or piling up moral maxims by the score, bade her be more careful for the future, and save her mother much anguish by letting the secret of her girlish indiscretion remain with their two selves.   (XLVIII: 312)

Practical morality apart, the G.O.P. controversy served to inscribe Woman ever more within discourses of fashion and consumerism: four out of the five *London Journal* G.O.P. articles either refer to them directly or focus on characters involved in them. This exactly tallies with G.O.P.'s general effect (White, 1970: 50; Rinehart, 1980).

Fashion, not Franchise

If the G.O.P. controversy with its emphasis on clothing had triggered the Ladies Supplements, a more insidious reason for the increasing association of women and the 'cheap family miscellany' was, I suggest, increasing demand for extending the franchise. Both Conservative and Liberal ministries had been attempting reform for some years, yet it was only men's enfranchisement that was being discussed: in a famous speech on the Bains Bill for lowering the borough franchise Gladstone talks only of 'men' (see Aldrich, 1983). Mill's intervention in the debate has been justly famous from Millett (1969) onwards. While direct involvement in politics was becoming more and more a possibility for working men over a long period, it was not until the huge extension of the franchise in July 1867 that the exclusion of political and theological news and debate from a mass-market periodical came more definitely to connote a different kind of 'femininity'. In England, enfranchisement was greatest in urban areas: in Birmingham the number of voters was tripled, in Leeds quadrupled, in Blackburn quintupled. In most large towns it was at least doubled. Most urban male householders were now able to vote (McCord, 1991: 259). That in turn meant that they had more of an incentive to read the kind of political news reported by the newspaper. While Stephen Coltham (1969) has offered a pessimistic account of the demise and low circulation of what he calls 'working-class' newspapers around the time of the 1867 Reform Act, he refers (and that in passing) to only one mass-market paper, *Reynolds's Weekly News*. According to Ellegård, this had a 25 percent rise in circulation between 1865 and 1870, from 150,000 to 200,000. The *Daily Telegraph* increased its sales only slightly less in the same period, from 150,000 to 190,000, and the *Journal*'s sibling, the *Weekly Times,* raised its circulation by 50 percent, from 100,000 to 150,000 (Ellegård, 1957: 20). While some small-circulation papers may have died, more and more newspapers were being bought.

Since the *London Journal* addressed above all the urban reader, greater enfranchisement of men seems to have had the effect of rupturing the long association of the 'feminine' with the disenfranchised male. If this had previously worked as an allegorical mask for addressing political concerns, it was no longer either necessary or representative of political reality. As a result, the exploitation and sufferings of Woman in fiction became more glued onto the female body. Disrupting one of its principal practices, this left a periodical like the *Journal* in a quandary. As during the Crimean War, it was faced with a choice of either changing its image radically to become more of a newspaper, and hence to continue to address primarily the masculine purchaser, or it could continue to direct itself to the now more sexually specific market of purchasers still without the vote. The first option was less attractive for one of the same reasons as during the Crimean War: The *London Journal* still had a brother in the *Weekly Times*. The appearance of the Ladies' Supplement just under a year after the 1867 Reform Act indicates the pursuit of the second option. While the Ladies' Supplements are a reaction to G.O.P., *Bow Bells* and the burgeoning numbers of literate women, I believe that debates around the Reform Act also spurred the *London Journal* to make the feminine adhere more closely to the female.

A directed address to women readers was yet to come, however. In the late 1860s women were still corralled into a separate space, for the Ladies' Supplement was physically detached from the rest of the magazine. It did not overtly penetrate the *Journal*'s body apart from the small advertisement to it on the back page of each issue. A separate pagination running from one supplement to the next created a chronological, vertical, continuity between each Supplement rather than a synchronous, horizontal one between the Supplement and the issue or part of the *Journal* it came with. Unlike the Ladies' Page of *Bow Bells*, the Ladies' Supplement ran *in parallel* with the main body of the magazine, fencing women into their own enclosure. This in turn suggests a continued allegiance to non-sex-specificity in the main body of the magazine. This is perceptible in the fiction too. The *London Journal* continues to run androcentric serials, including several masculine appropriations of the sentimental and sensational by Ernest Brent. While Mitchell (1989: 157) seems to suggest Brent's were stories directed at women, I read them rather as *gentlemanly*, bowdlerized in the sense I outlined in Chapter 8.

By 1872 there were signs of a more definite but still not total commitment to the Woman Reader. The Ladies' Supplements no longer continued their separate cumulative pagination, each now having its own. And as late as 1873-74, James Grant's *Shall I Win Her?*, set largely in South Africa, was an anticipation of Rider Haggard's imperial adventure stories. His work for the *Journal* from 1876 centred on the romantic heroine's adventures and psyche, however, and may, if we want a make-believe of a beginning, provide a date for when the *London Journal* was transformed into a women's magazine.

If the above defines the gender of the text in terms of its imagined consumer, more remarkable was the change in the gender of authors' names. From Stiff's repurchase of the *Journal* in 1859 to the introduction of the Ladies Supplements in 1868 both women and men in more or less equal proportion had been contributors of the serial novels and tales, 1 : 1.19 respectively. This is a figure calculated on the basis of genderable names that include those of anonymous works whose authors I have discovered. It therefore includes knowledge not necessarily available to readers of the periodical. A slightly larger number of women than men appeared anonymously but this does not greatly upset the near balance of masculine to feminine author names. Readers would have understood the magazine as produced by both men and women in virtually equal proportion, not as exclusive of one sex or the other. Between 1868 and the end of 1879, however, the proportion of women's names increases some 50 percent. In the years from 1880 through 1883 the situation changes again: anonymity now becomes the rule. The proper names of authors are almost always effaced behind by-lines so the sex of the producers is withheld.

From 1868 to 1883 the majority of Notices to Correspondents comprised matrimonial advertisements. These had started in 1849, been eliminated by Mark Lemon, and returned under Stiff. From the 1870s there was a perceptible move towards a greater number of female names in this space, which suggests more women readers, but the proportion of men remained significant even in 1883.[3] Nevertheless, I suspect that the figures for men are misleading and that the number of male *readers* was actually lower. By this stage men may well have bought the magazine specifically to use the matrimonial advertisement service. What is particularly interesting is how these advertisements stress the social and especially the economic position of their writers and what kind of partner (s)he wants. Rather than declare life-style interests as in today's Personal columns, which may be considered as searches for the merger of cultural and social capitals, matrimonial adverts in the *London Journal* zone were dominated by the search to merge and maximalize social and economic interests, as we see in the 'Sewing Machine Girl' story. It is interesting to note too that, contrary to the opinions of some critics, the *Journal* did enable prospective partners to meet, even if not directly through its pages. Rather it arranged the exchange of *cartes de visite* on receipt of the appropriate number of stamps, and directed correspondents to the *Weekly Times* as the place to insert second-stage advertisements whereby meetings could be arranged (see, for example, LVII: 16, 32, 48). Thus a newspaper could be bought by women in the same way that men could buy the *London Journal*, that is, to look for specific information, not for the periodical as a whole.

Women's Talk, Women's Space

Increased gender exclusivity is clearest in the language of the Ladies' Supplements which gradually became ever more verbose and 'technical'. Men might have used the fashion pictures for their own visual pleasure with little necessity to change subject positions, but most would have been excluded by the technical language of clothes, which figured in the *Journal* much more than other discourses that constituted late nineteenth-century women's language, such as cooking, singing or playing the piano.

Fig. 1. – Toilette de Ville in cashmere. Small casaque, Louis XIV., trimmed with a velvet ribbon and embroidered round the edge; sleeves coudés, with a flouncing at the end, and trimmed in the same manner as the casaque. Overskirt also in cashmere, trimmed with velvet and a rich twisted fringe. Chapeau Rabagas in velvet, trimmed with a feather at the top, ribbon, and a lace fall.
Fig.2. – Toilette de Bal. Corsage à basques, forming points at the side, and slightly pleated to the figure. The head of the corsage is trimmed with a bouilloné of tulle, surrounded with ruches; jockeys at the shoulders; satin bow at the back of the waist and at the edge of the overskirt, which is caught up at the back and sides. The overskirt is trimmed round the bottom with a velvet ribbon and deep lace; underskirt in taffetas, is trimmed with flounces, cut out in vandykes, and surmounted either with bouillonés or ruchings in tulle. On the first flounce a satin bow. Flowers in the hair.

---

[3] The average male to female ratio of genderable names in Notices to Correspondents (rounded to the nearest integer) is 51:61 in 1873; in 1875, 67:69; in 1880, 22:38; in 1883, 13:24.

Fig.3. – Toilette d'Intérieur for a Young Girl. – Corsage trimmed with a double ruche and bias-pieces indicating the cuirasse. Tunique princesse trimmed with black galoon, and caught up en tuyau at the sides; skirt trimmed with ribbons of black velvet. Bow of ribbon in the hair.

Fig.4. – Toilette d'Intérieur for a Young Married Lady. – Robe de chambre, close-fitting, in reps or cashmere, trimmed de revers, bows of ribbons and bias-pieces of taffetas; the basques of the corsage joined together. Skirt of taffetas, trimmed with a deep pleated flounce. Chemisette embroidered. Coiffure Maintenon, trimmed with a touffe of flowers on the left side.

(Description of coloured plate presented with part 337, LVII: 192; Figure 10.1)

Copyright.   THE LONDON JOURNAL,   *Entered at Stationers Hall*

Figure 10.1 Coloured Fashion Plate, 1d with Monthly Part
Source: March 1873, LVII.

Not the gender 'common' bowdlerism of the *Journal* in its earlier years, this is language specific to women (and those few men involved in *haute couture*). In Thomas Wright's 1867 description of what happens after dinner on a typical working-men's Sunday, the power relations that this kind of language was laced into are particularly clear:

> When left to themselves after dinner, the men charge and light their pipes, and enter into desultory conversation upon things in general, and the all-pervading Reform question is naturally the first touched upon... Bill joins the ladies [in the kitchen] ... In a few minutes after [*sic*] Mrs Jones goes upstairs to dress her hair and put her best cap on, and Bill embraces the opportunity – and Nelly – to snatch a kiss. When Mrs Jones returns to the

kitchen Nelly praises her cap, and this leads to a rather technical conversation between them upon the subject of fashion and dress, Bill being occasionally appealed to as to how *he* likes some particular fashion. While this talk is going on, Jones, who has had his nap, joins them, and being in his turn appealed to for an opinion upon some of the merits of some of the fashions upon which his wife and Nelly are discoursing, expresses views adverse to modern fashions generally, and begins to talk of the time when he was a boy, and is still holding forth upon that delightful period when the conversation is broken up by the arrival of his daughter Polly ...   ([Wright] 1867: 232-3)

Men's talk is 'naturally' political while the women's corresponding discourse concerns fashion. Politics serves to unite men while fashion unites women. Each is excluded from the other in various ways. Spatially corralled in the kitchen (inevitably invoking the 'kitchen literature' of Chapter 2), the women do not, it seems, discuss the 'Reform question'. While there is an attempt to include the young male lover in their discourse, the use of the italic 'he' in the original suggests an ironic attitude to its realization. Significantly, we are not told what fashions Bill does or does not like: he is silent, for he cannot enter their discourse without compromising his masculinity. The patriarch Jones deals with the women's 'technical conversation' by blocking it through his own domination of verbal space. His monologue is not so blatantly violent as a diversion onto a masculine topic (like politics), but appropriates and reorientates discursive space into gender common discourses everyone knows the vocabulary for, the age-old *ubi sunt* topos: a version of bowdlerization indeed. As in Bowdler, we can see the gender violence of his intervention, and his fear at the alliance of women through their own exclusive language. Since men owned and ran the *London Journal*, perhaps the initial reluctance to back women as a community of readers was motivated similarly.

After Pierce Egan II's death in 1880, the *Journal* sufficiently shifted ground and personnel to be able to parody elements of masculine news. An anonymous 'Special Paris Correspondent' aped the male 'Special Correspondent' who reported wars from the front. She – for the writer had a feminine persona – sent the news of the latest fashions chattily in a way that encouraged the social bonding of 'Science'. A representative passage shows the intense economic importance of dressmaking:

Thanks to weather and politics, the Paris season has been very dull. There have been but few balls and few receptions, and therefore scarcely anything can be gleaned from fashion's doings. Needless to say, trade is very depressed, and in every class of society gaieties have been left in the background.
     A pretty promenade dress I noticed in the Bois, was made of grey coteline, a thick ribbed yet supple material, profusely trimmed with terry velvet ribbon in garnet-colour ...
                    (Ladies' Supplement no. 467: 15, LXXVII, 3 March 1883)

Men's language – politics – is projected as a hindrance to what is implied as a matter of real importance to women, social performances and the appropriate costumes to wear at them. The *Journal*, like many other women's magazines, offered an endless joy in the continual disciplining of the body that is fashion.

Even if we do not entirely 'fabricate ourselves' through fashion (Cf. Craik, 1994: 16), clothes can nonetheless offer a huge variety of identities and aesthetic pleasures. *London Journal* novels certainly exploited the idea that clothes make the Woman. The two heroines of Harriet Lewis's *The Double Life* (1869), mother and daughter, adopt innumerable sartorial disguises both to conduct the lives they wish to lead and to escape the detectives hired to probe into their double lives.

At the same time, the *Journal* was not offering simply an exclusive space for women, but also a source of 'useful knowledge' or what the epigraph to this section calls 'science'. As the detailed account of Figure 10.1 shows, descriptions of the clothes were impersonal, anonymous and formulaic in their paratactic cataloguing. If their style seems to belong to the world less of the magazine than of the sales catalogue, they could also be read as instruction manuals not only by the thrifty who made up their own clothes, but also and especially by the large number of workers in the fashion trade. The Ladies' Supplements might help readers make money (cf. Hitchman, 1881: 393 on *Bow Bells*'s patterns). In 1883, Thomas Wright claimed that genteel dressmakers and milliners were the main purchasers of penny weeklies. The *Journal* never admitted its potential for financial utility, preferring to halo the Supplements with a magical nimbus, an auratic fantasy that everyone could afford the luxurious gowns on display. But use value in its strictest sense has never been part of the mythical appeal of fashion: fashion, rather, offers ideal versions of the self. By ignoring the potential utility of the supplements, the *Journal* was only modelling sales strategies that needlewomen who made up its patterns could employ with their own customers.

Initially, *London Journal*'s fashion plates showed two mannequins who gracefully and complaisantly conversed with one another in a setting where only women (and a very few perfect children) would ever be depicted. Their eyes were unrealistically large, mirroring the privilege spectators were supposed to assign to looking at them. They adopted stiff poses that celebrated the shapes and details of their dresses. Their faces were generalized signs of beauty, allowing the viewer more easily to overcome the images' otherness from herself than if the face had been an individualized realist portrait.[4] This could also be said for the descriptions of clothes in the Ladies' Supplement: they were ideals that in practice would be modified to fit individual bodies and circumstances.

In April 1870 motives for an increasing confidence in the woman reader/purchaser are revealed. Two mannequins are still genteelly conversing, but one is joyfully seated on a green tasselled armchair at a sewing machine, while the other is interested in her activity. There is no mention of the machine in the commentary. Sewing machines, commercially available since 1851, had been confined to workshops, and had come to have industrial connotations. From the 1860s, however, there were determined efforts by manufacturers to strip the machine of these associations in order to encourage its purchase for the home. One of the ways they tried to rebrand it was to have it included in fashion illustrations (Forty, 1986: 96-98). Sewing machines were already being advertised on the

---

[4] This was an objection to the introduction of fashion photography, which was introduced curiously late: see Craik, 1994: 93.

monthly covers of the *Journal*, as well as hosiery and haberdashery establishments. The fashion print thus functions as a secondary plug for advertisers, backed with the authority of an apparently Parisian origin: product placement *avant la lettre* indeed.

Other prints specified the setting these clothes moved in: in summer, an arcadia of suburban villa *nature civilisée*; in winter, elegant salons with candelabra, classical vases of flowers that matched the dresses in a harmony of nature and couture (December 1870), pianos and gilt clocks on mantelpieces over happily blazing fires (February 1871). Even if the *Journal* did not always advertise the time-pieces and pianos as shown in the plate, the background nevertheless kept readers informed of what they were supposed to desire for their homes and gardens, weaving a non-conflictual utopian space that promoted consumption as the discipline that achieved harmony in life. This was an even more ideal vision than the closely related one promoted by *cartes de visites* with their fake backgrounds and sitters' Sunday best (cf. Plunkett, 2003: 182-5).

Although by 1855 the practices of the fashion plate had penetrated the *Journal*'s fiction illustrations, the illustrations still comprised predominantly hieroglyphics of passion borrowed from the codified poses of the theatre. From the 1870s pictures such as Figures 10.2 and 10.3 become far more common. In these, just as much as to encode specific feelings, the characters' attitudes highlight the essential elements of costumes that are precisely drawn more often than earlier. The backgrounds too tend to be more detailed, presenting images of contemporary ideal home decoration similar to those of the fashion plates.

[HOW TRIX TOOK IT.]

Figure 10.2 'How Trix Took It', May Agnes Fleming, *A Terrible Secret*
Source: LVIII: 81.

February 22, 1878.]   THE LONDON JOURNAL.   121

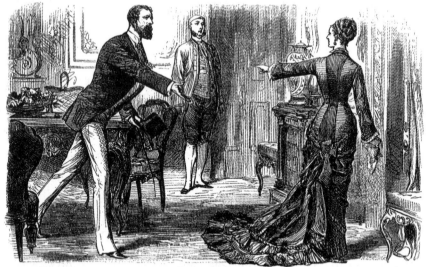

[AN ABRUPT DISMISSAL.]

HIS SWORN BRIDE.

By PIERCE EGAN.

Author of *" The Poor Girl," " The Pride of Birth,"* &c., &c.

CHAPTER XXI.

*" Fearfully her glance
Fell, as in doubt, on faces new and strange,*

So the very next day they were located in their new abode, Edith suggested a walk.

" It will be as well," she remarked, with a furtive glance at Ethel, " to know something of the place in which we are to end our days secluded and forlorn ; devoted all day to nothing but making frocks and underclothing for the little dirt-encrusted scrubs, the village gutterlings who swarm here, and in the even-

sharp—and driving my poor little brat, if I had been afflicted with one, with blows and expletives, off to the cliffs to gather samphire, or break its miserable neck in some of the clefts—it would not much matter which."

" Edith !" cried Ethel, turning to her with a look of reproof or reproach, it was not quite clear which.

" There was nothing else before me if that fine

Figure 10.3 'An Abrupt Dismissal', Pierce Egan, *His Sworn Bride*
Source: LXVII: 121.

If fiction illustration merges into fashion plate, the reverse is also true, for the fashion prints are tinged not only with watercolour but also with narrative. One of the stories that they suggest is the visit to the elegant home. From the 1870s there are usually several different kinds of dress in the same plate, arranged so that domestic clothes are placed furthest from the door, with outside clothes nearest it, as if the mannequin had just come in from the street. In the middle a ball gown, the public face of indoors, might be displayed to the admiring guest (see Figure 10.1). The linkage through narrative decoding of illustration to fashion print derives from their common relation to contemporary gallery art where the 'problem' picture was much in vogue, and where Tissot was using techniques from fashion prints for his sumptuous and enigmatic pictures of social life. Tissot seems, in fact, a common stylistic reference point through the common use of elongated, elegant bodies (see e.g. Figure 10.3.). This is not parergy, as metamorphic resentment seems absent. Rather it is another way that a harmonious fantasy space is pictured, a space where cultural boundaries fall and the dressmaker can inhabit the same culture as the lady that she dresses, or wants to dress as.

It is this particular congruence of fiction and fashion that defines the *London Journal* as a 'woman's magazine'. As I mentioned above, it returns the axis of interest back to Paris, where not only the fashion plates and designs but the language of fashion originate. And just as the 1867 extension of the franchise lay behind *London Journal*'s metastasis into consumerism, so the Siege of Paris in the autumn of 1870 and the ensuing Commune facilitated the refinement of its use of fashion. Communications between Paris and London were severely disrupted by the Prussian invasion, which meant that fashion prints could no longer be sent (see Ginsburg, 1982: 10). From October 1870 the names of the printers, Moine et Falconier, together with the names of artists, disappeared from the fashion plates. The plate for November is unfortunately missing from the BL run; from December there appear what seem to be intended as *imitation* Moine et Falconier plates. I write 'imitation' with some hesitation, as their names do not appear, but nonetheless there is a clear attempt to pass these plates off as if there had been no change in their source. The style remains similar and the lettering on the print remains almost identical. However, the mannequins' faces are now slightly longer, and the lettering, although very similar to the Paris plates, has tiny orthographic differences, the most obvious of which is the addition of a comma after 'The London Journal' – from which one can imagine how very close these plates are to the Parisian style. From February 1871 the significant words 'Copyright' and 'Entered at the Stationer's Hall' start to be printed on them. The siege of Paris did not only send Tissot over to Britain, then, but precipitated the *London Journal* into printing its own fashion plates. This had distinct advantages. The 'copyright' plate of February 1871 is the first that features pianos and clocks in the background. The advertisements on the monthly covers could now be tied into the plates with greater ease, enabling an even more harmonious space where the woman reader could feel at home with and – at least in fantasy – as, the lady consumer. The domestic space, no longer so blatantly dominated by men, could become voluptuously comforting for women, a place where she might feel at home, realize herself in her boudoir mirror, privately lose herself in feminine *jouissance*. It seems a particularly clear example of the transformation of communal politics to self-pleasuring that operates in this book as a sign of the *Journal*'s transgendering, a variant of what Jean Chalaby (1998) has reminded us is a shift in the press in general over the nineteenth century. As she succinctly puts it, once participants in the public sphere 'wrote to transform the world, journalists [later] to brighten it' (Chalaby, 1998: 193).

In the *London Journal* such a sensuous, sensual space and science is the confirmation of Mrs Madison's rule cited in the epigraph to this chapter 'to remember yourself in the dressing-room and forget yourself in the drawing-room'. But what does this forgetting oneself in the public zone of the drawing room mean? Of course it means abandoning politics, but does it not also lay one open to attempted seduction? And then is not the boudoir space itself a male creation, a seduction of the woman reader by the text's male producers? In other words, is the *London Journal* not setting up a theatrical, performative space, playing on and with its own artificiality, not for 'radical' or 'subversive' reasons, but to seduce with an image of *safety*? Is this the connection between gender and the increased stress on the self-reflexive performative that relies on an autonomous imaginary (see Chapter 7)? Is it perhaps a mirror of the seduction of melodrama where an actor performs a villain performing the desexualized, safe gentleman in order to seduce the heroine – and seducing the audience in the process, drawing them into the performance and validating the performative itself?

The issue now arises of the possibility of the heroine's and audience's resistance to this complex game of seduction. The next chapter shuttles between Paris and London to discuss how the *London Journal* treats Zola's analysis of this very question.

Chapter Eleven

1883. The Revenge of the Reader; or, Zola Out and In

Was will das Weib?
What does Woman want?
> (Freud, letter to Marie Bonaparte; quoted in Jones, 1953-57, II: 421)

Lorsque Mouret rentra dans son cabinet, il étouffait de sanglots contenus. Que voulait-
elle donc?
When Mouret returned to his office, he was choking with stifled sobs. What *did* she want?
> (Zola, 1883b: 444)

Like *Lady Audley's Secret*, Zola's novel has multiple existences both inside and outside the *London Journal*. Unlike the Braddon, *Au Bonheur des dames* is radically changed not only by its translation into a British mass-market magazine but in its very composition. I shall argue that the difference between the two versions of the Zola, the French version published in volume form and the drastically – surgically – altered one in the *London Journal*, enables meditation on attempted strategies of control that the male editor and proprietor of the *Journal* exercised over what their female clientèle were to read. Before discussing the *London Journal* version, I shall examine the French version of *Au Bonheur des dames* in order to establish what was at stake. I shall concentrate on the heroine's relations with the hero, Octave Mouret, the proprietor of a department store, who himself has conquered his clientèle, *la femme*.

Zola *chez lui*

Au Bonheur des Dames is the story of the creation of one of those department stores like the Bon-Marché or the Louvre, which have overturned and renewed commerce amongst us. I show it struggling with all the small shops, which are gradually devoured by it. To do that, I have set up a rival shop, an old shop which incarnates old-fashioned customs, and which the department store kills, which gives me a family drama. Furthermore, there are several other episodes of lesser importance with other little shops of the area. But that is only the business side of things. The passion side, the most important, is represented by a girl, Denise, who comes to Paris with her two young brothers. She enters the Bonheur des dames, where she endures all the sufferings of a beginner. Then the founder of the shop, Octave Mouret, falls in love with her; and so the antagonism that I wanted to establish begins. This Octave Mouret has based his huge business on the exploitation of Woman: he speculates on her coquetry, he flatters his customers, he installs them at his place like queens, the better to empty their purses. And here he is in love with a girl who will avenge all women. He who only believed in force, who mocked love, here he is at the feet of Denise, dying of passion. Initially he wanted to make her his mistress. Then, on the girl's refusal, he comes gradually around to marrying her after having given her more and more elevated positions in his shop. She has overcome him with her simplicity and her honesty. I repeat, it is the vengeance of Woman. Mouret, who has earned an immense fortune, suffers frightfully and gives everything to be loved by Denise.

   These are the bare bones of the subject. Naturally, I have put in it the depiction of the customs of our present-day great business ...
          (Zola, 1978-95, IV: 329-30, letter to Frank Turner, Médan, 10 October 1882)[1]

When Frank Turner, the translator of *Au Bonheur des dames* for the *Journal*, had told Zola that a summary of his novel was needed before it would be accepted by the two British publishing houses, Zola replied with the summary above. Since he did not know who the houses were, he hedged his bets, initially placing a narrative of an impersonal agency, the shop itself, at the heart of the book. In 1882 this was a new and therefore risky commodity to sell (see Zola, 1883d: x-xi), and so he quickly laid more stress upon the romantic-moral elements of the work: on the love affair between Mouret and Denise, on the heroine's incarnation of virtue that triumphs over vice and, perhaps paradoxically, on how this proves her to be the vengeance of women.

   When *Au Bonheur des dames* first came out the critics read it as a moral text. Apparently void of explicit sexual description and class struggle, they were pleased. It is a story where a virgin triumphs. '[L]a vertu est récompensée et le vice puni' wrote the journalist Albert Cim,[2] in a phrase that takes us back to Richardson again: *Pamela; or Virtue Rewarded*. In many ways this is a reading that it is justifiable to make. Angus Wilson, in the book that introduced Zola to British academia in the 1950s, understood the novel in the same way and consequently disparaged it: the 'dreary refinement of Denise's character lays [*sic*] like mildew over the whole novel' (Wilson, 1952: 121). More recent readings have preferred to see Denise as a utopian-socialist or oppressive form of the Goethian *Ewig-Weibliche* (or a combination of both), still charging Denise with carrying conventional morality (see, for example, Bowlby, 1985: 79-80). And it is true both that the moral dimension of the novel is left to Denise alone to ponder and that her sufferings in the shop provoke reflection on the cruelty of the department store employment system.

   As a sympathetic heroine, Denise is an appropriate figure to carry the ethical aspects of the novel. When her cousin, the daughter of the ruined small shop, symbolically dies through neglect by both her father and fiancé, Denise has nightmares about the store which she has helped to 'devour' shops like her uncle's.

---

[1] Throughout this chapter, I have preferred to give my own translations of French texts unless I refer to specific translations. I make no apology for their ugliness in English. They are as literal as will make sense and are intended to bring out various stylistic features in the original, such as the many passionate parataxes, which more elegant and readable translations efface (cf. Zola, 1883d and 1883e).

[2] Zola, 1978-95, IV: 46, quoting a review in *Le Radical* (14 March 1883).

Was it true that it was necessary for birds to eat spiders and for spiders to eat flies in a 'struggle for life'? Yet when she awakes, Denise immediately realizes not only that she can save no-one, but that that's fine – 'cela était bon' (Zola, 1883b: 461). While she may institute changes that to Mouret seem 'socialist', creating a 'phalanstery' of commerce, she does so for commercial reasons, 'non par des raisons sentimentales, mais par des arguments tirés de l'intérêt même des patrons' (Zola, 1883b: 438). Even her virginity is kept not for sanctioned, absolute, moral reasons but because '[e]lle se faisait de la vie une idée de logique, de sagesse et de courage' (Zola, 1883b: 241) – because she conducts her life according to logic, wisdom and courage. Hers is not the conventional morality of sentiment, but that of the capitalist, 'scientific' logic of Herbert Spencer's survival of the fittest. She doesn't have sex because the consequences might ruin her life. This is not virtue for its own sake, but practical morality such as dished out to the dressmaker by the pro-capitalist overseer, the 'lady of the period', that I referred to in the previous chapter.

Denise does not entirely lack traits of the Woman stereotypically passive and essentially good. They are certainly there for whoever wishes to find them. It has been claimed that Zola did not follow the course that his friends 'plus pessimistes' would have preferred, that is, to make Denise 'consciente de son pouvoir' (Mistler, in Zola 1883a: 702), and I cannot with conscience unmake readings already made that 'prove' her ignorance of her power. But I will remark that it is pessimistic to create a woman conscious of her power only for those who would threatened by an image of feminine agency. I want to argue instead that Denise can just as easily be understood as actively transforming herself from a penniless girl from the provinces to the 'toute-puissante' wife of a wealthy department store owner. The role of Good Woman she plays ups her price, enabling her rise to power, like a cynic's version of Richardson's Pamela, who holds out until she gets the exact price she wants for her virginity. Such strategic consciousness of power would indeed be 'pessimistic' for some, contesting the essential nature of the Good Woman reading of Denise and turning her partly into a Lintonesque Girl of the Period who ends victorious and happy through her manipulation of fashion and consumerism. Perhaps this is what Zola meant by 'the revenge of Woman' – the triumph of a woman who exploits the idea of Woman-as-Commodity better than men. In that case, Denise might model resistance to and triumph over male controllers of commodity culture, and in particular a resistance to the voluptuously harmonious and seductive space I described in Chapter 10.

I do not want to go to the opposite extreme and claim Denise is unequivocally powerful. Far less than in Richardson's heroine, readers are not allowed to penetrate deep and long into Denise's psyche. Instead we have to draw conclusions from exterior signs and tiny narratorial gestures. At one point, the narrator comments that Denise 'n'aurait pu jouer un jeu' better suited to throw Mouret at her feet (Zola, 1883b: 431; 'she could not have played a better game'). When Mouret offers Denise marriage, the narrator asks in wonderment if even at this 'price' she will not be had. Then Mouret offers her more – a home for her brothers too – and she accepts. Other characters in the novel are baffled by Denise. As in the summary, where the heroine is little more than a first name viewed from afar, the romantic plot is portrayed mostly from Mouret's point of view. This allows the reader to collude with other characters in the novel who are aware of his feelings and who understand the signs that he produces. Everyone knows that he is about to offer marriage to Denise by the way he has dressed the shop all in white. But no one can interpret Denise. What does this woman want?

> The intrigue which for months had kept the assistants enchanted with Denise's long resistance, had suddenly come to a crisis: it had been learnt the day before that the girl was going to leave the Bonheur, despite Mouret's supplications, on the pretext of a great need for rest. And opinions were open: would she leave? would she not leave? From department to department, a hundred sous were being bet for the following Sunday. The clever-clogs were betting a lunch on the card of a final marriage. Yet others, those who believed in her departure, were not risking their money any more without good reasons ... In any case, both sides agreed that this little salesgirl had conducted the affair with the science of a female rake of genius, and that she was playing a supreme match in leading him on like this by the hand. Marry me or I'm off.   (Zola, 1883b: 490)

The shop workers assume women want a happy marriage, the end of virtually all popular novels. They also assume she has her own 'science', which in terms of the *London Journal* we may read as a variant of a woman's 'science of life', a calculus of dress and address.

When the reader is shown what is going on in Denise's mind, however, a different narrative is suggested. The passage above continues:

> Denise, however, hardly dreamt of these things. She had never made either a demand or a calculation. And the situation that had made her decide to leave had rightly resulted from the judgements which were being passed on her conduct, to her continual surprise. Had she wanted all that? Had she shown herself tricksy, coquettish, ambitious? She had simply come there, she was the first to be astonished that she could be loved thus. Today, again, why was anyone seeing cleverness in her resolution to leave the Bonheur? It was so natural anyway! She was heading for a nervous illness, for intolerable anguish, amid the gossip rising incessantly in the shop, Mouret's burning obsessions, the fights she had to free herself from herself, taken by fear that she would give in one day and then regret it for the rest of her life. If that was a wise tactic, she didn't know it ...

> (Zola, 1883b: 490-91)

Style indirect libre such as here is very common in the novel, as in Zola in general. By its nature ambiguous, the thoughts of a character reported by the narrator whose mediation is signalled by the third person, two points of view jostle with each other, neither taking absolute precedence as with direct speech or third person narration. Readers have already been invited to regard Denise's thoughts, especially about Mouret, with irony. While the signs of her erotic attachment to Hutin are obvious both to herself and to readers, for a long time readers must infer what she feels for Mouret through ambiguous physiological signs, rather than through her thoughts as they are reported to us. Halfway through the novel Denise is fired, yet boards right next door to the shop.

She kept dreaming about Hutin, full of malaise. Every day she saw him pass beneath her window. Now that he was second [in command of the department] he walked alone, amid the respect of the ordinary salesmen. He never ever raised his head, she believed she suffered from the vanity of this boy, she used to follow him with her eyes, without fear of being surprised. And, as soon as she perceived Mouret, who likewise passed every evening, a trembling agitated her, she would hide herself quickly, her heart thumping ...

(Zola, 1883b: 242)

Until chapter X, when Mouret's letter arrives asking her to 'dine' with him, Denise herself does not know that she loves him. But if the reader has decoded the external signs, such as in the passage above, and discovered an internal state through them, s/he will have guessed Denise's internal state over a hundred pages earlier. It is through reading Denise *symptomatically*, in the way the shop assistants try but fail to do, that readers may understand her more than she does herself.

Reading symptomatically permits the reader to see how Denise comes to play the same game with Mouret as he plays with women when he seduces them: masking oneself as the object one wishes to seduce. Mouret persuades women to buy at his store by giving them ideal versions of themselves. Only when they are at his mercy, lost in *jouissance*, does he allow the reflective mask to drop from the violence behind it. In the hilarious climax of Mme Desforges's at-home, he is telling the friends of his current mistress about his store.

But in that soft voluptuousness of the dusk, amid the warm odour of their shoulders, he nonetheless remained their master beneath the ravishment that he affected. He was Woman, they felt penetrated and possessed by that delicate sense that he had of their secret being, and they abandoned themselves, seduced; whereas he, certain from then on of having them at his mercy, appeared, enthroned brutally above them, like the despotic king of chiffon.

'Oh! monsieur Mouret! monsieur Mouret!' they stammered, in low, rapturous voices in the depths of the shadows in the salon ...   (Zola, 1883b: 124)

This is very different from the tactic that Mr Jones had employed to ensure masculine domination of verbal space. Instead, it models the relationship between periodical and feminine reader with which I ended Chapter 10.

This narcissistic structure is not, however, gender-specific. In a less overt way than Mouret's specular conquest of Woman, Denise mirrors Mouret by offering an even more efficient version of his will to sell and his discourse. There are no descriptions of how Mouret is attracted to Denise physically. Indeed, most people consider her rather ugly. What he becomes obsessed by are his conversations with her. Their first, when she tells him her business plan (Zola, 1883b: 410-11), has an especially powerful effect.

Now she had come to having long friendly conversations with Mouret. When she had to go to his office to take orders or to give a report, he kept her to chat, he liked to listen to her. It was what she laughingly called 'making a decent man of him'. In her rational and shrewd Norman mind, all sorts of projects were bubbling out, those ideas about the new commerce which she had dared to sketch out already at Robineau's, and of which she had expressed a few that beautiful evening of their walk in the Tuileries. She could never do anything, see any task being done, without being pressed by the need to put it in order, to improve the mechanism.   (Zola, 1883b: 437)

Without her rewriting of the notion of the *brave homme* (the 'decent man') from the domestic morality of continence into her narrative of commercial success, Mouret would never have taken the million francs on the day of the final sale. Just like Mouret's, ideas that stem from her *tête raisonneuse et avisée* 'ravish' the customers (*ravirent la clientèle*; Zola, 1883b: 437, 438). If she is the 'vengeance of Woman' on Mouret, through him women are nonetheless the final victims of her sales strategies. Denise is hardly a feminist committed to collective action to empower all women.

Denise's mirroring of Mouret does not simply repeat his discourse back to him in amplified and elaborated form. He had been enabled to start his empire through his older wife who had died and left him the original shop. The connection between Denise and his wife, Mme Hédouin, is a *leitmotif* of the novel, and parallels Mouret's Sedgwickian relation with an older man. Just as Mouret enters into a business alliance with the banker Baron Hartmann through a shared mistress, so Denise enters into an alliance with Mme Hédouin through Mouret. In a gender-switched version of the triangulation that comprised a key strategy of homosocial bonding in Chapters 8 and 9 above, Mouret is passed between the two women just as Mme Desforges is passed between him and Hartmann. The final paragraph of the novel, at the moment that Denise has finally obtained what she wanted, underscores her triumphant alliance with Mme Hédouin.

A last noise rose up in the Bonheur des Dames, the distant acclamation of a crowd. The portrait of Mme. Hédouin was still smiling with its painted lips. Mouret had fallen to sit on his desk, into the million [francs], which he no longer saw. He could not leave Denise, he kept desperately clasping her to his breast, telling her that she could leave now, that she could spend a month at Valognes, which would stop people talking, and that he would then go to fetch her himself, to bring her back on his arm, all-powerful.

                                                                    (Zola, 1883b: 528)

Denise becomes 'all-powerful', *toute-puissante* (the last words of the novel) by mirroring Mouret both in his homosociality and by offering him an improved version of himself in the same way that Mouret captures women by selling them an image of themselves beautified. Both Denise and Mouret play on and with the narcissism of those they wish to catch. Each offers a version of love that is in the strictest sense homoerotic.

It is therefore indeed possible to read Denise as not fitting her description as a conventional heroine of what Hemmings (1966: 147) called a 'prim mid-Victorian novel'. While the narrative of the Virgin Triumphant is present, above all in the last third of the novel, we can also see that Denise learns how to manipulate that story to her own advantage. For contemporaries who wished to find it, this strategy would have had a double justification. If *Pamela/Shamela* and their derivatives offer literary models with high symbolic capital, there were also the 'scientific' observations Zola made of society. Denise's character corresponds to his description of the metropolitan female shopkeeper in his lengthy article 'Types de femme en France' (1878), in which the wives of Parisian shop owners are altogether more efficient and more intelligent than their husbands, keeping the books better and entertaining better relations with their customers. While in the provinces such successful women would be subject to gossip, says Zola, in Paris they can flourish. Denise's first act in the novel is to come uninvited to Paris from provincial Valognes, and it is in Paris that she develops her skills.

In order to arrive at this view of 'Denise', it has been necessary to study her as a sign, to analyse the proper name into its constituent sememes. But I also have to admit the fracture of the sign into contrascriptions: pragmatic calculation as well as *das Ewig-Weibliche*. For overall, it is never quite clear if Denise has *consciously* been playing the mirror game. To grant her unambiguous agency is to view her from the point of view of liberal humanism. She may also be read as a better-evolved entity in the machine narrative of Spencerian Progress, a Good Woman, or a product of sado-masochistic male fantasy. These and other readings of Denise have all been made. The only certainty is that she remains a figure held at a distance by the novel: it is never fully sure what this woman wants. And this itself may offer a form of resistance to the analyst.

Analysing Gender

The commercial competition that Denise ponders and assists in was predominantly an androcentric activity. She may help Mouret and adopt masculine traits, but all the *patrons* of the competing shops are men, while *la clientèle* are women. According to late Darwinian theory, men competed with each other for women (Darwin, 1871: II, *passim*). Women were simply links between men, not 'definite subject[s]' (Bowlby, 1985: 79). Mouret's mistress, Mme Desforges, realizes, even though she does not wish to admit it to herself, that Mouret is simply using her to obtain an introduction to her former lover, the banker Baron Hartmann. Although the masculine homosocial basis of commerce is contested by Denise's relationship with the dead Mme Hédouin, the Sedgwickian triangle remains dominant. Since women are not taken literally by force from one man by another, men vie to seduce purchasers, so that what Woman wants and how she wants it become a focus. For that reason Mouret *l'analyse en grand moraliste* (Zola, 1883b: 299) – he analyses Woman like a great moral philosopher.

There is a passage towards the end of *Au Bonheur des dames* which functions as a quasi-symphonic recapitulation of many of the work's themes and images. The reader is swept up to the heights of the store and inside the proprietor's own eyes and head. As at each of the three great sales in the novel, he looks down from his *poste favori* (Zola, 1883b: 163) into the 'immense nave' of his shop, a great panoptical gesture. In the following passage, yet another of *style indirect libre*, readers are shown how Mouret believes he has conquered *la femme* even while fearing that she might suddenly escape control and riot. The last and greatest sale of the novel is just coming to a close:

And Mouret was still looking down at his nation of women in the midst of this blaze [of electric light upon the entire shop decked in white cloth and clothes]. The black shadows were standing out vigorously against the pale background. Long eddies were breaking up the crowd, the fever of this great sales day was passing like an attack of vertigo, rolling back the disordered swell of heads. People were beginning to leave, the wreckage of the materials was strewn on the counters, the gold sounded in the cash-desks; while la clientèle, despoiled and violated, were going away half undone, with the assuaged voluptuousness and the secret shame of a desire satisfied in the depths of a sleazy hotel. It was he who possessed them like that, who held them at his mercy, by his continual accumulation of goods, by his lowering of prices and his 'returns', his fancy goods and his publicity. He had conquered the mothers themselves, he reigned over them with the brutality of a despot, whose caprice was ruining households. His creation was bringing a new religion, the churches, which were being deserted by tottering faith, were being replaced in souls hitherto unoccupied with his store. Woman came to spend empty hours at his place, the thrilling and unquiet hours which she had experienced once in the depths of chapels: a necessary expenditure of nervous passion, a recurring struggle of a god against the husband, a cult endlessly renewed of the body, with the divine afterlife of beauty. If he had closed his doors, there would have been a rising in the street, the desperate cry of female devotees to whom the confessional and the altar are abolished. In the luxury they had accumulated over ten years, he saw them, despite the hour, persist in crossing the enormous metal structure, along the suspended stairways and suspension bridges. Mme Marty and her daughter, swept up to the very top, wandered around the furniture. Held back by her children, Mme Bourdelais could not tear herself away from the fancy goods. Then, coming as a group, Mme de Bove still on Vallagnosc's arm, followed by Blanche, stopping in each department, daring to look again at the materials in her proud manner. But of the accumulated clientèle, of that sea of bodices swollen with life, beating with desire, all blooming with bunches of violets as though for the popular wedding of some sovereign, he ended by only making out the bare bodice of Mme Desforges, who had stopped in the glove department with Mme Guibal. In spite of her jealous grudge, she too was buying and he felt himself the master one last time, he held them at his feet, under the dazzle of the electric flames, like cattle from whom he had extracted his fortune.

With a machine-like step, he went along the galleries, so absorbed that he abandoned himself to the push of the crowd...   (Zola 1883b: 521-2)

After the first sale, the shop had been compared to a battlefield where *un peuple des femmes* (Amazons) has fought and disrobed *dans un coup de désire* (Zola, 1883b: 162-3). A 'coup' is a political takeover as well as a sudden access of passion, and this alternative allows in a political reading of the sign 'Woman' that the novel, never once mentioning the question of women's legal and political rights, resolutely refuses. Susanna Barrows has seen the perceived threat of feminism behind the figure of the dangerous horde of women in many nineteenth-century French texts. One of the most notorious images of feminine resistance and demand in the 1870s and 1880s was that of the incendiary *pétroleuses* setting Paris alight during the 1871 Commune – the very event that had helped the *London Journal* to consolidate the magical coherence of its consumerist space. *Au Bonheur des dames* was written only a short time after women had successfully demanded the right to secondary education in France. Furthermore, in 1880 an amnesty had been granted against the communards, many of whom had been deported. There was fear that the *pétroleuses* were coming back (Barrows, 1981). 'Woman' had, therefore, to be contained. As with the *London Journal* Ladies' Supplements, shopping was one activity into which women could have their energies redirected. And for those men who knew how to control women's shopping, this redirection of the 'expenditure of nervous passion' could result not only in the negative virtues of avoiding threat, but in the positive ones of economic profit. Mouret's seductions then arrive as overdetermined both by an ideology of gain and by a fear of gender revolution.

It may appear that Woman in the panoptical passage above is a ragbag of miscellaneous contrascriptions, by no means all potentially incendiary. Woman has transferred its supposedly 'natural' religious tendency to consumerism (as in the *Journal's* first 'Girl of the Period' article), but in Zola this paradoxically segues into the recurrent image of Maenadic riot. The governing trope of 'Woman' is actually that 'necessary expenditure of [undifferentiated] nervous passion': 'Woman' is liquidity, a very common nineteenth-century trope that appears in a variety of guises, from concern with monthly blood-loss to the definition of the expressive 'poetess'.[3] 'Man' on the other hand is what controls that 'expenditure' with the controlling valves of a machine, a common comparator of the department store (Bowlby, 1985: 80). Woman's liquid 'expenditure' is thus fuel for commerce, controlled by and circulated between men. The analogy of department store and machine forms another link between *magasin* and magazine for it can also be applied to the control of women's passions by that other kit-made machine that works on women's bodies and excites passion: mass-market fiction. As in the long quotation in Chapter 2, a few years later Vizetelly was to write of girls 'expending' their pennies for their own copies when they were too excited by J.F. Smith to wait for the instalment they shared with other girls.

Yet Zola knew that if Woman's passions were to feed the commercial machine, this undifferentiated fuel had to undergo what seems to be a personalizing, individualizing, process. 'Woman' needed to be broken down into specific women with specific names, for women had to feel comfortably 'at home' ('*chez elles*'; Zola, 1883b: 315, 321), as though they were in private spaces they themselves had individually made, even though they were *chez Mouret*. This is precisely the 'home' that Mouret makes, a man-created and controlled space that, intended for women, is coded feminine. Masculine origins are effaced through using the addressee to define the gender. Now Zola had made it clear from the first introduction of the named women who reappear in the panoptical passage above that they are all psychological types, not real individuals (Zola, 1883b: 119). Mouret's triumph lies in his ability scientifically to *analyse* the sign Woman, to break it down into its component parts as defined by various types of desire. But he still has control of the entire category 'Woman', not just of one or some of its desiring parts, for he has control of his whole department store which, systematically broken down into different departments and seduction practices, is

---

[3] On menses, see Showalter, 1987: 56-7, 67 and elsewhere. Armstrong (1993: 332-67) shows how the 'poetess' was especially associated with 'expressive theory', an idea that emotion must be 'expressed' like milk or tears.

designed to appeal to all types of women, and thus to the whole of 'Woman'. It goes without saying that the real threats to the shop, the unnecessary workers and the thieves – all women – are also surveyed, analysed, categorized and dealt with accordingly (Zola 1883b: 322 and ch. 6; and cf. Abelson, 1989, esp. ch 7). Only when Mouret cannot work out what a woman desires, does she triumph over him. And gets exactly what she wants.

Au Bonheur des dames forms part of the same cultural matrix as Charcot, who started his analyses of Woman in 1870, twelve years before the novel was written. Only two years after its publication, Freud would be studying under Charcot at the Salpêtrière asylum (Showalter, 1987: 146-55). Soon he would be moving towards his own system that would in the twentieth century be used to analyse and classify people according to what and how they want. It would even, through Freud's nephew Edward Bernays, be used to persuade them to buy. Thirty years later, instead of dignifying Mouret with the term *grand moraliste*, Zola might have called him a *psychanalyste*.

Zola Abroad

As I remarked in Chapter 7, *Au Bonheur des dames* was not a success in the *London Journal*. Its last third, about two hundred pages in the Gallimard edition, is compressed into a mere one column. Tinsley later published a more complete (but still expurgated) version of the same translation in three volumes. This latter has already received some comment from Ross (Zola, 1883d: xx, xxii), who avers that its expurgations concern sexual references. The same at first seems to apply to the *London Journal* version. The sexual adventures of Denise's younger brother Jean are deleted, for example, as from the Tinsley volumes. The preparations for bed together made by Denise's friend Pauline and her boyfriend are likewise dropped (Zola, 1883b: 200-201; cf. LXXVII: 167-68). Yet other very suggestive passages that the volumes eschew are left intact, such as the unmistakably sexual climax of Mrs Deforges's at-home, complete with Mouret's masquerade as a woman, and the description of the shop after the first great sale as though 'an army of women ... had disrobed there' (LXXVII: 136).[4]

Two *London Journal* illustrations to *The Ladies' Paradise* actively exploit current iconographic conventions of sexuality. One shows the sales assistant Mingot, looking like a moustache-twirling villain from stage melodrama, predatorily holding the hand of a listless Mrs Deforge while she is trying on gloves (Figure 11.1). It inserts the innocuous caption, a quotation from the novel, into a story of attempted seduction. This is, of course, faithful to the spirit of the original, but not to this particular passage. Surprisingly, given the frequent collapse of the difference between fashion and fiction illustration, this is the only illustration to the novel that shows the textures and voluptuous materiality of women's costumes that

---

[4] Note: Mrs Deforge = Mme Desforges. When referring to the *London Journal* version, I shall retain the spellings and names offered there.

The Ladies' Paradise so insists upon. Are we to read this unusual divorce as a sign of anxiety about it?

THE LONDON JOURNAL.

120   [FEBRUARY 24, 1883.

Figure 11.1 '"Quite perfect, madam," repeated Mingot. "Six and a quarter would be large for a hand like yours."' Zola, *The Ladies' Paradise*
Source: LXXVII: 120.

The other illustration, a picture entitled 'An evil counsellor for Denise', shows Pauline talking to the heroine in the conventional garret of a poor seamstress (Figure 11.2). Pauline is dressed like a cocky prostitute with rather too large a feather in her hat. While the illustration and caption suggest that Pauline is trying to get Denise to prostitute herself, all that she is doing according to the novel is inviting her for a day out in the suburbs! While it is true that Pauline sleeps with her boyfriend, all mention of this is omitted in the *London Journal* version as I have said. The salacious suggestion of the illustration therefore clashes what the periodical's words convey. Rather it indicates a reading of, and an attitude towards, the original: Pauline must be a vulgar prostitute if she has sex outside marriage, even if she does not get paid for it.

The important point is that it was not sex *per se* that was being deleted from the novel or excluded from the *Journal*. In Notices to Correspondents there are numerous clear references to unmarried pregnancy with no hint of reproach – according to the *Journal*'s practical morality, what is done is done (see, for example, 'One in Distress', LVII: 32). What is of concern in the *London Journal* version of the Zola is the possibility that Denise might be an active agent. While there is no exact equivalent for Denise of *Pamela*'s parodic sister *Shamela* that provides evidence that contemporaries did read Denise as calculating, I want to argue that the *Journal* fulfils this role by, as Mistler put it, 'pessimistically' interpreting her and other women as *conscientes de leur pouvoir*. The excision of the final third is designed to prevent exactly this reading by rewriting Woman as unequivocally powerless.

Figure 11.2 'An Evil Counsellor for Denise', Zola, *The Ladies' Paradise*
Source: LXXVII: 152.

In the *Journal* version, Mouret's revelation to Baron Decker of how he brutally exploits women is allowed to stay, as are the descriptions of how he traps mothers through their children (LXXVII: 268), how women become helpless before his displays of goods (LXXVII: 120), and the analysis of types of women consumers (LXXVII: 108). Men are shown to control women, and women do not resist them. Yet the *Journal* cut all passages from which women readers might directly learn strategies to gain power as consumers. Mme Guibal relates how she buys a dress, notes the pattern, has the dress made up more cheaply, then sends the original back for a refund (Zola, 1883b: 330). She also buys items like smart door-curtains and returns them as unsatisfactory after using them for a ball (Zola, 1883b: 329). Passages such as the following, a variation on the 'Maenadic riot' topos, are snipped out too.

And in that last hour [of the second sale], camping there as in a conquered country, just like an invading horde installed amongst the wreckage of the goods. The salesmen, deafened, exhausted, were now nothing but their things, of whom they disposed with the tyranny of female sovereigns...   (Zola, 1883b: 334)

Women may 'disrobe' in the shop but they are not to take charge of it. In the *London Journal* readers never learn of Denise's eventual power in the shop or of her commercial improvements. All indications that she may be actively in control over Mouret – however ambiguous they may be – are ruthlessly chopped out, the *Journal* instead selectively and clumsily quoting the last three pages of the novel to bring Denise and Mouret together. It radically alters the very last paragraph. Instead of collapsing and hanging on to Denise with a desperation whose magnitude is emphasized by the use of the imperfect tense in the original French, Mouret is propped up by active verbs and a decisive discourse style. Denise's determination to leave for Valognes had not previously been introduced, and is metamorphosed into a command by Mouret. The portrait of his dead wife no longer smiles with painted lips, and Denise certainly does not end 'toute-puissante'.

> Mouret held her close in his embrace, told her with sweetest words that she could now leave as she had wished, that she would stay a month at Valognes, which would close the lips of the world, that he would fetch her thence himself, and that she should never have cause to rue the day she entered as a poor girl the brilliant walls of *The Ladies' Paradise*.
>   (LXXVII: 286)

Denise is rewritten as a poor girl rescued by a king of chiffon.

Exactly as in Mouret's shop, a magazine that addressed women was coming to mean a space that made women feel at home and in charge, rather than a space where they were obviously lectured by men (as Beeton had done in his *English Woman's Domestic Magazine* of the 1850s). Just as Mouret masquerades as a woman to seduce, so male journalists on women's magazines were becoming obliged to 'cross-dress'. Arnold Bennett wrote for *Woman* 'as a more 'advanced woman' than any of his readers' under a series of female pseudonyms. Indeed Bennett's rhetoric, as Margaret Beetham describes it, suggests more than a passing resemblance to Mouret's. Denying 'his economic and cultural power over the women contributors and instead invest[ing] them with the power he holds himself, as editor and shareholder', he offered women an illusion of freedom in spaces they themselves have supposedly created (Beetham, 1996: 189). The earlier strategies that the *London Journal* had exercised, techniques that granted a man his masculinity through endless definition of 'Woman', were less and less saleable in the zone of the penny fiction magazine.

As in the shop the addressee has come to define the gender of the commodity text itself: exactly, a 'women's magazine'. Obviously, the notion of the 'domestic' here has metastasized dramatically from the pseudo-political homosocial masquerade of the early *London Journal* into a man-induced, man-controlled, feminine *jouissance*. *Au Bonheur des dames* revealed these strategies and showed women consumers using them to their own advantage; the removal of such passages indicates, I think, anxiety about the potential power of the *London*

Journal's own readers. It is as if this power were imagined as a malignant cancer that required drastic surgery to keep it at bay. This is fear of the metastasis of the reader and ultimately the reason for the alternative title of Part 3. Chapter 2 pointed out that contemporary accounts of mass-market reading indicated a widespread return of desire for a supply-led transformation of culture and a general anxiety about the demands of mass-market readers. Its form in the *London Journal* is powerfully gendered and leads towards what Andreas Huyssen (1988) has presented as the feminization of the mass market in general under modernism. What is offered as a substitute for women's empowerment as consumers (or indeed as voters) is the pleasure of the psychological.

Precisely because of its surgical excision of large parts of *Au Bonheur des dames*, the *Journal* grants Denise proportionally more space than in the original, so she becomes much more prominent than either Mouret or his shop. The details of her sufferings in the first two-thirds of the novel, both emotional and physical, remain intact. As a result, she is metamorphosed into a heroine whose sufferings for virtue's sake are rewarded: it would be very difficult indeed to read the *London Journal* version in any other way than as a story where 'la vertu est récompensée et le vice puni'. She becomes a Pamela with – importantly – a subtle interiority that marks her as the social equal and deserving bride of her lord, but shorn of ambiguity, including the potential for readers to interpret her actions as manipulative survival strategies à la Shamela. For the reader, the pleasures of decoding her interior subjectivity from external signs oust any pleasures of the revenge of Woman. The *Journal* also deletes the shocking deaths of Denise's cousin and aunt, and the hefty passages concerning the ruination of her relations and her generous friends. The ethical question of Denise's nightmare of Spencerian logic is therefore effaced too. Morality is instead rendered unproblematically prim, proper and conventional, an 'optimistic' picture of a woman *ignorante de son pouvoir*. Both potentially feminist and impersonal 'scientific' readings are foreclosed. The *London Journal*'s Denise is remarkably unambiguous.

When compared to the *London Journal* heroines I described in Chapter 9, this concern to remove agency from Denise seems surprising. Yet by the early 1880s the *Journal*'s priorities had been transformed. Sally Mitchell has described the heroine in fiction from the *Journal* and from the *Family Herald* during the 1870s, differentiating her from the heroine of 'the reading of the middle class', mainly through the 'overwhelmingly physical nature of the action' (Mitchell, 1989: 151). The penny fiction heroine *uses* her body:

> The aristocratic romance operates from the same emotional ground as the middle-class women's novels of the sixties: the heroine is threatened, persecuted, and finally vindicated. The difference is that in the middle-class novel the threats are social – loss of status, need to work, exclusion from the family role. In penny magazines both threat and resolution are primarily physical ...
> The dramatic climax in which a woman uses her body to protect her husband's crops up in a number of stories ... writers judge women and men on the same grounds and find the same qualities admirable in both. Intellect is not very important in fiction built around physical action; even in detective stories the solution generally comes about by accident

instead of ratiocination. Still, it is often the heroine who falls through the rotten floorboard and finds the missing will, and she does have enough sense to realize its significance ...

Penny magazine stories assume that able-bodied women will support themselves ... The actress has become at least as popular as the governess as a surrogate ...

Women play a more central role in achieving their desires ... There is, however, a hypocritical distinction between what a woman can do and what she can be seen to do ...

Though the penny magazine editors preach male dominance, the fiction continually shows women exercising secret power...

(compiled from Mitchell, 1989: 152, 153, 154, 158)

Many illustrations support the priority of physical action in serials from the 1860s, but there is far greater variety in *London Journal* fiction of the 1870s than Mitchell suggests: her comments on the 'unique' nature of a story by Ernest Brent are indicative not of its exceptional status but of a diversity that can only with difficulty be accommodated into an argument based on a notion of an undifferentiated penny press. While each novel clearly follows a set of generic practices, each is as different and as sophisticated as the reader cares to make it (cf. Geraghty, 1992: esp. 223, on soap-operas). Harriet Lewis's *Lady Trevor's Secret* (1877) includes complicated treatment of the masquerade of gender and class through clothes, for example, continuing the insistent discussion of this in the mass-market novel. In May Agnes Fleming's *A Wonderful Woman* (1872), the heroine is a cross-dressing, boisterous hoyden whose actions, highly questionable according to masculine earthly law, are in the end decisively recognized and rewarded. In Fleming's *Carried By Storm* (1878-79), one of the heroines turns a whip on a man who tries to whip her, flees thinking she has killed him and finds work as a singer, before eventually making the man she has always loved fall in love with her through her performance – not that she marries him. This could easily be read as a beautifully reflexive narrative about the complicated attitudes of the mass-market novelist who both desires and despises her public.

Notable exceptions from Mitchell's stereotype continue in the *Journal* into the 1880s. *Countess Lovelace* (1883) by Emma Watts Phillips, with its symbolic names, corruptly luxurious settings, army characters, open sexual bartering and international cast suggests a version of the world of Ouida's *Moths* (1880). Enormously successful, *Moths* was considered the most scandalous of all Ouida's works, with the reputation for being the first novel in England to show a divorced woman living happily ever after. A poll of the readers of the American *Literary News* in 1882 named Ouida and Zola at the top of the list of 'authors having the worst influence'. According to Bigland (1950: 152), *Moths* was spoken of in the same breath as Charlotte Brontë's *Villette* and Mrs Gaskell's *Ruth*: libraries 'were besieged with people clamouring for copies'. It cannot really be surprising that economic literature like the *Journal* should try to repeat such a commercially successful performance. Countess Lovelace, the central character of Watts Phillips's novella, turns out to be a French prostitute, abandoned, pregnant, on the streets of Paris by the hero's father. She is also the mother of a virtuous girl who narrowly escapes an incestuous relationship with her brother. The Countess eventually ends up 'happily' married to a paralytic but very wealthy major general to whom she had once tried to sell her daughter.

> She distributes her favours with extraordinary impartiality for so capricious a woman.
> The last news we have of her is that she has presented the hero of hundred fights with twins, the news of which startled no one more than the major-general himself.
>
> (LXXVII: 86)

Her story, when she reveals it to the reader through a confrontation with her son's father, is that of *Ruth* or Barrett-Browning's Marian in *Aurora Leigh*, though without any indication of Magdalen reform. Sex is not excised here. Rather the Countess is unquestionably the vengeance of Woman on a society of stupidly lustful men. As such she, like several other heroines, both undermines Mitchell's stereotype and, apparently, my argument over the *Journal*'s problematisation of women's agency.

It is important to remember that the *London Journal* is a periodical with very specific conventions and hierarchies in its format. *Countess Lovelace* was neither placed in a prominent position nor long. Amongst the heroines of short stories there is also very great variety.[5] Mitchell's description in fact holds true for *London Journal* heroines in *front-page* serials of the 1880s (with the caveat that they are not quite as physically energetic as she suggests). These are the 'official' novels with which the *Journal* wishes to identify itself, the public face of the magazine. Obviously intended as a lead serial from the amount of money paid for it, the status of its author and, of course, the position of its initial appearance, *The Ladies' Paradise* must be measured against its peers, not short stories or second- or third-string novels. It is therefore more appropriate to compare it to *A Terrible Suitor* which replaced it on the front page and maintained that position for many weeks, and to *Fairest of All*, a slightly later serial that also held the front page for an exceptionally long time. These do confirm Mitchell's characterization, but I read them more as developing J.F. Smith's trial narratives, so that not only the hero but now especially the heroine are anchored into sexual stability, a fixity that enables marriage, and social and sexual reproduction.

In *A Terrible Suitor* the heroine Ilda is very active, 'spirited' in her resistance to the villainous suitor who is blackmailing her father. Her generosity to an old woman enables her to discover both that her terrible, villainous suitor is already married and the hiding place of the document with which he is blackmailing her father. In the final episode, the latter, forgetting his daughter's key role in his deliverance from blackmail, remarks that he was saved by Ilda's true beloved –

---

[5] See, for instance, Percy B. St John, 'Too Handsome by Half', LXXVI: 77-8; 'How Dorothy Escaped', LXXVI: 252-54; 'Kate's Adventure', LXXVI: 13-14, 'His Own Fault', LXXVII: 156-58; 'My First Transgression', LXXVIII: 52-3, 'Too Young and Pretty', LXXVIII: 220-22. See also stories by other authors (possibly reader-contributors): 'Cigarette', 'The Bride of a Day', LXXVI: 45-6; E.A., 'Happily Jilted', LXXVI: 236-37; E.D. 'Nellie's Interesting Foreigner', LXXVII: 28-30; A.G., 'Tony Truelove's Valentine', LXXVII: 132-33; A.G., 'Dr Fairflax's Wonderful Cure', LXXVII: 172-74; L.V.P., 'Hester', LXXVII: 348-51.

who has in fact done very little indeed. This sudden and curious elevation of the hero's achievements acts both to nullify Ilda's activity and as a pointer to how her beloved has now entered full masculinity and is therefore an appropriate husband for her. For just as the narrative plays with the sexual ambiguity of the heroine's 'spirited' nature, so the hero's 'womanly refinement' had initially been remarked (LXXVII: 114-15). Violating the conventions of sexual difference and thus creating a tension that requires resolution, front-page *London Journal* novels eventually provide the solution by erasing inappropriate gender traits from hero and heroine. While this may be achieved by means such as found in *A Terrible Suitor*, at other times the sexualized and gender-ambiguous male turns out not to be the hero after all. Gaston Dantree of 'somewhat effeminate' and even 'fatal' beauty (Fleming, *A Wonderful Woman*, LVI: 3) is revealed to be married already. In the same novel the heroine Katherine, whose name explicitly recalls the heroine of *The Taming of the Shrew*, and who has passed herself off as a man twice and enjoyed a career on the stage, ends up happily married to a good man, thus proving her true femininity.

None of these variants occurs in *Au Bonheur des dames* as I have described it, for Denise's story is not even an inversion of the sexual stability narrative: the heroine gradually learns the techniques not of femininity or even masculinity but of homoerotic narcissistic gender masquerade.

To define the *London Journal*'s official serials by their resolutions is, however, to ignore two major points. Firstly, the novels are located in a periodical which now contains at least three other serials running concurrently. Gender ambiguity may be resolved in one story, but continues in all the others. The spectacle of a rite of passage is repeated again and again in the overlapping serials so that sexual stability is never fully achieved in any issue of the magazine. Such intertessellation works to forestall resistant readings that a heroine's activity is unjustly rewarded, since it encourages readers to lurch from resolution into instability again simply by turning the page: if one heroine is reduced to passivity and married motherhood, others will still be having adventures in the same issue. Secondly, resolution is never stressed in the *Journal*. The end is always skimmed over in a column or less of conventional banalities, since it is far more important to move narrative desire from one issue to another than allow satisfying closure to any one novel. Hence the rapid resolution of Denise's sufferings would not have read as so glaringly incoherent to habitual users of the magazine as it does to those of us who expect the elegant closures or artful terminal ambiguities of consecrated volume-form novels.

As with the rewritten *Au Bonheur des dames*, the narratives concentrate on the heroines, giving them far more space than anyone else. But rather than physical activity, the heroine's worth hangs on the refinement and correctness of her feelings and (far less stressed) her generalized, non-denominational piety, of which her activity is only the outward manifestation. Madge, the heroine of *Fairest of All*, not only saves her rival in love from drowning but afterwards proves herself much more capable than the feckless hero of ensuring that the woman lives. All the while, her anguished thoughts are given in detail. She eventually gets her man (and, although she has been working as a servant, finds out she is of aristocratic birth) precisely because she is able to overcome her selfish desires. Such a story grants pleasures of a very particular kind. Since the heroine is now characterized by an identity and interiority all her own, interiority can become a utopian space where she can apparently exist most fully, free of men. It is also an inherently democratic space: anyone can turn out to be a 'lady' by birth if a 'lady' in spirit and accordingly have her identity confirmed by voluptuous couture. The luxurious spectacle of the inwardly suffering woman is legitimated by a variety of other discourses too. Firstly, returning again to a central tenet of the culture of sensibility, mental sufferings typologically recalled those of Christ. Front-page heroines are genealogically descended from *Clarissa* via melodrama, with Clarissa's paradise of heaven replaced by a happy, reproductive family and freedom from the labour market. Suffering wins the leisure and liberty that a 'lady' has. Secondly, the psychological was coming to be seen increasingly as the province of women both in terms of fiction and in the psychological sciences. Hugh Stutfield infamously condemned women's fiction in 1897 with the sentence 'Psychology ... is their never-ending delight'.[6] Charcot's experiments and Freud and Breuer's *Studies on Hysteria* are as indicative of the association of interiority with the feminine as George Egerton's interest in 'psychological moments' in *Keynotes*. Mass-market heroines may not be drawn with the psychology of learned treatises, but rather with a kind of early pop psychology, the function of which is to validate them as high-status individuals. The *Journal*'s offer of a fantasy feminine interior space with its luxuriously subtle sensations is thus a retreat from and resistance to a brutal masculine world. As I have repeated, it is also a site that masculinity creates and tries to control.

The *Journal*'s retuning of Denise and the other women in *Au Bonheur des dames* thus ensures harmony with the official front-page narrative. Yet anxiety about the power of women addressees of the magazine insistently returns. The heteronomous side of the cultural field within which the *London Journal* operated meant providing the illusion of women in power while men in fact remained in control: this is the function of the psychological, the magic space of women's *jouissance* granted by men. But *Au Bonheur des dames* showed too clearly how women could turn the tables on men precisely in the area of the psychological. The *Journal*'s massive alterations to Thiers' *History of the Consulate* (1845-52) had in the end been openly admitted and the reasoning behind it explained: it was thought too offensive for the market (see p. 26 above). There is no similar announcement regarding *The Ladies' Paradise*. While we cannot know the real reasons for the rewriting of the novel, it will be clear by now that lack of popularity was not the only one. Pierce Egan III was not happy editing the *Journal* and Johnson wanted to sell it. Perhaps, unlike Oscar Wilde a few years later, they felt unease at being associated with a women's magazine. Perhaps Johnson and the old hand Percy B. St John, having become successful in a previous generation when a different gender dynamic was in play and already anxious about the masquerade they had been forced to adopt by the changing nature of the field, were uneasy that depiction

---

[6] On women and the psychological sciences, see Showalter, 1987, *passim* and esp. ch 6.

of women's control of the *magasin* might suggest women readers' control over the magazine. Perhaps, as I have also suggested, coupled with the return of discourses demanding the transformation of society through control of supply, it was a desire to prevent the fantasized metastasis, the cancerous spread, of 'the revenge of Woman' that resulted in the drastic surgery. The producer not the consumer was to remain in absolute control.

In terms of market research this was a primitive reaction: to remain in control they should rather have followed Mouret and tried to find out What Women Wanted in detailed surveys of the psychological constitution of their actual and potential markets as today's Values, Attitudes and Lifestyles marketing studies do. Their failure to do so means that we know virtually nothing about how real readers of the *London Journal* would have reacted to the original or did react to the amputated version. An enormous variety of options was open. Non-academic reading can operate in a 'meaningless' way, as Ang (1995) and Hermes (1995: 12-17) remark, or with varied degrees of meaningfulness at different moments, on the level of the most minute lexia, as well as the largest, depending on what specific context it is performed in. A particular phrase or a scene may resonate with a reader while the rest is immediately forgotten – to take the entire work as the only valid lexia is to remain imprisoned within narrow High Culture notions of the Unity of the Book. The case of a certain Mrs Smith's reading of a dime-novel by Laura Jean Libby, as told by Michael Denning (1998: 197-200), would be a radical misprision of the original according to academic standards. But, as Denning points out, it has its own logic, which partly depends on the way the dime-novel was published in parts. Mrs Smith may not have read the whole story. She may have made up her version to cover the gaps. Even assuming a reader read the whole of *The Ladies' Paradise*, she may remember the spell cast over Denise by the shop window on the first page as having reference to her own life, and she may ignore the 'Virtue Rewarded' option.

As Baudrillard (1996) hypothesized, consumers of culture might resist by simply consuming and leaving no or ambiguous traces of how they consumed. This is precisely the strategy of Denise, who even at the end remains an enigma. By resisting analysis, she may figure not only the revenge of Woman on men but of the Victorian consumer of mass-market fiction on the condescension of the investigative High.

I began by noting the material absence of nineteenth-century mass-market periodicals from our libraries and have ended by dissolving my engagement with the magic of commodity texts back into the mystery of their reading. If this seems to risk a free-market version of deconstruction that many have justly condemned, it is intended only to stress the extremely local conditions under which meanings are made and how both each utterance and its decoding are necessarily interventions in a field of power. I have been concerned to investigate a hitherto marginalized norm of the nineteenth century, while never seeking to turn it into anything more heroic than it was. If it has been a rediscovery of my own story repertoire – the imaginary of a child of provincial parents 'between the two nations' hypnotized by the metropolis, fascinated and appalled, old enough to hear the echoes of practical morality and romance narratives that could have, and maybe did, ripple down from

J.F. Smith – that is only one aspect of the polymorphous magic of the commodity-fetish. My socio-political aim has not been to discover the 'subversive' potential of a commodity text, but to show that the excluded, the vilified, the marginalized are already contained within a centre which is much more complex and riven than it thinks it is and likes to be thought of.

Is that critical aim itself a current norm of the academy now, a distinguishing badge of the liberal British inspectors of culture? Perhaps so. But when the descendents of the nineteenth century mass market still quite happily simplify, seduce, scapegoat and sensationalise, such a complicating intervention remains a necessity.

Appendix

The *London Journal*'s Circulation Figures

3 March 1845	20,000 ('Address to Our Readers', III: 16, 7 March 1846)
4 October 1845	75,000, weekly and monthly issues together ('P.E. (Birmingham)' in Notices to Correspondents, II: 64)
November 1845	75,000, with back issues nearly 100,000 (8 November 1845, 'Quid Nimio' in Notices to Correspondents, II: 144; 'G.W.M. Reynolds', quoted from the *Glasgow Examiner*, 8 November 1845, II: 191)
January 1846	150,000 of issue 1 have been sold ('A Constant Reader' in Notices to Correspondents, 3 January 1846, II: 272, though 'F.H.M' is told in Notices to Correspondents, 24 January 1846, II: 320, that 130,000 of issue 1 have been sold)
24 January 1846	80,000 weekly, but constant demand for back numbers ('F.H.M.' in Notices to Correspondents, II: 320)
28 February 1846	120,000 including back numbers ('A.B.C. (Belfast) in Notices to Correspondents, II: 400)
7 March 1846	80,000 weekly but monthly parts and back numbers make the circulation 120,000 for each number ('Address to our Readers', III: 16)
1 August 1846	Myles the Bookseller of Dundee sells 100 dozen every week (=1300); Heywood of Manchester sells 9,000 of the current number, excluding back numbers ('P.W. (Dundee)' in Notices to Correspondents, III: 352)
August 1846 to February 1847	100,000 (general address in Notices to Correspondents, III: 416, 29 August 1846; 'A North Briton' in Notices to Correspondents, IV: 16, 12 September 1846; 'J.S. (Maidstone)' in Notices to Correspondents, IV: 64, 3 October 1846; 'Humanitas' in Notices to Correspondents, IV: 336, 30 January 1847)
20 June 1847	'close upon 90,000', but with sales of monthly parts, etc. 140,000 ('T.M.B.' in Notices to Correspondents, V: 272)
9 January 1848	170,000 (*Weekly Times*, 1848: 606)
mid-1849	80,000 during the serialization of *Godfrey Malvern* (Anon., 1866: 102)
23 June 1849	readership of 500,000 (John Wilson Ross, after-dinner speech reported in *Weekly Times*, 1849: 453)
26 October 1849	100,000 (*Daily News*, 26 October 1849: 2, 'Report to the Committee on Public Libraries')
1850	170,000 (Ellegård, 1957: 37, quoting *Encyclopaedia Britannica*, 11th edn)
22 February 1851	'Upwards of 120,000 per week' ('A Common Tradesmen' in Notices to Correspondents, XII: 400)

1851	200,000 (Heywood in *Report*, 1851: 373, 376, 377; 'M. de S.' in Notices to Correspondents, 16 August 1851, XIII: 384, 'not less than a million readers and increasing' supports Heywood's figure)
18 October 1851	'500,000 readers' ('Henri (Blackburn)' in Notices to Correspondents, XIV: 112)
late 1851-52	300,000-400,000 during *Minnigrey* (Anon., 1866: 102); 512,000 during *Minnigrey* (advertisement on monthly cover, *London Journal* n.s. XIII: 17 May 1890, and repeatedly)
10 July 1852	276,000 copies of no. 312 sold 'up to this time' i.e. to no. 387, after almost seventeen months ('Harriet of Aberdeen' in Notices to Correspondents, XIV: 288)
24 July 1852	'upwards of a million [readers] a week' ('Scrutator' in Notices to Correspondents, XV: 320)
24 September 1852	'250,000' of a free engraving ('G. Davis' in Notices to Correspondents, XVI: 48)
late 1853-54	500,000 during *Woman and her Master* (Anon., 1866: 102)
1854	450,000 (Dalziel, 1957: 23)
19 March 1855	2,000,000 readers weekly (*Weekly Times*, 1855: 194)
1855	450,000/ 510,000 (Altick, 1998: 359, 394; Ellegård, 1957: 37); 512,000 in speech by Chancellor of the Exchequer reported 28 April 1855, XXI: 144; but 510,000 in Hansard, ser.3, CXXXVII (1855), col. 783 (19 March 1855)
August 1855 to November 1855	'upwards of half a million' ('W.R.' in Notices to Correspondents, 18 August 1855, XXI: 400; 'J.C.' in Notices to Correspondents, 10 November 1855, XXII: 176)
1856	26,520,000 over the year (= about 500,000 weekly) (de Clarigny, 1857: 228)
November 1857 to January 1858	400,000 (advertisements for *London Journal*, *Weekly Times*, 15 November 1857: 7, 3 January 1858: 7 and 11 January 1858: 7)
10 April 1858	400,000 (advertisement for *Kenilworth*, XXVII: 96)
25 April 1858	467,000 (advertisement for *London Journal*, *Weekly Times*, 25 April 1858: 7)
May 1858	'two million readers' (advertisements for *London Journal*, *Weekly Times*, 9 May 1858: 7 and 16 May 1858: 7)
21 August 1858	500,000 (Collins, 1858: 440), but Brougham (1858: 11) is sceptical, giving 350,000
1858-59	250,000 (Anon., 1866: 163)
1860	300,000 (Ellegård, 1957: 35)
1860-61	*c.* 350,000 (Cross, 1985: 190)
1860	313,000 (*Times*, 25 July 1862: 12)
1864	500,000 (Altick, 1998: 358, though his source is not stated)
1865	200,000 (Ellegård, 1957: 35)
1867	120,000 (Ellegård, 1957: 37)
1870	150,000 (Ellegård, 1957: 35)
July 1871	400,000 (W.S. Johnson in *The Times*, 4 August 1871: 11)

References

The following omits articles in periodicals and newspapers for which I have supplied references in the text.

Pre-1929

Ackland (1894), Joseph, 'Elementary Education and the Decay of Literature', *Nineteenth Century*, XXXV: 412-23.

[Ainger] (1859), [Alfred], 'Doubleday', 'Books and their Uses', *Macmillan's Magazine,* I: 110-13.

Alexander (1876), William, 'Literature of the People – Past and Present', *Good Words*, XVII: 92-96.

[Alison] (1834), [Archibald], 'The Influence of the Press', *Blackwood's Edinburgh Magazine*, XXXVI: 373-91.

Almar (1840), George, *Oliver Twist, a Serio-Comic Burletta in Three Acts*, London: Chapman & Hall.

Anon. (1820), '*Ivanhoe: A Romance*, By "the Author of Waverley", &c.', *Eclectic Review*, n.s. XIII: 526-540.

Anon. (1833), 'The Present Taste for Cheap Literature', *Bee; or the Collector of Literary Sweets*, 1 March: 9-10.

Anon. (1845a), *A Week in London; or, How to View the Metropolis*, London: Cradock & Co., new edition.

Anon. (1845b), *City Scenes; or, a Peep into London*, London: Harvey & Darnton.

Anon. (1845c), 'New and Cheap Forms of Popular Literature', *Eclectic Review*, 4th n.s., XVIII, July: 74-84.

Anon. (1847), 'Popular Serial Literature', *North British Review*, VII, May: 110-36.

Anon. (1848), 'Our Weekly Gossip', *Athenaeum*, 1 January: 24.

Anon. (1851a), 'The Copyright Question', *Critic*, n.s. X: 251.

Anon. (1851b), 'Revelations of the Newspaper Press', *Critic*, n.s. X: 499-500.

Anon. (1851c), 'The Duty on Paper and the Working Classes', *Working Man's Friend and Family Instructor*, V, 25 January: 85-88.

Anon. (1856), 'Weekly Romance', *Saturday Review*, I, 8 March: 364-5.

Anon. (1859), 'Cheap Literature', *British Quarterly Review*, XXIX, April: 313-45.

Anon. (1862), 'Mr Charles Reade's Novels: *The Cloister and the Hearth*', *The National Review*, XIV, January: 134-49.

Anon. (1866), 'Penny Novels', *Macmillan's Magazine*, XIV, June: 96-105.

Anon. (1889), *The Cost of Production ... of a Book*, printed for The Incorporated Society of Authors.

Anon. (1918), 'An Old-Time Favourite Re-Appears', *Spare Moments*, LIX, 12 October: 644.

Austin (1870), Alfred, 'Our Novels: The Sensational School', *Temple Bar*, XXIX, June: 410-24.

Bagehot (1858), Walter, 'The Waverley Novels', *National Review*, VI, April: 444-72.

Bagehot (1852), Walter, 'The French Newspaper Press' from 'Letters on the French Coup d'État of 1851', *The Inquirer*, January and March, reproduced in *Collected Works*, ed. Norman St John-Stevas, 8 vols, III, London: The Economist, 1968: 71-6.

Barker (1880), Joseph, *The Life of Joseph Barker Written by Himself, edited by his Nephew John Thomas Barker*, London: Hodder & Stoughton.

Baxter (1869), R.D., *The Taxation of the United Kingdom*, London: Macmillan & Co..

Bertram, James Glass (1893), *Some Memories of Books, Authors and Events*, London: Constable & Co.

Bowdler (1807), Thomas, *The Family Shakespeare*, London: Ward & Lock.

Bowdler (1861), Thomas, *The Family Shakespeare*, London: Richard Griffin.

Braddon (1861-62), Mary Elizabeth, *The Black Band; or, The Mysteries of Midnight*, ed. with an Introduction by Jennifer Carnell, Hastings: The Sensation Press, 1998.

Braddon (1862), Mary Elizabeth, *Lady Audley's Secret*, ed. David Skilton, Oxford: Oxford University Press, 1987; ed. Jenny Bourne Taylor with Russell Crofts, Harmondsworth: Penguin, 1998.

Braddon (1862), Mary Elizabeth, *Lady Lisle*, London: Ward & Lock.

Braddon (1863), Mary Elizabeth, *Aurora Floyd*, ed. P.D. Edwards, Oxford: Oxford University Press, 1996; ed. Jennifer Uglow, London: Virago, 1984.

Braddon (1864), Mary Elizabeth, *The Doctor's Wife*, ed. Lyn Pykett, Oxford: Oxford University Press, 1998.

British Parliamentary Papers (1971), *Select Committee Reports, Returns and Other Papers Relating to Newspaper Duties and the Law of Libel 1814-88*, 2 vols, Shannon: Irish University Press.

Brougham (1857), Henry, 'Of Revolutions; Particularly that of 1848', *Works*, 11 vols, London and Glasgow: R. Griffin & Co., 1855-61, VIII: 263-334.

Brougham (n.d. [1858]), Henry, *Cheap Literature for the People*, London: Partridge & Co.

[Burn] (1855), [James D.], *The Language of the Walls and a Voice from the Shop Windows; or, the Mirror of Commercial Roguery*, Manchester: Abel Heywood.

Burnand (1904), Sir Francis C., *Records and Reminiscences, Personal and General*, 2 vols, London: Methuen & Co.

Burt (1924), Thomas, *An Autobiography, with Supplementary Chapters by Aaron Watson*, London: T. Fischer Unwin.

Bussey (1879), Harry Findlater and Thomas Wilson Reid, *The Newspaper Reader: The Journals of the Nineteenth Century on the Events of the Day*, London: Blackie.

Bussey (1906), Harry Findlater, *Sixty Years of Journalism: Anecdotes and Reminiscences*, London: Simpkin, Marshall, Hamilton, Kent & Co.

[Carlyle] (1838), [Thomas], 'Memoirs of the Life of Sir Walter Scott, Baronet', *London and Westminster Review*, XXVIII, January: 293-345.

Chadwick (1875), Sheldon, *Working and Singing: Poems, Lyrics, and Songs on the Life-March*, London: Benson.

[Chapman] (1852), [John], 'The Commerce of Literature', *Westminster and Foreign Quarterly Review*, o.s. LVII, n.s. I, April: 511-54.

Chrisholm (1895), Hugh, 'How to Counteract the "Penny Dreadful"', *Fortnightly Review*, n.s. LVIII: 515-529.

Clarigny (1857), Cucheval de, *Histoire de la presse en Angleterre et aux États Unis*, Paris: Amyot.

Clarke (1869), Marcus, *Long Odds*, Melbourne: Clarson, Massina & Co.

Clayton (1911), Herbert B., 'Sir John Gilbert as Illustrator', *N&Q*, 11th series, IV, 30 December: 521-22.

'Clericus Londiniensis' (1846), *Churchman's Monthly Penny Magazine*, I: 57-78.

Coleman (1903), John, *Charles Reade as I Knew Him*, London: Treherne & Co.

Collet (1899), Collet Dobson, *History of the Taxes on Knowledge*, London: T. Fisher Unwin, 2 vols.

[Collins] (1858), [Wilkie], 'The Unknown Public', *Household Words*, XVIII, 21 August: 439-44.

[Croker] (1845), [J.W.], 'Thiers' Histories', *Quarterly Review*, LXXVI, September: 521-583.

[Dallas] (1859), [E.S.], 'Popular Literature – The Periodical Press', *Blackwood's Edinburgh Magazine*, LXXXV, January / February: 96-112, 180-95.

Darwin (1871), Charles, *The Descent of Man and Selection in Relation to Sex*, 2 vols, London: John Murray.

Dickens (1965-), Charles, *The Letters of Charles Dickens*, general eds. Madeline House, Graham Storey and Kathleen Tillotson, Oxford: Clarendon Press.

Dickens (1879), Charles [the Younger], *Dickens's Dictionary of London. An Unconventional Handbook*, London: Charles Dickens.

Dix (1854), John, *Lions: Living and dead; or, Personal recollections of the 'Great and Gifted'*, London: Tweedie.

Dixon (1847), J. Hepworth, 'The Literature of the Lower Orders', *Daily News*, 26 October, 2 November.

Downey (1905), Edmund, *Twenty Years Ago: A Book of Anecdotes Illustrating Literary Life in London*, London: Hurst & Blackett.

Edwards (1900), Henry Sutherland, *Personal Recollections*, London: Cassell & Co.

Edwards (1906), John Passmore, *A Few Footprints*, London: Watt & Co.

Eliot (1856), George [Mary Ann Evans], 'Silly Novels by Lady Novelists', *Westminster Review*, n.s. X, October 1856: 442-61.

Evans (1967), Edmund, *The Reminiscences of Edmund Evans*, ed. Ruari McClean, Oxford: Clarendon Press.

Fern (1855), Fanny, *Ruth Hall: A Domestic Tale of the Present Time*, ed. Susan Belasco Smith, Harmondsworth: Penguin, 1997.

Francis (1890), J.C., letter in *Star*, 13 March: 1.

Frost (1880), Thomas, *Forty Years' Recollections: Literary and Political*, London: Sampson, Low & Co.

Frost (1886), Thomas, *Reminiscences of a Country Journalist*, London: Ward & Downey.

'G.B.P.' (1847), 'The Present State of Cheap Literature', *Liverpool Mercury*, 1 June: 3.

Ginswick (1849-51), J., edited by, with an Introduction, *Labour and the Poor in England and Wales, 1849-1851*, London: Cass, 3 vols, 1983.

Grand (1892), Sarah [Frances Bellenden-Clarke], *The Heavenly Twins*, with an Introduction by Carol A. Senf, n.p.: Michigan University Press, 1992.

Green (n.d. [1850]), Rev. Samuel, *The Working Classes of Great Britain; their Present Condition and the Means of their Improvement and Elevation*, London: John Snow.

Greenwood (1873), James, 'Penny Awfuls', *St. Paul's Magazine*, XII, February: 161-68.

Greg (1862), W., 'Why are Women Redundant?', *National Review*, XIV, April: 434-60.

Hansard (1855), *Parliamentary Debates: House of Commons Official Report, 3rd series, commencing with the Reign of William IV*, CXXXVII, 2 March to 2 May, London: Cornelius Buck, 1855.

Harrison (1873), John Pownall, 'Cheap Literature – Past and Present', *Companion to the British Almanac*, London: Society for the Diffusion of Useful Knowledge: 60-81.

Hazlitt (1824), William, 'The Spirits of the Age (No. IV): Sir Walter Scott', *New Monthly Magazine*, n.s. X, April: 297-304.

Hemyng (1884), Bracebridge, *The Bondage of Brandon*, London: Maxwell.

Hitchman (1881), Francis, 'The Penny Press', *Macmillan's Magazine*, XLIII, March: 385-98.

Hitchman (1890), Francis, 'Penny Fiction', *Quarterly Review*, CLXXI, July: 150-71.

[Hoare] (1850), [C.J.], 'The Penny Press', *Englishwoman's Magazine and Christian Mother's Miscellany*, n.s. V, October: 721-23.

Hole (1863), James, *The Working Classes of Leeds*, London: Simpkin, Marshall & Co..

[Hughes] (1861), [Thomas] 'Anonymous Journalism', *Macmillan's Magazine*, V, December: 157-68.

Humphery (1893), G.R., 'The Reading of the Working Classes', *Nineteenth Century*, XXXIII, April: 690-701.

Hunt (1850), Leigh, *The Autobiography of Leigh Hunt; with Reminiscences of Friends and Contemporaries*, ed. J.E. Monpurgo, London: Cresset Press, 1949.

J.F. McR. (1890), 'Letter to the Editor', *Speaker*, 15 March: 289.

Jackson (1885), Mason, *The Pictorial Press*, London: Hurst & Blackett.

Jay (1918-19), Frank, 'Peeps into the Past', *London Journal*, New Series as supplement to *Spare Moments* LX-LXI.

Jeffrey (1849), Francis, *Contributions to the Edinburgh Review*, Philadelphia: Carey & Hart.

[Johns] (1887), [B.G.], 'The Literature of the Streets', *Edinburgh Review*, CLXV, January: 40-65.

Kavanagh (1847), Julia, 'The Literature of the French Working Classes – the Poets', *People's Journal*, III: 46-9.

Keon (1879), Miles Gerald, *Harding the Moneyspinner*, London: Bentley.

Kirwan (1845), A.V., 'Histoire du Consulat et de l'Empire', *Fraser's Magazine*, XXXI, May: 505-20.

Knight (1841-44), Charles, ed., *London*, 6 vols, London: Charles Knight.

Knight (1863-65), Charles, *Passages of a Working Life During Half a Century*, 3 vols, London: Bradbury & Evans.

'A Layman' (1820), *Observations University Presson Sunday Newspapers*, London: J. Hatchard & Son.

[Lewes] (1863), [G.H.], 'Our Survey of Literature and Science', *Cornhill Magazine*, VI, January: 132-39.

[Linton] (1868), [Eliza, Lynn], 'The Girl of the Period', *Saturday Review*, XXV, 14 March: 339-40.

Linton (1890), Eliza Lynn, 'Literature: Then and Now', *Fortnightly Review*, Vol. 47, pp. 517-31.

MacFarlane (1895), W.G., *New Brunswick Bibliography*, St John, New Brunswick: Press of the Sun Printing Co. Ltd..

Mackay (1852), Charles, *Memoirs of Extraordinary Popular Delusions and the Madness of Crowds*, London: Office of the National Illustrated Library, 2nd edn, intro. Norman Stone, Ware: Wordsworth, 1995.

Mackay (1877), Charles, *40 Years Recollections of Life, Literature and Public Life*, 2 vols, London: Chapman & Hall.

[McNeill] (1841), [John], 'Mr Thiers' Foreign Policy', *Blackwood's Edinburgh Magazine*, XXXIX, January: 127-40.

[Mansel] (1863), [H.L.], 'Sensation Novels', *Quarterly Review*, CXIII, April: 482-514.

Marx (1887), Karl, *Capital: a Critique of Political Economy*, trans. Samuel Moore and Edward Aveling, ed. Frederick Engels, London: Lawrence & Wishart (1954).

May's British and Irish Press Guide and Advertiser's Handbook and Dictionary, 1874-90.

Mayhew (1847), Henry and Augustus Mayhew, *The Greatest Plague of Life; or, the Adventures of a Lady in Search of a Good Servant by One who has been 'almost worried to death'*, London: Routledge.

Mayhew (1861-62), Henry, *London Labour and the London Poor*, 4 vols, London: Frank Cass & Co., 1967.

[Mayne] (1850), [F.N.], 'The Literature of the Working Classes', *Englishwoman's Magazine and Christian Mother's Miscellany*, n.s. V, October: 619-22.

[Mayne] (n.p., n.d. 1851?), [F.N.]*The Perilous Nature of the Penny Periodical Press*.

[Mayne] (1852), [F.N.] 'What Pernicious Literature Can Do', *Working Man's Friend*, n.s. I, 24 January: 266.

Mayo, Isabella Fyvie, *Recollections, of What I Saw, What I Lived Through, and What I Learned during more than Fifty Years of Social and Literary Experience*, London: Murray.

[Merle] (1829a), [Gibbons], 'Newspaper Press', *Westminster Review*, X, January: 216-37.

[Merle] (1829b), [Gibbons] 'Weekly Newspapers', *Westminster Review*, X, April: 466-80.

Mitchell, (1846–) Charles, *The Newspaper Press Directory*, London: Mitchell.

[Murray] (1836), [John], *Handbook for Travellers on the Continent*, London: John Murray.

Mursell, (1858-64), Arthur, *Lectures to Working Men*, 1st– 2nd series, Manchester: William Bremner, 1858; 3rd – 7th series, Manchester: John Heywood.

[Oliphant] (1855), [Margaret], 'Modern Novelists - Great and Small', *Blackwood's Edinburgh Magazine*, LXXVII, May: 554-68.

[Oliphant] (1858), [Margaret], 'The Byways of Literature. Reading for the Million', *Blackwood's Edinburgh Magazine*, LXXXIV, August: 200-16.

[Oliphant] (1867), [Margaret], 'Novels', *Blackwood's Edinburgh Magazine*, CII, September: 257-80.

Page (1914), John T., 'Sir John Gilbert', *N&Q*, 11th series, 31 October, X: 357-358.

Parker (1853), John, 'On the Literature of the Working Classes', *Meliora*, ed. C.J. Talbot, Viscount Ingestre, 2nd series, London: John W. Parker & Son: 181-97.

Payn (1881), James, 'Penny Fiction', *Nineteenth Century*, IX, January: 145-54.

Phillips (1891), Emma Watts, *Watts Phillips: Artists and Playwright*, London: Cassell & Co.

Pike (1894), Godfry Holden, *John Cassell*, London: Cassell & Co.

[Rae] (1865), [W.F.], 'Sensation Novelist', *North British Review*, XLIII, September-December: 180-204.

Ratcliffe (1913), Thomas, 'Sir John Gilbert, J.F. Smith and *The London Journal*', *N&Q*, 11th series, VII, 5 April: 276.

Reach (1844), Angus B., "The Coffee Houses of London", *New Parley Library*, 9 March, II:, 293-4.

Reade (1860), Charles, *The Eighth Commandment*, London: Trübner & Co..

Reade (1887), Charles R. and Compton Reade, *Charles Reade, Dramatist, Novelist, Journalist*, 2 vols, London: Chapman & Hall.

Report (1851), *from the Select Committee on Newspaper Stamps*, Shannon: Irish University Press, 1969.

Reynolds (1839), G.W.M., *The Modern Literature of France*, 2 vols, London: G. Henderson, 2nd edn, 1841.

Reynolds (1844-48), G.W.M., *The Mysteries of London*, 4 series, 8 vols, London: Vickers.

Reynolds (1844-46), G.W.M., *The Mysteries of London*, ed. Trefor Thomas, Keele, Keele University Press, 1996.

Richardson (1747), Samuel, *Clarissa; or, The History of a Young Lady*, ed. Angus Ross, London: Viking, 1985.

Robinson (1863), Emma, *Mauleverer's Divorce: A Story of Woman's Wrongs*, London: Routledge, Warne & Routledge.

Rogers (1913), Frederick, *Labour, Life and Literature: Some Memories of 60 Years*, ed. David Rubinstein, Brighton: Harvester Press, 1973.

[Rymer] (1842), [J. Malcolm], 'Popular Writing', *Queen's Magazine*, I, June: 99-103.

[Sala] (1854), [George Augustus], 'Travels in Bohemia', *Household Words*, IX, 8 July: 495-500.

[Sala] (1862), [George Augustus], *The Seven Sons of Mammon*, 3 vols, London: Tinsley.

Scott (1891), Clement and Cecil Howard, *The Life and Reminiscences of E.L. Blanchard, with Notes from the Diary of Wm. Blanchard*, 2 vols, London: Hutchinson & Co..

[Scott] (1863), [J.A.], 'The British Newspaper: the Penny Theory and Its Solutions', *Dublin University Magazine*, LXI, March: 359-76.

Seymour (1915), Charles, *Electoral Reform in England and Wales: the Development and Operation of the Parliamentary Franchise 1832-1885*, ed. Michael Hurst, Newton Abbot: David & Charles, 1970.

Smith (1759), Adam, *The Theory of the Moral Sentiments*, ed. D.D. Raphael and A.L. Macfie, Oxford: Clarendon Press, 1976.

[Smith] (1858), [William Henry], 'Debit and Credit', *Blackwood's Edinburgh Magazine*, LXXXIII, January: 57-74.

Southworth (1859), E.D.E.N., *The Hidden Hand*, ed. Joanne Dolesa, London: Rutgers University Press, 1988; ed. Nina Baym, Oxford: Oxford University Press, 1997.

Spicer (1907), A. Dykes, *The Paper Trade*, London: Methuen.

Spielmann (1895), M. H., 'The Rivals of *Punch*: A Glance at the Illustrated Comic Press of Half a Century', *National Review*, XXV, July: 654-66.

[Spielmann] (1898), [M. H.], 'Sir John Gilbert, R.A. P.R.W.S.: A Memorial Sketch', *Magazine of Art*, XXI: 53-64.

[Stephens] (1859), [Frederick G.], 'Cheap Art', *Macmillan's Magazine*, I, November: 46-54.

Stevenson (1888), Robert Louis, 'Popular Authors', 'Vailima edition', London: Heinemann, 26 vols, XII, *Random Memories,* 1922: 326-44 (orig., *Scribner's Magazine*, IV, July: 122-28).

Stowe (1851), Harriet Beecher, *Uncle Tom's Cabin*, ed. Christopher Bigsby, London: J.M. Dent, 1993.

Strahan (1870), Alexander, 'Our Very Cheap Literature', *Contemporary Review*, XIV, June: 439-60.

Strahan (1875), Alexander, 'Bad Literature for the Young', *Contemporary Review*, XXVI, November: 981-91.

Talbot (1853), C.J., Viscount Ingestre, 'Social Evils: their Causes and their Cure', *Meliora*, 2nd series, London: John W. Parker & Son: 90-103.

Tallis (1838), John, *London Street Views 1838-1840 ... with revised and enlarged views of 1847*, intro. Peter Jackson, London: Nattali & Maurice, 1969.

[Thackeray] (1838), [W.M.], 'Half-a-Crown's worth of Cheap Knowledge', *Fraser's Magazine*, XVII, March: 279- 90.

Thomas (1913-14), Ralph, 'Sir John Gilbert, J.F. Smith and *The London Journal*', N&Q, 11th series, VII: 221-223; VIII: 121- 22; X: 144; X: 183- 85; X: 223- 25; X: 262- 63; X: 301-2.

Thornbury (1869), George Walter, *The Vicar's Courtship*, 3 vols, London: Tinsley Bros.

Tinsley (1900), William, *Random Recollections of an Old Publisher*, London: Simpkins, Marshall & Co.

Trollope (1883), Anthony, *Autobiography*, ed. Michael Sadleir and Frederick Page, Oxford: Oxford University Press, 1980.

Trollope (1983), Anthony, *Letters*, ed. N. John Hall and Nina Burgis, 2 vols, Stanford: Stanford University Press.

Vizetelly (1904), Ernest Alfred *Émile Zola: Novelist and Reformer*, John Lane, 2 vols.

Vizetelly (1893), Henry, *Glances Back Through Seventy Years*, 2 vols, London: Kegan Paul & Co.

Waite (1887), Arthur E., 'Byways of Periodical Literature', *Walford's Antiquarian*, XII, July-November: 65-74.

Weir (1841-44), W., 'London Newspapers', in *London*, ed. Charles Knight, 6 vols, V: 337-52.

Wheatley (1891), Henry B., *London Past and Present: Its History, Associations, and Traditions*, 3 vols, London, John Murray.

[Wilson] (1834), [John], 'Noctes Ambrosianae LXVII', *Blackwood's Edinburgh Magazine*, XXXVI, August: 258-88.

[Wise] (1866), [J.R.], 'Belles Lettres', *Westminster Review*, n.s. XXX, October: 524-38.

[Wright] 1867 [Thomas], 'Journeyman Engineer', *Some Habits and Customs of the Working Class by a Journeyman Engineer*, London: Tinsley Brothers.

[Wright] 1876 [Thomas], 'Readers and Reading', *Good Words*, XVII: 315-20.

[Wright] 1883 [Thomas], 'Concerning the Unknown Public', *Nineteenth Century*, XIII, February: 279-96.

Zangwill (1892), Israel, *Children of the Ghetto: a Study of a Peculiar People*, Detroit: Wayne State University Press, 1972.

Zola (1878), Émile, 'Types de femmes en France', in Nicole Priollaud, Liana Levi and Sylvie Messinger, eds, *La Femme au 19eme siècle*, Collection Les Reporteurs de l'Histoire, 1993: 22-47.

Zola (1883a), Émile, *Au Bonheur des Dames*, ed. Henri Mitterand, with a Preface by Jean Mistler, Paris: Cercle du Livre Précieux, 1968.

Zola (1883b), Émile, *Au Bonheur des Dames*, ed. Henri Mitterand, with a Preface by Jeanne Gaillard, Paris: Gallimard, 1980.

Zola (1883c), Émile, *The Ladies' Paradise*, trans. Frank Belmont 'with the author's special permission', London: Tinsley Bros., 3 vols.

Zola (1883d), Émile, *The Ladies' Paradise*, trans. Kristin Ross, Berkeley: California University Press,1992.

Zola (1883e), Émile, *The Ladies' Paradise*, trans. Brian Nelson, Oxford: Oxford University Press, 1995.

Zola (1978-95), Émile, *Correspondance*, ed. B.H. Bakker et al., 10 vols, Montréal: Les Presses de l'Université de Montréal.

After 1929

Aarsleff (1983), Hans, *The Study of Language in England 1786-1860*, Minneapolis: Minnesota University Press.

Abelson (1989), Elaine S., *When Ladies Go A-Thieving*, Oxford: Oxford University Press.

Abercrombie (1998), Nicholas, and Brian Longhurst, *Audiences: A Sociological Theory of Performance and Imagination*, London: Sage.

Adrian (1966), Arthur A., *Mark Lemon: First Editor of Punch*, Oxford: Oxford University Press.

Aldritch (1983), R.E., 'Educating our Mistresses', *History of Education*, XII: 93-102.

Altick (1989), Richard, 'The Sociology of Authorship: The Social Origins, Education, and Occupations of 1,100 British Writers, 1800-1935', in Richard Altick, *Writers, Readers, Occasions: Selected Essays on Victorian Literature and Life*, Columbus: Ohio State University Press: 95-112.

Altick (1997), Richard, *Punch: the Lively Youth of a British Institution, 1841-1851*, Columbus: Ohio State University Press.

Altick (1998), Richard, *The English Common Reader: a Social History of the Mass Reading Public 1800-1900*, 2nd edition, Columbus: Ohio State University Press.

Anderson (1967), Olive, *A Liberal State at War*, London: Macmillan.

Anderson (1991), Patricia J., 'Cassells & Company Ltd.', *DLB*, 'British Literary Publishing Houses 1820-1880', ed. Patricia J. Anderson and Jonathan Rose, CVI: 72-82.

Anderson (1994), Patricia J., *The Printed Image and the Transformation of Popular Culture 1790-1860*, Oxford: Clarendon Press.

Ang (1991), Ien, *Desperately Seeking the Audience*, London: Routledge

Ang (1995), Ien, 'The Nature of the Audience', in John Downing, Ali Mohammadi, and Annabelle Sreberny-Mohammadi, eds, *Questioning the Media: A Critical Introduction*, 2nd edn, London: Sage: 207-20.

Ang (1996), Ien, *Living Room Wars: Rethinking Media Audiences for a Postmodern World*, London: Routledge.

Armstrong (1993), Isobel, *Victorian Poetry: Poetry, Poetics and Politics*, London: Routledge.

Armstrong (2000), Isobel, *The Radical Aesthetic*, Oxford: Blackwell, 2000.

Baguley (1976), David, *Bibliographie de la critique sur Émile Zola*, Toronto: Toronto University Press.

Baguley (1994), David, ed., 'The Nineteenth Century', V, *A Critical Bibliography of French Literature*, 5 vols, Syracuse: Syracuse University Press (1968-94).

Balée (1997), Susan, 'English Critics, American Crisis, and the Sensation Novel', *Nineteenth-Century Contexts*, XVII: 125-32.

Ballaster (1991), Ros, et al., *Women's Worlds: Ideology, Femininity and the Woman's Magazine*, London: Macmillan.

Barber (1961), Giles, 'Galignani and the Publication of English Books in France 1800-1852', *The Library*, 5th series, XVI: 267-86.

Barker (1984), 'Chambers's Saturday Journal' in Sullivan, III: 64-9.

Barnes (1957), Robert Money, *A History of the Regiments and Uniforms of the British Army*, London: Seeley Service & Co. Ltd.

Barrows (1981), Susanna, *Distorting Mirrors: Visions of the Crowd in Late Nineteenth-Century France*, London: Yale University Press.

Baudrillard (1996), Jean, 'The Masses: the Implosion of the Social in the Media', in *Media Studies: A Reader*, ed. and introduced Paul Marris and Sue Thornham, Edinburgh: Edinburgh University Press: 60-68.

Bauer (1953), Josephine, *The London Magazine 1820-1829*, Copenhagen: Rosenkilde & Bagger.

Baym (1993), Nina, *Women's Fiction: A Guide to Novels by and about Women in America 1820-70*, 2nd ed., Urbana: Illinois University Press.

Beer (1989), Gillian, 'Representing Women: Representing the Past', in *The Feminist Reader*, ed. Catherine Belsey and Jane Moore, Basingstoke: Macmillan: 77-90.

Beetham (1985), Margaret, '"Healthy Reading": the Periodical Press in Manchester', in *City, Class and Culture: Studies of Social Policy and Cultural Production in Victorian Manchester*, ed. Alan J. Kidd and K.W. Roberts, Manchester: Manchester University Press: 167-92.

Beetham (1990), "Towards a Theory of the Periodical as a Publishing Genre", in *Investigating Victorian Journalism*, ed. Laurel Brake, Aled Jones and Lionel Madden, London: Macmillan: 19-32.

Beetham (1996), Margaret, *A Magazine of Her Own? Domesticity and Desire in the Woman's Magazine, 1800-1914*, London: Routledge.

Beetham (1999), Margaret, 'The Lady, the Domestic Servant and the Consumption of Print', paper delivered at the 5th annual conference at Leeds Centre for Victorian Studies, Trinity and All Saints College, University of Leeds, Horsforth, 14 July.

Benjamin (1968), Walter, 'The Work of Art in the Age of Mechanical Reproduction', in *Illuminations*, ed. with an Introduction by Hannah Arendt, trans. Harry Zohn, New York: Schocken Books: 217-51.

Bennett (1980), Scott, 'Victorian Newspaper Advertising: Counting What Counts', *Publishing History*, VIII: 5-18.

Bennett (1982), Scott, 'Revolutions in Thought: Serial Publication and the Mass Market for Reading', in *The Victorian Periodical Press: Samplings and Soundings*, ed. Joanne Shattock and Michael Wolff, [Leicester]: Leicester University Press: 225-60.

Bennett (1990), Scott, 'The Golden Stain of Time: Preserving Victorian Periodicals', in *Investigating Victorian Journalism*, ed. Laurel Brake, Aled Jones and Lionel Madden, London: Macmillan: 166-83.

Berman (1983), Marshall, *All that is Solid Melts into Air: The Experience of Modernity*, London: Verso.

Berridge (1976), Virginia, 'Popular Journalism and Working Class Attitudes 1854-1886: A Study of *Reynolds's Newspaper, Lloyd's Weekly Newspaper* and *The Weekly Times*', Ph.D. dissertation, Birkbeck College, University of London.

Berridge (1978), Virginia, 'Popular Sunday Newspapers and Mid-Victorian Society', *Newspaper History: From the Seventeenth Century to the Present Day*, ed. George Boyce, James Curran and Pauline Wingate, London: Constable: 247-64.

Best (1971), Geoffrey, *Mid-Victorian Britain 1851-75*, London: Fontana.

Bevington (1941), Merle Mowbray, *The Saturday Review 1855-1868*, New York: Columbia University Press.

Bigland (1950), Eileen, *Ouida, the Passionate Victorian*, London: Jarrolds.

Biographical Dictionary of Modern British Radicals, ed. Joseph O. Baylen and Norbert J. Gossman, Sussex: Harvester Press, 4 vols. as 3, 1979-88.

Blainey (1985), Ann, *Immortal Boy: A Portrait of Leigh Hunt*, London: Croom Helm.

Booth (1991), Michael R., *Theatre in the Victorian Age*, Cambridge: Cambridge University Press.

Bory (1962), Jean-Louis, *Eugène Sue: le roi du roman populaire*, Paris: Hachette Littéraire.

Bostick (1979), Darwin F., 'Sir John Easthope and the *Morning Chronicle*, 1834-1848', *VPR*, XII: 51-60.

Bourdieu (1984), Pierre, *Distinction: A Social Critique of the Judgement of Taste*, trans. Richard Nice, London: Routledge, Kegan Paul.

Bourdieu (1988), Pierre, *Homo Academicus*, trans. Peter Collier, Cambridge: Polity Press.

Bourdieu (1990), Pierre, *The Logic of Practice*, trans. Richard Nice, Cambridge: Polity Press.

Bourdieu (1993), Pierre, *The Field of Cultural Production: Essays on Art and Literature*, ed. Randal Johnson, Cambridge: Polity Press.

Bourdieu (1996), Pierre, *The Rules of Art*, trans. Susan Emanuel, Cambridge: Polity Press.

Bowen (2000), John, *Other Dickens: Pickwick to Chuzzlewit*, Oxford: Oxford University Press.

Bowlby (1985), Rachel, *Just Looking: Consumer Culture in Dreiser, Gissing and Zola*, London: Methuen.

Bowlby (1993), Rachel, 'Make University Press Your Mind: Scenes from the Psychology of Selling and Shopping', in *Shopping with Freud*, London: Routledge: 94-119.

Boyle (1939), Louise Regis, *Mrs E.D.E.N. Southworth: Novelist*, Washington: Catholic University of America Press.

Brake (1994), Laurel, *Subjugated Knowledges: Journalism, Gender and Literature in the Nineteenth Century*, Basingstoke, Macmillan.

Brake (2001), Laurel, *Print in Transition, 1850-1910: Studies in Media and Book History*, Basingstoke: Palgrave.

Brake (1990), Laurel, Aled Jones and Lionel Madden, eds, *Investigating Victorian Journalism*, London: Macmillan.

Briggs (1990), Asa, *Victorian Cities*, Harmondsworth: Penguin.

Brooks (1981), Michael, 'The *Builder* in the 1840s: The Making of a Magazine, The Shaping of a Profession', *VPR*, XIV: 87-93.

Brooks (1976), Peter, *The Melodramatic Imagination: Balzac, Henry James, Melodrama and the Mode of Excess*, London: Yale University Press.

Brown (1992), Lucy, 'The British Press, 1800-1860', in *The Encyclopedia of the British Press*, ed. Dennis Griffiths, Basingstoke: Macmillan.

Brown (1982), Philip A.H., *London Publishers and Printers c.1800-1870*, London: British Library Publications.

Burke (1940), Thomas, *The Streets of London Through the Centuries*, [London]: Batsford.

Burns (1961), Wayne, *Charles Reade. A Study in Victorian Authorship*, New York: Bookman Associates.

Butt (1957), John and Kathleen Tillotson, *Dickens at Work*, London: Methuen.

Buzard (1993), James, *The Beaten Track: European Tourism, Literature and the Ways to Culture, 1800-1913*, Oxford: Clarendon Press.

Caine (1992), Barbara, *Victorian Feminists*, Oxford: Oxford University Press.

Carnell (2000), Jennifer, *The Literary Lives of Mary Elizabeth Braddon: A Study of her Life and Work*, Hastings: The Sensation Press.

Carter (1982), Harold and Sandra Wheatley, *Merthyr Tydfil in 1851: a Study of the Spatial Structure of a Welsh Industrial Town*, Cardiff: Cardiff University Press.

Chalaby (1998), Jean K., *The Invention of Journalism*, London: Macmillan.

Chandler (1981), John H. and H. Dagnell, *The Newspaper and Almanac Stamps of Great Britain and Ireland*, Saffron Waldon: Great Britain Philatelic Publications.

Clark (1986), Anna, 'The Politics of Seduction in English Popular Culture, 1748-1848', in *The Progress of Romance: the Politics of Popular Fiction*, ed. Jean Radford, London: Routledge, Kegan Paul: 47-70.

Clark (1996), Anna, 'Gender, Class and the Nation: Franchise Reform in England, 1832-1928' in *Re-Reading the Constitution: New Narratives in the Political History of England's Long Nineteenth Century*, ed. James Vernon, Cambridge: Cambridge University Press: 230-53.

Clery, Emma, 'Women, Publicity and the Coffee-House Myth', *Women: a Cultural Review*, II, 1991: 168-77.

Cogswell, Fred, 'Early, May Agnes Fleming', *Canadian Dictionary of National Biography, 1871-1880*, X, 1972: 268-69.

Coltham (1969), Stephen, 'English Working-Class Newspapers in 1867', *Victorian Studies*, XIII: 158-80.

Coulthorpe-McQuin (1990), Susan, *Doing Literary Business: American Women Writers in the Nineteenth Century*, Chapel Hill: North Carolina University Press.

Couturier (1991), Maurice, *Textual Communication: A Print-Based Theory of the Novel*, London: Routledge.

Craik (1994), Jennifer, *The Face of Fashion: Cultural Studies in Fashion*, London: Routledge.

Cross (1985), Nigel, *The Common Writer: Life in Nineteenth-Century Grub Street*, Cambridge: Cambridge University Press.

Cunnington (1937), C. Willett, *English Women's Clothing in the Nineteenth Century*, London: Faber and Faber.

Curran (1978), James, 'The Press as an Agency of Social Control: an Historical Perspective', in *Newspaper History: From the Seventeenth Century to the Present Day*, ed. George Boyce, James Curran and Pauline Wingate, London: Constable: 51-75.

Curran (1991), James and Jean Seaton, *Power without Responsibility: The Press and Broadcasting in Britain*, 4th edn, London: Routledge.

Cvetkovich (1992), Ann, *Mixed Feelings: Feminism, Mass Culture and Victorian Sensationalism*, New Brunswick: Rutgers University Press.

Dalziel (1957), Margaret, *Popular Fiction 100 Years Ago: An Unexplored Tract of Literary History*, London: Cohen & West.

Darnton (1990), Robert, *The Kiss of Lamourette: Reflections in Cultural History*, London: Faber & Faber.

Davidoff (1987), Leonore, and Catherine Hall, *Family Fortunes: Men and Women of the English Middle Class, 1780-1850*, London: Routledge.

DeGategno (1994), Paul J., *Ivanhoe: The Mask of Chivalry*, New York: Twayne.

Denning (1998), M., *Mechanic Accents: Dime Novels and Working-Class Culture in America*, 2nd edition, London: Verso.

Derrida (1987), Jacques, *The Truth of* Painting, trans. Geoff Bennington and Ian McLeod, Chicago: Chicago University Press.

Dictionary of American Biography, ed. Allen Johnson and Dumas Malone, London: Humphrey Milford/Scribner's, 1928- .

Dictionary of Literary Biography, ed. Joel Meyerson et al., Detroit: Bruccoli Clark/Gale Research Co., 1978- .

Dictionary of National Biography, ed. Leslie Stephen, Sidney Lee et al., Oxford: Oxford University Press, 1917- .

Dizionario Biografico degli Italiani, ed. Alberto Ghisalberti, Rome: Istituto della Enciclopedia Italiana, 1960- .

Dorling (1983), H. Taprell, *Ribbons and Medals*, ed. and revised by Alec A. Purves, London: Osprey.

Eagleton (1983), Terry, *Literary Theory*, Oxford: Blackwell.

Edgecombe (1994), Rodney Stenning, *Leigh Hunt and the Poetry of Fancy*, London: Associated University Presses.

Edwards (1997), P.D., *Dickens's 'Young Men': George Augustus Sala, Edmund Yates and the World of Victorian Journalism*, Aldershot: Scolar Press.

Eliot (1995), Simon, 'Some Trends in British Book Production, 1800-1919', in *Literature in the Marketplace: Nineteenth-Century British Publishing and Reading Practices*, ed. John O. Jordan and Robert L. Patten, Cambridge: Cambridge University Press: 19-43.

Ellegård (1957), Alvar, *The Readership of the Periodical Press in Mid-Victorian Britain*, Göteborg: Göteborgs Universitet.

Engen (1985), Rodney K., *Dictionary of Wood Engravers*, Cambridge: Chadwick Healey.

Epstein Nord (1995), Deborah, *Walking the Victorian Streets: Women, Representation and the City*, Ithaca, New York: Cornell University Press.

Feather (1988), John, *A History of British Publishing*, London: Routledge.

Feltes (1986), N.N., *Modes of Production of Victorian Novels*, London: Chicago University Press.

Fish (1980), Stanley, *Is There a Text in this Class? The Authority of Interpretative Communities*, London: Harvard University Press.

Fisher (1988), Leona W., 'Mark Lemon's Farces on the "Woman Question"', *Studies in English Literature*, XXVIII: 649-70.

Fisher (1997), Trevor, *Prostitution and the Victorians*, Stroud: Sutton Publishing.

Flint (1993), Kate, *The Woman Reader 1837-1914*, Oxford: Clarendon Press.

Forty (1986), Adrian, *Objects of Desire: Design and Society since 1750*, London: Thames & Hudson.

Foster (1984), Vanda, *A Visual History of Costume: the Nineteenth Century,* [London]: Batsford.

Fowler (1997), Bridget, *Pierre Bourdieu and Cultural Theory: Critical Investigations*, London: Sage.

Fox (1988), Celina, *Graphic Journalism in England during the 1830s and 1840s*, London: Garland.

Frith (1995-1996), Simon, 'Editorial', *New Formations*, no. 27, Winter: v-xii.

Gallagher (1985), Catherine, *The Industrial Reformation of English Fiction 1832-1867*, London: Chicago University Press.

Geraghty (1992), Christine, 'A Woman's Space: Women and Soap Opera', *Imagining Women: Cultural Representations and Gender*, ed. Frances Bonner, Lizbeth Goodman, Richard Allen, Linda Jones and Catherine King, Cambridge: Polity Press: 221-36.

Gerrard (1998), Teresa, 'New Methods in the History of Reading: "Answers to Correspondents" in *The Family Herald* 1860-1900', *Publishing History*, XLIII: 51-69.

Gilbert (1979), Sandra M. and Susan Gubar, *The Madwoman in the Attic: the Woman Writer and the Nineteenth-Century Literary Imagination*, London: Yale University Press.

Ginsberg (1980), Carlo, *The Cheese and the Worms: the Cosmos of a Sixteenth-Century Miller*, trans. J. and A. Tedeschi, 2nd edn, Harmondsworth: Penguin.

Ginsburg (1982), Madeleine, *An Introduction to Fashion Illustration*, London: Her Majesty's Stationary Office.

Gray (1972), Donald J., 'A List of Comic Periodicals Published in Great Britain 1800-1900, with a prefatory Essay', *VPN*, no. 15: 2-39.

Gray (1982), Donald J., 'Early Victorian Scandalous Journalism: Renton Nicholson's *Town* (1837-42)', in *The Victorian Periodical Press: Samplings and Soundings*, ed. Joanne Shattock and Michael Wolff, [Leicester]: Leicester University Press: 317-48.

Habegger (1981), Alfred, 'The Well Hidden Hand', *Novel: a Forum on Fiction*, XIV: 197-212.

Hall (1992), Catherine, *White, Male and Middle Class: Explorations in Feminism and History*, Cambridge: Polity Press.

Hankinson (1993), Graham and Philippa Cowking, *Branding in Action: Cases and Strategies for Profitable Brand Management*, London: McGraw-Hill Book Co.

Harrison (1994), Brian, *Drink and the Victorians: The Temperance Question in England 1815-1872*, 2nd edn, Staffordshire: Keele University Press.

Harrison (1971), J.F.C., *Early Victorian Britain, 1832-51*, London: Fontana.

Harrison (1990), J.F.C., *Late Victorian Britain, 1870-1901*, London: Fontana.

Hayden (1970), John O., ed., *Scott: The Critical Heritage*, London: Routledge.

Hemmings (1966), F.W.J., *Émile Zola*, 2nd ed., Oxford: Clarendon Press.

Hermes (1995), Joke, *Reading Women's Magazines: An Analysis of Everyday Media Use*, Cambridge: Polity Press.

Hewitt (1996), Martin, *The Emergence of Stability in the Industrial City, 1832-67*, Aldershot: Scolar Press.

Hildreth (1976), Margaret Holbrook, *Harriet Beecher Stowe: a Bibliography*, Hamden: Archon.

Hillier (2002), Jean, and Emma Rooksby, eds, *Habitus*, Aldershot: Ashgate.

Houfe (1981), Simon, *The Dictionary of British Book Illustrators and Caricaturists 1800-1914*, 2nd edn, Woodbridge: Antique Collectors Club.

Howe (1947), Ellic, ed., *The London Compositor: Documents Relating to Wages, Working Conditions and Customs of the London Printing Trade 1785-1900*, London: The Bibliographical Society, (1785-1900).

Hughes (1991), Linda K. and Michael Lund, *The Victorian Serial*, London: Virginia University Press.

Humpherys (1991), Anne, 'Generic Strands and Urban Twists: The Victorian Mysteries Novel', *Victorian Studies*, XXXIV: 455-472.

Hutcheon (1988), Linda, *A Poetics of Postmodernism: History, Theory Fiction*, London: Routledge.

Huyssen (1988), Andreas, *After the Great Divide: Modernism, Mass Culture, Postmodernism*, London: Macmillan.

Ings (1996), Katherine Nicholson, 'Blackness and the Literary Imagination: Uncovering *The Hidden Hand*', in *Passing and the Fictions of Identity*, ed. Elaine K. Ginsberg, London: Duke University Press: 131-50.

Iser (1978), Wolfgang, *The Act of Reading: A Theory of Aesthetic Response*, London: Routledge.

James (1963), Louis, *Fiction for the Working Man 1830-1850*, Harmondsworth: Penguin (1974).

James (1972), Louis, '"Economic" Literature: the Emergence of Popular Journalism', *VPN*, no. 14: 13-20.

James (1976), Louis, ed., *Print and the People 1819-1851*, London: Allen Lane.

James (1982), Louis, '"The Trouble with Betsy": Periodicals and the Common Reader in Mid-Nineteenth-Century England', in *The Victorian Periodical Press: Samplings and Soundings*, ed. Joanne Shattock and Michael Wolff, [Leicester]: Leicester University Press: 349-66.

Jay (1995), Elisabeth, *Mrs. Oliphant: 'A Fiction to Herself'*, Oxford: Clarendon Press.

Johanningsmeier (1997), Charles, *Fiction and the American literary Marketplace. The Role of newspaper Syndicates 1860-1900*, Cambridge: Cambridge University Press.

Johannsen (1950), Albert, *The House of Beadle and Adams and its Dime and Nickel Novels: the Story of a Vanished Literature*, 3 vols, Norman: Oklahoma University Press.

Johnson-Woods (2000), Toni, 'The Virtual Reading Communities of the *London Journal*, the *New York Ledger*, and the *Australian Journal*', in *Nineteenth-Century Media and the Construction of Identity*, ed. Laurel Brake, Bill Bell and David Finckelstein, Basingstoke: Macmillan: 350-61.

Johnson-Woods (2001), Toni, *Index to Serials in Australian Periodicals and Newspapers. Nineteenth Century*. Canberra: Mulini Press.

Johnston (1994), Judith, 'Invading the House of Titian: the Colonisation of Italian Art. Anna Jameson, John Ruskin and *The Penny Magazine*', *VPR*, XXVII: 127-43.

Jones (1984), Aled, 'Tillotson's Fiction Bureau: the Manchester Manuscripts', *VPR*, XVII: 43-49.

Jones (1996), Aled, *Powers of the Press: Newspapers, Power and the Public in Nineteenth-Century England*, Aldershot: Ashgate.

Jones (1953-57), Ernest, *Sigmund Freud: life and work*, 3 vols. London: Hogarth Press.

Jordan (1995), John O., and Robert L. Patten, eds., *Literature in the Marketplace: Nineteenth-Century British Publishing and Reading Practices*, Cambridge: Cambridge University Press.

Joyce (1994), Patrick, *Democratic Subjects: The Self and the Social in Nineteenth-Century England*, Cambridge: Cambridge University Press.

Joyce (1995), Patrick, ed., *Class*, Oxford: Oxford University Press.

Joyce (1996), Patrick, 'The Constitution and the Narrative Structure of Victorian Politics', in *Re-Reading the Constitution: New Narratives in the Political History of England's Long Nineteenth Century*, ed. James Vernon, Cambridge: Cambridge University Press: 180-203.

Keller (1998), Kevin Lane, *Strategic Brand Management: Building, Measuring and Managing Brand Equity*, London: Prentice-Hall International.

Kelley (1984), Mary, *Private Woman, Public Stage: Literary Domesticity in Nineteenth-Century America*, Oxford: Oxford University Press.

Kelly (1993), Thomas, *A History of Adult Education in Great Britain from the Middle Ages to the Twentieth Century*, Liverpool: Liverpool University Press.

Kent (1962), Christopher, 'Higher Journalism and the Mid-Victorian Clerisy', *Victorian Studies*, XIII: 181-98.

Kent (1987), Susan Kingsley, *Sex and Suffrage in Britain 1860-1914*, London: Routledge.

King (1999), Andrew, 'Including the Nude: The Great Exhibition, Class, Gender and Nationality in a Victorian Mass-Market Magazine', *Studii de limbi şi literaturi moderne: Studii de Anglistică şi Americanistică*, Timişoara: Mirton: 161-80.

King (2000), Andrew, 'Defining Positions: A Pragmatic Approach to Periodical Illustrations', *Nineteenth-Century Media and the Construction of Identity*, ed. Laurel Brake, Bill Bell, & David Finckelstein, Basingstoke: Macmillan: 77-92.

King (2002), Andrew, "Sympathy as Subversion? Reading *Lady Audley's Secret* in the Kitchen", *Journal of Victorian Culture*, VII: 60-85.

Klancher (1987), Jon P., *The Making of English Reading Audiences 1790-1832*, London: Wisconsin University Press.

Knoke (1991), David and James H. Kuklinski, 'Network Analysis: Basic Concepts', in *Markets, Hierarchies and Networks: the Co-ordination of Social Life*, ed. Grahame Thompson, Jennifer Francis, Rosalind Levačić, and Jeremy Mitchell, London: Sage: 173-83.

Lalumia (1984), Matthew Paul, *Realism and Politics in Victorian Art of the Crimean War*, Ann Arbor: UMI Research Press.

Law (2000), Graham, *Serializing Fiction in the Victorian Press*, Basingstoke: Palgrave.

Law (2000), Graham, and Norimasa Morita, 'The Newspaper Novel: Towards an International History', *Media History*, VI: 5-17.

Lee (1976), Alan, *The Origins of the Popular Press in England 1851-1914*, London: Croom Helm.

Lessing (1962), Doris, *The Golden Notebook*, London: HarperCollins, 1993.

Levine (1987), Phillipa, *Victorian Feminism 1850-1900*, London: Hutchinson.

Lloyd-Jones (1952), A., '*Bow Bells*', *N&Q*, CXCVII, 22 November: 526.

Lohrli (1973), Anne, *Household Words ... Table of Contents, Lists of Contributors and their Contributions*, [Toronto]: Toronto University Press.

Macherey (1978), Pierre, *A Theory of Literary Production*, trans G. Wall, London: Routledge & Kegan Paul.

Maidment (1982), Brian, 'Victorian Publishing and Social Criticism: the Case of Edward Jenkins', *Publishing History*, XI: 41-69.

Maidment (1984), Brian, 'Magazines of Popular Progress and the Artisans', *VPR*, XVII: 83-94.

Maidment (1987), Brian, *The Poorhouse Fugitives: Self-Taught Poets and Poetry in Victorian Britain*, Manchester: Carcanet.

Maidment (1992), Brian, *Into the 1830s: Some Origins of Victorian Illustrated Journalism. Cheap Octavo Magazines of the 1820s and their Influence*, [Manchester]: Manchester Polytechnic Library.

Maitzen (1995), Rohan, "'This Feminine Preserve': Historical Biographies by Victorian Women', *Victorian Studies*, XXXVIII: 371-394.

Marchand (1941), Leslie A., *The Athenaeum: A Mirror of Victorian Culture*, Chapel Hill: North Carolina University Press.

Maxwell (1992), Richard, *The Mysteries of Paris and London*, London: University Press of Virginia.

Mays (1995), Kelly J., 'The Disease of Reading and Victorian Periodicals', *Literature in the Marketplace: Nineteenth-Century British Publishing and Reading Practices*, ed. John O. Jordan and Robert L. Patten, Cambridge: Cambridge University Press: 165-94.

McAleer (1992), Joseph, *Popular Reading and Publishing in Britain 1914-1950*, Oxford: Clarendon Press.

McCalman (1988), Iain, *Radical Underworld: Prophets, Revolutionaries and Pornographers in London 1795-1840*, Cambridge: Cambridge University Press.

McCarthy (1997), Thomas J., *Relationships of Sympathy: the Writer and the Reader in British Romanticism*, Aldershot: Scolar Press.

McCord (1991), Norman, *British History 1815-1906*, Oxford: Oxford University Press.

McCracken (1993), Ellen, *Decoding Women's Magazines: From* Mademoiselle *to* Ms., London: Macmillan.

McDonald (1997), Peter D., *British Literary Culture and Publishing Practice 1880-1914*, Cambridge: Cambridge University Press.

McMullen (1992), Lorraine, 'May Agnes Fleming: 'I did nothing but write'', in Carrie MacMillan, Lorraine McMullen and Elizabeth Waterston, *Silenced Sextet: Six Nineteenth-Century Canadian Women Novelists*, London: McGill-Queens: 52-81.

Miller (1986), D.A., 'Cage aux folles: Sensation and Gender in Wilkie Collins's *The Woman in White*', in *The Nineteenth-Century British Novel*, ed. Jeremy Hawthorne, London: Edward Arnold: 95-124.

Millett (1969), Kate, *Sexual Politics*, 2nd edn, London: Ballantine Books, 1988.

Millgate, Jane (1987), *Scott's Last Edition*, Edinburgh, Edinburgh University Press.

Mitchell (1962), B.R. and Phyllis Deane, *Abstract of British Historical Statistics*, Cambridge: Cambridge University Press.

Mitchell (1977), Sally, 'The Forgotten Woman of the Period: Penny Weekly Family Magazines of the 1840s and 1850s', in *A Widening Sphere: Changing Roles of Victorian Women*, ed. M. Vicinus, London: Indiana University Press: 29-51.

Mitchell (1984), Sally, '*Sharpe's London Journal*', in Sullivan, III: 393-97.

Mitchell (1989), Sally, *The Fallen Angel: Chastity, Class and Women's Reading 1835-1880*, Bowling Green: Bowling Green University Popular Press.

Moers (1976), Ellen, *Literary Women*, intro. Helen Taylor, London: The Women's Press.

Moore (1992), Arlene, "The Letters of Harriet and Leon Lewis to Robert Bonner", *Dime Novel Roundup*, LXI: 2-7.

Moretti (1998), Franco, *Atlas of the European Novel 1800-1900*, London: Verso.

Morgan (1989), C.J., 'Demographic Change 1771-1911', in *A History of Modern Leeds*, ed. Derek Fraser, Manchester: Manchester University Press: 46-71.

Morrison (1995), Elizabeth, 'Serial Fiction in Australian Colonial Newspapers', in *Literature in the Marketplace: Nineteenth-Century British Publishing and Reading Practices*, ed. John O. Jordan and Robert L. Patten, Cambridge: Cambridge University Press: 306-324.

Mountjoy (1985), Peter Roger, 'Thomas Bywater Smithies, Editor of the *British Workman*', *VPR*, XVIII: 46-56.

Mullane (1990), Janet, 'E.D.E.N. Southworth' in *Nineteenth Century Literary Criticism*, ed. Mullane, Janet, Robert Thomas Wilson et al., London: Gale Research Inc., 1981-, XXVI: 429-449.

Mullin (1987), Donald, *Victorian Plays: A Record of Significant Productions on the London Stage, 1837-1901*, New York: Greenwood Press.

Mulvey (1989), Laura, *Visual and Other Pleasures*, Basingstoke: Macmillan.

Murphy (1994), Paul Thomas, *Toward a Working-Class Canon: Literary Criticism in British Working-Class Periodicals, 1816-1858*, Columbus: Ohio State University Press.

Myerson (1983), Joel, 'Ann Stephens, *The London Journal* and the Anglo-American Copyright in 1854', *Manuscript*, XXXV: 281-86.

Nead (1988), Lynda, *Myths of Sexuality: Representations of Victorian Women*, Oxford: Blackwell.

Nead (1997), Lynda, 'Mapping the Self: Gender, Space and Modernity in Mid-Victorian London', in *Rewriting the Self: Histories from the Renaissance to the Present*, ed. Roy Porter: 167-85.

Nead (2000), Lynda, *Victorian Babylon: People, Streets and images in Nineteenth-Century London*, New Haven: Yale University Press.

Nemesvari (1995), Richard, 'Robert Audley's Secret: Male Homosocial Desire in *Lady Audley's Secret*', *Studies in the Novel*, XXVII: 515-28.

Neuberg (1977), Victor E., *Popular Literature: A History and Guide from the Beginning of Printing to the Year 1897*, London: The Woburn Press.

Nicoll (1959), Allardyce, *A History of English Drama 1660-1900*, 2nd edn, vol. V, Cambridge: Cambridge University Press.

Nicoll (1946), Allardyce, *A History of Late Nineteenth - Century Drama 1850-1900*, 2 vols, Cambridge: Cambridge University Press.

Noel (1954), Mary, *Villains Galore ... The Hey-day of the Popular Story Weekly*, New York: Macmillan.

Nowell-Smith (1958), Simon, *The House of Cassell 1848-1958*, London: Cassell & Co..

Nunn (1987), Pamela Gerrish, *Victorian Women Artists*, London: The Women's Press.

Ong (1982), W.J., *Orality and Literacy: The Technologizing of the Word*, London: Methuen.

Palmegiano (1976), E.M., 'Woman and British Periodicals 1832-1867: A Bibliography', *VPN*, no. 9: 1-36.

Palmer (1991), Jerry, *Potboilers: Methods, Concepts and Case Studies in Popular Fiction*, London: Routledge.

Parker (2000), Mark, *Literary Magazines and British Romanticism*. Cambridge: Cambridge University Press.

Pearl (1955), Cyril, *The Girl with the Swansdown Seat*, London: Frederick Muller.

Perkin (1993), Joan, *Victorian Women*, London: John Murray.

Plunkett (2003), John, *Queen Victoria: First Media Monarch*, Oxford: Oxford University Press.

Poovey (1988), Mary, *Uneven Developments: The Ideological Work of Gender in Mid-Victorian England*, Chicago: Chicago University Press.

Pryce (1988), W.T.R., 'Language Areas and Changes *c.* 1750-1981', in *Glamorgan County History*, ed. Prys Morgan, Glamorgan History Trust Ltd., VI: n.p.

Pykett (1994), Lyn, *The Sensation Novel: From the 'Woman in White' to the 'Moonstone'*, Plymouth: Northcote House.

Pykett (1995), Lyn, *Engendering Fictions: The English Novel in the Early Twentieth Century*, London: Edward Arnold.

Radway (1984), Janice, *Reading the Romance: Women, Patriarchy and Popular Culture*, London: Verso.

Reed (1997), David, *The Popular Magazine in Britain and the United States, 1880-1960*, London: Toronto University Press.

Rendall (1990), Jane, *Women in an Industrialising Society: England 1750-1880*, Oxford: Blackwell.

Reynolds (1988), David S., *Beneath the American Renaissance: the Subversive Imagination in the Age of Emerson and Melville*, London: Harvard University Press.

Riffenburgh (1994), Beau, *The Myth of the Explorers: The Press, Sensationalism and Geographical Discovery*, Oxford: Oxford University Press.

Rinehart (1980), Nana, ''The Girl of the Period' Controversy', *VPR*, XIII: 3-9.

Roberts (1972a), F. David, 'Early Victorian Newspaper Editors', *VPN*, no. 14: 1-13.

Roberts (1972b), F. David, 'More Early Victorian Newspaper Editors', *VPN*, no. 16: 15-28.

Rodolff (1981), Rebecca, 'The *Weekly Chronicle*'s Month-by-Month Reception of *Pendennis* and *David Copperfield*', *VPR*, XIV: 101-11.

Rogers (2000), Helen, *Women and the People: Authority, Authorship and the Radical Tradition in Nineteenth-Century England*, Aldershot: Ashgate.

Rose (2001), Jonathan, *The Intellectual Life of the British Working Classes*, New Haven: Yale University Press.

Rosenthal (1958), Harold, *Two Centuries of Opera at Covent Garden*, London: Putnam.

Royle (1980), Trevor, *Precipitous City: the Story of Literary Edinburgh*, Edinburgh: Mainstream.

Said (1991), Edward, *The World, The Text and The Critic*, London: Vintage.

Saunders (1992), David, *Authorship and Copyright*, London: Routledge.

Schaffer (2000), Talia, *The Forgotten Female Aesthetes: Literary Culture in Late Victorian England*, Charlottesville: Virginia University Press.

Scholes (1989), Robert, *Protocols of Reading*, London: Yale University Press.

Scholnick (1999), Robert J., '"The Fiery Cross of Knowledge": *Chambers's Edinburgh Journal*, 1832-1844', *VPR*, XXXII: 324-58.

Schom (1987), Alan, *Émile Zola: A Bourgeois Rebel*, London: MacDonald.

Sedgwick (n.d. [1993]), Eve Kosofsky, *Between Men: English Literature and Male Homosocial Desire*, 2nd edn, New York: Columbia University Press.

Sheets-Pyenson (1985), Susan, 'Popular Science Periodicals in Paris and London: the Emergence of a Low Scientific Culture, 1820-1875', *Annals of Science*, XLII: 549-72.

Shevelow (1989), Kathryn, *Women and Print Culture: The Construction of Femininity in the Early Periodical*, London: Routledge.

Showalter (1977), Elaine, *A Literature of Their Own: British Women Novelists from Brontë to Lessing*, Princeton: Princeton University Press.

Showalter (1987), Elaine, *The Female Malady: Women, Madness and English Culture, 1830-1980*, London: Virago.

Simmons (1973), James L., *The Novelist as Historian*, The Hague: Mouton.

Sinnema (1998), Peter, *Dynamics of the Printed Page: Representing the Nation in the Illustrated London News*, Aldershot: Scolar Press.

Sommerville (1996), C. John, *The News Revolution in England: Cultural Dynamics of Daily Information*, Oxford: Oxford University Press.

Springhall (1990), John, '"A Life Story for the People'?: Edwin J, Brett and the London 'Low-Life' Penny Dreadfuls of the 1860s', *Victorian Studies*, XXXIII: 223-46.

Springhall (1994), John, 'Disseminating Impure Literature': the 'Penny Dreadful' Publishing Business since 1860s', *Economic History Review*, XLVII: 567-84.

Srebrnik (1986), Patricia, *Alexander Strahan, Victorian Publisher*, Ann Arbor: Michigan University Press.

Steele (1988), Valerie, *Paris Fashion: A Cultural History*, Oxford: Oxford University Press.

Stephens (1987), W.B., *Education, Literacy and Society, 1830-70: the Geography of Social Diversity in Provincial England*, Manchester: Manchester University Press.

Sullivan (1984), Alvin, ed., *British Literary Magazines*, 4 vols, London: Greenwood Press.

Summers (n.d. [1940]), [Alphonsus Joseph-Mary Augustus] Montague, *A Gothic Bibliography*, London: Fortune Press.

Sutherland (1976), John, *Victorian Novelists and Publishers*, London: Chicago University Press.

Sutherland (1988), John, *The Longman Companion to Victorian Fiction*, London: Longman.

Taylor (1989), Helen, *Scarlett's Women: Gone with the Wind and Its Female Fans*, London: Virago.

Tebbel (1972-81), John, *A History of Book Publishing in the United States*, 4 vols, London: R.R. Bowker.

Thomis (1982), Malcolm and Jennifer Grimmett, *Women in Protest 1800-1850*, London: Croom Helm.

Thompson (1963), E.P., *The Making of the English Working Class*, Harmondsworth: Penguin, 1991.

Thompson (1971), E. P. and Eileen Yeo, eds., *The Unknown Mayhew: Selections from the Morning Chronicle 1849-1850*, London: Merlin Press.

Thompson (1945), Flora, *Lark-Rise to Candleford*, Oxford: Oxford University Press.

Thorogood (1991), Julia, *Margery Allingham: A Biography*, London: Heineman.

Tilley (1995), Elizabeth, 'Gender and Role-Playing in *Lady Audley's Secret*', in *Exhibited by Candlelight: Sources and Developments in the Gothic Tradition*, ed. Valeria Tinkler-Villani and Peter Davidson, with Jane Stevenson, Amsterdam: Rodopi: 197-204.

Tillotson (1954), Kathleen, *Novels of the 1840s*, Oxford: Clarendon Press.

Todd (1972), William B., *A Directory of Printers and Others in Allied Trades: London and its Vicinity 1800-1840*, London: Printing Historical Society.

Tosh (1999), John, *A Man's Place: Masculinity and the Middle-Class Home in Victorian England*, London: Yale University Press.

Treuherz (1993), Julian, *Victorian Painting*, London: Thames & Hudson.

Tuchman (1989), Gaye with Nina E. Fortin, *Edging Women Out: Victorian Novelists, Publishers, and Social Change*, London: Routledge.

Turner (2000), Mark, *Trollope and the Magazines: Gendered Issues in Mid-Victorian Britain*, Basingstoke: Macmillan.

Vann (1994), J. Don, 'Comic Periodicals', in *Victorian Periodicals and Victorian Society*, ed. J. Don Vann and Rosemary VanArsdel, Aldershot: Scolar Press: 278-90.

Vincent (1989), David, *Literacy and Popular Culture: England 1750-1914*, Cambridge: Cambridge University Press, 1993.

Vries (1995), Leonard de, *History as Hot News: the World of Early Victorians through the Eyes of the ILN 1842-1865*, London: John Murray.

Walkowitz (1992), Judith, *City of Dreadful Delight: Narratives of Sexual Danger in Late-Victorian London*, Chicago: Chicago University Press.

Ward (1989), Ken, *Mass Communications and the Modern World*, London: Macmillan.

Warner (1985), Marina, *Monuments and Maidens: The Allegory of the Female Form*, London: Weidenfeld & Nicolson.

Warren (1993), Joyce W., ed., *The (Other), American Tradition: Nineteenth-Century Women Writers,* New Brunswick: Rutgers University Press.

Waterloo (1989), *Directory of Scottish Newspapers and Periodicals 1800-1900*, compiled by John S. North, 2 vols, Waterloo, Ontario: North Waterloo Academic Press.

Waterloo (1997), *Directory of English Newspapers and Periodicals 1800-1900*, compiled by John S. North, 10 vols, Waterloo, Ontario: North Waterloo Academic Press.

Webb (1955), R.K., *The British Working Class Reader 1970-1845*, New York: Augustus M. Kelly.

Wellesley (1966-1979), *Index to Victorian Periodicals*, ed. Walter E. Houghton et al., 5 vols, London, Routledge, Kegan Paul.

Wheeler (1994), Michael, *Heaven, Hell and the Victorians*, Cambridge: Cambridge University Press.

White (1970), Cynthia, L., *Women's Magazines 1693-1968*, London: Michael Joseph.

Wiener (1978), Joel, 'Circulation and the Stamp Tax', *Victorian Periodicals: A Guide to Research*, n.p.: Modern Language Association of America: 149-74.

Wiener (1991), Joel, 'Vizetelly & Co.', *DLB*, CVI, 'British Literary Publishing Houses', ed. Patricia Anderson and Jonathan Rose: 314-20.

Williams (1973), Raymond, *The Country and the City*, London: The Hogarth Press.

Wilson (1952), Angus, *Emile Zola: an Introductory Study of his Novels*, London: Secker & Warburg.

Wilson (1993), Elisabeth, "Is Transgression Transgressive?" in *Activating Theory: Lesbian, Gay and Bisexual Politics,* ed. Joseph Bristow and Angela Wilson, Lawrence & Wishart: 107-17.

Wolff (1974), Robert Lee, 'Devoted Disciple: the Letters of Mary Elizabeth Braddon to Sir Edward Bulwer-Lytton, 1862-1873', *Harvard Library Bulletin,* XXII: 5-35, 129-61.

Wolff (1979), Robert Lee, *Sensational Victorian: the Life and Fiction of Mary Elizabeth Braddon,* New York: Garland.

Wright (1988), D.G., *Popular Radicalism: the Working-Class Experience 1780-1880,* London: Longman.

Wynne (2001), Deborah, *The Sensation Novel and the Victorian Family Magazine,* Basingstoke: Palgrave.

Zboray (1997), Ronald J. and Mary Saracino Zboray, '"Have you read ...?" Real Readers and their response in Antebellum Boston and its Region', *Nineteenth-Century Literature,* LII: 139-70.

Žižek (1994), Slavoj, *Metastases of Enjoyment: Six Essays on Woman and Causality,* London: Verso.

Index